D0079297

KOREA
AT THE
CENTER

A publication of the Northeast Asia Seminar

Rediscovering Russia in Asia
Siberia and the Russian Far East
Edited by Stephen Kotkin and David Wolff

Mongolia in the Twentieth Century
Landlocked Cosmopolitan
Edited by Stephen Kotkin and Bruce A. Elleman

Korea at the Center
Dynamics of Regionalism in Northeast Asia
Edited by Charles K. Armstrong, Gilbert Rozman,
Samuel S. Kim, and Stephen Kotkin

KOREA
AT THE
CENTER

Dynamics of Regionalism in Northeast Asia

Edited by
Charles K. Armstrong,
Gilbert Rozman, Samuel S. Kim,
and Stephen Kotkin

M.E. Sharpe
Armonk, New York
London, England

Copyright © 2006 by M.E. Sharpe, Inc.

All rights reserved. No part of this book may be reproduced in any form
without written permission from the publisher, M.E. Sharpe, Inc.,
80 Business Park Drive, Armonk, New York 10504.

Every effort was made to identify the owners of the illustrations reprinted herein in order to
secure permissions for publication. If any acknowledgment is missing, please inform the
publisher so that the omission can be rectified in any future printing.

Library of Congress Cataloging-in-Publication Data

Korea at the center : dynamics of regionalism in Northeast Asia / edited by Charles K.
Armstrong ... [et al.].
   p. cm.
  Includes bibliographical references and index.
  ISBN 0-7656-1655-6 (hardcover : alk. paper)
  1. Regionalism—East Asia. 2. East Asia—Economic integration. 3. Korea—Foreign
relations—East Asia. 4. East Asia—Foreign relations—Korea. I. Armstrong, Charles K.

  JQ1499.A38R437 2005
  327.51905—dc22   2005000073

Printed in the United States of America

The paper used in this publication meets the minimum requirements of
American National Standard for Information Sciences
Permanence of Paper for Printed Library Materials,
ANSI Z 39.48-1984.

BM (c) 10   9   8   7   6   5   4   3   2   1

Contents

Preface

It may seem odd to single out regionalism in an age of globalization, especially since globalization has by no means displaced nationalism. But between the national and the global there lies something that is connected to both, yet distinct from either—a regional order that does not preclude nationalism but makes cooperative use of it; a regional order that partakes of trends in globalization but retains a regional flavor and focus. It is this spotlight on regionalism—an idea and a set of activities often lost in the preoccupation with nationalism and with globalization—that sets off our volume.

A second distinguishing feature, we believe, is the focus on Korea at the center. Our volume, moreover, emphasizes Korea's centrality not just today, but through various incarnations of regional orders over the past century or so. Situated among three great powers (China, Japan, Russia) and of great interest to a fourth (the United States), the Korean peninsula has long divided countries seeking advantage in the region. But it has remained their shared preoccupation. Despite the tensions, we argue, the peninsula holds the possibility of pulling these neighbors still closer together.

Korea's centrality provides a key both to understanding the modern history of Northeast Asia and to finding a path toward a new era of an emergent broad, open regionalism. To be sure, as the Berlin Wall fell but the demilitarized zone remained, it was evident that volatile conditions endured on the Korean peninsula. But at the same time, there are unmistakable circumstances that have made the Korean peninsula the center of ways of thinking and acting on a pan-regional level.

This volume has grown out of two international conferences: a workshop on the Princeton campus in 1996, funded by the Northeast Asia Council of the Association of Asian Studies as well as Princeton's East Asian Studies program; and a larger gathering in 2003 on the Princeton campus held jointly with Columbia University, and funded by Columbia's Weatherhead Institute as well as Princeton's Institute for International and Regional Studies, East Asian Studies program, Davis Center for Historical Studies, and Woodrow Wilson School. The editors are grateful to all for their support. Lois Ornstein managed all conference logistics. Joyce Howe prepared the index. We also would like to thank M.E. Sharpe, which has also published two previous volumes in this series of works on transnational Northeast Asia: *Rediscovering Russia in Asia* (1995) and *Mongolia in the Twentieth Century* (1999).

Korean-language materials have been rendered according to the McCune-Reischauer transliteration system, minus the diacritical marks; Japanese according to the modified Hepburn system; Chinese by pinyin; and Russian, according to the Library of Congress system. Exceptions are made for a few well-known individuals, for example, Park Chung Hee, Chiang Kai-shek, and Boris Yeltsin.

Stephen Kotkin

Introduction

Common images of Korea have failed to capture its importance. Once known as the "hermit kingdom," Korea traversed the twentieth century in the unappealing, brutalized roles of "colony," "battlefield" (where the cold war turned hot), and "divided state frozen in time." No wonder many consider it to be crunched between the powers that really matter in Northeast Asia: Japan, the imperialist state of the first half of the century and the regional economic power over the second half; Russia, Japan's rival and headquarters of communism that spread across the region and kept it divided; China, the civilizational fountainhead of East Asia fast ascending to reclaim its prominence; and the United States, which increasingly insisted on using its unparalleled global power to shape relations in Northeast Asia. In comparison to this constellation of heavyweights, the divided states of South and North Korea may seem insignificant. Yet a neighborhood experiencing great-power flux is precisely what gives the Korean peninsula the special opportunity to play a critical role in the emergence of substantial regional linkages. Tracing Korea's centrality through three periods, this book assesses the case for the peninsula as the indispensable factor and in recent years the moving force in the coalescence of a broad, open Northeast Asian regionalism.

Korea's centrality takes various forms. Historically, it served as the transmitter of Chinese culture and practices to Japan. Even if this function declined over a millennium, it left Korea well positioned as intermediary. In the half-century of its colonialism, the Japanese sought to reverse the flow, making Korea the conduit to China. Although historic ties were interrupted in various directions from 1945, some of the linkages could be reconnected. In the cold war era, South Korea drew Japan's attention as the latter began to regain a firm footing on the Asian mainland, while North Korea took advantage of a balancing role in the decades of the Sino-Soviet dispute. Of course, the opportunities for realizing any centrality were limited, yet each side of the Thirty-eighth Parallel made important inroads. Few anticipated that the end of the cold war would dramatically raise the still-divided Korean peninsula's prospects for involving many states in the search for Korea's regional centrality.

Through a burst of economic integration driven by the Japanese miracle and the subsequent ascent of China, the Korean peninsula has moved to the hub of the region again. Economically, South Koreans now have grown hopeful about occupying the middle post in a high-tech urban belt linking Beijing and Tokyo; via energy pipelines, which would pump oil and perhaps gas from Asiatic Russia to China and Japan; via a Eurasian railroad corridor reducing the transit time for goods shipped across more than 6,000 miles; and in a giant free trade area that China and Japan lack sufficient trust to develop without a third party present. Japan eagerly anticipates a free trade area (FTA) in 2005, while Koreans look to China for a follow-up FTA that would signify regional balance rather than one-sided dependency. Over the horizon, multilateral support for North Korean economic openness would add impetus to regional integration.

Could it really come to pass—a Northeast Asia characterized by mutually beneficial, deep links across political boundaries? As everyone knows, two wars in which Korea was the spoils (but not a participant) had once determined its future: the Sino-Japanese war of 1894–95 (which was not initially about control over Korea, but once Japan had secured its position, ambitions rose for direct rule over Korea); and a decade later, the Russo-Japanese war, which put Korea's future directly on the line. China's half-century of marginalization had begun, and Korea was left in Japan's hands for forty years. Then came the hugely destructive World War II. Liberation brought division, followed by the bloodiest conflict of the cold war. No peace treaty has ever been signed. In the 1990s, and again in the 2000s, talk of nuclear crisis erupted. But it might be noted that the bomb spread in Northeast Asia in part as a result of regional cooperation; in any case, for better or for worse, the nuclear worries did compel joint consideration of genuinely regional security. What is more, in the commotion, both Koreas have been eyeing a central role, hoping that security uncertainties and seeming great power imbalances could raise their profile. The South in 2000 with Kim Dae Jung's sunshine policy showed that it could seize the initiative, and the North in 2003–4 through six-party talks established itself as a force that could not be ignored. There was even talk of a coming of age.

If the goal of a broad, open regionalism in Northeast Asia remains elusive, it has at least become thinkable. By broad, open regionalism, we mean: (1) rapidly increasing economic ties backed by a joint strategy of economic integration; (2) growing political ties nurtured by summits and organizations that set goals for collective action; (3) advancing social integration through labor migration, business networks, and a common agenda on outstanding problems; (4) shared consciousness of regional identity enhanced by some signs of shared culture in the face of globalization; and (5) a widening security agenda to resolve tensions and ensure stability. We explore times when some or all of these goals have turned the attention among the great powers onto Korea. We argue that Northeast Asia has in the first decade of the 2000s entered a period when regionalism will intensify along with new awareness of Korean centrality in strategic, economic, and political balancing.

This perspective should provoke a reexamination of local history that transcends parallel, nonintersecting nationalist narratives. In its enduring geography, North-east Asia consists of three linked entities: China, Japan, and Korea (whether whole or divided). For centuries before the 1840s, these countries stood side by side with only the Mongols and then the Manchus briefly disrupting, at times of conquest, their existence. They formed a pocket of Confucian tradition with high levels of premodern literacy and urbanization far from the international system that was eventually forged with Western Europe at its core. Beginning in the second half of the nineteenth century, Russia and the United States, coming from opposite directions, made their presence strongly felt in the region. In 1945 the United States and the Soviet Union, improbably brought together by the imperative to defeat Germany and Japan, quickly divided Korea, a division that persists after a major war to overcome it. Any discussions of Korean centrality in Northeast Asia, therefore, must range between two long-time historical partners and four great power contenders.

We trace the bumpy path of Korea's place in Northeast Asia through three periods, in each of which it acquired significance commensurate with changing prospects for regionalism. In the 1880s to the 1900s, Japan's rapid economic and military ascent gave it the power to attempt to impose its will on a weak Korea, moving in the direction of a kind of regionalism under colonial control. Before its run as regional hegemon ended in 1945, Japan had tried to extend its reach militarily with the seizure of Manchuria, the invasion of China, and then full-scale war from the Pacific to Southeast Asia, and culturally with forced assimilation of Koreans in the vanguard. By touting liberation from domination by the white race, Japan pretended that its motives were pure. The Soviet Union had similar designs, masked by the ideology of communist liberation from class exploitation. First, Russia had challenged Japan for hegemony in Korea and over Northeast China. Then, the successor Soviet state took advantage of an alliance with the United States and last-minute entry into the Pacific front to try to use the end of World War II to impose its brand of regionalism in the name of the socialist bloc. Later it aimed to use the Korean War and the cold war to spread its influence and assert control. More recently, Japan and China have sought to use the end of the cold war to shape a form of regionalism befitting an age of globalization, but also serving nationalist objectives. The first period led to vertical regionalism by a colonizer that ended in war, the second to a bipolar regionalism that gave way to the split of the socialist side and rising autonomy within each bloc, and the third to a more horizontal search that is still at an early stage. Despite these sharp differences over time, however, we find continuities in the pursuit of one or another type of regionalism with Korea occupying a pivotal role.

Accordingly, through the three periods we trace what stand out as the economic foundations for regionalism. Prior to the 1880s they remained doubtful. China and Japan became more inward looking in the Ming/Qing and Tokugawa eras, respectively, while Choson Korea confined its trade with both to tightly prescribed locations. Unlike in Europe, ties across this region were meager—as, of course, were economic connections beyond Northeast Asia. Partly under Western influence, the infrastructure for regional economic linkages finally started taking shape by the early twentieth century, but Japan quickly became the driving force in Korea, while Russia began to take the lead across much of Northeast China. In the second distinct period, when colonial integration reached its apex followed by nation building on the basis of this foundation, we observe substantial political and social networks for economic growth. Japan built much of this, and Soviet assistance to North Korea and China in the 1950s expanded it. There are many signs of continuities between the development realized by the Japanese and the postwar economic recovery and expansion, led initially by the once-colonized areas in both Koreas and Northeast China. By the 1980s, if not before, however, it had become clear that the mammoth factories of the military-industrial complex had little to offer countries restructuring for economic integration beyond the command economies of socialism. The new challenge centered on conversion of defense enterprises and enticement of foreign direct investment. North Korea, the Russian Far East, and even Northeast China trailed southern coastal China in adapting to these changes. In the third period, though, we see full-scale economic integration, marked by cross-investments and multiple sources of dynamism. An extraordinary expansion of trade and direct investment is stimulating the commercial connections of this still ongoing period. The path to a region-wide FTA and a further surge in regional economic integration may still appear unimaginable to observers attuned to political tensions. But the third wave of regionalism shows no signs of abating as South Korean–Chinese trade and South Korean–Japanese FTA talks lead the way.

Beyond economics, the political discourse about regional relations inclusive of Korea dramatically changed over more than a century. At the turn of the past century, Koreans desperately (and often naively) sought sponsorship from one power after another, but many were ambivalent about Japan as an Asian state that they hoped would share the secrets of its newfound modernization. Driving the process was a twisting and turning Korean search for a modern identity. By contrast, the Japanese and Russians moved deliberately from vigorous efforts to expand their regional influence to embrace of the discourse of empire building. A broad regionalism was held hostage, as elsewhere, to national aggrandizement. In the aftermath of war, North Korea fell within the socialist camp, initially guided by Soviet efforts to create a closed region uncontaminated by the capitalist bloc. Pressures for communist international solidarity made for a particular kind of regionalism, and soon the Sino-Soviet split as well as North Korea's *juche* (self-reliance) doctrine fixed further new divides. Below the parallel, South Korea found itself under U.S. tutelage. Gradually, a revitalized Japan under U.S. leadership maneuvered to enlist South Korea in its designs for capitalist regionalism based on the developmental state. Although South Korean political ties with Japan were strained, a virtual alliance centering on the United States encouraged linkages.

Rival strategies were refracted through the political calculus in Pyongyang and Seoul. By the 1990s, China's calculus, too, became manifest as a driving force in regionalism, alongside Japan's enthusiasm for a broad regionalism in the aftermath of the end of the cold war and Russia's attempts to remain relevant in Northeast Asia. Rapidly expanding ties between China and South Korea affected the region. So far, however, political progress toward a breakthrough in a broadened, open regionalism falls far short of the economic integration that has been achieved. Yet, dreams of a corresponding political regionalism keep appearing as economies open wider.

Movement of people is both a crucial motor and a measuring stick of such regionalism. By the start of the twentieth century Japanese officials and merchants were moving vigorously into China and Korea, while Chinese and Korean laborers and small-scale entrepreneurs had taken up residence in the Russian Far East. Although Chinese students coming to Japan energized the revolutionary movement at home, few heterogeneous communities of elites emerged in this period. The Japanese colonial era changed that. New scholarship emphasizes the importance of human movements in the 1930s and early 1940s for the postwar recovery and development across the region. Finally, in recent years, concern focusing on the environment and human security is bringing nations closer. This is not yet leading to open borders or large-scale movements of people. Although the number of Chinese in South Korea, Japan, and the Russian Far East is growing, we cannot yet speak of a breakthrough toward the stable heterogeneous communities typical of a broad, open regionalism.

Perhaps comparisons to Europe are not fair, but that kind of regional accommodation across Northeast Asia has yet to emerge. And yet historical roots exist and recently the search for such an identity has intensified. We detect new consciousness of Northeast Asia with Korea at the center—and not just in the Koreas. The theme of how countries view regionalism reappears in various chapters, as we look for continuities as well as a chronology in the pursuit of a broad regionalism since the end of the cold war. At the ASEAN+3 summit in 2001, there was finally an agreement to establish the East Asian Community, starting with a 2005 summit. If countries agreed on a plan to manage the crisis-ridden situation in North Korea—however fraught that process remained—the possibility would be present for a consensus on the unavoidability of regional approaches to all questions, political as well as economic, social, and cultural. In sum, even globalization frequently must take regional forms to proceed.

Gilbert Rozman

Part I

Competing Visions of Regional Order

Late Nineteenth/Early Twentieth Centuries

Let us begin unconventionally for Northeast Asia, not with China, or even Japan, but with Korea. From about the 1650s until the 1850s, Korea's real status failed to correspond to its central geographic position. Situated between three larger and more powerful states, it faced not aggression but mostly benign neglect. Having been invaded in the 1590s by a newly integrated Japan that was on its way to a century of extraordinary premodern development—quadrupling of urban population, consolidation and bureaucratization of elites, rapid integration of a national market—Koreans found reassurance that Japan's new rulers chose a decentralized balance of power and inward-looking posture. In addition, having suffered incursions from a newly expansionist Manchu banner state in 1627 and 1636, Koreans were relieved that once the Manchus had seized imperial power in Beijing, interest in new attacks faded. Even as commerce flourished in China as in Japan, narrowly circumscribed channels to Korea replaced old trade networks. The Chinese concentrated commerce on overland tribute missions, which were reduced to only once a year, or periodic trade fairs even as the Japanese allowed commerce only through monopoly traders confined to the island of Tsushima. Thus, despite being a peninsula defined by open coasts, Korea had little contact with foreign merchant ships. While the royal court in Seoul embraced this relative separation, it endured because Korea's huge neighbors wanted it that way.

To be sure, there is a longer, different history of the Korean peninsula (a history whose relevance may be growing), whereby Korea had kept a central role in the region for almost a millennium—and had done so even after Japan had retreated from active engagement on the peninsula in 663 and China had abandoned periodic efforts to invade around the same time. But from the seventeenth century, forces of autonomy in each state left little room to connect the region. Certainly the means existed for possible regional integration: Large ships were well known, including Portuguese and Dutch vessels that plied the world's waters and docked at the few ports open to them; specialized, domestic commerce grew and expanded the range of goods available to exchange; and organized merchant groups amassed ample resources to stretch their operations. Strong states, however, rejected not only opening borders to representatives of European powers but also wide-open contact with their neighbors in East Asia. Attuned to a worldview that privileged perfecting harmonious state–society relations within a single country, they had no guiding thought in favor of welcoming even the Confucian outside world with which they were long familiar.

Matters changed in the nineteenth century, as sudden incorporation of parts of East Asia into the global order became the driving force for the creation of a new regional order. In the 1880s Korea appeared as a vacuum that each of the contending powers feared would be filled by another state. Each state started with the intent to deny anyone else a chance to dominate Korea while working to maintain its independence. China moved first to bolster its position, based on traditional rights, by converting its loose hegemony in 1882 from a ritually hierarchical tribute system to imperial stewardship backed by troops on Korean soil. But China proved too weak to hold what it had long left alone to sustain its influence. Russia, after obtaining the Maritime Zone in a treaty with China, became an active neighbor by building the city of Vladivostok and sending merchant and military ships along Korea's coast. Yet, Russian influence peaked in 1896–97, as the Korean king desperately sought its assistance. Korean nationalists soon organized in opposition and Russian leaders proved to be willing to cut a deal with Japan in order to get a freer hand in Manchuria. In the event, it was Japan that became the driving force in building on forces of world integration with designs for regional integration. Thus did Korea reemerge as a crossroads of Northeast Asia.

Against this competitive background, visions of a new regional order diverged. While China clung to its Sinocentric order, both Korea and Japan were reconceptualizing this part of the world to give their own countries a certain centrality. Incipient national identities clashed with both the established Chinese civilizational identity and the impending Western worldview on the horizon. In this volume's chapter by Takashi Inoguchi we are reminded that a conflict with China's insistence on clinging to a China-centered world order, combined with Korea's refusal to shift away from a Korea-centered order that tightly limited contact with Japan, drove the new Meiji government in search of a place in the Western-centered order to focus on opening Korea. Inspired by its embrace of the hegemonic global order, Japan joined Russia in striving to reshape the regional order to give it an enduring advantage as the nexus between the two. If officials in Tokyo did not proceed from a strategy for regional control, the "power vacuum in Korea" nevertheless kept inducing them ever deeper into the struggle for such leadership. Cognizant of China's delayed rethinking of a Sinocentric order that entangled it in peninsular affairs beyond its capacity and Russia's premature insistence on spheres of influence that overexposed its forces before they had securely established themselves in Northeast Asia, Japan kept ratcheting up expectations for its security role in Korea.

Russian factions, for their part, had differed on how to approach Korea and Northeast China as well. As Alexander Lukin argues in his chapter, the prevailing approach emphasized patience and no further territorial expansion. Although from 1884 there were temptations to become assertive, the position that gained the upper hand was to support Korean independence, first against China and then, more urgently, against Japan. In 1896–97, Korean leaders turned to Russia, leading to extensive involvement but still caution. Yet, military interests, led by officials intent on acquiring a naval base in Korea, decided aggressively to challenge Japan. Koreans had drawn Russia into their power struggles, and then Russians, too, played a large role in drawing Japanese more deeply into Korean politics. In the event, the Japanese, victorious in the Sino-Japanese War and then the Russo-Japanese War, found no obstruction in gaining full control over Korea. The re-emergence of Korean centrality ended abruptly with Korea reduced to a colony and Japan growing more assertive in using its toehold there to subject the entire region to its imperial authority.

Simply put, Koreans lacked a unified and consistent strategy that would allow them to steer a path through the diplomatic machinations and oppose the assertion of Japanese hegemony. On the contrary, Korean actions played into that outcome. Hahm Chaibong's chapter traces a pattern of Koreans seeking saviors and then putting up little resistance when the outside power infringed on national independence, whether orthodox Confucians accepting China's resident control, the king and a pro-Russian cabinet calling for Russia to exercise dominant influence, or the Enlightenment Party agreeing to Japan's "Protectorate." Mostly, Koreans were content to retain the old regional order. Later, some idealized Pan-Asianism, without realizing that this stance allowed Japanese nationalism to rush into the void. But a number of Korean modernizers, as Hahm shows, consciously looked to Japan as a model to lead the way for the entire region.

Late nineteenth- and early twentieth-century political and geopolitical changes in the regional order took place against the background of a sharp rise in trade, albeit from a very low starting point, as documented in the chapter by Kirk W. Larsen. By 1883, three treaty ports in Korea had joined the country not only to Western entrepôts but also to nearby ports in southwest Japan and northern China. Importantly, Larsen has uncovered dynamism in the Korean economy *prior* to Japanese involvement. The upshot, though, was that Korean traders and farmers became closely linked to Japan. At the ports of Wonsan and Inchon, Chinese merchants more than held their own for a time. Before long, however, textiles from

Japan superseded British goods, strengthening Japan's hand at the expense of the Chinese merchants. Through integration of trade, transportation, and communications, the Japanese developed an infrastructure conducive to their political control as well as to making this peninsula the bridgehead for further continental economic penetration. Japan defeated China not only militarily but also by utilizing their rapidly modernizing economy to draw Korea's economy closer. The lessons for all concerned would be bitter.

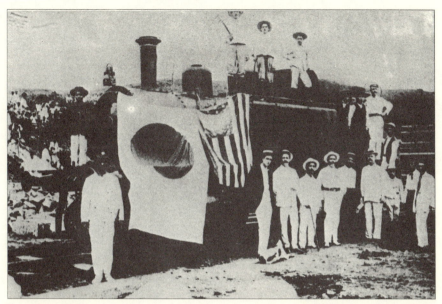

The first railroad in Korea was built as a joint venture between the Japanese and Americans. The Kyongin railroad line was finished in 1896. (Reproduced with permission of *Donga Ilbo*, Seoul, Korea.)

The first streetcar ran in May 1899 after its completion by an American company the prior year. Streetcar is seen coming out of its depot in the East Gate area of Seoul. (Reproduced with permission of Somundang, Seoul, Korea.)

The opening ceremony for Kanto Normal School for Koreans, 1908. *Chosenkoku shinkei.* (Photograph by Hayashi Buichi; Published by Hayashi, Kameko, Japan.)

Japanese soldiers and border stone marking the boundary between Korea and Kanto, Manchuria. The stele was first erected in 1712. The Japanese finalized the exact location of the boundary with the Chinese in 1909. (*Shiho bunko,* Japan)

Crossing to China over Yalu River. *Majima shashincho* (Photographs of Majima).
(Sotokufu rinji majima hasyutsujo, Japan)

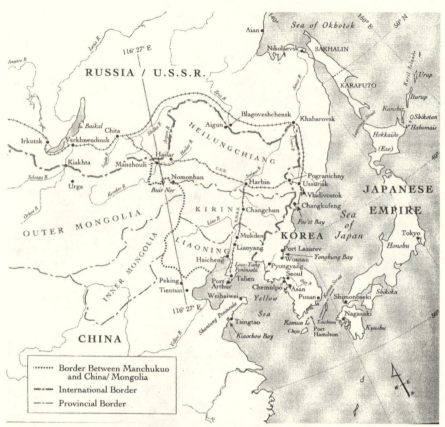

Map of Northeast Asia, 1905-41 (From G. Patrick March, *Eastern Destiny: Russia in Asia and the North Pacific.* Westport CT: Praeger, 1996. Used with permission of Greenwood Publishing Group.)

1

Korea in Japanese Visions
of Regional Order

Takashi Inoguchi

During the past fifteen hundred years, the Korean peninsula has frequently been at the forefront of Japanese debates about Japan's place in its region. In particular, two turning points decided Japan's involvement in East Asia prior to 1945. The first occurred in 663, after the Japanese defeat in southwestern Korea (then called Paekche) forced them to retreat from the continental bridgehead that had been established. With the exception of the invasion of Korea by Hideyoshi at the end of the sixteenth century, this retreat from active involvement on the Asian mainland endured for twelve hundred years, ensuring a level of Japanese autonomy from continental Asia far beyond that of (for example) England from continental Europe.

The second major turning point was Japan's submission to Commodore Matthew Perry's coercive naval diplomacy in 1853, obliging Japan to open its ports and country to Western powers. While the seventh-century defeat discouraged Japan from active involvement in Asia, the 1853 "opening" led to Japanese reengagement with the continent. In the latter half of the nineteenth century, competition with other powers for influence over Korea led to a rethinking of Japan's place in Northeast Asia. Thus, whether Japan has been engaging with or disengaging from mainland Asia, geographic realities and historical connections (good and bad) put Korea at the center of Japan's interest in the continent.

An Interconnected History

Control over Korea has long had a profound impact on Japan's fortunes. In the mid-seventh century A.D., the Koguryo kingdom, whose territory spread across Manchuria and northern Korea, engaged in a series of violent conflicts with China's Sui dynasty and Sui's successor, the Tang. In 660, Koguryo's peninsular rival, the Silla kingdom of southeastern Korea, allied with Tang to defeat Koguryo. The combined forces of Silla and Tang then overcame the Paekche-Japan coalition in southwestern Korea in 663, and most of the Korean peninsula was unified under Silla control.[1] These regional upheavals led to new power configurations in Silla-dominated Korea and in Yamato-dominated Japan. Strong dynasties in China and even longer-lasting united dynasties in Korea left little scope over the next millennium for Japanese armed intervention on the continent. Instead, advancing from their nucleus of power in the Yamato area, Japanese leaders turned to state-building at home.

Although it is most likely that the ruling elites of Yamato-dominated Japan were direct descendants of Koreans (as indicated by Emperor Akihito's explicit reference in his official speech made in reply to President Kim Dae Jung during the latter's state visit to Japan in 1998), the newly consolidating regime in Japan took swift measures at making its separation and distance from the continent solid and enduring and at expanding and consolidating its territory and authority toward northeastern and southwestern Japan, which had been controlled by more "indigenous" peoples. Their new goals were centered on distancing Japan from Sino-centric civilization and creating a separate world order on the Japanese archipelago. This retreat from the continent and subsequent consolidation of the Japanese state appears comparable to England's retreat from Europe and its subsequent vigorous state formation.[2] In fact, however, Japan's retreat was much greater and longer lasting. Furthermore, Korea's unity and stability—and its continued close relationship to China—contrasted with the ongoing flux across Europe that invited renewed English participation.

Japan demonstrated its determination to place itself outside the Chinese world order by—among other acts—sending official correspondence to China in the name of the Japanese "emperor" (unlike a proper tributary state such as Korea, which could claim only to have a "king," implicitly subordinate to the Chinese emperor), and by receiving "tributary" missions from the Korean peninsular states of Silla and Parhae, the latter of which had more or less inherited the territory of Koguryo.[3] Through most of the next twelve hundred years—again, with the exception of Hideyoshi's disastrous expedition to conquer Korea in the late sixteenth century—Japan's foreign policy doctrine was to keep stable, friendly, and commercially profitable relations with the continent (China and Korea) as long as they remained at arm's length. Despite Japan's later receptivity to Confucian teachings, one of the consequences of this distancing was to solidify a civilization gap; even some Western observers, from Arnold Toynbee to Samuel Huntington, have thus drawn a sharp distinction between Japanese and Chinese civilization.[4]

Commodore Perry's gunboat diplomacy led quickly to the establishment of a U.S.-Japan Treaty of Amity in 1854.[5] Under the circumstances of the mid-nineteenth century, Japan's conception of world order also made the Western world its principal reference, replacing earlier reference to the Chinese world order. In sharp contrast to the contemporary Korean leader, the Taewongun, who fought and repulsed such Western demands in the 1860s and 1870s, the leaders of Tokugawa

Japan, faced with superior force, were realistic enough to recognize that Western power was unconquerable and the trend of Westernization irreversible. Japan could not possibly challenge the Western nations' predominance in technology, commerce, institutions, and knowledge. What Japan did instead was to create a new regime adaptable to a Western world order. The Meiji Restoration of 1868 was crafted to execute Japan's fast Westernization while insisting that the Japanese spirit would remain intact (*wakon yosai*—Japanese spirit, Western technology). "Revitalizing" the Japanese "spirit" had an international as well as a domestic dimension: Leaders were concerned with proving that Japan could shape the evolution of its region and, thereby, prove its equal standing to Western powers.

Meiji Japan generally complied with the Westphalian conception of state sovereignty;[6] both internally and externally, Japan established new institutions and sources of legitimacy. At a time when the Japanese government employed only a few thousand Japanese, more than five hundred foreigners were employed in the key sectors of government-led institutions and enterprises to ignite rapid Westernization. Former samurai warriors became energetic bureaucrats, establishing a central government bureaucracy, modern army, and national police force. Externally, the Ryukyu archipelago was formally subordinated to Japan, and Korean diplomacy became controlled directly by Tokyo, rather than via the Tsushima domain, as it had been previously. Beginning with Korea, Japanese strategic thinkers reinterpreted existing notions of a Japanese order with an eye toward regional involvement and intervention on the Asian mainland. The "Korea problem" in modern Japanese foreign policy thus emerged.

The Tokugawa World Order and Korea

The Tokugawa regime had long been aware of Western dominance in the world. Japanese world maps used in the mid-Tokugawa and late Tokugawa eras represent well the changing Japanese conceptions of world order—quite literally, the West loomed much larger than before.[7] Westerners were very active in Japan beginning in the sixteenth century, when Portuguese brought guns and Spaniards introduced Christianity. A total ban on Christianity by the Tokugawa regime in the seventeenth century was triggered by the success of Christian missionaries in converting some of the *daimyo* of southwestern Japan to Christianity. Those lords could have grown into a united opposition to the Tokugawa regime, as they had more access to Western ideas, institutions, and technology. The total monopoly of foreign commerce by the Tokugawa regime was similarly motivated. Central control of foreign trade was regarded as indispensable for maintaining a power disparity between the Tokugawa regime in Edo and the *daimyo* distributed over three hundred domains and as a corollary for enhancing the legitimacy of the Tokugawa regime. In harmony with the time-tested diplomatic tradition of Japan, the Tokugawa regime set up its own port called Deshima at Nagasaki to monopolize foreign commerce, mostly with the Dutch and Chinese, while delegating power to three domains—Tsushima, Satsuma, and Matsumae—to control ties with Korea, the Ryukyus, and the indigenous Ainu of the North (later Russia would be added).

The Satsuma domain conquered the Ryukyu kingdom in the late sixteenth century, but while extracting resources from the Ryukyus, it forced the kingdom to maintain the pretense that it was an independent kingdom that continued to send tributary missions to the Qing.[8] The Matsumae domain engaged in commerce with the Ainus on Hokkaido and became the spearhead for Japanese settlement of the northern island. As Russians started to visit Japan requesting ports, water, and energy, the Matsumae domain even became a foreign office on behalf of the Tokugawa regime, following instructions to deny the Russians entry. Most significant was the Tsushima domain, which played the role of an emissary-cum-tributary vis-à-vis Choson Korea, while serving also as foreign office toward Korea. Korea, understandably suspicious of Japan since the Hideyoshi invasion, sent its own emissary-cum-tributary very frequently to the Tokugawa regime.[9] Thanks to the buffer of Tsushima, Tokugawa Japan and Choson Korea were successfully able to coexist without questioning their respective visions of world order. This fragile balance could be maintained as long as both Japan and Korea had few foreign connections and little pressure to adjust their international relations, but the arrival of Western powers forced first Japan and then Korea to face conflicting realities.

The official Korean worldview held that China was the center of civilization, although in private (and sometimes in public), Choson intellectuals put Korea at the center of the East Asian world order, seeing the Qing dynasty as only semicivilized, ruled by Manchu "barbarians." Japan, in terms of Confucian social structure, ritual, and etiquette, was even less civilized, from this point of view.[10] Somewhat similarly, Nguyen Vietnam regarded itself as the southern half of Chinese civilization, whereas the northern half of the civilization was commonly called China.[11] Tokugawa Japan went even further in its rethinking, following Japan's long separation from the events on the Asian mainland. Doubting that it was really an heir to Chinese civilization, Japanese had long envisioned their country as distinctive and apart from the Sinocentric world order. They visualized a separate world order, although overlapping with the Chinese one, which put Edo at the center.[12] Perhaps in part because of this, Japan was much more successful than Korea at relinquishing what remained of a traditional East Asian, Sinocentric worldview and reimagining Northeast Asia in terms of modern power politics, with Korea very much the focus of its strategic concerns.

Korea at the Center of Japanese Regional Strategic Thinking

Japan went through fifteen years of internal debates and strife after the Perry visit and the Treaty of Amity with the United States in 1854. After the domains were abolished, including the Tsushima domain in 1871, the entire framework of diplomacy had to change. Very complex and multifaceted diplomatic traditions manifested themselves simultaneously. First, the Qing administration continued to believe in the persistence of a China-centered world order, whose authority had to be claimed over Korea, Taiwan, and the Ryukyu kingdom. Second, Korea continued to believe in the persistence of a Korea-centered world order, insisting that it could deal with Japan only through the Tsushima domain while Korea remained closed. Third, Japan was in the midst of shifting from the Chinese-referenced Japanese order to the Western-referenced Japanese order in a long transition that accelerated from 1871 and did not reach its culmination until 1895. It was a multifaceted entity during this transition. Comparing itself to the West, it aspired to become a modern country and sought to abolish unequal treaties concluded in the 1850s and 1860s, which accorded the West extraterritoriality and deprived Japan of tariff autonomy. Against Korea it acted like the Western powers, demanding to open ports as well as the entire country. Vis-à-vis Qing China, it refused to acknowledge the Qing authority over the Ryukyu kingdom and over Korea. Of course, all of this was taking place as the Japanese consolidated their control over Hokkaido and Okinawa as new territory, where minority groups experienced elements of imperial expansion. Given this diversity, we argue that the period between the Kanghwa (1876) and Shimonoseki (1895) treaties exhibited four strikingly different diplomatic/domestic traditions in Japanese foreign relations, territorial expansion, and consolidation. Korea became the focus that brought these varied approaches together.

In the early 1870s Korea refused to deal with the Meiji regime directly, insisting that it deal only with the Tsushima domain, which had disappeared. The diplomatic tie was broken between Korea and Japan, and Japan replayed with Korea what Perry had done. It began with coercive diplomacy and proceeded to the conclusion of a treaty to open ports and a country. The treaty of Kanghwa was concluded with Korea in 1876. In a similar vein, the Ryukyu kingdom was abolished and then, a little strangely, it was reestablished in 1872 after all the other domains had been abolished. Finally, it was transformed into Okinawa prefecture in 1879. In 1871 Ryukyu fishing ships drifted across to Taiwan and some Ryukyu fishermen were killed by Taiwanese people. Japan registered its protest to the Qing. Negotiations were prolonged, each side sticking to its own vision of world order over the Ryukyus and to its perceived place in the world. Japan dispatched troops and killed some Taiwanese in 1874. The Qing acknowledged Japan's action as legitimate because they thought that the Taiwanese involved were "outside (Chinese) civilization" and paid war indemnities to Japan thanks to the British role as an intermediary, which must have been puzzled by the mindsets of the two Oriental "inscrutables." As seen in China, this acquiescence was in return for Japan's agreement to evacuate Taiwan.[13]

Although the Japanese had taken steps forward in realizing the Japanese vision of regional and national order by 1876, the year of the Treaty of Kanghwa, it was merely the beginning of a path toward narrowing the disparity between vision and practice. The transition between 1868 and 1876 was made largely in response to the need to consolidate Japan's now expanded home territory in relation to what the Tsushima, Matsumae, and Satsuma domains had managed in their diplomatic activities, allowing Japan's conception of regional order and Korea's and China's conceptions of regional order to coexist. Once Hokkaido and Okinawa were firmly established as home territories, the difficulties with Korea, Taiwan, and Qing China itself still had to be addressed according to the Japanese conception of regional order.

The logic of Japanese activities toward China was roughly as follows: Japan opened its country to the West. The West imposed its self-righteous and unjust unequal treaties on Japan. But Japan had been striving to make the country rich and the army strong (*fukoku kyohei*), thereby trying to achieve a status sooner rather than later on a par with the West.[14] Looking at Japan's neighbors, Korea and China, the situation was not good. They obstinately stuck to their old-fashioned and outdated practices to suit their old beliefs. Because the Japanese felt obliged to get rid of the outdated beliefs and practices of their own in order to eradicate the Western prejudice against despotic and decadent Orientals, officials deemed that their country must act in perfect observance of the Western practice of international law and use of force among nations. Through such diplomatic and military actions toward its neighbors, Japan tried to achieve three aims simultaneously.

First, there was a desire to assert Japan's vision of regional order in parallel to its own consolidation of internal rule by the new modernizing Meiji regime. As Iwakura Tomomi, one of the key leaders of antiexpansionism put it: "We will not be able to restore our national rights without first making concrete achievements and establishing real power. To accomplish this, we must consolidate political control at home and expand our wealth. Our work will not have lasting results if we seek rash and hasty achievements."[15]

Second, the Meiji regime wished to undermine Korea's and China's largely outdated yet still powerful visions of regional order, which would serve the purpose of facilitating the decay of outdated ideas and institutions in Korea and China. In the words of Enomoto Takeaki, "There is no doubt that to control the port of Pusan is 'strategically' indispensable to Japan. It is also our major policy requirement to open Korea, to let Korea have intercourse with foreign countries and to have trade at Kanghwa or Hanyang (Seoul). It would provide immense 'political' prestige to our country, since no other country has done this before. This is all the more true since only the Japanese, among the similar races like the Chinese, Vietnamese, and Siamese, think of it and do it."[16]

Third, the Japanese leadership tried to dissociate Japan from its neighbors so that the newly civilizing and rapidly modernizing Japan could not be lumped together with the despotic and decadent neighbors within the club of civilized nations called the West. As Fukuzawa Yukichi explained: "We cannot wait for our neighbour countries to become so civilized that all may combine together to make Asia progress. We must rather break out of formation and behave in the same way as the civilized countries of the West are doing. . . . We would do better to treat China and Korea in the same way as do the western nations."[17]

Fukuzawa, the foremost thinker and educator and writer in Meiji Japan, is best known for articulating these streams of thought during this important transition from Kanghwado through Shimonoseki. His writings offer a fascinating array of thought and passion during the transition. They have an element of the logic and momentum of internal unification spilling over its adjacent space, reminiscent of the French Revolution and the Napoleonic Wars. Saigo Takamori, who argued that Korea be conquered by Japan but failed to persuade the government and rose up against the government in vain, is sometimes likened to Napoleon.

Japan's second aim had elements of the logic of democracy promotion. Fukuzawa, president of Keio, which is the oldest university in Japan, gave opportunities for education to such Korean reformers as Kim Okkyun and Park Yunghyo and sought to stimulate the study of Japanese modernization as a force for engineering regime change in Korea. Despite this enthusiasm, he was so disappointed by the failure of modernizing reforms in Korea that he published a widely noted piece called "Depart from Asia" (*Datsu-a ron*) in which he argued that Japan could not do much about the despotic and decadent Asia and it had better focus its efforts on its own modernization in harmony with the West. Needless to say, other streams of thought went in the direction of building Japan's civilizing bridgehead in Korea by colonizing Korea slightly later when Qing occupied Hanyang (Seoul) after Korea's reformists failed in their regime change attempt. An argument that grew increasingly popular was that Japan's neighbors must be civilized, if not by the West, then by Japan. A surge in support for this way of thinking occurred after Japan defeated the Qing in 1895 and found its influence in Korea heightened.

A third aim for Japan was to achieve diplomatic recognition as a civilized and modernizing country so that the West could bestow on it an equal status. Japan's aspirations were frustrated, however, immediately after the victory over the Qing in the form of the tripartite intervention of France, Germany, and Russia, which were alarmed by Japan's swift expansion of influence in East Asia and forced Japan to return some of the territories it had obtained.

The Treaty of Shimonoseki symbolized two things to Japan. First, it registered the victory of a civilizing Japan over a decaying Qing. Its victory enabled Japan to further seek its position on a par with the West. Second, its victory was overshadowed by the tripartite intervention whereby Japan was forced to return the Liaodong Peninsula. Furthermore, though extraterritoriality was relinquished, tariff autonomy was retained until 1911. But most important, by 1895, three threads of thought started to converge: that of the modernizers, focusing on internal consolidation; the civilizationists, focusing on the diffusion of new ideas and institutions both at home and abroad; and the realists, focusing on catching up and competing with the West. This marked the end to the "let one hundred flowers bloom" period of the Meiji era. Once the modernizers achieved victory at home and fastened onto parliamentary monarchy, once the civilizationists parted from fellow Asians whom Japanese thought were similarly victimized by the West, and once the realists despaired at what they considered a shameful tripartite intervention, most were co-opted by the modernizing Meiji regime. As Tokutomi Soho argued, "It is no exaggeration to state that the return of the Liaodong peninsula decided my fate. Thereafter I became a different man spiritually. Japan was forced to succumb to the Powers' will only because it was weak. I was convinced that, without power, justice and morality had no value at all."[18]

Japanese had become accustomed to viewing their nation as victimized by the Western powers. The outcome of the war of 1894–95 left them with renewed frustration that they had been denied fair treatment. The result was a sharpened sense that Northeast Asia had become a proving ground that would test Japan's worthiness as a "normal" great power. It was under these circumstances that Russian expansionist behavior drew Japan's rapt attention. The Trans-Siberian Railroad was beginning to transport Russian soldiers to the region. Plans were taking shape to construct as a foreign concession the Chinese Eastern Railway through Manchuria. Rising concern about Russian capabilities as well as intentions had many sources, but the foremost worry in the late 1890s was the Russian involvement in Korea. That country's chronic political instability gave Russia an opening to exert considerable influence. Instead of leaving Asia, Japanese found themselves drawn ever more deeply into the mainland. Motives varied: to prevent a threat to national security by Russian control over Korea; to prove to the Western powers that Japan was their equal by drawing Korea into Japan's sphere of influence; or even to realize the image of a Japanese world order in which Korea became the next extension after power had been consolidated in the Kuril and Ryukyu islands, and, from 1895, Taiwan had been transferred from Chinese to Japanese control. For the decade leading to the Russo-Japanese War the struggle over Korea took center stage.

Prior to 1895 Japanese became accustomed to arguing that their role was to defend Korean independence as well as to sponsor its modern transformation. After all, Korean conservatives had been clinging to the notion of China's special place on the peninsula in opposition to reformers, who largely welcomed a greater role for Japan in support of opening their country further and of launching modernization reforms. It was tempting for Japanese to take pride in their country as a progressive force, as both a model and a protector. In place of the specter of China's outdated presence, the aftermath of the Sino-Japanese War brought a more threatening image of Russia's potential future influence as an imperialist power that would leave Japan stranded from the Asian mainland. It was not long before Japan's perception of its own involvement began to slip from protector to possessor, albeit with noble claims for the regional mission ahead.

As the Japanese media commemorated the centennial of the outbreak of the Russo-Japanese War on February 10, 2004, they offered different versions of its historical significance. *Mainichi shimbun* briefly linked the victory over the military great power Russia with annexation of Korea, the Sino-Japanese War, and the Pacific War, arguing that Japanese should return to the spirit of the 1855 Shimoda Treaty with Russia, which peacefully delineated the border.[19] In contrast, *Sankei shimbun* gave abundant coverage to reviving memories of Japan's positive contribution as a lesson to inspire renewed pride and a more vigorous foreign policy after sixty years of defeatism since 1945. It concluded that, contrary to the message from antiwar Japanese media of the times, the war with Russia was unavoidable and proved a turning point in world history by inspiring colonial peoples' liberation from white rule. It showed the value of a nation uniting behind a war.[20] *Sankei* on the day of the centennial also published an opinion piece by Kobori Keiichiro, who glorified the spirit of the Japanese people that resulted in victory. He noted that under the brainwashing of the U.S. occupation and the Tokyo Trials, the Japanese people had lost their historical memory. Postwar teaching and textbooks then perpetuated a soiled anti-Japanese history, distorting the glorious achievements of the Japanese nation. By recalling the decisive historical event in 1905 and renewing memories of glory, a national movement can begin toward the reconstruction of Japan. If this opinion seems extreme to many, it is no longer the voice of just a few in Japan. Insistence on reinterpreting the war years of the 1930s and 1940s may still be rather uncommon, but pride is now widely evident in recollections of Meiji era policies in Northeast Asia.

Within Japan there are diminished signs these days of the prevailing view in the West that beginning at least by the time of the establishment of a protectorate over Korea in 1905 Japan was on the path toward imperialism, which destabilized Northeast Asia and imperiled relations with other powers. Although the United States and other powers had not opposed Japan's early steps that stabilized Korea, the increasingly assertive Japanese posture that followed has been harshly attacked as the prime humiliation for the peoples of the region. Victory in 1905 represents, in the eyes of observers in the West as well as in Korea and China, the fountainhead of arrogance and unbalanced foreign policy that brought tragedy to other nations. It was premised on widely shared reasoning that "vigorous foreign policies and enterprises were a sign of internal health and power."[21] At the heart of the divergence is the question of Korea's formal submission to Japanese rule in 1910. Was it a voluntary union for which Japan should have no need to apologize or was it an inseparable step on the path of imperialism that left a dismal legacy for regional trust? The debate inside Japan has been renewed.

Conclusion

Commodore Matthew Perry's coercive naval diplomacy of 1853 led Japan to depart decisively from the Asian continent, to relinquish its remaining attachment to the traditional Sinocentric world view, and to profoundly rethink the regional order. Although Japan had developed its own vision of regional order helped by a natural geographical distance and further reinforced by the self-conscious policy of amity at arm's length with the Asian mainland over ten centuries, Japan's vision of regional order was not entirely free from the Chinese world order, partly because of geographical proximity, partly because of historical ties, and partly because Japan had benefited from its interactions with the continent in order to enhance legitimacy to its domestic leadership by associating with its big and small brothers vis-à-vis potential or actual domestic contenders, and to gain commercially and technologically from its trade with the continent. The turning point of 1853 is comparable to the event of 663, when Japan retreated from the Asian continent and consolidated its rule at home in the Japanese archipelago. But the results, in a way, were opposite: One led to isolation, the other to opening. The Western world order of the mid-nineteenth century painted the world map in various colors: solid color to the West, pale color to the semi-independent, that is, Asia, and white color to nonindependent, that is, Africa. On this world map, Asia was a place for the West to open ports and countries and to remold old-fashioned ideas and institutions. Asia meant something different once Japan subscribed to the Western-referenced world order.

Whereas the Chinese-referenced world order once gave comfort and benefit to Japan for a good amount of time, thanks in large part to the geographical and political distance Japan kept vis-à-vis the continent, it worked dysfunctionally for Japan once the West stood at the gate. The Chinese-referenced world order constrained Japan when it coped with the West standing at the gate. The Japanese grand strategy was to join the West. It meant building a rich country and a strong army at home whereas abroad it meant honing skills of diplomacy and war. It meant that Japan "behave well" in the Western world order by building a "civilized" country and that Japan "keep its friendly distance" from the Continent. But as history evolved, Japanese visions of regional order went awry in two directions: asserting itself in defiance of the Western world order and getting deeply mired in Continental politics. Thus, the late nineteenth century marked a watershed in the evolution of the Japanese vision of regional order.

2

Russian Views of Korea, China, and the Regional Order in Northeast Asia

Alexander Lukin

In the second half of the nineteenth century, China and Korea were important Russian partners in Northeast Asia. However, Russian views of these countries differed significantly. By that time Russia had a three-hundred-year history of relations with China, and thus the role of China's image in Russian culture and politics was much greater. Various groups in Russia saw China very differently. For some, it was a symbol of Oriental wisdom, good government, and a proper approach to nature worthy of emulation; for others, it was a stagnant country in decay where the idea of progress could be instilled only with cannons and rifles. Foreign policy recommendations also varied, ranging from the idea of fighting Western powers in alliance with Beijing and securing China's unity to recommendations of dividing China in concert with Western powers. The approach to Korea was more unified. Korea was seen by most as an underdeveloped but friendly country with a pleasant and hardworking population that had suffered foreign intrigues and oppression. While elements within the Russian establishment had designs on Korean territory, many in Russian society sincerely sympathized with Koreans and wished to help them in the struggle for their country's independence. The problem of Chinese and Korean immigration also played a role in shaping the Russian perception of both countries, but it did not directly influence Russian views on foreign policy.

In the field of practical foreign policy in the Far East, several factions espousing different views vied for supremacy in Russia. One view, represented by the foreign minister, Vladimir Lamsdorff, maintained that Russia's interests lay in Europe and the Near East and it should therefore avoid being too active in the Far East. The second faction, represented by the finance minister, Sergei Witte, stood for steady and gradual economic penetration of Manchuria and only to a limited extent in Korea as well as the avoidance of war with Japan at all costs. The third group, associated with the war minister, Aleksei Kuropatkin, argued that Russia should come to terms with other powers in Europe and switch its attention to the Far East. It believed that military annexation of Manchuria was possible, but that Japan should be compensated with political domination in Korea. These three factions united to oppose the fourth one (Alexander Bezobrazov and his supporters), which advocated a proactive Korean policy despite Japanese objections. The resulting Russian course of action in the region was inconsistent and led to a disastrous war with Japan. As a result of its defeat, Russian influence in the region deteriorated and Russia had to agree to the political loss of Korea and to coordinate its actions in Manchuria with Japan.

Russia and Asia

Russian views of China and Korea in the nineteenth century can be understood only within the more general framework of the Russian worldview at the time. From the second half of the eighteenth century, when French became the language of polite society, Russian thought was under the profound influence of European, particularly French, thinkers. Followers of the French Enlightenment saw the East differently but had one thing in common: Their approach was instrumental. The East was studied not for its own sake but to provide an example (either positive or negative) to European rulers or to support general theories of human society.

Like the European Sinophobes, the Russian nineteenth-century Westernizers often used China as a negative opposite to the advanced West, which presented a social and spiritual ideal for Russia. Different Westernizing schools of thought saw China as a symbol of various ills: a godless and nonspiritual society (if they were religious themselves), stagnant and immobile (if they believed in technological progress), or tyrannical and despotic (if they were nonreligious fighters for liberty). Among the most prominent Russians who wrote along these lines were the philosophers Aleksandr Herzen and Vladimir Solov'ev, the writer Dmitri Merezhkovskii, and others.

In the nineteenth century, the Eurocentrist concept of unidirectional progress became only one trend in Russian thinking that came under criticism both from official and nonofficial circles. The view of Westernizers that progress was possible only in the West came under serious criticism from both supporters of the official concept of "Orthodoxy, Aurocracy, Nationality"—such as Minister of Enlightenment (education) Count Sergei Uvarov and historian Mikhail Pogodin—and nonofficial Slavophiles and Pan-Slavists, including the poets Aleksei Khomiakov and Fedor Tiutchev and the philosopher Nikolai Danilevskii.

Another line of thought developed the idea of Russia's special mission in Asia and China in an even more radical fashion. Its proponents—mainly but not exclusively coming from the military—argued that Russia should deal with the backward Asians militarily, conquer them, and impose civilization forcefully under Russian rule. There were several components in the application of this approach to China: the belief that China was weak and its army ineffective; the idea that the Chinese, like all Asians, were uncivilized barbarians or at least had long ago fallen far behind the level of progress in the world; and the perception that Russia's unique mission and its contribution to world civilization was the firm and speedy "civilizing" of China and other Asian countries. This was the view of most military officers dealing with Asia, such as the great explorer Nikolai Przheval'skii and Nicholas II's war minister, General Aleksei Kuropatkin.

In the latter part of the nineteenth century, extreme Westernizers—and even some supporters of the now official position that Russia was different from Europe—turned to advocacy of Russian expansion in Asia. These feelings increased, especially after Russia's loss in the Crimean War and the growth of dissatisfaction with Europe. A peculiar mixture of Westernism and Russian patriotism emerged: While Europe was seen as hostile and unwilling to accept Russia's greatness, Russia was to turn to China to realize both its great destiny and its civilizing potential.

An Unwelcome Immigrant

By the end of the nineteenth century, China had become not just a theoretical problem for Russia but an acute political one as well. The Russian Far East was developing rapidly due to: the construction of the Trans-Siberian Railway, including the part that went through China's territory (the Chinese Eastern Railroad), acquired through a Russian concession ("the alienation zone"); the emergence of several Russian settlements, including the city of Harbin; the deployment of Russian troops in Manchuria during the Boxer Rebellion; and the creation of a Russian naval base in Port Arthur. All of these measures were closely linked to strategic concerns. It was thought that if Russia did not penetrate further into China, other world powers would get there first and would undermine Russia's position. To be sure, the military threat at the time from a weak China was not believed to be real, unlike the threat from Japan. However, in various circles of Russian society, another fear existed: that of Chinese ethnic penetration and of the sinification of Russian territories.

The greatest fear of the ethnic "China peril" naturally concerned the Russian Far East, which had been confirmed as Russian territory only in 1860, and where many Chinese and Koreans were settling either illegally or as contract laborers. Originally, the Chinese (and Manchu) population of the area numbered only a few thousand, and most Chinese came to the Russian Far East after it became Russian. Chinese (as well as Korean and Japanese) immigration was originally stimulated by very liberal regulations, adopted in 1861, which encouraged both Russians and foreigners to settle in the Amur and maritime regions by providing them with public land and waiving taxes for twenty years.

The number of Chinese in Russia continued to grow, and workers were still hired by private companies. According to an 1897 census, 57,000 Chinese lived in Russia (excluding Chinese Muslims), with 41,000 of them living in the Far East. In 1910, official statistics suggested that there were more than 115,000 Chinese in Russia, but, according to unofficial estimates, there were about 150,000. During the working season, this number as much as doubled.[1] Between 1910 and 1914, the Chinese population of the Russian Far East grew to between 80,000 and 100,000, with the majority residing in the maritime and Amur regions.

The number of Korean and Japanese residents also grew.[2] In 1910, the entire Russian population of the Russian Far East amounted to about 1.2 million, with the Chinese constituting 10 to 12 percent of the population.[3] When Russia joined World War I, there was a desperate need for workers, so most limitations were forgotten. Another 100,000 Chinese laborers were hired, and Chinese workers spread far beyond the Lake Baikal region, including European Russia from Murmansk to the Black Sea. According to figures provided by the officer of the Chinese Embassy in Russia who was in charge of labor affairs, during the war 150,000 Chinese laborers worked in Russia, with about 50,000 of them in the frontline zone.[4] In 1916, the total population of Vladivostok was 88,576, of whom 28,770 (about a third) were Chinese.[5]

The Chinese were often seen as spies or as potential "guides" for the "rear army" of the neighboring country, which could rise immediately if a signal were given. The government feared that the influx of Chinese, as well as Korean and Japanese settlers, could lead to its losing control over its Far Eastern territories. This was the essence of the so-called yellow question, which was widely discussed at the time. The fear significantly intensified after Russia lost its war with Japan in 1905, and respect for the Russian government in the region significantly decreased.[6]

Images and Foreign Policy

Until the mid-eighteenth century, Russia's policy toward China was quite cautious. The image of a remote but large, strong country that could create unnecessary problems for Russia's unpopulated and poorly protected regions played an important role. At the beginning of the eighteenth century, Peter the Great instructed the Church to send missions to China in which priests should have been "not so much learned as they are wise and obliging," and learned "not to arouse anger in the Chinese leaders or in the Jesuits."[7] From that time on, the government in St. Petersburg did its best to adhere to the treaties that were concluded at the end of the seventeenth century and the beginning of the eighteenth century and not to provoke Beijing. According to the Treaty of Nerchinsk (1689), which was signed after the Qing dynasty forces defeated the Russian garrisons on the Amur, Russia had to recognize that the Amur basin belonged to China. However, the Treaty of Nerchinsk and the following treaties of Bura and Kiakhta in 1727, which further clarified the boundary (still leaving much of its eastern part undefined), gave Russia important advantages. Russia was allowed to establish an ecclesiastical mission with a language school in Beijing (officially to serve the spiritual needs of the Russian captives or defectors who resided there); two towns (Kiakhta and Tsurukhaitu) were opened for trade; and Russians were allowed to send periodic trade caravans to Peking, which the Chinese recorded as tribute missions.

Russia found itself in a privileged position. China opened its ports for trade with other countries only in 1842, under the Treaty of Nanjing, and no other country was allowed to have permanent representatives in China until 1861, when formal diplomatic missions were established as a result of the Second Opium War. So, despite the loss of some territories that were believed to be remote and unimportant, Russia benefited greatly from its peaceful relations with China. For example, before 1850, the Kiakhta trade (which effectively became the major trade center with China) had accounted for 15 to 20 percent of the total customs revenues of the Russian empire, while customs revenues accounted for about 20 percent of all government revenues from both direct and indirect taxes. Russia imported 90 to 95 percent of its tea (which became a very popular drink in the nineteenth century) from China and became a major tea supplier to Europe. Before ports were opened for European trade, Russia gained a lot from transit trade between Europe and China. China was also important for Russian exports.[8] Thus, Russian supporters of close relations with China claimed that these relations were special and that the Russian attitude to China was much better than that of other European countries. The Chinese emperor, Yi Zhu (reign title: Xianfeng), himself wrote, "China and the Russian barbarians have been friendly and at peace for over a century without a breach. This is very different from Britain and France."[9]

The situation changed radically in the middle of the nineteenth century. Many factors played a role in Russia's decision to claim the Far Eastern territories, which, according to the Treaty of Nerchinsk, belonged to China:

- the decline of trade as a result of the growing naval trade between China and Europe;
- Russia's rivalry with Britain, which reached the Far East;
- the deterioration of Russia's influence in Europe as a result of the Crimean War;
- the fact that Russian settlers were moving closer to these areas;
- the overestimation of Russia's military power by Beijing; and
- the fact that China, as a result of a series of internal rebellions and wars with European powers, was weak and unable to defend its own remote and virtually unpopulated territories.

Because of all these reasons, thanks to the activities of the governor-general of Eastern Siberia, Nikolai Murav'ev, and naval commander, Gennadii Nevel'skoi, Russia, in the late 1850s, acquired large territories in the Far East between the Amur and Ussuri rivers under the treaties of Aigun, Tianjin (1858), and Beijing (1860), which were negotiated with the weakened Qing empire. However, these territorial gains were not seen in Russia as an occupation of Chinese territories but as a recovery of land that had originally (before the Treaty of Nerchinsk) belonged to Russia. Besides, there was no real border in the area, and the Chinese authorities at the time did not even have a concept of fixed borders in the European sense.

The return of the Kulja region and the Ili area to China, according to the Treaty of St. Petersburg as signed in 1881, and Russia's support of China's territorial integrity after China's defeat in its war with Japan were often cited in Russia as examples of Russia's exceptional friendliness to China. In fact, before and immediately after the signing of the anti-Japanese Treaty of Alliance in 1896, which allowed Russia to build a railway through Chinese territory in Manchuria, the pro-Russian mood in Beijing was widespread and there were high hopes that Russia would support China against its rivals. At that time, a senior Chinese statesman in charge of Russian policy, Li Hongzhang, wrote in his diary that, in his view, Russia was much more solid and powerful than the British Empire and that "if Russia did not want to control us in all our home affairs, what a strong alliance would be possible between us."[10]

The concept of special friendly relations with China should be judged against the background of the heated debate about Russia's China policy, which was going on in the second half of the nineteenth century. Generally, the struggle was between two main approaches toward China. One position was that it was in Russia's interest to maintain good relations with China and to insist on international guarantees of China's territorial integrity. This was not an altruistic position, but a realistic one based on the belief that Russia was not able to digest more territories in the Far East, which was densely populated by non-Russians, and that it should therefore first concentrate its efforts on developing what it already had in Central Asia, Siberia, and the Amur basin. Supporters of this position also feared that further Russian territorial expansion would unite European powers and Japan against it and that, by insisting on China's territorial integrity, other powers would be stopped from gaining any advantages in China at Russia's expense and China's sympathy would be secured, which was important for promoting Russia's economic interests in Manchuria. The other position held that Russia should divide China (and Korea) with the other powers and acquire as much territory as possible, while handling the consequences with diplomacy and armed force.

The first approach was generally dominant during the reign of Alexander III and later had its main adherent in the finance minister, Count Sergei Witte. The latter managed to persuade Nicholas II not to usurp more land from China, and he ensured that his contract with Li Hongzhang for the lease of Chinese territory for the Chinese Eastern Railway was formally mutually beneficial and was voluntarily granted by the Chinese. One of the official reasons for the railway's construction was to provide a better means of transferring Russian troops to help China in case of a new conflict with Japan. Of course, Li Hongzhang had a personal interest in seeing the railway completed, as he had accepted a personal bribe. However, at the time, China had reasons to be sympathetic to Russia because Russia had managed to persuade the other powers to convince Japan not to occupy the Liaodong Peninsula after the Chinese-Japanese war, by persuading Japan to satisfy itself with imposing an indemnity on China and occupying Taiwan. The main architect of this policy was Witte, who managed to go ahead with the agreements, despite proposals of various high-ranking officials and courtiers that Russia should come to an agreement with Japan to occupy Manchuria.[11]

However, the situation changed radically in 1898, when Tsar Nicholas II, following Germany's example of occupying Qingdao, demanded that China lease Russia the southern part of the Liaodong Peninsula so that Russia could build a port there. This time, China reluctantly agreed under the direct threat of military force, and Russian-Chinese relations were damaged. From that time forward, Russia was seen in China not as a counterbalance of the expansionist powers but as one of them. Relations became even worse after Russia sent an expeditionary force to Beijing to join the international action during the 1900 Boxer Rebellion, and, at the same time, under the pretext of securing Russia's interests, occupied Manchuria. Among the main proponents of the new, activist policy were the foreign minister, Count Mikhail Murav'ev, and the minister of war, General Aleksei Kuropatkin, who finally managed to outmaneuver Witte in persuading Nicholas II to his own position. Kuropatkin, among others, insisted that Russia should not withdraw its troops from Manchuria but should instead establish a friendly, half-independent state under the direct control of the Russian government, modeling it after the Bukharan emirate.[12] It is ironic that Kuropatkin, being one of the most active proponents of Russia's expansionism in China, talked of a special Russo-Chinese relationship. Only months before, Russian troops had been sent to Manchuria. In 1900, he wrote:

> Among Asiatic nations, our relations with China are the most ancient and peaceful. Despite the vast extent of our border and despite our ties with China going back over two centuries, the peace between us has never been broken. More than once we helped China out of difficult situations, in 1860 in her struggle with England and France, in 1876 during the insurrection in Kulja and in 1895 during the struggle with Japan.[13]

His position on Russian policy toward China was, nevertheless, quite straightforward, as discussed above.

Due to the pressure of those who supported territorial gains in China, the realistic policy of Witte was rejected, and, from 1898, the Russian government engaged in active territorial expansion in China. The defeat in the war with Japan, which was a result of this course of action, as well as Russia's adventures in Korea (the so-called *Bezobrazovshchina*), led to disastrous consequences for Russia.

Russian Views of Korea

While the first descriptions of Korea and initial contacts between Russians and Koreans (which occurred mainly in China) date back to the seventeenth century, Russians only began to visit Korea two centuries later. The first Russians to set foot on Korean territory are believed to have been members of the expedition of Vice Admiral Efimii Putiatin on the frigate *Pallada,* which had been sent to Japan to establish diplomatic relations. Putiatin sent two letters to the Korean authorities but received no response. Following the example of the Japanese, he then asked permission for "the Russian ships sailing in the vicinity to call at Korean ports to replenish water and food supplies as well as repair damage caused by storms and other unexpected circumstances."[14] Putiatin visited Komun Island and the port of Wonsan, which he named Port Lazarev. The expedition's stay in Korea was described by prominent Russian writer Ivan Goncharov, an expedition member, in a popular book on *Pallada*'s travels.[15]

However, official relations with Korea had to wait a decade after Russia regained control over the left bank of the Amur under the 1858 and 1860 treaties with China making Korea Russia's neighbor. First official contacts were on a local level and were very friendly. In the summer of 1861, Russian border authorities under the command of Captain Turbin were marking the border with China at the lower stream of the Tumen River in accordance with the Russo-Sino treaties when they were visited by several local Korean officials. The Russians showed the text of the treaty to the Koreans who knew nothing of it. The record of the Ussuri border commission states: "These officials were very friendly and invited Captain Turbin to visit their town. It should be noted that Koreans who hate Manchurians and Chinese, were very pleased to have new neighbors."[16]

Russia's Far Eastern Policy and Korea

Russian policy toward Korea in the second half of the nineteenth century can be understood only against the background of power politics in Northeast Asia, specifically Russian rivalry with China, Britain, and Japan. On the one hand, Russia wanted to secure its interests in the region and not lag behind the other powers in gaining a stake in Korea. On the other hand, the Russian government was aware of Korea's remoteness from the historical center of its empire, the lack of communications, which made rapid transfer of troops impossible, and the superior naval power of her rivals. This made for a reactive and conservative Russian strategy in Korea aimed at maintaining the status quo and foiling Chinese, and later Japanese, attempts to strip Korea of its independence. Explaining this policy, the leading Russian expert on Russo-Korean relations, Boris Pak, wrote:

> The remoteness of the newly acquired Amur region, difficulty in communication and the weakness of the military force in defending the region—all led to status quo Russian diplomacy not only in Korea, but also in China and Japan. Fear that in case of war, Russia's competitors would exploit the strategic position of the Korea peninsula and close off the Korean Strait to Russian ships, drove the tsarist government to support Korean independence. In addition, the tsarist government believed that any move to open Korean ports would harm its commercial interests because Russian merchants and industrialists were unable to compete there with the largest European and U.S. trade companies.[17]

However, unlike other Western powers, Russia had the advantage of sharing a border with Korea. From the 1860s to the mid-1870s, Russia persistently asked Korean authorities to enter into trade talks, but the Koreans failed to react. In August

1873, Russia refused Japan permission to move its troops across Russian territory toward Korea in an attempt to subjugate the country. Even the Korean-Japanese treaty in 1876, which opened Korean ports to foreign trade, did not influence the Russian foreign ministry to change its "wait and see policy." The ministry recommended instead "a similar agreement with Korea to secure our border and future trade interests in Korea" only in the eventuality of other powers following Japan's lead.[18]

According to Aleksei Narochnitskii, in his pioneering study of the international relations in the Far East in the nineteenth century, the tsarist government did not initiate the forcing of unequal treaties on Korea and believed that the penetration of Korea by Western powers was undesirable. Until 1884 it regarded China's suzerainty over Korea as a useful obstacle to Japanese and American colonial ambitions in Korea and believed that "vassal relations with China served as a guarantee of its future independence" and that Russia should therefore "encourage the Chinese government not to give up its claims over that country."[19]

However, after Britain and Germany signed treaties of friendship and commerce with Korea in 1883, Russia decided to follow suit. On July 7, 1884, the Russian consul in Tianjin, Karl Waeber, signed the Russian-Korean Treaty of Friendship and Commerce. The treaty opened the ports of Inchon (Chemulpo), Wonsan, and Pusan to Russian trade, and permitted Russians to rent or buy land and build houses, warehouses, and factories in the cities of Seoul and Yanghwajin. They were granted freedom of movement within a hundred Korean li of the opened cities. With a passport issued by the Russian consul and stamped and signed by local Korean authorities, Russians could move freely anywhere in Korea. Russia also received most-favored-nation status, which meant that its subjects enjoyed the same privileges granted to the citizens of other countries. Conceding to Korean concerns that any special privileges to Russia would lead to similar demands by other powers, Russia agreed to base its own agreement with Korea on the Korean-British and Korean-German treaties and excluded two provisions regulating border and border-trade issues that were important to Russian interests These problems were dealt with in a separate Russo-Korean convention, signed in August 1888.

The development of Russian relations with Korea after 1884 was greatly influenced by Korea's domestic situation, especially the coming to power of the so-called Progressives in December of that year (the Kapshin Incident). Three days after assuming power, the Progressives were overthrown by Chinese troops led by Yuan Shikai, and Japan used this as a pretext to send its own troops to Korea. In April 1885, a Sino-Japanese agreement was reached in Tianjin that gave Japan the right to send troops to Korea under certain conditions and deprived China of the right to interfere in Korea's internal affairs. Confronted by Sino-Japanese rivalry for control over Korea and the failure to secure countervailing support for Korean independence elsewhere, Paul Georg von Möllendorf, an adviser to the Korean government, turned to Russia for military assistance.

In the middle of December 1884, von Möllendorf proposed via Russian diplomatic representatives in Japan that the tsarist government declare Korea a Russian protectorate and send the Russian navy to Inchon to protect King Kojong. In Russia a discussion over the possible reaction began. The foreign minister, Nikolai Giers, asked the naval minister how many ships it had in Chinese waters, and the possibility of military action was examined. In the Russian newspaper *Novoe vremia* it was said:

> If possible we should limit ourselves to opposing the seizure of Korea by any European power, since we have no intention of conquering Korea as the French are conquering Tonkin. However, to limit ourselves to merely opposing the seizure of Korea by another power would in effect be a politics of nonaction . . . in a region where the enlightened actions of Britain and Germany can work against us in our own Asian sphere of influence.[20]

But in the end caution prevailed. Russia sent its diplomat in Tokyo, Aleksei Speier, to Seoul to study the situation, under strict instructions "to refrain from making any statement that may be interpreted as an obligation on behalf of the imperial government."[21] The Russian government rejected von Möllendorf's proposal to occupy Port Lazarev and to send military instructors to Korea. In this regard Giers wrote to Tsar Alexander III advising that "a conflict, be it with China or Japan, would demand from us such efforts and sacrifices that can hardly be compensated for by the limited advantages that we may gain from our preeminent position in Korea."[22]

In the following years, the dominant opinion of the Russian elite was that the Russian government should support Korean independence. For example, in 1886, in a letter devoted to Russian strategy in Korea, addressed to the director of the Russian Foreign Ministry Asia Department, I.A. Zinovev, the governor-general of the Amur region, A.N. Korf, argued that

> our policy in this state should not pursue any mercenary end and should maintain instead the integrity and the greatest level of independence possible for Korea. To expand our presence, which is already overstretched, is definitely impossible. It is necessary first to firmly and solidly consolidate the Amur region, where life is still barely possible, and which we lack the funds to defend. Under these conditions, enlargement of Russian control over Korea would be highly unwise and unconsidered.[23]

Korf recognized that Port Lazarev "has the advantage that our naval vessels would be able to stay there for the winter, and, in the event of war with any maritime power, threaten its colonies and fleet all year round and not just eight months a year as at present." However, in Korf's opinion, to secure a new port, Russia would have to increase the number of troops in the Far East as well as connect it to the mainland, which would be impossible until the Russian Far Eastern territories were properly developed and a railroad from European Russia to the Far East had been built.[24]

In the second half of the 1880s the Russian government identified China as the main threat to Korean independence after it won Britain's support in its attempts to broaden its suzerain rights in Korea. At the same time, St. Petersburg obviously underestimated Japanese power and the danger of its aggression. This was the opinion, expressed by the Special Conference devoted to the Korean question convened in the summer of 1888.[25] It was only after the beginning of the Sino-Japanese War when Japan's superiority became evident that Russian diplomats began to express their fears that Japan would subject Korea to a dependency more severe than Korea's old dependency on China. The Russian envoy to Beijing, Count Artur Kassini, reported during the days of the war:

> Even if Japan is not considering a full seizure of Korea . . . it wants to interfere into the internal life of that country so deeply and to bind her to itself under such harsh obligations that all the future good deeds it exhibits would amount to no more than the most despotic protectorate, a much more severe overlord for Korea and far more uncomfortable to her neighbors than the weak bondage of vassal dependency that has until this time connected this kingdom to the Celestial Empire.[26]

After Japan in effect created a protectorate over Korea and demanded the ceding of the entire South Manchurian coast at the peace talks, the Russian government began to think of counteraction. At a special conference, convened on February 1, 1895, it was decided that Russian naval forces in the Pacific should be reinforced in order to make them stronger than those of Japan. It also instructed the foreign ministry to come to an agreement with European powers to put collective pressure on Japan if it tried to undermine fundamental Russian interests during the peace talks. The conference made clear that the main Russian aim in Korea was to maintain that country's independence.[27]

Russian society saw the Shimonoseki peace treaty, which recognized Korea's independence from China (but not from Japan), as a Japanese attempt to establish sole domination over Korea. The liberal *Russkaia mysl'* commented in the summer of 1895: "The recognition of Korean independence would not have contradicted our interests if it had not led to the effective dominance of Japanese influence in Korea. It is unlikely that the Japanese would not demand significant concessions from the Koreans as well."[28] Successful English, French, and German interference in the peace talks increased Russia's influence in Korea, where a strong anti-Japanese movement had begun. Pro-Russian ministers were appointed to the Korean cabinet and the Korean army military unit trained by the Japanese instructors was dissolved. In an attempt to restore their influence, the Japanese organized the murder of Queen Min, which infuriated the Korean population even further. This move backfired when King Kojong, fearing assassination or capture by the Japanese, fled to the Russian legation in Seoul giving Russia the opportunity to influence all government decisions.

During King Kojong's stay at the Russian legation from February 11, 1896, to February 20, 1897, Russia's influence grew rapidly. But Russia still reacted cautiously to Korean proposals of broader cooperation. A special Korean envoy to Russia, Min Yong-hwan in April 1896 asked Russia for the following: (1) Russian protection of the king until the creation of a new Korean army; (2) Russian instructors for the military and police; (3) three Russian advisers—one each for the Royal Household, the cabinet, and industrial and railroad enterprises; (4) a loan of ¥3 million to repay a Korean debt to Japan; and (5) the establishment of telegraph lines between Korea and Russia.[29] Despite the favorable situation, Russia was cautious and met only part of Korea's requests to avoid conflict with Japan. Moreover, in June 1896, it signed an agreement with Japan (known as the Lobanov-Yamagata agreement), which carved up Korea into Russian and Japanese spheres of influence and allowed both countries the right to send troops to Korea "if tranquility and order in Korea are disturbed or seriously threatened by internal or external causes."[30]

Russia dispatched a group of military instructors headed by Colonel D.V. Putiata, but it was not as large as what the Koreans had asked for. The granting of a Russian loan was discussed for a long time and finally delayed by the Korean government itself, pressured by the British commissioner of the Korean Maritime Customs Service, John McLeavy Brown. At the end of September 1897, a Russian customs official, Kiril Alekseev, arrived at Seoul and was appointed the chief finance adviser and commissioner of customs. However, his authority was limited from the very beginning because McLeavy Brown, supported by Britain and Japan, refused to hand over supervision to him. Russia preferred to come to an agreement with Japan, and in less than a year Alekseev was recalled to Russia.

Russian pliancy was partly caused by the change of domestic climate in Korea. By 1898 the nationalist movement was on the rise and it pushed the government to limit Russian influence. In March, the king had to agree to remove Russian military instructors. In April, the Japanese foreign minister, Nishi Tokujiro, proposed a new agreement to the Russian envoy to Japan, Baron Roman Rosen, which would recognize Korea as belonging to the Japanese sphere of interests, with Manchuria in the Russian sphere of interests. While Russia refused to recognize unlimited Japanese dominance in Korea in the Nishi-Rosen agreement signed on April 25, 1898, it did recognize the predominant Japanese economic interests there and pledged not to hinder the development of trade and industrial relations between Korea and Japan. This meant significant concessions to Japan in Korea. Some historians argue that in failing to give Korea assistance when it needed it most, immediately after the Sino-Japanese War, Russia lost an opportunity to consolidate its influence in Korea and preserve Korea's independence.[31] However, Russian strategy in Korea has never aimed at sole domination there, which was considered a dangerous aim. After 1897 the group within the Russian government headed by Count Witte, which advocated an activist policy in Manchuria and an agreement in Japan over Korea, gained the upper hand in St. Petersburg.

Russo-Japanese Rivalry and the War of 1904–1905

The Nishi-Rosen agreement did not stop Russian-Japanese rivalry in Korea; on the contrary, Russia apprehensively watched the growth of Japanese political influence over the Korean government, and conflicts over telegraph lines and territorial leases increased. On December 14, 1897, Tsar Nicholas II ordered the Pacific fleet to enter Port Arthur. The relatively low-key Japanese reaction to this action was due, among other things, to Japanese hopes that after acquiring a port in the Pacific that would remain navigable during winter, Russia would not encroach on the Korean shore. The Japanese miscalculated. Russian naval officers did not consider Port Arthur ideal for a naval base. At a special conference on November 14, 1897, in the presence of Tsar Nicholas II, Vice Admiral P.P. Tyrnov questioned the viability of berthing Russian naval ships in the Port Arthur and Dalnii bays on the Liaodong Peninsula during winter. He advised against Port Arthur for the time being, and recommended acquiring a port in Korea that would remain navigable during winter. Representatives of the ground forces shared this opinion. Thus, on December 15, 1897, General Staff officer Prince A. Volkonskii sent a secret memorandum to the staff's training committee entitled "On the Necessity of Strengthening Our Strategic Presence in the Far East," in which he stressed the need to acquire an alternative port in southern Korea. He argued:

> A single glance at the map is enough to understand the strategic significance of Korea in the struggle for the Pacific. The fleet that possesses a port on the southern shore of Korea will enjoy a commanding position in the Asiatic parts of the ocean and could ply along internal operational lines against China, Japan toward the south, and against the British shipping route from India to Eastern China. . . . If . . . one of the southern ports (Kojedo) is in Russian hands, the operational line of our fleet for destinations in the Yellow and Chinese Seas would be shortened by two sailing days. Occupation of one of the more northern ports in the Korean Strait (for example, Port Arthur or Dalianwan) would not give us this advantage but it would bring our naval base closer to the Manchurian railway.[32]

Counter-Admiral F.V. Dubasov also argued: "Our main naval base should be nowhere else but in Masampo (Masan)," the bay at the entrance of Koje island.[33] To achieve this aim, Russia decided to buy land in the Masan bay area, a move that met strong Japanese opposition. In 1900, Russia finally succeeded in buying the land but was pressured by the Japanese to withdraw all military personnel by 1903 and abolish plans to create a naval base there.

The Forest Concession on the Yalu River and Internal Russian Discussions on Korean Policy

By the end of the 1890s, a powerful group demanding a more active Korea policy had emerged in St. Petersburg. Driven both by commercial and political interests, the so-called Bezobrazov group included several powerful bureaucrats and well-connected courtiers and adventurers such as A.M. Bezobrazov, Colonel V.M. Vonliarovskii, minister of the Imperial Court Grand Duke Aleksandr Mikhailovich, General-Adjutant Count Illarion Vorontsov-Dashkov, the Russian representative in Seoul (since 1898) Nikolai Matiunin, Count F.F. Yusupov, Admiral A.M. Abaza, and others. The group acquired the rights to manage the forest concession on the Amnok (Yalu) River. Supported by Admiral E.I. Alekseev, who was appointed vice-regent of the Far East in 1903 with broad authority to oversee all government agencies in the region as well as by the tsar himself, the group began to build a fortified region on the Russian-Korean border by smuggling in military personnel disguised as civilian concession guards.

The views of the group were expressed in *A Humble Memorandum*, which was presented by Bezobrazov to the tsar in 1901. The fundamental position of the group was that a war with Japan in Korea was unavoidable and Russia should be well prepared for it. Bezobrazov argued, "If one assumes that the opponent acts rationally, North Korea would definitely be the theater of future clashes. Therefore, it seems important to prepare initially for an active defense and later for a decisive offensive in this future cockpit of military operations." Bezobrazov continued that if Russia did not occupy the strategic Yalu, Japan would. He also believed Russian troops stationed in Manchuria since the Boxer Rebellion should be withdrawn and strategic attention switched to Northern Korea instead, a policy that, incidentally, coincided nicely with the group's commercial interests. Bezobrazov reassured the supporters of an active policy in Manchuria that "Russia could surround Manchuria and in effect conquer the country without occupying it directly."[34]

Bezobrazov's group clashed with the powerful group that supported an active policy in Manchuria and backed Russia's agreement with Japan on Korea. Members of the pro-Manchuria group included the foreign minister (in 1900–1906), Count Vladimir Lamsdorff, the finance minister, Count Witte, and the war minister, General Kuropatkin.[35] In 1898 the Foreign Ministry believed that "at present any active Russian interference into Korean affairs may cause Japanese dissatisfaction" and decided to adopt a wait-and-see policy on Korea for the following five years. This frustrated the Bezobrazov group's plans for "developing Korea." Bezobrazov wrote in this respect: "This five-year delay . . . is a dangerous miscalculation. In five years Korea could become a well-fortified area, a kind of Plevna on a larger scale. . . . In five years Korea could practically and legally become a possession of the international capital."[36]

The Ministry of Finance opposed the Bezobrazov group initiatives even more actively. It had financed multiple Russian projects in Manchuria, including the building of the Chinese Eastern Railroad, industrial development, and fortifications in Port Arthur and Dal'nii. Therefore, at the very beginning of the forest project, Witte proposed that all nongovernment enterprises in Korea be managed "privately, without state assistance." As a strong supporter of a Manchurian-oriented Russia policy,

Witte was very critical of Bezobrazov's plans, even more so because they needed large-scale state financing. Witte thought that government money could be better spent in Manchuria, thereby avoiding a conflict with Japan. In general, Witte believed that "external peace was a necessary condition for any effort aimed at the internal reconstruction of an exhausted country."[37]

As a military strategist, Kuropatkin believed that if Russia prioritized Manchuria over Korea, war with Japan could be avoided. After returning from a trip to the Far East in 1903, he wrote in his diary that "the Japanese headed by the Mikado continue to believe in the possibility of a peaceful settlement of the problems in Korea and Manchuria." He concluded that "the Japanese will not start a war, but if we do not stop our military-political activities in Korea, war will be inevitable."[38] After a fierce internal struggle, Bezobrazov's group finally gained the support of the tsar resulting in the decisions of the special conference on April 8, 1903, presided over by Nicholas II, but which Witte and Lamsdorff refused to sign. Russian military activities in Northern Korea combined with other disputes finally led to the Russo-Japanese War in 1904, which Russia lost.

The Russian defeat opened the way for the Korea-Japanese agreement signed in November 1905, which established a Japanese protectorate over Korea. At first Russia tried to show its disagreement by treating Korea as a sovereign country. Thus, the first postwar Russian consular general, G.A. Planson, attempted to get agreement not from the Japanese government but from the Korean emperor. Japan protested and Russia had to comply with Japanese demands. After repeatedly asking St. Petersburg for protection, Emperor Kojong sent a separate Korean delegation to an international peace conference in The Hague in 1907. The Korean delegation went to Europe via Vladivostok and St. Petersburg and on its way passed a letter to Tsar Nicholas II asking for assistance. However, despite the fact that the head of the Russian delegation, A.I. Nelidov, presided over the conference, under pressure from Japan, the United States, Britain, France, and Germany, it did not recognize the credentials of the Korean delegation.

The reason for Russia's reluctance to be more supportive of Korean independence was that in the situation of weakness after defeat in the war with Japan, Witte's line finally won in St. Petersburg. It was believed now that a new conflict with Japan in the Far East would be too dangerous and that it was more reasonable to divide spheres of influence with Tokyo keeping northern Manchuria under Russian dominance while ceding Korea and southern Manchuria to Japan. Therefore, despite Kojong's repeated appeals for help in 1909–10, Russia failed to react and did not protest either the abdication of Kojong or the new Korean-Japanese agreement that gave Japan effective control of Korea in July 1907.

Maintaining peace with Japan was seen as more important in St. Petersburg, and a weakened Russia nevertheless had to agree to Japanese demands. Russia preferred to trade granting the Japanese a free hand in Korea in exchange for Japanese recognition of Russia's special rights in Outer Mongolia. This was the gist of the secret agreement, signed by the Russian foreign minister, A.P. Izvol'skii, and the Japanese minister to Russia, Motono Ichiro, on July 30, 1907. Thus, Russia agreed to Japan's establishing a protectorate in Korea and did not protest its full annexation later in 1910. This document effectively put an end to official Russo-Korean relations, although Russia's general consulate in Seoul was closed down only in 1925. Russia also became tougher on the Korean anti-Japanese resistance movement, which formed some of its units from Korean refugees in Russia and attacked Japanese forces in Korea from the Russian territory. (Before 1910 Russia saw anti-Japanese resistance as a positive factor that undermined growing Japanese influence in the Far East.) In 1910, the leader of the Korean resistance, Yi Pom-yong (who was forming Korean resistance units on the Russian territory), was ordered to leave the maritime region for Irkutsk, and 1911 saw the last major guerrilla intrusion to Korea from Russia.[39]

The weakening of the Russian position in the Far East did not mean that Russia had lost all interest in Korea. Between 1905 and 1910, many fundamental works on Korea were published in Russia, among them studies by Russian military officers, including P. Rossov's *Korea at the End of 1905 and the Beginning of 1906* (which described the Korean resistance movement in detail) and *The National Self-Consciousness of Koreans*; P. Vaskevich's *On the Current Situation in Korea*; and V.D. Pesotskii's *Korea on the Eve of Annexation*. In 1912 a well-known Japan and Korea expert, N.V. Kiuner, published a two-volume *Statistical, Geographical, and Economic Outline of Korea*.[40] Thus, while general public interest in Korea almost entirely disappeared after Russia's defeat in the war with Japan, in its place were deeper professional and practical studies. By that time, the Korean question in Russia had also become an internal problem, insofar as Russian authorities had to deal with growing numbers of Korean emigrants.

Korea as a Source of Immigration

Almost immediately after Russia and Korea became neighbors, the problem of mass Korean immigration to Russia emerged, which had a profound influence on Russia's perception of Korea and Koreans. At first, the reasons for Korean emigration to Russia were purely economic. The population of Korea's Hamgyong Province bordering the Russian Far East suffered from poverty caused by frequent crop failures, high taxes, and corrupt local officials, while on the Russian lands just across the river there was a lot of free land and a high demand for labor. According to Russian records, the first thirteen Korean families crossed the Tumen River into Russia in 1863. By 1866–67, Korean immigration had grown until nearly the entire population of two border villages crossed into the Russian Ussuri region, and both governments realized they had a problem on their hands.

At first, Russia recognized all Korean immigrants as Russian subjects as they did Chinese and other foreigners who did not violate Russian law. According to the first census of the Korean population in Russia, conducted in 1867, 999 Koreans lived in the south Ussuri region. The next year saw the arrival of another five hundred people, but when famine in 1869 drove seven thousand Koreans across the border, the Russian government began to worry. It dispatched Count Y.N. Trubetskoi, the border commissar in the south Ussuri region, to Korea. In an official letter, he informed the local Korean officials that "the Russian government . . . cannot passively watch the swelling tide of homeless people washing over the Russian border and . . . finds it necessary to take decisive measures to stop this menace. But in consideration of its historic and good neighborly ties with Korea, it will take joint measures in agreement with the Korean authorities to avoid any future misunderstandings."[41] The Korean government responded by introducing border controls and improving the living standards of the border communities. In spite of these measures, Korean immigration continued in the 1880s at the rate of three thousand people per year. They were mostly workers of various specialties and unskilled laborers. Korean merchants residing in Russia soon gained control of Russo-Korean trade.

In 1882 the Korean population of the Maritime region totaled 10,761, compared with 67,708 Russians and Ukrainians residing there.[42] Although Russo-Korean trade was significantly smaller than Korean trade with other Western countries in the 1880s and 1890s after Korea was opened to foreign trade, Korea was of key importance to the Russian Far East, as it was the only market at the time where the population of the south Ussuri region and the troops deployed there could buy cattle and meat.

The Russo-Korean treaty of 1884, signed by Karl Waeber, Russia's envoy to Korea, and Choson foreign minister Kim Yun-shik established the status of Koreans in Russia. According to the treaty, all Koreans who had arrived on Russian territory before 1884 were to be given full citizenship. But the Korean side refused to ratify this agreement, arguing that it could not publicly abandon its subjects. Nevertheless, this agreement became the basis of Russian policy toward Korean immigrants. In 1891, all Koreans residing in Russia were divided into three groups. Members of the first group, those who had settled in Russia before 1884, were granted full rights as Russian subjects and received 40.5 acres of land per family. The second group consisted of Koreans who had moved to Russia after 1884 and who wished to become Russian subjects. They were forbidden the right to use public land and had to liquidate their holdings and return to Korea within a two-year period. The third group comprised Korean temporary residents who had come to Russia in search of work. They had no right to start holdings and could only stay in Russia if granted permission by the Russian authorities. In 1995, there were 13,111 Koreans of the first category, 2,400 of the second, and 3,000 of the third in the Amur region.[43]

However, according to Boris Pak, the flight of Koreans to Russia that started in 1860 was too small to be called an exodus. Significant emigration started only after the establishment of the Japanese protectorate and gained new momentum after Japan's annexation of Korea in 1910. Masses of Koreans began to flee to Russia wishing to settle there permanently. The main reason was Japanese colonialism, which manifested itself, among other ways, in the seizure of Korean lands. After the loss of independence, political factors also began to play a role. Many members of the anti-Japanese national liberation movement were among the Korean emigrants. In 1907, even the Korean emperor was thinking of fleeing to Russia.[44] As a result, the Korean population of the Amur region grew from 34,399 in 1906 to 50,965 in 1910, according to official Russian data. The real figure, which should include nonregistered immigrants, was probably higher by at least 30 percent.[45] At the same time, the proportion of Koreans granted the status of Russian subjects declined from 49 percent to 33 percent. This was the result of the position of the local authorities who wanted to keep the Amur region "Russian." Nevertheless, by the end of 1915, the number of Koreans had grown to 72,600.

The Russian Far East authorities reacted negatively to the flow of Korean immigrants after the Russo-Japanese War. This became especially visible after the appointment in 1905 of P.F. Unterberger as governor-general of the Amur region. Unterberger was a strong supporter of populating the Amur region with Russians only. His term as governor-general coincided with the agrarian reforms pursued by Prime Minister Petr Stolypin, which led to an increase of the Russian population in the Russian Far East. As a result, in 1917, 748,300 Russians and Ukrainians lived in the Amur region. However, the Korean population also grew. In 1917, 100,000 Koreans resided in the Amur region, which meant that despite all efforts by the Russian authorities, the proportion of the Korean population (about one to seven) had remained stable since 1882. Apart from Koreans, as of 1916, there were 78,000 Chinese and 49,000 Japanese, as well as about 20,000 various ethnic minorities residing in the Russian Far East.[46]

Korean immigration provoked heated debate within the Russian government, society, and press in the first decade of the twentieth century. In the view of Unterberger and his supporters, Korean immigration presented a threat because Koreans did not assimilate even after becoming Russian subjects and would thus be patriotic during a war. He also argued that leasing them land "corrupts our rural population, which gets out of the habit of independent farming and indulges in idleness and hard drinking." Therefore "in the event of war, instead of a disciplined Russian population ready to stand up for their homeland, we risk dealing with a faint-hearted and weak population that would burden rather than help our troops."[47]

According to the Foreign Ministry representative in the Amur region, V. Grave, Unterberger once remarked,

> I am not a foe of Koreans, as is often thought. But I cannot agree with the opinion of my predecessors who believed that the uninhabited region should first and foremost be populated, even if only by Koreans. I would prefer a Russian desert to a cultivated Korean region. In time the region will be filled with Russians, the land will be cultivated by them, and not by Koreans. This will occur, perhaps, in a hundred years. But at least I will not be blamed for allowing the plunder of the Russian land by yellow-faced foreigners.[48]

Such views came under fire both in St. Petersburg and the Russian Far East. Advocating a more moderate policy toward Korean immigrants during public discussion of the issue in 1910, a St. Petersburg newspaper *Russkie vedomosti* explained: "To many of them, particularly after the Japanese had virtually seized their country, Russia is the second fatherland to which they want to belong to forever. . . . Koreans turn the worst land into fertile oases and in this way, thanks to their work, the overall agricultural productivity of the Amur region can be raised." The paper argued that "it is absolutely impossible to agree with the Amur regional administration on the threat posed by Koreans to the region. . . . On the contrary, circumstances demand a favorable approach . . . to Koreans on behalf of the Russian authorities."[49]

Even severe critics of the use of foreign labor in the Russian Far East sometimes made an exception for Koreans. This was the position of a well-known Far Eastern journalist and public figure, Sergei Merkulov. On September 15, 1910, he argued in another newspaper, *Novoe vremia*:

> By dint of their character and political status, Koreans are the only representatives of the yellow race who are inclined to become loyal Russian subjects and love Russia as their new homeland, although the lower classes maintain their beliefs, language, and culture. As laborers, Koreans are preferable to all other peoples of the yellow race. As a rule, they come here not in search of temporary work but because they wish to settle permanently with their families.[50]

These discussions influenced the passage of several new draft laws. In 1909, the State Council and the State Duma approved the Law "On Imposition of Some Restrictions for Foreign Subjects on the Territory of the Amur General Governorship and the Trans-Baikal Region of the Irkutsk General Governorship." This law, which was signed by the tsar on June 1, 1910, forbade leasing state land to foreign nationals and hiring them to work for the state. On April 8, 1910, the Council of Ministers decided to limit the rights of Koreans in Russia. However, this decision, as well as new regulations limiting border crossings and the right of abode in Russia for Chinese and Korean subjects, drafted by the State Duma in 1909, failed to win appropriate support and were rejected. In the end, the milder approach to Korean emigrants won, and, in April 1911, the Council of Ministers gave the right to grant status as a Russian subject to the minister of interior, thus withdrawing it from the Korean-hostile local authorities.

Conclusion

Russian views of Northeast Asia at the end of the nineteenth and beginning of the twentieth centuries varied significantly. Some thought of this region as a great opportunity for Russia, advocating activist foreign military policy, despite the possible reaction of other countries. Others stood for caution and the economic development of Russian interests in limited areas, namely, northern Manchuria, because in their view, too much activism would bring dangerous conflict with other powers, especially Japan. There were also those who believed that Russia should abandon its active policy in Asia and switch its entire attention to Europe. All three positions influenced Russian policy before 1905, clashing with each other and making the resulting course inconsistent. Russia's defeat in the war seemed to have proved the position of the second group and the policy of cutting a deal with Japan on the spheres of influence in this region got the upper hand. Russia's revival after its defeat in the war with Japan and internal disturbances of 1904–5 led to gradual return of activism in Manchuria, but this process was stopped by the beginning of World War I and the Russian Revolution of 1917.

3

Civilization, Race, or Nation?

Korean Visions of Regional Order in the Late Nineteenth Century

Hahm Chaibong

Choosing a Civilization and a Race

"If I had means to choose my home at my pleasure, Japan would be the country. I don't want to live in China with its abominable smells or in America where racial prejudice and discrimination hold their horrid sway, or in Corea as long as its infernal government lasts. O blessed Japan! The Paradise of the East! The Garden of the World!"[1] This is an entry in Yun Ch'i-ho's diary for November 1, 1893. Yun (1865–1945) was a renowned Korean patriot and a respected leader of the Enlightenment Party, the group of politicians and intellectuals of the late Choson dynasty who advocated modern reforms. What this passage reveals, perhaps more clearly than any other, is that Yun, like many other Asian intellectuals of the time, regarded the rapidly and successfully modernizing Japan as the model to follow. He saw Japan, not the West, as the best exemplar of modern civilization. In this, the question of "race" was a major factor. Yun saw Japan playing the role of the leader of nations of Asia, of the "Yellow race." In an earlier version of the "flying-geese" model or "East Asia Free Trade Agreement," Yun and other would-be modernizers of late Choson envisioned Korea, China, and Japan marching together to the beat of modernization with Japan in the lead.

However, all the hopes that Yun placed on Japan turned out to have been tragically misplaced when Japan colonized Korea in 1910, having imposed a "protectorate" five years earlier. For those looking at the history of this period from the postannexation, "nationalist" vantage point, Yun was the archetype of naive and ultimately treasonous intellectuals and politicians who placed the fate and future of Korea in the hands of a foreign power. In their eagerness to identify themselves with Japan, regarding it not only as the model but also the benefactor and patron of Korean aspirations for modernization, they turned a blind eye to what should have been only too obvious: Japan's machinations to colonize Korea. The lesson that many nationalists derived from the case of Yun and others like him was that to commit oneself to anything larger and broader than a "nation," narrowly defined in the ethnic and historical sense, is to open the door to foreign domination. Any effort to identify Korea with universal or more encompassing categories such as civilization or race inevitably leads to the dilution of Korea's racial and cultural identity and ultimately the loss of political independence.

The worldview that encapsulated such sentiments was articulated by the likes of Sin Ch'ae-ho (1880–1936) and Pak Un-sik (1859–1925), the founders of "nationalist historiography" (*minjok sagwan*) in Korea. From this perspective, what was lacking in Yun's conception of global and regional order was nationalism. Nationalism, as opposed to "civilizationism" or "racism" of the pan-Asian sort evinced here, would prioritize and privilege the Korean nation regardless of how dirty its people, how backward its society, or how infernal its government. Nationalism, by definition, is a commitment to one's nation in spite of all its shortcomings. Had he been a true nationalist, Yun would have said, "My country, backward or not!" From the perspective of Korean nationalism, then, it was insufficient nationalist spirit on the part of many modernizers of nineteenth-century Choson that ultimately led to its fall.

For the past century, Korean political discourse has been conducted within these two extreme poles of "civilizationism," on the one hand, and "nationalism," on the other. Even after Japan colonized Choson, there were those who collaborated with the Japanese saying that it was the quickest and surest way to modernize Choson. Among those who rejected the Japanese version of modernity after the annexation of Korea, Christianity and communism provided two important alternative models of modernity, neither of which was beholden to the Japanese.[2] These were clearly continued efforts on the part of Korean intellectuals to evaluate, criticize, and prod Korea to achieve a global standard. Many refused to turn "parochial." On the other hand, there were those who argued that reliance on foreign powers and appeals to different conceptions of global civilization or regional order threaten national independence. Today, such questions still animate modern Korean political discourse. For example, what is the role of the United States and its army, which, after all, occupy the very grounds once occupied by the imperial armies of Qing China and Japan? How much can we trust the Japanese and the Chinese with whom South Korea is enjoying an unparalleled degree of economic, social, and cultural interaction? How much of foreign values and institutions should Koreans accept in the name of globalization and regional integration without, thereby, losing their national culture and identity?

Defending Confucian Civilization

"As Western barbarians invade, to not fight is to sue for peace, and to sue for peace is to sell out the country." So read the inscriptions on steles erected throughout the kingdom in the aftermath of the "victory" of the Choson army over U.S. and French incursions in 1866 and 1871. The steles, called the *ch'okhwabi*, literally meaning "stele for denouncing efforts to sue for peace," were the most visible manifestations of the resolve of Taewongun (1820–1898), the prince regent, to defend the country against Western barbarians. But what exactly was he defending?

One of the great misfortunes of Choson was that the dynasty was undergoing major reforms of its own just as it started to come into contact with the West. Taewongun, the father of King Kojong, came to power when his second son acceded to the throne in 1863, as the previous king, Cholchong, died without an heir. As soon as he became prince regent, Taewongun began undertaking reforms to restore the glory of the dynasty and the power of the monarchy. Through sound fiscal management and personnel policy, Taewongun was able to enrich the coffers of the state treasury while bringing back a semblance of coherent, centralized government to a dynasty that had long been in decline.

Although opposed by many, especially those belonging to the hereditary class of scholar-bureaucrats, or *yangban,* Taewongun's reforms were clearly of the traditional kind.[3] His reforms were not efforts to try to adopt, copy, or otherwise follow the West in any way. In fact, from his limited contacts with the West, Taewongun had become convinced that the only thing it had to offer was barbarism. Given the atrocities committed by American and French soldiers during their incursions in 1866 and 1871, respectively, this was not surprising. When American soldiers desecrated his father's grave based on a bizarre plan to force concessions from Taewongun in exchange for his father's remains, and when the French expeditionary force that landed on Kanghwa Island looted and burned the royal depository, Taewongun needed no further proof. When the Roman Catholics of Choson refused to perform ancestor worship, claiming that it was idol worship, and tried to call in French troops to "punish" the Choson government for persecuting them, it was clear that what Western religion had to offer was only barbarism and treachery.[4] The fact that his reforms were at least partially successful in restoring the power and prestige of the monarchy and that he was successful in repulsing two incursions on the part of the United States and France, convinced Taewongun that his reforms were working, that they would enable Choson to stand up to the West.

For Taewongun, however, his isolationist policy was more than just an effort to protect the monarchy and the territorial integrity of Korea. It was also a way to defend the true civilization, Confucianism. The "orthodoxy" referred to in the steles renouncing any effort to sue for peace with the West, was neo-Confucianism. That Choson thought of itself as part and parcel of a greater Confucian civilization, centered in China, was clearly manifested in its dealings with modernizing Japan. Immediately after the Meiji Restoration, the Japanese government sent a communication to the Choson court informing them of the change in government that had taken place in Japan while expressing its wish to maintain cordial relations. The communication was conveyed to the magistrate of the Waegwan, the "special trade zone" that was set up to allow for limited commerce with Japan following the post-Hideyoshi invasion settlement reached between Choson and the Tokugawa Bakufu.

The communication, carried by the *daimyo* of Tsushima, the traditional intermediary between the Choson court and Tokugawa Bakufu, opened thus: "It is a privilege for me to inform you that our government has changed back into the emperor's hands, and we are glad to have good relations with you forever."[5] An Tong-jun, the magistrate of Waegwan and a handpicked man of Taewongun, refused to accept the communication noting that there were numerous violations of long-standing protocol, including references to the Japanese ruler as an "emperor" and terms such as "imperial decree."[6] Such references were not acceptable because, as far as Choson was concerned, there was only one emperor and he was in the Middle Kingdom, not in the "barbarian outpost" of Wae (Japan).[7] Choson refused the overtures of Meiji Japan to establish a new level of diplomatic relations, not in its own name but in the name of the Chinese emperor. The Japanese were violating not only Korean interests and sensibilities but also the norms and protocols of civilization itself.

In his defense of the Confucian civilization, Taewongun was anything but an exception. Even though he and the *yangban* elite had serious disagreements on how best to uphold the orthodoxy, there was no doubt that the preservation of the orthodoxy was their common goal. Yi Hang-no, the Confucian scholar-bureaucrat who commanded enormous respect among the literati of the time, was, if anything, even more isolationist than Taewongun. He was supremely confident that as long as Choson followed the way of the Confucian sages and kings it would be able to repulse the Western barbarians and preserve the true civilization. Among the many policy recommendations that he made in regard to Choson's foreign policy was the restoration of the Mandongmyo, a shrine dedicated to the memory of the Ming emperor Shenzong, who had sent troops to help Choson during the Hideyoshi invasion.[8] Taewongun closed the shrine in 1865 as it had become one of the centers of the ultra-orthodox schools of neo-Confucianism that exerted a powerful influence on Choson politics. The shrine was closed along with hundreds of private Confucian academies as part of the prince regent's bold and sweeping reforms designed to curb the power of the literati. Yi wanted the restoration of the shrine dedicated to a Ming emperor, clearly demonstrating that the epicenter of his civilization was China. That the Ming emperor was "Chinese" apparently did not matter to him or, more accurately, never occurred to him. He was not thinking in terms of "nationalities." He was thinking only in terms of civilizations.

It was not just the elite that regarded China as the center of civilization. In 1894, the Tonghak peasant army rose up against the misrule of the dynasty and against the intervention of "Japanese barbarians" in domestic affairs. Tonghak, literally meaning "Eastern Learning," was an indigenous religious movement based on eclectic teaching that drew from sources as diverse as Confucianism, Buddhism, and Christianity. In the rebels' famous Muchang Manifesto of May 1894, Chon Pong-jun, the leader of the Tonghak army, declared:

> Man is the most precious being in the world because he has morality. The proper relationship between ruler and subject as well as between father and son constitutes the fundamental fabric of human morality. If the ruler is benign and the subject upright, and the father affectionate and the son filial, then we can establish

good family and state and, thereby, enjoy boundless felicity. Now, our Sovereign is benign, filial, kind and loving; He is also equipped with a brilliant mind as well as sage wisdom. Therefore, if He is assisted by wise and honest ministers, the harmony of Yao and Shun, or the golden age of the Wen-ti and Ching-ti shall be easily achieved within the predictable future.[9]

In a passage that could have been a quote straight from Mencius, the rebels, who were rising up against Japanese intervention, had no qualms about discoursing on Confucianism, a decidedly "Chinese" philosophy, invoking Chinese mythology, and citing the rule of two Han dynasty emperors as examples of ideal rule. In modern nationalist historiography of South Korea, Chon is a veritable "nationalist" hero who gave shape and voice to the national, and hence, modern, sentiment of the Korean "people" (*minjung*). However, his writings only referred to Chinese philosophical, historical, and political sources to criticize the misrule in his native Choson. For him, the only measure of good government was Confucian. The fact that it was Chinese philosophy and history that he referred to did not even occur to him or to his audiences (nor to most modern "nationalist" historians either). Indeed, in his memorial, Chon did not even mention the direct rule of Qing over Choson that was still in force at that time.[10]

Modern-day Koreans would feel much less sense of betrayal in reading Chon's words than Yun's, but that in no way detracts from the point that they were both appealing to "foreign" or "alien" standards in evaluating and criticizing Korean politics, society, and culture. Had he been a true nationalist, Chon would have cited the examples of great Korean kings and emperors from Korea's own history. Instead, what Chon wanted for Choson was a return to Confucian ideals and institutions. However, it would have made no sense to Chon to refer to anything in "Korean" history before Choson because, according to Confucian historiography, it was before the introduction of Confucianism, and as such, was a period of barbarism and "false learning" (Buddhism). Hence, despite their disagreements over policy and clash of class interests, Taewongun, Yi Hang-no, and Chon Pong-jun found common ground in defending the Confucian civilization to the last. Even though Taewongun, Yi, and Chon are described in Korean history books as patriots and even nationalists in their own way, it is clear that what they were defending was not the Korean nation per se, a concept that was alien to them, but the civilization that Choson embodied and represented. They were not nationalists but "civilizationists." They defended Choson not simply because it was theirs, but because it represented the undisputed standard of civilization.

Modernity, the New Civilization

Even as Taewongun and other orthodox Confucians were trying their best to uphold and defend the "true civilization" besieged from all sides, a group of intellectuals and scholar-bureaucrats was undertaking a serious reevaluation of its merits.

For the likes of Kim Ok-kyun, Pak Yong-hyo, So Chae-p'il, Yu Kil-chun, and Yun Ch'i-ho, it was no longer self-evident that the Confucian civilization centered in China was the true one worthy of defense. It was not only that the Confucian civilization lacked the scientific and military prowess of the West but also that it fell behind the West in terms of its own standards of "human heartedness and justice."[11] Once it was decided in their minds that the modern civilization of the West was the true one, the members of the Enlightenment Party tried to move quickly to introduce modern civilization to Choson. They were under no illusion that this would be an easy task. However, it was helpful to have the example of neighboring Japan, which was undertaking radical and spectacularly successful modern reforms. Moreover, with Japan seemingly willing to help with Korea's efforts at modernization, they had found an ally as well as a model for putting Choson quickly on the path to modernity.

Subsequent history proved the Enlightenment reformers' assessment of Choson's prospects to have been overly optimistic. However, as far as they were concerned, it was not the Japanese interference that ultimately negated their efforts, but rather the obstructionism of the Choson court and the Confucian establishment. Even after Taewongun was forced from power in 1874, little headway was made in terms of modern reforms. In fact, the removal of Taewongun from power was a victory for the orthodox Confucians who had opposed the prince regent's "unorthodox" reforms. As far as the isolationist policy was concerned, the orthodox Confucians were, as we have seen, in complete agreement with Taewongun.

What finally forced the "opening" of Korea was not a voluntary change in policy on the part of the Choson court, but outside intervention. In 1876, Choson opened its ports by signing the first modern treaty with Japan after she had threatened the hapless kingdom with a naval show of force off the coast near Kanghwa Island. In addition to the threat from the Japanese, the Choson court received encouragement from the Qing court to open its ports. In fact, the Qing government had been urging Choson to open relations not only with Japan but also with the United States and France, believing this to be the best way to check the growing Japanese influence over the peninsula.[12] For Choson, this was advice from its most trusted "ally," and it readily accepted the treaty. The first clause of the treaty stated that Choson was a "self-governing country," which historians have regarded as a clause of momentous consequence. However, the Choson court regarded it as little more than a minor adjustment to the Sinocentric tributary system, the institutional manifestation of the great Confucian civilizational order of which they were so proud to be a part. "This affair is nothing but the restoration of an old relationship of friendship," said King Kojong himself immediately after the treaty was signed.[13] After all, Choson had always been a de facto "self-governing" country for centuries under the Chinese tribute system.[14]

Such an interpretation of the watershed event did not bode well for modernization of Korea. The court and the Confucian elite continued to "muddle through," thinking that the old regional order was still very much intact. It was only in 1881, five years after the Kanghwa Treaty was signed, that Choson sent missions to China and Japan to get a firsthand look at the reforms under way there. Again, given that the destination was China and Japan, both countries within the old regional system, even such missions were deemed of less significance at the time than has since been interpreted. In November 1881, Choson sent some thirty-eight students to Tianjin to learn modern technology. Because they had little background in technological training, most of them having been chosen on the basis of their expertise in Confucian classics, and also due to financial difficulties, all of them returned to Choson within a year. The most concrete result of the mission was that Kim Yun-sik, the head of the delegation, returned with many books on modern science and machinery donated by the Qing government, while four technicians from Tianjin accompanied the returning mission to set up Choson's first modern factory in 1883.[15]

The mission to Japan had greater success. In February 1881, Choson sent off a sixty-two-member mission. The members had to meet in Pusan secretly before embarking for Japan so as not to alert the orthodox Confucians who still largely dominated the court. The mission arrived in Nagasaki on May 8, 1881, and dispersed to study Japanese central and prefectural governments, armament industry, postal service, and education system for three months.[16] They also met with various political and intellectual leaders of Japan. One of the most important results of the mission was that three members of the party, Yu Kil-chun, Ryu Wan-su, and Yun Ch'i-ho, were left behind in Japan for further studies: Yu and Ryu at Keio in the care of the great Japanese intellectual, Fukuzawa Yukichi, and Yun at Doshisha University. The reformists of Choson were thus able to start nurturing true converts to modernization while building deep links to Japan.

However, even as half-hearted and confused attempts at learning about the modern civilization were just getting under way, a powerful reaction from the traditionalists scuttled the process in very short order. In 1881, the Choson government established its first modern army with the help of Japanese advisers. A year later, soldiers from the old army, disgruntled by the government's preferential treatment toward the new-style army, started a riot that quickly grew into a full-blown rebellion. The rebels assassinated a number of high-ranking officials whom they thought were modernizers. They also asked Taewongun, sidelined since 1874, to come back to power. Taewongun was only too happy to oblige and he returned triumphantly to the palace at the head of the rebellious army. His first order of business was to rescind and nullify what few modern reforms the government had undertaken since his involuntary retirement.

In desperation, Queen Min and her clan, who had by then formed the most powerful political faction in the government, sought Qing's intervention.[17] Having anxiously watched the events unfold on the peninsula as Japan increased its presence over her erstwhile "subject country" (*shuguo*), the Qing saw this as the perfect opportunity to reassert its claims of suzerainty over Choson. And reassert it did. At the "invitation" of Queen Min, Li Hongzhang dispatched an army of three thousand to promptly put down the rebellion while taking Taewongun prisoner and incarcerating him in Tianjin. Once in Choson, the Qing went about establishing direct control over Choson government. Beginning in 1882, Choson, which had always been a de jure "subject country" of the Qing, came much closer to being a de facto one than ever before or since.

From the perspective of the Enlightenment Party, events were unfolding in a hopeless direction. The spectacle of the power struggle between Taewongun, on the one hand, and the King Kojong and Queen Min, on the other, which resulted in the Qing military occupation, was too much to bear. Instead of forging ahead with modernizing reforms so as to quickly follow in Japan's footsteps, Choson was in the grips of two reactionary forces vying for power. Seeing any chance of the country undertaking serious modern reforms slip away, the desperate leaders of the Enlightenment Party, Kim Ok-kyun, Pak Yong-hyo, So Chae-p'il, and Yun Ch'i-ho, staged a coup d'état on December 4, 1884. By kidnapping the king, the coup leaders were able to grab power and promulgate a dizzying array of reform measures closely modeled after the ones undertaken by Japan during the Meiji Restoration.

However, the intervention of the Qing army, led by Yuan Shikai, brought the Kapshin Incident (1884) to a bloody and ignominious end in just three days. The support expected from the Japanese forces never materialized as they fled the Qing army, which was far superior in both numbers and armaments. The coup leaders barely escaped with their lives. Their families were not as lucky. So Chae-p'il's parents and wife committed suicide; with no one left to take care of him, So's two-year-old son starved to death. For the next ten years, the Enlightenment Party members wandered through foreign lands while Choson was ruled by the Qing's "Resident-General," Yuan Shikai. As far as the Enlightenment Party leaders were concerned, the ruling elite of Choson and the Chinese were ruining the country as the window of opportunity for Choson to modernize closed rapidly.

Japan to the Rescue

> From what I gather in the Japanese papers it is evident that the reformation in Corea is only on paper. The truth of the business is that the King and the Queen and Taewonkun and their officers are incapable of and worse still unwilling for the radical renovations that are vitally necessary to the country. Since the Coreans are thus incapable and unwilling to better their condition, it may be a mercy to them for Japan or England to take possession of the peninsula altogether. The Chinese literature and Confucianism have ruined the poor Coreans beyond recovery. It may take centuries to restore them to life. Oh for a thorough scouring out of the rotten, Confucianized, good-for-nothing officers from the government.[18]

Yun Ch'i-ho wrote this in his diary in 1894, fully ten years after the failed Kapshin coup. Kim Ok-kyun had been killed in Shanghai in 1893 by an assassin sent by the vengeful Queen Min. Pak Yong-hyo was trying to maintain his image of a leader of the Enlightenment movement subsisting on what meager financial support he could receive from his remaining friends in Japan. So Chae-p'il had become a naturalized citizen of the United States, attending medical school, and becoming the first Korean to receive a medical license in his adopted country. One can only imagine the sense of frustration and despair that the Enlightenment Party members felt during those long years of exile.

Then, in 1894, Japan intervened in Choson once again. That year, the aforementioned Tonghak army rose up in protest against government corruption and misrule. Japan immediately dispatched troops under the pretext of helping the Choson government put down the rebellion. Having handed over the rule of the peninsula to the Chinese for the past ten years, Japan did not wish to miss this chance to right the balance. The Korean peninsula became the battleground for the Qing and Japanese armies. As the Japanese military emerged victorious in the lopsided battles of Pyongyang and the sea battle on the Yellow Sea, Yuan Shikai's ten-year "residency" came to an end.

For the Enlightenment Party members, this was the opportunity that they had been praying for. Indeed, the members of the Enlightenment Party saw the Sino-Japanese War as a war between the representatives of two civilizations, the decrepit Chinese versus the modern Japanese:

> The battles of Marathon and Salamis preserved Grecian independence. The Saracenic conquest in Europe received its fatal blow at the hands of Charles Martel. These are regarded among the momentous events in history: for upon them depended the question of whether Asiatic conservatism or European progress should rule the world. The present war is more than a conflict between the regenerating civilization of the West and the degrading barbarism of the East. The success of Japan would mean the salvation of Corea and the reformation of China. The reverse would plunge the peninsula Kingdom into the bottomless pit of Chinese corruption while the celestials would be confirmed in their belief that the Empire needs no renovations. For the good of the whole East, may Japan succeed![19]

The Treaty of Shimonoseki, which concluded the Sino-Japanese War in 1895, stated in its first clause that Choson was an independent sovereign nation without any obligation to China. As far as the Enlightenment Party was concerned, this was first international recognition of Choson as a fully independent nation. So Chae-p'il suspended his medical practice in the United States to return to Choson to set up the *Independence Newspaper* and founded the Independence Club. In commemoration of Choson's newfound independence, the Club erected an "Independence Arch" (*Tongnimmun*) on the site of Yongunmun, the gate at the northwestern outskirts of Seoul where traditionally the Choson kings went to greet visiting emissaries of Chinese emperors. Today, the fact that behind the Independence Arch lies the infamous Sodaemun Police Prison, the hated symbol of Japanese occupation and the place where thousands of Korean men and women who fought for independence were tortured and executed, leads many to believe that the arch was constructed to celebrate Korean independence from Japan. However, at the time the arch was constructed the brutal Japanese occupation was still a decade away. The more immediate occupation from which Choson was freeing itself was the Chinese one.

For those celebrating Choson's independence from five hundred years of vassalage, Koreans had only Japan to thank. Japan was the only trustworthy ally in their long struggle to modernize Choson. It was Japan that forced the "opening" of Choson, and it was the Japanese officials and intellectuals who invited them to Japan to be educated in the ways of modernity. Now, Japan defeated the hated China and gave Choson its first independence in centuries. It is little wonder, then, that many Koreans chose to see only the benign side of Japan's intentions.

For its part, Japan installed a pro-Japanese cabinet composed of many of the members of the Enlightenment Party who had been languishing in a decade-long exile. Pak Yong-hyo was appointed co-prime minister while Yu Kil-chun assumed an important post in the Foreign Ministry. Yun Ch'i-ho became an adviser to the king and the queen. Together, with moderate reformists such as Kim Hong-jip, they began to undertake a series of measures that came to be known as the Kabo (1894) Reforms. Once again, following the model of the 1868 Meiji Restoration (and the failed Kapshin coup), the new government abolished the Confucian civil service examination and introduced a modern education system. It also ordered the cutting of men's queues and otherwise tried to abolish the traditional system of social status. The government structure was completely overhauled to closely approximate a constitutional monarchy, a modern legal system was promulgated, and the military was modernized.

However, almost from the start, the modernizing reforms that the Enlightenment advocates tried to implement faced determined resistance from all sides. Ch'oe Ik-hyon, a disciple of Yi Hang-no, the architect of the ideology of isolationism during the Taewongun years, came with an ax in his hand to memorialize the king when he was ordered to cut his queue. Remaining true to his and his teacher's Confucian civilization, Ch'oe reportedly said "You may cut off my head, sire, but you may not cut off my queue." For its part, the court, especially the faction led by Queen Min, who had been playing Taewongun off against the Chinese to great effect (and to the great dismay of the Enlightenment Party) now began to maneuver against the Enlightenment Party and their patron, Japan. The king, at the behest of the queen, began to seek Russian help to balance the growing influence of Japan. The policy of "ridding Japan by using Russia"[20] gained momentum when Russia, with the help of Germany and France, forced Japan to return the Liaodong Peninsula to China, which it had been granted as a concession in the Sino-Japanese War. As it became clear that the Great Powers were not yet ready to cede complete control of Choson over to Japan, the Japanese position in Choson was suddenly weakened. Emboldened by the "Triple Intervention," Kojong and Queen Min began to actively court the Russians.

Alarmed at seeing their influence over Choson receding, Japan resorted to extreme measures. With the tacit consent of Taewongun and while the Enlightenment

Party members looked the other way, the new Japanese minister to Choson, Miura, mobilized a band of Japanese thugs to murder the Queen in the palace. However, the brutal and blatant assassination only turned public opinion against Japan and those seen to be acting on its behalf. The king, understandably angry and fearing for his own life, decided the Enlightenment Party was not to be trusted. On February 11, 1896, the king and his party moved into the Russian consulate, seeking Russian protection and pronouncing Pak Yong-hyo and others in the reformist cabinet traitors. Pak had to flee the country again, and the reform process came to an end. What few reforms had already been implemented were rescinded in the ensuing reaction.

Once again, the modernizers' reform efforts failed in the face of the intransigence, or outright opposition on the part of the royal family, the Confucian literati, and the masses. Once again, Choson fell into the hands of a reactionary ruling coalition between the court and a foreign power, this time Russia—which had little interest in Korea's modernization or independence. For the next ten years, Russia exercised enormous influence over Korea's affairs. With the active cooperation of the king, Russia placated other powers by granting foreign concessions, ranging from mining to lumber to railway rights. Korea now became the classic example of a colony being carved up by rapacious great powers. The pro-Russian cabinet that was formed by the likes of Yi Po-jin, Yi Un-yong, and Yi Wan-yong vacillated between modern reforms and traditional policies, trying to forge what they thought was a compromise. The result, however, was chaos. As a bureaucrat named Chong Pom-jo remarked, "The old laws were abolished but the new laws have not yet been decided and it is truly a state of lawlessness."[21]

As far as the Enlightenment Party was concerned, all hope was lost. By 1904, when Japan intervened to repulse Russia, it was thought that the opportunity for an independent modernization effort was lost. When Japan imposed a protectorate over Choson in 1905, it was the traditional "Righteous Army" (*Uibyong*) in the age-old tradition of Confucianism that arose to put up sporadic resistance. By and large, the Enlightenment Party members acquiesced to the Japanese move. Yun Ch'iho had already written the following in 1889:

> To me the question of Corean independence is of no concern. With a government like the present one, independence will bring no relief to the nation. On the other hand, with a better government—a government that will take patriotic and sympathetic interest in the welfare of the people even dependence is no real calamity. Besides a healthy and prosperous nation may at any time recover its independence, but a people kept poor, ignorant, and weak by a weak, poor, ignorant, and outrageously selfish government—what good will independence do to such a people?[22]

Just as the orthodox Confucians put up no resistance against Yuan Shikai's residency, the Enlightenment Party members accepted the Japanese "protectorate" with what seems in hindsight astonishing equanimity.

Racial Harmony and Regional Cooperation

Another reason that the Enlightenment Party almost invariably chose Japan as the role model was because of "race." Many of its members admired the United States as the best model of modern civilization. Yun Ch'i-ho, So Chae-p'il, Yu Kil-chun, Yi Sung-man (Syngman Rhee), and Yi Sang-jae were all baptized because, to them, Protestantism was what made America a great nation. However, what prevented them from wholeheartedly embracing the United States over and against Japan was American racism, which many of them had the opportunity to witness first-hand. When Pak Yong-hyo and Yun Ch'i-ho went to San Francisco after the failed coup of 1884, they walked straight into a region that was most directly affected by the Chinese Exclusion Act of 1882:[23]

> Nothing seems to be more absurd and foolish for anyone than to be deceived by the boastful pretensions of the Americans to "the inalienable right" or liberty of man. Their orators, preachers, poets, and statesmen talk much about the equality, liberty, and fraternity of men. But in practice the Americans have shown that their doctrine of equality, etc., is only skin deep. That is, if you want to enjoy the so-called inalienable right of man in this "Land of Freedom" you must be white. The persecution of the Chinese in the West, the treatment of the Negro in the South, and dealings with the Indian by the whole nation are fair commentaries on the bragged about "American doctrine" of the "inalien-able right of man." I do not blame, for a moment, the national or racial preju-dice of the Americans. But I do blame the perfect inconsistency between their acts full of the basest prejudice and their doctrine full of the loftiest and never to be realized catholicity.[24]

Firsthand experience with racism in America convinced the Enlightenment Party members that their future lay with Japan. Japan was now not only the model of modernization but also the leader among the nations of East Asia, protecting and defending the honor, prestige, and rights of the East Asian race. Thus, during the Russo-Japanese War, Yun and others were squarely on Japan's side:

> The meanest Japanese would be a gentleman and scholar compared to a vodka-drunk, orthodox Russian. Between a Japanese and a Korean there is community of sentiment and of interest, based on the identity of race, of religion, and of written characters. Japan, China, and Korea must have one common aim, one common policy, one common ideal—to keep the Far East the permanent home of the yellow race, and to make that home as beautiful and happy as nature has meant it to be.[25]

Pan-Asianism based on racial solidarity was a discourse widely disseminated and shared by intellectuals of East Asia in the nineteenth century.[26] This was a reflection of the sense of crisis felt among the intellectuals of East Asia since the Sino-Japanese War that Asia was falling prey to white imperialists: "Alas! The lands of the East have so quickly fallen under the control of the white race."[27] Pan-Asianism relied on cultural and racial commonality as well as geopolitical proximity, emphasizing the mutually dependent nature of China, Japan, and Korea. Embraced by the likes of "Confucian reformists" such as Chang Chi-yon and Pak Un-sik, it emphasizes the fact that the three countries of Asia faced a common enemy in Western imperialists.[28] In his famous essay written in protest against the Protectorate Treaty of 1905, Chang argued that the Japanese who, as members of the "same culture and same race" (*tongmun tongjong*), should have stood with the Koreans and the Chinese against the Western white race instead of invading and oppressing their own. Japan, who was the first to successfully achieve civilization and enlightenment, should have become the leader of all of Asia, civilizing and enlightening China and Choson in turn, thereby ensuring the common prosperity of the three countries of Asia.[29] As became painfully clear in the case of *Ilchinhoe*, a pro-Japanese political organization, which presented a memorial to King Sunjong, asking him to give up his throne and merge Korea fully with Japan,[30] such arguments provided logic according to which an independent Choson was deemed superfluous.

My Nation, Civilized or Not

The logic of civilization and enlightenment, racial and regional harmony all compromised Choson's political sovereignty and independence. All these discourses posited a standard outside Korea, be it China, Japan, or the West, to which Korea could not measure up. If it tried to, and asked for outside assistance in the process, the helping hand inevitably turned against it. What was necessary was a way to create a standard that was internal to Choson by which it could be measured. Such a standard was found in the discourse of *minjokjuui* or "nationalism" most ably articulated by Sin Ch'ae-ho.

In an essay aptly called "A New Reading of History" (*Toksa sillon*) published in 1908, Sin introduced the concept of *minjok* (ethnic nation) into the Korean lexicon. The term was the Japanese translation of "nation," already widely used by Japanese and Chinese intellectuals. First, Sin posited the *minjok* as the only legitimate unit of history: "The history of a state is the selected record of the rise and fall of a nation. Without a nation there is no history and without history the nation will not have a clear conception of a state. This is why a historian must bear a heavy responsibility."[31] The proper subject of history was to be "nation," not—for example—"civilization."

> One who writes history must first reveal one particular race that is the master of that country and take it as his subject. Afterward, he should record how its politics rose and fell, how its industry prospered and failed, how its martial prowess advanced and retreated, how its living habits and customs changed, how it accepted those races that came from the outside, and how it interacted with countries of other regions. Only then, can it be called history. Otherwise, it will be a

history without spirit. A history without spirit begets a nation without spirit, which, in turn, produces a country without spirit.[32]

Moreover, the "race" needed to be defined narrowly enough so that one did not make the mistake of lumping Koreans together with the Chinese and the Japanese. Thus, Sin distinguished six different races among "Our country's race" (*urinara injong*) and lists the Mongols and the Japanese as "others." The point here was to identity the "proper" and "true" Korean race by distinguishing it from other "races" of, interestingly enough, Korea itself, and others. Sin defined Korean *minjok* as the people of Puyo, an ancient Korean kingdom, said to have originated in Manchuria. The Korean *minjok* was then given a common ancestor in the mythical figure of Tangun.[33] Now, the Korean "race" could coincide with the Korean "nation," which became the subject of real history of the Korean nation-state.

What this concept of *minjok* afforded its putative members was a way of looking at other civilizations without falling prey to the "civilizationist" perspective of orthodox Confucians or Enlightenment Party members. Confucian and modern civilizations were no longer the ideals to which the Korean *minjok* must aspire. Instead, they were foreign impositions by other more powerful *minjok*, or imports by local elites who lacked the sense of pride in one's own "culture." At best, foreign civilizations were things from which a *minjok* needed to learn things so as to better struggle against other *minjok*. The ultimate aim was to ensure the survival of the "bloodline," the "family" in its purest form. The "character" or the "soul" of the *minjok* was not to be contaminated by foreign influence.

The logic of civilization was to want to become what one was not. It was to posit an objectively higher or better state of being for oneself and for one's people. The logic of nationalism, on the other hand, was to want to become what one was, an "authentic" Korean. Now it became possible for Koreans to "discover" themselves, "recover" lost history, and "become" themselves. The advantage of this nationalism was that it was a project in which only Koreans could participate. No one else, no matter how hard they tried, could ever hope to become an authentic Korean. "Koreanness" was an identity secure from foreign invasion, political or intellectual. It was a standard to which only Koreans could aspire.

Who, then, were the true Koreans? What qualities represented true "Koreanness?" What were the characteristics of Koreans that had persisted throughout a five-thousand-year history and that continued to provide Koreans with their distinctive identity? One thing that was clear to those nationalists, living through the darkest period in their nation's history, was that true Koreanness had little to do with Chinese Confucianism, Japanese modernism, American Christianity, or Soviet Marxism. Nor did it have much to do with being culturally sophisticated, urbane, or well educated. Instead, many turned to the peasants as the guardians of true Koreanness.[34] The fact that Korea was still an overwhelmingly agrarian society, with peasants making up more than 80 percent of the population, scarcely touched by foreign influences, political or cultural, made them the logical choice to become the "real Koreans." They were the ones who held onto the essence of Korean national character throughout centuries of foreign invasion, rule by elites who "forgot their roots" by importing foreign ideologies to oppress and exploit the masses, and of course, direct foreign domination.[35]

Korean nationalism thus came to take on an extremely xenophobic and "nativist" tone. Because the "peasants" became the embodiment of Korean racial instinct, character, and spirit, Korean nationalism also became susceptible to class analyses of the sort offered by various leftist discourses. For many, to be on the side of the peasants, that is, to be on the side of "Koreanness," meant to be "anti-imperialist" and "anticapitalist." The combination of nationalism and leftism provided fertile grounds for "leftist-nationalism" of the sort found in the post-1945 North Korean state and in the so-called *minjung* movements that reached their apogee in 1980s South Korea. North Korea's *juche* (self-reliance) ideology and South Korea's *minjung* ideologies provided Koreans with the theoretical as well as the emotional weapons by which to counter the imperialisms and capitalisms lurking around every corner of Korean history. For the North Korean regime, the imperialists and capitalists perpetuated national division by taking over the South. As far as the *minjung* ideologues were concerned, South Korea was being ruled by pro-Japanese collaborators and pro-American capitalists, in turn controlled by American imperialists. The Korean peasants, suffering so long from foreign domination and exploitation by the upper class, were now being exploited as industrial workers, forced to work under atrocious conditions while living in horrid squalor in the innumerable shantytowns that sprang up around Seoul and other cities in South Korea during its rapid industrialization.

Thus, the nationalist discourse of the sort articulated by Sin Ch'ae-ho became the basis for both oppositional politics in South Korea and the xenophobic ideology of the North Korean regime. That North Korean archaeologists recently claimed to have found the remains of Tangun and his wife, remarkably well preserved and now enshrined in an enormous mausoleum, shows the ludicrous extremes to which that regime can carry things. However, despite the almost comic nature of this claim, it does reveal the power of nationalist discourse and how much the North Korean regime is beholden to it. The rapid rise of "anti-Americanism" in South Korea also shows that leftist-nationalism once popular among radical students in the 1980s is now finding a wider audience.[36] This also shows that as South Koreans have become more confident and self-assured, having achieved successful industrialization and democratization, nationalist sentiment is on the rise. The problem is that the only sort of nationalism familiar to South Koreans is the sort based on Sin Ch'ae-ho's xenophobic, nativist, and hence racist logic.

Conclusion: A Lesson Too Well Learned

The regional order of East Asia in the late nineteenth century showed Korean nationalists the futility of trying to find a civilizational or regional solution to the crisis that befell them in the aftermath of the destruction of the Confucian order. Their allegiance to a standard of civilization alien to Choson contributed to their acquiescence in the face of foreign domination when the "nation-state" (China or Japan) that represented the civilization (Confucian or Modern) came to annex Choson. To some, a new standard of civilization, one that would not be the provenance of a particular foreign power, needed to be articulated. That new standard would be "nationalism." History has taught Koreans a painful lesson in nationalism and the Korean "nation" became one of its best students.

Of course, the irony is that South Korea came to enjoy its success precisely because it unabashedly imported, adopted, and otherwise copied everything from the Japanese economic model to American liberal democracy to the "Wall Street standard." South Korea has gone against everything that true nationalism would recommend. Indeed, modern South Korea was created by those who, like Yun Ch'i-ho, Pak Yong-hyo, Kim Song-su, and Yi Kwang-su, tried to follow the Japanese way. They were succeeded by the likes of Syngman Rhee, who tried to follow the American way.[37] Then Park Chung-hee shamelessly adopted the Japanese model of economic development. Since the Asian financial crisis of 1997, South Korea has gone out of its way to adopt American-style free-market economic practices and institutions.

As far as the nationalists are concerned, these were all "collaborators" in one way or another. The very success of South Korea in terms of globalization and regional integration continues to sow its own seeds of nationalist discontent. What then is the future prospect for globalization and regional integration for Korea and the Northeast Asian region? With the continuing modernization of South Korea and greater integration into the global and regional community, there is bound to be a lessening of the virulent form of nativist nationalism. However, for the foreseeable future, Korean political discourse will continue to be conducted within the terms of "civilization," "race," and "nation," arising from the historical experience of the late nineteenth century.

4

Trade, Dependency, and Colonialism

Foreign Trade and Korea's Regional Integration, 1876–1910

Kirk W. Larsen

On February 26, 1876, representatives of Korea's Choson and Japan's Meiji governments signed the Treaty of Kanghwa. This treaty began what is generally known as the Open Port period in Korea, an era that saw significantly intensified contact and exchange with the outside world. Foreign trade played an important role in Choson Korea's growing integration into regional and global markets. Through the conduits of designated treaty ports, the people of Korea produced, consumed, bought, and sold goods in unprecedented amounts and varieties. Choson Korea's increasing involvement in foreign trade also facilitated the integration of the Korean peninsula itself into something that far more resembled a single national market in 1910 than it did in 1876. These twin processes of integration owe much to the designs and actions of competing imperialist powers as they vied for opportunity, advantage, and dominance in Korea. They also, however, were directly influenced by the aims and activities of individual merchants and firms who cooperated with their home governments when convenient but went their own way when necessary.

An examination of Choson Korea's foreign trade during the Open Port period sheds much light on how Korea came to participate in regional and global trading patterns. It also illuminates the ways in which the disparate and diverse regions of the Choson Kingdom itself were knit together to form an identifiably single Korean market. However, many of the key elements of this national integration were not in place until nearly the end of the Open Port period. Thus, it is useful to consider trade not only at the national level but also at the regional level. For much of the Open Port period, Japan-dominated Pusan, with its heavy emphasis on the exports of Korean agricultural products, was rather different from Wonsan, where abundant gold attracted both Chinese and Japanese merchants. Both were different still from Inchon—a port that was more likely to elicit comparisons with Chinese treaty ports than with Japanese cities—and where most merchants focused on imports. By the end of the period, this regional diversity was rapidly diminishing as the Japanese commitment to formal colonial rule and the integration of the Korean market combined to facilitate growing and irrevocable Japanese dominance of Korea's foreign trade.

Pre–Open Port Period Trade

Before the Open Port period, Korea's trade was limited to four restricted venues. The most significant was the traditional tribute mission trade. In addition to offering Korean goods to the imperial Chinese court as tribute and receiving gifts in return, Choson envoys were also allowed to bring personal goods and engage in private trade. Korean silver, ginseng, and paper were exchanged for Chinese silks, medicines, books, and other luxuries. Many merchants vied to be included in tribute missions, bringing with them sizable amounts of silver to trade for Chinese goods.[1] Trade with Japan was limited to visits by Tsushima merchants to the Japan House (*waegwan*), a complex maintained by the Choson government in Tongnae (located in present-day Pusan).[2] Japanese merchants traded silver and other metals, spices, and medicines for Korean cotton cloth, rice, ginseng, and other goods.[3] Trade was also permitted at designated periodic trade fairs along the Sino-Korean border at Chunggang, Hoeryong, and Kyongwon. This exchange was heavily regulated and moderated by both governments. Korean merchants sometimes grumbled that the border trade amounted to little more than subsidizing poor Manchu families who exchanged animal skins and shoddy blue cotton cloth for cattle, paper, salt, and other necessities.[4] A final avenue of exchange, difficult to quantify, was smuggling. Anecdotal evidence points to the presence of smuggling on both the southern and northwestern coasts of Korea. The ill-fated *General Sherman* expedition of 1866, for example, was guided by a Chinese merchant who had a working knowledge of the local terrain, not to mention the good sense to abandon the expedition before it sailed too far up the Taedong River.[5]

Taken together, these patterns of foreign trade were not entirely insignificant but all indications point to the conclusion that foreign trade was seldom if ever an important element of the late Choson economy. The Choson state aimed far more often to restrict foreign trade rather than encourage it and there is little evidence of any attempts to officially profit from foreign trade by assessing tariffs or other customs duties. In official communications with China, late Choson kings pointed to the kingdom's poverty and a general lack of suitable goods to trade as reasons for Korea's reluctance to engage in it.[6] Nor did many Westerners see a great deal of commercial potential in Korea; one British observer quipped "there is no abundance of anything in the country except magpies."[7]

Although a small number of Korean officials began to make tentative calls for more engagement with the outside world in the 1870s, it was outside pressure that forced the door open. Japanese demands, backed by a flotilla of gunboats, combined with behind-the-scenes persuasion from the Qing empire to convince Choson Korea to negotiate the 1876 Treaty of Kanghwa, thus opening the door for greater levels of interaction and trade. One of the key provisions of the 1876 treaty mandated the opening to foreign residence and trade of two ports in addition to Pusan. The first three treaty ports—Pusan, Wonsan, and Inchon—became the primary conduits through which foreign goods entered Korea and Korean goods left for points abroad.

Pusan: The "Natural" Treaty Port

Given its proximity to Japan and its historical role as the channel through which the limited trade between Japan and Korea was carried out, Pusan was the natural choice to function as Korea's first treaty port. Pusan's proximity to the agriculturally rich Kyongsang region only added to its significance and potential, particularly in the eyes of Japanese rice and soybean exporters, who would dominate the port's commerce for the next several decades.

Korea's geography increased the difficulty and cost of overland travel from Pusan to other areas of the peninsula. However, the nearby Naktong River allowed for goods from Pusan to be shipped upstream (at least by small sailing craft) for nearly 200 miles. In addition, Pusan was the center of a regional coastal trade long before 1876 with wholesale merchants (*kaekchu*) plying the coasts as far north as Ulsan and as far west as Yosu. The level of commercial activity in and around Pusan would only grow after 1876.[8]

The two most important and enduring characteristics of Pusan during the Open Port period are the port's role in the export of Korean agricultural goods to Japan, and the almost unchallenged Japanese dominance of the port and its trade. It is only at the beginning and the end of the Open Port period that Pusan's main functions went beyond the facilitation of Korean agricultural exports. In the first few years following 1876, Pusan was Korea's only open port and hence the place where all goods legally sold in Korea by Japanese merchants first entered Korea. Some of the goods sold in Pusan were transported, either by the arduous overland route or by small Korean junks, to Seoul and other parts of Korea. Pusan's entrepôt role diminished in 1880 with the opening of Wonsan, which quickly became the port that provided goods for most of the east coast. The 1883 opening of Inchon, the port that served the Korean capital, still further reduced the amount of goods entering Korea via Pusan. It was not until the completion of the Pusan–Seoul railroad in 1905 that the port would regain its Korea-wide significance and influence. No longer just the gathering point for a regional agricultural market, Pusan was now the obvious starting point for virtually all goods served by the railroad and its ever-increasing number of branch lines. And, as Japanese ambitions grew, Pusan became the starting point for much of the commercial and colonial expansion into Manchuria and beyond. By the end of the Open Port period, Pusan had regained its position as the port that handled the greatest amount of Korea's exports. Soon after Japan's annexation of Korea, the port would once again handle the greatest amount of Korea's total foreign trade.[9]

It is in the area of penetrating, rationalizing, and seizing the Korean agricultural market that Pusan played its most significant role. Its proximity to Korea's most fertile agricultural lands made the port the ideal location for facilitating agricultural exports. Many of the Japanese who flocked to Pusan after 1876 hoped to use the vast disparity between the price of rice in Korea and Japan to acquire "quick and easy riches."[10] Exports of rice and beans increased dramatically during the Open Port period. In 1878, Korean exports to foreign countries included ¥50,600 worth of rice. This amount increased fourteenfold by 1880, fortyfold by 1890, seventyfold by 1900, and one-hundred-twenty-fold by 1910; exports of soybeans grew in a similarly spectacular fashion.[11] The amount of rice exports often fluctuated wildly, depending on the quality of harvests in both Korea and Japan. At times, Korea was actually a net importer of rice.[12] The value of soybean exports often rivaled and even exceeded that of rice. The growth of bean exports was much more steady and stable than that of rice. This is due in part to the fact that beans were generally more resistant to drought and other climatic changes. Often grown on marginal land, beans were clearly designed more for export (to Japan and later to China) than for home consumption.[13]

The opening of Pusan and the increase in Korea's agricultural exports served to augment the integration of the agriculturally productive southern region of Korea. Japanese rice merchants initially were willing to deal with Korean middlemen who transported agricultural products to Pusan. But after a few years, a growing number of Japanese merchants attempted to bypass the middleman by going directly to the producers. After 1894, many local Korean officials used tax money to speculate in rice and beans, which they would sell to Japanese merchants, pocketing the difference between the selling price and their designated tax quota.

As increasing numbers of Korean producers, middlemen, and officials became involved in the trade in agricultural products, the transportation and distribution infrastructure improved, albeit often frustratingly slowly from the viewpoint of foreign merchants. Japanese merchants and shipping lines continuously implored the Choson government for permission to ply the prohibited waters of the Naktong River and to be able to call at unopened ports. In the absence of such permission, many visited their markets illegally; some chartered Korean boats.[14] In addition, the opening of Mokp'o (1897) and Kunsan and Masan (1899) allowed producers in the environs of these ports a more direct path to Japan, thus enabling them to save the costs of transporting the goods to Pusan.

Korean farmers became increasingly attuned to and involved in wider regional— and even global—markets. For example, in times of poor harvests in Korea, the Choson government often subsidized imports of rice from abroad in an effort to relieve the suffering of Korean farmers and to bring down the domestic price of rice. However, at least some imported rice invariably found its way to Japan. In 1894, some 340,000 piculs (1 picul is equivalent to about 133 pounds) of rice were imported from China. Observers noted, however, that Japanese rice merchants bought up much of this rice, mixed it with Korean rice, and exported it to Japan.[15]

Korean agricultural producers were increasingly intertwined in a complex web of trading networks. Chinese rice intended for hungry Korean peasants ended up going to Japan where it may have fed a Japanese factory worker or may even have been exported once again to Europe or the United States.[16]

From 1876 onward, Japanese activity in Pusan steadily increased. The establishment of a government-subsidized monthly steamship line running between Pusan and Nagasaki further facilitated Japanese travel to and commerce in Pusan. The Japanese in Pusan numbered more than two thousand as early as 1880, a figure that would increase tenfold by the end of the Open Port period. They looked to Japan for nearly all of their necessities. In 1893, Sakurai Gunnosuke observed that Pusan's total trade was little more than the provision for the needs of Pusan's Japanese residents.[17] While this may be an exaggeration, local Japanese demand did constitute a significant portion of the port's trade. Indeed, in the later years of the Open Port period, some foreign observers saw little to distinguish Pusan from port cities in Japan. Peter Duus writes:

> The town looked comfortingly Japanese, not all that different from a port town at home. A cluster of Japanese inns, some of them three stories high, were visible from the docks, and several dozen large Japanese-style shops lined the downtown streets. In the center of town not a single Korean-style dwelling was to be seen. Only the white-garbed Koreans on the dock and in the street revealed the unfamiliar. In fact, the new arrival did not have to deal with Koreans at all, except to get his bags to the inn.[18]

The Japanese predominance in the port was mostly due to its geographical proximity to Japanese ports and to the long-standing tradition and experience of Japanese commerce in Pusan. However, Japanese merchants and the diplomats who represented their interests were not above using whatever means available—legal or illegal—to discourage and intimidate potential competitors. Such was the case in 1883, when a crowd of Japanese merchants threatened to burn down a shop established by Kobe-based Chinese merchants. The Japanese consul in Pusan, Maeda Kenkichi, declared himself unwilling to restrain the Japanese merchants, claiming that the port of Pusan was open only to Japanese. The Chinese merchants had no choice but to postpone the opening day, a decision that cost the merchants dearly, and ultimately shut down their operations in Pusan.[19] Although a handful of other Chinese firms made a brief foray into the Pusan market in the years 1899–1901, the Japanese supremacy in Pusan was almost wholly unchallenged.[20]

Wonsan: Gold-Driven Prosperity

After years of difficult negotiations, the Japanese managed to secure the opening of Wonsan in 1880. Pusan had been a logical choice for an open port due to its proximity to both Japan and the fertile southern regions of Korea, not to mention the centuries-long tradition of Japanese trade in the port. Wonsan, however, had none of these qualities. Situated on Korea's forbidding and largely desolate east coast some 250 miles north of Pusan, Wonsan offered no immediately apparent commercial enticements to the foreign merchant. The selection of the port was more due to strategic concerns about Russian designs in Korea than to any thought of commercial gain. When Inchon opened in 1883, many Japanese merchants who had businesses in Wonsan closed up shop and moved to the more promising west-coast port.[21]

However, Wonsan and its environs did possess ample amounts of one important commodity: gold. The presence of relatively large quantities of easily accessible gold transformed the port from a potentially lifeless backwater to a vibrant center of trade that accounted for a respectable portion of Korea's overall trade for much of the Open Port period. Gold was significant not only for the Wonsan region but for Korea's trade in general. In fact, for most of the period it was gold not rice or beans that was Korea's most valuable export.

Despite its isolation and apparent lack of commercial potential, Wonsan accounted for roughly one-fifth of all imports into Korea and just over 28 percent of all Korean exports for the period 1880–1900. Most of this significance can be explained by the relative abundance of gold and the purchasing power this conferred upon local residents. One observer concluded that "the most powerful motor of trade at this port is the Gold produced in Northern Corea and exported here. It alone has hitherto paid for the bulk of Foreign Imports, and, indeed, without it, the Foreign trade, as well as the revenue, would be reduced to a minimum."[22] Beans, the hides of cattle and other animals, and marine products were also exported in some quantity. However, gold accounted for the majority of Wonsan's exports, averaging some 63 percent of the port's entire exports throughout the Open Port period. In fact, Wonsan's exports of gold accounted for more than half of all of Korea's exports of the metal until the 1897 Japanese adoption of the gold standard. After 1897, Japanese demand for gold increased dramatically, transforming the metal into another means of paying for Japanese imports Korea-wide.

Japanese merchants in Wonsan vastly outnumbered their Chinese counterparts throughout the Open Port period.[23] Given this numerical superiority, the difficulty of the long journey between China and Wonsan, and the Japanese domination of shipping lines to and from the port, one might expect Japan's commercial domination of Wonsan to rival what it enjoyed in Pusan. However, Chinese merchants made swift inroads in Wonsan; in 1892, one observer concluded that "the import trade is almost entirely in the hands of the Chinese, who have now five firms established there, all of which made money in 1892, though it was considered to be an unprofitable year."[24]

Chinese merchants were able to use their proximity to and experience with the cotton textile markets in Shanghai to obtain and distribute British cotton textiles at lower prices than the same items offered by the Japanese. Since cotton textiles made up the lion's share of imports into Wonsan, Chinese domination of this trade greatly enhanced their position. In addition, the relative lack of a rice market in the

Wonsan region diminished the urgency with which Japanese merchants sought to push their imports upon Korean consumers. Chinese merchants, on the other hand, were eager to obtain as much gold dust as was available.

It is not easy to explain the Chinese resurgence that took place around the turn of the century. By this time, Japanese-manufactured cotton goods—especially cotton thread and piece goods—were beginning to make inroads into British goods' domination of the Korean market. In addition, the growing Japanese demand for and monopolization of Korea's gold exports reduced the amount of gold that could be used to purchase Chinese imports. However, Korean patterns of consumption were not always predicated on price considerations alone. The Wonsan region enjoyed a relatively high degree of purchasing power and prosperity due to the abundance of gold. Without the constant specter of famine and ruin watching over their shoulders, residents of the region may have considered the quality of goods, their suitability to individual and regional tastes, and even the amicability of relations with merchants and retailers when they made their purchasing decisions. If such was the case, British textiles, especially shirtings, Chinese silks, and Chinese merchants, all had clear advantages over their Japanese counterparts.[25]

Exports of gold are often omitted in calculations of Korea's foreign trade during the Open Port period. Gold's function as currency in many parts of the world renders problematic the consideration of the precious metal as a simple product like rice or textiles. However, it is clear that for Korea, at least until 1897 (the year Japan adopted the gold standard), gold did not in any way serve as a medium of exchange.[26] Stores of gold held by the Korean government were infinitesimal even when compared to the nearly empty coffers of silver and copper. A wide variety of materials—iron, copper, silver, paper, hemp cloth, and rice—circulated as media of exchange at various times during the Choson period, but gold was never widely used for this purpose.[27] If one considers gold as "merchandise" rather than currency, it becomes clear that gold was Korea's chief export during much of the Open Port period, not rice or soybeans. Moreover, foreign merchants routinely took considerable amounts of gold on their persons or in their personal luggage so as to avoid the export duty.[28] Estimates of the amount of gold that illicitly left Korea each year vary; one contemporary observer estimated that 90 percent of the gold exported left the country without being reported. However, the consensus seems to have been that it was safe to at least double the amount declared to the Korea Maritime Customs Service.[29]

Regarding gold as an item of export rather than as currency helps explain Korea's chronic imbalances of trade and payments. Choson Korea had virtually no overseas assets. Therefore, every item imported into Korea would of necessity have been paid for by "money or money's worth obtained within the limits of the kingdom." And yet, the tables and charts painstakingly compiled by customs officials did not add up; rather, they revealed persistent deficits. Including declared gold exports in calculations of Korea's total exports narrows but does not entirely close the gap between imports and exports. However, once smuggled gold is taken into consideration, the mysterious payments imbalance all but disappears.[30]

The export of gold from Korea is of particular importance to Sino-Korean trade. For the fifteen-year period, 1885–1900, gold accounted for an average of 72.3 percent of all Korean exports to China. Legal restrictions on the export of gold to countries other than Japan were put in place in the late 1890s, a process that led to a dramatic and irrevocable decline in Korean gold exports to China.

Roughly the same pattern of rise and dramatic fall is evident in China's position in Korea's exports of gold as a whole. Customs officials and other observers of Korea's trade were quick to note that once Chinese merchants entered Korea in earnest, exports of gold to China grew rapidly.[31] This pattern continued well after the Sino-Japanese War, with China's share of Korean gold exports peaking around 1898 and falling off sharply thereafter. This change is largely due to the Japanese decision to adopt the gold standard and the subsequent obtaining of a monopoly on purchases of gold dust and bullion in Korea for Japanese banks. Legal exports of gold to China dwindled to insignificance though it is unlikely that the clandestine gold trade completely dried up.[32]

The opening of Wonsan and the attendant increase in the port's exports of gold dust and other commodities heralded the increasing connections of Wonsan with points both to the north and south along the coastline, with areas in the interior, and with regional markets and trading networks. After 1880, the Mitsubishi Steamship Company received a government subsidy to add Wonsan to the ports of call for its Korean lines. A year later, the line was extended as far north as Vladivostok.[33] Russian, Chinese, and British steamship lines also provided service, albeit often intermittently, that connected Wonsan with a growing number of ports in the region.[34] Wonsan's growing connections with a number of smaller Korean ports along the coast were facilitated largely by Korean ships. Only with the opening of Songjin (1899) and Ch'ongjin (1908) did foreign vessels begin to call on additional ports on Korea's eastern shore with any regularity.

Wonsan used its abundance of gold to purchase both foreign goods and Korean commodities, the latter being primarily comprised of rice and other foodstuffs. The port also became an important transshipment point for Korean products such as dried *myongt'ae* (Alaska pollack) originating from Pukch'ong, and soybeans grown in many areas along the eastern coast.[35] In addition, Wonsan provided goods for the remote Korean interior as far away as areas in eastern Pyongan Province.[36]

While Japanese and Chinese merchants accounted for the vast majority of foreign merchants in Wonsan itself, the port also played a prominent and important role in Choson Korea's growing trade with Russia. Korean gold, cattle, and other products left Wonsan destined for Vladivostok in ever-increasing numbers.[37] In addition, Vladivostok became an important destination for both Korean and Chinese seasonal migration, a development that troubled some Russian authorities in the city.[38] The establishment of a trading post at Kyonghung in

1888 facilitated Korean-Russian trade at the Choson kingdom's northern border. Until 1901, some foreign goods entered Russia first and then Korea overland either via Kyonghung or via smuggling routes in an effort to avoid the onerous exactions placed upon trade by local Korean officials outside the treaty ports.[39] However, in 1901 this dynamic reversed as Vladivostok adopted the tariff levels of European Russia, thus making it cheaper to import goods into Korea directly. Moreover, some of the Korean imports ultimately made their way overland to Russia.[40] The Russo-Japanese War severely disrupted trade between Korea and Russia, but shipping lines and the flow of goods resumed soon after the cessation of hostilities.[41]

Inchon: Importer's Prize

The 1883 opening of Inchon as Korea's third treaty port was a victory for determined Japanese negotiation in the face of almost equally determined Korean resistance. Whatever the implications of the opening of the port for Korean-Japanese diplomatic relations, the first sight of Inchon did little to stir the pulse of foreign merchants.[42] Descriptions of the port and its surroundings almost universally included complaints about the difficulty of actually getting ashore.[43] Once they managed to get ashore, foreign merchants found little in the way of local population or industry that would indicate any great commercial potential.[44] Farther north than the most productive agricultural regions of Korea and lacking the Wonsan area's easy access to gold, Inchon had, at first glance, little to offer.

That foreign merchants braved these obstacles to make Inchon the busiest port in Korea for most of the Open Port period was primarily due to Inchon's one great asset: its proximity to Seoul, the capital of the Choson kingdom. Within two years of its opening, Inchon would handle more of Korea's trade than any other port. In fact, until 1908, Inchon generally handled as much trade as the rest of Korea combined. It would relinquish its position as Korea's chief port only after the Japanese annexation of Korea in 1910.[45]

Unlike the other two previously opened ports, trade in Inchon was unequivocally import driven, with the market in Seoul its chief attraction. Getting people and goods from Inchon to Seoul was no easy task. By land, the trip over the sometimes barely passable road by ox or pony often took most of a day. Small boats cruising up the Han River to Yanghwajin, Map'o, or Yongsan, three communities on the river that were closest to Seoul, had to navigate treacherous, shallow, sandbar-filled water. However, Seoul offered a far greater concentration of wealth and demand than anywhere else in the country and many resolute foreign merchants found their ventures to be difficult but profitable. Merchants from Japan and China, and later from Western nations, vied for this market.

Unlike export-oriented Pusan and Wonsan, most merchants in Inchon focused on imports first, and exports as a means of paying for imports if possible. This tendency is particularly evident in the case of Chinese merchants. In fact the lack of Korean goods suitable for export to China was a constant complaint from both the Chinese commercial community and its potential customers.[46]

In many respects, Pusan was a Japanese monopoly. Inchon, on the other hand, much more closely resembled a wide-open Chinese treaty port, complete with a General Foreign Settlement, a Western-dominated municipal council, and Western merchants (albeit in small numbers until 1905). Like many Chinese treaty ports, Inchon was populated by foreigners from a variety of countries, including Japan, China, Russia, the Philippines, Great Britain, France, Germany, Belgium, Switzerland, Austria-Hungary, the Netherlands, Turkey, Egypt, and the United States.[47] Many officials in the Korean Customs Service had served in posts in the Chinese Maritime Customs Service before coming to Korea; many returned to China after their service in Korea. The same can be said for a good number of Western diplomats, missionaries, and traders in Inchon and Seoul.

From the opening of the port, Japanese and Chinese merchants competed fiercely for control of Inchon's imports. The share of the port's total trade controlled by Chinese merchants generally rivaled and occasionally exceeded that of Japanese merchants until 1904 with significant but temporary setbacks during the Sino-Japanese War (1894–95) and the Boxer Rebellion (1900). After 1904, the share of trade controlled by Chinese merchants shrank considerably, but so did the share controlled by merchants from Japan. Picking up the slack were growing numbers of Western merchants who established a significant on-the-ground presence in Inchon for the first time. The Japanese could console themselves with the fact that Japan was losing market share in a shrinking market, while their dominance of the resurgent Pusan trade continued unabated.

Even before the arrival of large numbers of Western merchants, Westerners had a hand in influencing Inchon's trade dynamics by aiding and encouraging Chinese commercial activity in the port. British consuls and other officials repeatedly noted that Chinese merchants did a brisk business in importing Manchester cotton textiles. During the Sino-Japanese War British diplomats fiercely resisted attempts by Japanese officers and merchants to confiscate Chinese land and goods and otherwise make doing business in Korea more difficult for Chinese merchants.[48] Later, Russia, seeking to counterbalance the growing Japanese presence in Korea, subsidized a shipping line that stopped in Inchon on the way from Vladivostok to Shanghai, which significantly aided Chinese merchants in the port. In an attempt to break the Japanese banking monopoly in the port, a branch of the Sino-Russian bank was opened in Inchon in 1898; although short-lived, this had the effect of significantly reducing for Chinese merchants the costs of foreign exchange, paying customs duties, and acquiring loans.[49]

The intense competition for Inchon's trade meant that the port was connected to a variety of other ports and trading and distribution networks. As was always the case in Open Port period Korea, Japanese shipping companies dominated the maritime carrying trade to and from the port. However, Russian and Chinese steamship lines also called at Inchon; smaller sailing craft were ubiquitous as well. The

Japanese lines connected Inchon with ports in China, other ports in Korea, and cities back home, particularly Osaka. But as the Open Port period progressed Inchon saw increased connections with various Chinese ports across the Yellow Sea. In 1907, for example, Japanese, Chinese, Russian, British, and Norwegian ships collectively made more than a hundred trips between Inchon and Andong, Chefoo (Yantai), Dalian, Niuchuang, and Shanghai.[50]

Goods and Networks

The types of goods entering Inchon, most of which were destined to end up in Seoul, can be generally classified into three broad categories: goods traditionally exchanged via tribute missions, goods intended for consumption by foreigners in Korea, and foreign manufactured goods intended for Korean use. Although tribute missions continued until 1894, once Inchon was opened it became the more natural conduit through which many of the traditionally exchanged goods flowed. One of the primary dynamics of this expanded and intensified traditional trade was the Korean export of ginseng and import of Chinese silk and grasscloth.

Trade in ginseng between China and Korea had gone on long before the opening of Korea to maritime trade. By the time of Kojong's reign, royal control of ginseng exports accounted for a significant portion of royal revenue.[51] While some ginseng surely continued to find its way to China via annual tribute missions, once Inchon was opened, the vast majority of ginseng exports left Korea via that port. No matter who controlled the market in Korea, virtually all ginseng exports ended up in China. And, despite wild fluctuations in the amount exported in any given year (often the result of the attempts of the Korean government to manipulate prices), the export of ginseng constituted a significant element in overall Korean exports. Moreover, ginseng was extremely susceptible to smuggling; Chinese, Japanese, and Koreans all participated in the lucrative if illicit trade.[52]

The other half of this traditional trade was the Korean import of Chinese textiles, particularly silk and grasscloth. Despite Japanese efforts to compete directly with the Chinese as well as pressure the Choson government to put up barriers to the import and consumption of Chinese textiles, Japanese merchants never seriously challenged the Chinese predominance in this area.[53] Chinese producers and merchants paid close attention to an exacting and ever-changing Korean market. One British observer noted:

> The silk for the Corean market is specially manufactured in the neighborhood of Chinkiang, and is quite different from anything worn in China. Coreans like bright and fancy colors, children especially appearing on holidays in clothes of the most dazzling hues. It is amusing in this remote part of the world to hear the Chinese purveyor complaining of the impossibility of keeping pace with the ever-changing fashions of the Coreans.[54]

Chinese merchants also did a brisk business in grasscloth, with imports of the fabric often rivaling and occasionally exceeding those of silk. These Chinese-manufactured goods accounted for over a quarter of the value of all textiles imported into Korea in 1909 and an average of nearly 19 percent of the value of all textile imports over the decade 1900–1910, a clear demonstration of the staying power of traditional networks and patterns of commerce, distribution, and consumption.

Sundry Goods and Enclave Trading

A second major category of imports into Inchon consisted of a wide variety of goods intended not for Korean consumption but for the use of Korea's growing foreign community. A large and consistently growing portion of the imports into Korea meticulously recorded by Customs Service officials were placed in the "sundries" category. For example, well over a hundred such items are listed in the 1893 Customs Service Report for Inchon. These include everything from cigarettes to "braid, llama" from fireworks to iron safes; from needles to pomatum; from watches to "worm tablets, in bottles." An examination of a 1901 report on trade in Inchon reveals that while Japanese merchants imported greater quantities in many categories of sundry goods, they had a monopoly on only a very few (among them hair oil, used newspapers, and straw rope).[55] Any individual item taken alone constituted a tiny fraction of the port's total trade, but taken together, these various and sundry goods accounted for an average of just over 30 percent of all foreign imports into Inchon over the period 1883–1907.

Japanese merchants imported Japanese goods for the use of the growing Japanese communities in Korean treaty ports. Chinese merchants imported goods for their own communities and provided for the needs of many Westerners in Korea as well.[56] The share of both Chinese and Japanese merchants in the import of foreign sundries (and of foreign manufactured goods in general) declined with the arrival of Western merchants who imported many such goods directly.

Aside from the various sundry goods originally intended for use by foreign communities within their treaty port enclaves, other foreign manufactured goods found a steadily increasing demand among the Korean populace at large. Most prominent among these were matches and kerosene, items that, along with British cottons, had "the honor of representing an alien civilization."[57] The influence of these items on Korean lives and lifestyles probably cannot be overstated, as they allowed greater numbers of Koreans to extend their productive or leisure time well into the night. Tobacco, wine and spirits, and coal and coke were also imported in growing amounts.

Cotton Textiles

For much of the Open Port period, foreign cotton textiles constituted the single largest import into Korea. The cotton textiles market was the object of fierce competition between Japanese and Chinese distributors and between Japanese and

British manufacturers. In general terms, the Chinese would win the battle for control of distribution of British cotton textiles in Korea. However, given that Japanese textiles occupied an ever-growing share of the Korean market, the Chinese victory would prove pyrrhic. Moreover, the cotton textile trade demonstrated a complexity that belies the simple application of ethnic or national identifications to the merchants who warehoused, distributed, and sold machine-woven cotton goods in Korea.

Western, particularly British, cotton goods were a significant and permanent feature in Korea's imports during the Open Port period. However, for most of the period, British merchants did not attempt to do business in Korea, having been long accustomed to using "established indigenous merchants within the treaty port system" to market their textiles in East Asia.[58] This usually meant relying on Chinese merchants. Japanese merchants frequently "complained that they had to buy almost all the foreign goods bound for Korea from Chinese houses in Nagasaki."[59]

After the establishment of maritime relations between China and Korea in 1882, Chinese merchants based in Japan took advantage of unprecedented representation and protection afforded by Qing officials on Korean soil to compete directly for the import trade in Korea.[60] Merchants from China possessed several advantages over their Japanese counterparts. The first was simple geography: Inchon, the chief port of the Korea trade, especially in imports, was closer to Shanghai, the main distribution center of British textiles, and closer still to Tianjin, an important regional distribution center, than to any port in Japan. The second advantage was proximity to and experience with the Shanghai textiles market. Chinese merchants were able to react more swiftly to fluctuations in exchange rates, prices, supply, and demand.[61] Third, most Chinese merchants who imported British textiles had larger amounts of capital than their Japanese counterparts, many of whom were small-scale merchants trying to make the rice trade pay by importing Manchester gray shirtings or T-cloths. Fourth, and more generally, the widespread Korean antipathy toward Japan meant that Korean consumers generally preferred Chinese merchants to Japanese (all else being equal).

The Japanese challenge to Chinese commercial superiority in Korea came not in the transshipment of British machine-woven cotton goods but rather in the development of Japanese-produced goods that competed directly with their British counterparts. Many of the first Japanese forays into what was previously British territory took place in Korea. Combining the advantages of late industrialization, proximity to Korea, attention to Korean demand, and the benefits of the growing colonial presence in Korea, Japanese merchants were able to challenge the British monopoly in cotton goods. This challenge was first felt in lower quality goods such as yarn and piece goods, but eventually even the high-quality shirtings market was not immune to Japanese competition.

Japanese yarn, initially of considerably lower quality than yarn from India or Britain, was competitive largely because of price. However, the quality of the yarn gradually improved while its price remained competitive. In addition, Japanese spinners paid close attention to Korean needs.[62] An additional Japanese advantage was the willingness of Japanese peddlers who traveled to the interior to take virtually any available commodity in exchange for yarn.[63]

Imports of piece goods, an area increasingly dominated by Japanese manufactured articles, followed roughly the same pattern as yarn.[64] Japanese machine-woven imitations of native Korean cloth gained in popularity not only because of their low price but also because Japanese manufacturers paid close attention to Korean needs, seeking to match the texture, size, and other qualities of Korean cotton cloth.[65] Japanese-made sheetings appeared in larger quantities in the late 1890s. British observers noted that Japanese sheetings were "rapidly increasing in quality, are both heavier and cheaper than their English competitors, and are said to stand much better the pounding and scrubbing which is inseparable from the Corean system of washing."[66] The Japanese challenge to British textiles in Korea ultimately extended even to high-quality goods such as unbleached (gray) and bleached (white) shirtings.

The factors that help explain the British decline and Japanese ascent are myriad and diverse. Some stress the fact that British producers and merchants simply did not work as hard to discover and meet the tastes of Asian consumers as did their competitors from the Continent, the United States, and Japan. The inability or unwillingness of the British merchant to get his hands dirty in the field was taken as emblematic of an empire in decline. Other scholars have stressed more impersonal shifts in factor endowments that gave comparative advantage to Japan.[67] All of these factors played a part in the textiles trade in Korea. In the end, however, it was the Japanese commitment to formal empire in Korea that trumped the Sino-British informal one.

It should be noted that the massive influx of foreign cotton goods did not necessarily signify the immediate demise of the domestic textile industry. This phenomenon is particularly apparent in the case of cotton yarn. One of the first products of Japan's effort to industrialize—cotton yarn spun in Japan and sold in Korea—constituted an important stepping stone for a Japanese textile industry bent on expansion and improvement. However, as is evident in the nature of the good, Koreans bought yarn to weave into cloth themselves. Foreign yarn had the benefit of being of higher quality and, especially after the Japanese entry into the market, was of comparable price to yarn produced in Korea. Thus every spool of yarn imported into Korea reduced the demand for foreign woven cloth.[68] Although more research needs to be done on this subject, it is apparent that it is at least worth considering whether sizable yarn imports into Korea may have had the same impact as imports of yarn into China and Japan where they resulted in "the paradoxical strengthening of the long-established domestic weaving industry and thus obstructed the entry of Western cotton piece goods."[69]

Contemporary observers and subsequent generations of scholars alike have tended to write about merchants from a particular country as if they formed an undifferentiated monolith. While the composition of merchants in Pusan and

Wonsan may have been closer to this generalized ideal, Inchon was home to a diverse range of merchants connected to one another and to merchants of other nations that often belied the simple depictions of them as "Japanese," "Chinese," or "Western." For example, the Chinese in Inchon were divided into three major groups. The "Northern League" hailed largely from neighboring Shandong Province and accounted for the largest number of merchants in Inchon. A "Guangdong League" did a brisk trade in textiles as well as tobacco, liquor, canned goods, foodstuffs, and various sundries. A "Southern League" made up of merchants from Jiangsu, Zhejiang, and Jiangxi Provinces dealt mostly in piece goods and silk.[70] In addition, the Chinese seizure of the transshipment trade of British textiles in Inchon came not so much at the expense of Japanese merchants but of the Chinese Nagasaki-based "Zhejiang clique."[71]

Domestic and Regional Integration

The period after 1895 saw significant increases in the amount of Korea's foreign trade as well as the intensification of Korea's integration both as a national market and into regional networks and markets. The opening of additional ports, the establishment and expansion of shipping lines, the construction and operation of telegraph lines, and the construction of a railroad network in Korea all served to tie the heretofore distinct disparate regions of Korea much closer together. The primary dynamic behind much of this integration, however, was the intensification of Japanese colonial designs for and activities in Korea. Thus, a more unified Korea became inexorably connected to the Japanese metropole.

From the Treaty of Kanghwa to the Sino-Japanese War, the three open ports of Pusan, Wonsan, and Inchon dominated Korea's foreign trade. After 1895, Choson Korea's commercial connections with the outside world were amplified by the opening of additional ports. Ports in the southern part of the peninsula like Mokp'o (1897), Kunsan (1899), and Masan (1899) afforded Japanese rice and bean buyers greater direct access to Korean producers and allowed them to avoid the expense of transshipping the goods to Pusan before their departure for Japan. The opening of Chinnamp'o—also known as Namp'o—(1897) gave foreign merchants legal access for the first time to the relatively populous and prosperous Pyongan region. Other ports—Songjin (1899), Uiju (1907), and Chongjin (1908)—further facilitated the foreign commercial penetration of Korea.[72] However, by and large the opening of new ports did not significantly alter the preexisting patterns and dynamics that characterized Korea's foreign trade in the 1880s and early 1890s. The agriculturally prosperous south continued to attract Japanese rice and bean merchants who dominated the trade there. Wonsan continued to export significant quantities of gold and enjoy close connections with the Russian Far East as well as Japan and China. Inchon remained the chief conduit through which foreign manufactured goods entered Korea (and through which Korean ginseng headed for China).

More significant for many Koreans was the gradual yet inexorable integration of various parts of the Korean peninsula into what more closely resembles a national market. Shipping—both sail and steam—the telegraph, and most significantly, the railroad bound the Korean peninsula together in unprecedented ways.

Shipping

Korean coastal shipping networks had existed long before the arrival of foreign merchants to Korea in the late nineteenth century. While certainly less expensive than transporting goods overland, these networks left much to be desired in the eyes of foreign merchants and observers. Complaints abounded about the expense and the unreliability of Korean shipping ventures, not to mention the fact that Korean sailing ships were often "rickety and leaky" and most were uncovered, which considerably raised the probability of damage to cargo.[73] The advent of more modern steamships, both Korean- and foreign-run, reduced the costs and risks of coastal transport.

Korea's connection to foreign ports by steamship was initiated and dominated by Japanese shipping ventures. As mentioned previously, the Meiji government was quick to subsidize Japanese steamship lines connecting Pusan with Nagasaki, Kobe, and various Chinese ports. The Japanese shipping network expanded to include additional Korean ports as they opened as well as Vladivostok to the north. By all accounts, Japanese firms carried the lion's share of cargo entering and leaving Korea. Foreign competition appeared from time to time in the guise of Qing-subsidized China Merchants Steamship Company lines connecting Korean ports, particularly Inchon, with Yantai, Tianjin, Shanghai, and points beyond. Chinese shipping lines were interrupted by war and unrest, especially during the Sino-Japanese War, the Boxer Rebellion, and the Russo-Japanese War (1904–5). Moreover, Chinese merchants in Korea often exchanged their goods for gold dust or ginseng, both of which were usually carried on board as personal luggage or smuggled, which meant that many Chinese steamers returned to China with their holds virtually empty. Russian attempts to establish shipping lines between Vladivostok and Korean, Japanese, and Chinese ports were intermittent and did little to seriously challenge the Japanese monopoly. Curiously, British steamship companies displayed little to no interest in extending their lines to Korea; as one British consul in Korea remarked:

> Accustomed as one is to see the British merchant flag predominating everywhere, it is curious to find a country with any foreign trade with not a single British ship entering any of its ports for a space of 12 months, not even under charter; in this respect one would almost imagine that Corea held a unique record.[74]

Equally significant was the expansion of intercoastal shipping lines and networks within Korea itself. Here there was a much greater variety of ships, companies, and networks competing for a growing market. Korean, Japanese, and Chinese sailing vessels were a frequent sight along much of Korea's rugged coast and among its innumerable coastal islands. Many were tramp vessels owned by an individual or family who moved from port to port based on whatever contracts were available. Others developed regular schedules and networks and were sponsored by powerful shipping families such as those hailing from Marifumura, Japan.[75] Foreign merchants often chartered Korean vessels to engage in interport and intercoastal trade.

The proliferation of these shipping networks signaled the development of two major networks of long-distance internal trade. One was along the east coast and consisted of the exchange of southern cotton cloth for northern hemp and *myongt'ae*; the other was along the west coast and consisted of the import of provincial rice, ramie, and cotton cloth into Seoul. Both of these networks expanded considerably until the Russo-Japanese War and the development of railroads.[76]

Foreign companies such as the German Myer and Company and the Chinese Tongshuntai also vied for the lucrative tribute grain shipping routes between the agriculturally productive south and Seoul. The latter firm also sought to connect Inchon and Seoul with both an overland transport company utilizing huge carts pulled by as many as forty oxen and a shipping line whose crown jewel, the 100-ton steamer *Hanyang,* dominated the river trade until it was seized by the Japanese in the Sino-Japanese War.[77]

Telegraph Lines

The establishment of telegraph lines in Korea greatly enhanced the speed and reliability of communications between various points on the peninsula.[78] The Qing empire dominated Korea's telegraph lines until its defeat in the Sino-Japanese War, after which Japan seized the upper hand in control of Korea's modern communications. A line between Inchon and Seoul was completed by September 1885, a branch office was opened in Pyongyang in October, and the line to the border town of Uiju was completed by the end of November of the same year, thus linking Korea with the outside world in a manner unprecedented in its long history. After some delays Korea's telegraphic network was expanded to include lines connecting Seoul to Pusan (1888) and Wonsan (1891).

Much of the Inchon–Seoul–Uiju line was destroyed during the Sino-Japanese War, and when the lines were rebuilt, the Qing empire was not in a position to interfere or assert any sort of authority. Korean autonomy over the lines was to be short-lived, however, as Japan extended its control over key Korean institutions, including the telegraph. Russian attempts to connect areas of northern Korea with its own growing communications grid were fiercely resisted by both the Korean and Japanese governments.[79] Under Japanese aegis, telegraph lines extended to Masan, Chinju, and several points in southwestern Korea. By the time Korea became a Japanese protectorate in 1905, few significant commercial or population centers remained outside telegraph range.

Merchants, diplomats, and government officials alike used this new form of communication to their advantage. The establishment of the telegraph allowed for instantaneous communication between ports, and, therefore, greater sensitivity to fluctuations in price, currency, and demand. Enterprising merchants could react more quickly to harvest shortfalls and changes in the market.[80]

Railroads

The construction of railroad lines in Korea greatly accelerated the commercial integration of the peninsula. Plans for railroad construction date back to the reformist cabinet of 1894. But war, unrest, and lack of capital slowed actual construction for many years. Concessions were initially granted by the Choson government to the American James B. Morse for the construction of a line between Seoul and Inchon and to Fives-Lille, a French company, to construct a line between Seoul and Uiju on Korea's northern border. Railroad concessions became objects of diplomatic and commercial wrangling among Russia, Japan, and Korea. In the end, all of Korea's railroads passed into the hands of Japanese businesses, and, ultimately, the Japanese government. Railroad construction was often opposed and resisted by a suspicious local populace and by anti-Japanese "righteous armies" (*uibyong*) but the might of the Japanese military was not to be gainsaid.[81] The Seoul–Inchon line was completed in 1900, the line between the capital and Pusan in 1905, and the Seoul–Uiju line, constructed by the Japanese military, was completed in the same year.

The impact of the establishment of railroads on Korea's commercial patterns was immediate and considerable. Observers were quick to note the salutary effect of greatly reduced distribution costs on the levels and profitability of trade in Korea.[82] In addition, few were surprised to discover that Japanese attempts to facilitate the integration of Korea by railroad, although having the effect of increasing trade generally, were biased toward Japanese commercial interests. According to one observer, Japanese railroad officials used "every possible means" including the manipulation of railroad rates to encourage trade in Pusan at the expense of Inchon.[83]

The construction of an expanding rail network also had the effect of linking Korea ever more closely to the outside world. One observer noted that once the Trans-Siberian Railway was completed in 1904, a passenger could make a journey from London to Inchon within an unprecedented twenty-one days.[84] Coming relatively late in the Open Port period, the railroad had an immediate and significant impact on Choson Korea's growing commercialization, trade, and integration.

Colonial Consolidation

Korea was officially annexed by Japan in 1910, but this did not have a dramatic impact on the peninsula's trading patterns, at least not immediately. Ultimately, however, annexation would inexorably reduce the amount of non-Japanese involvement in Korea's foreign trade. Japanese commercial activity in Korea had been a quasi-colonial enterprise since at least 1905. The massive influx of goods related to Japanese administration had little to do with Korean demand or Japanese competitiveness, but reflected rather the growing Japanese commitment to colonial rule and development in Korea.[85] Japanese statesmen may not have been motivated primarily by commercial concerns but they were not above promoting the interests of Japanese businesses in Korea whenever possible. The use of Japanese steamship lines and Japanese-controlled railroad lines to the benefit of Japanese merchants and the detriment of competitors has already been mentioned. In addition, while official Japanese attempts to influence Korean demand, as in the cases in which the wearing of Chinese-style silks and the use of long pipes were prohibited in 1894–95, were not terribly successful, the persistent and ultimately successful pursuit of control over Korea's gold and ginseng exports wrested these profitable trades away from competitors. Attempts to standardize and regulate the Korean currency, culminating in the virtual imposition of the Japanese yen as Korea's currency, also worked to the advantage of Japanese merchants.[86]

Moreover, the composition of the Korean-Japanese trade would gradually become simpler, eventually earning the pithy description of "rice for cotton."[87] In the end, Choson Korea was far more integrated—both as a national market and as an important participant in regional trading networks—in 1910 than it was in 1876. But it was increasingly integrated into a colonial infrastructure not of its own choosing.

Part II

Competing Regional Orders

Colonialism, the Cold War, and Their Legacies

World War II constituted a watershed in Northeast Asia. The short-lived Japanese push for total regional supremacy, and with it Japan's longer experiment with colonial empire in East Asia, went down in total defeat, capped by the explosion of the first atomic weapons. In the war's aftermath, the power and presence of the United States attained an unprecedented level. The Soviet Union, too, greatly extended its Asian-Pacific reach, initially as an ally of the United States. With the creation of separate regimes in Seoul and Pyongyang in 1948, however, two opposing blocs—distinct regional systems—faced off against each other on a divided Korean peninsula. Japan narrowly escaped Korea's divided fate, owing to the protective posture of Japan's main wartime enemy and conqueror, the United States, which kept the Soviets out. The sudden new bipolar strategic situation in Northeast Asia was hardened with the victory of the Chinese communists in 1949. Overall, the shifts of the 1940s stand out as momentous.

And yet, some would date Northeast Asia's great watershed to the Korean War, which began in 1950. In that light, Bruce Cumings suggests here, as he has elsewhere, that global political economy undergirded the advent of a new international system. To put the matter another way, a new economic order—not just a new political order—was formed by U.S. "hegemony," which Cumings defines as the demarcation of limits whose transgression brings retaliation. The U.S.-led system, he writes, was more open, and therefore stronger, than previous imperialisms. Readers may wonder to what extent U.S. power in the Pacific resulted from implementation of a strategy, as opposed to circumstances and the unsystematic pursuit of perceived interests. Cumings does adduce internal policy ruminations about a

"great crescent," but he concludes that it was the Korean War—a contingency—
that put the new realities in place and new forces in motion.

Amplifying Akira Iriye's argument about the exceptionalism for Japan of the
1941–45 period—against the background of Japan's willing, opportunistic subor-
dination to the international system across the twentieth century—Cumings underscores how readily the Japanese took to U.S. supremacy. He argues that Japan
became the prime beneficiary of the U.S. wars in Asia, and he notes that U.S.
dominance also created the conditions, and the logic, for the postwar reestablish-
ment of Japanese ties to its former colonies, Korea and Taiwan. At the same time,
however, when his discussion moves to South Korea, Cumings's "hegemony" argument becomes more implicit as he stresses South Korean agency. He suggests
that it was precisely the South Korean economic success that broke the back of the
once attractive communist model (an outcome often attributed, at least in Asia, to
the Japanese miracle, and secondarily, to communist China's reforms). Cumings
prefers not to discuss the imperatives behind containment—the Soviet system and
behavior—but instead to demonstrate the motivation (lucre) and critical economic
dimension of America's cold-war political strategy, whose structures are still largely
with us, despite the Soviet capitulation.

Whereas Cumings stresses continuities in terms of Japan's place in the international system despite the ascension of the United States, Daqing Yang emphasizes
continuities in terms of Japanese-built (and especially planned) infrastructure.
Looking backward from the recent proposals to reconnect the railway links across
the Korean peninsula, Yang points out what might be considered an irony—that in
the interwar period, Japanese language had no equivalent for "infrastructure," even
as the Japanese built massive infrastructure and wielded it as a form of regional
integration. Whether Japanese actions were, as Yang suggests, imitative of the Nazis,
or isomorphic with European developments, could be debated. The important point,
Yang shows, is how colonial-era infrastructure continues to function, occasionally
with very different purposes, across the region. And yet, in the postwar period, it
was the Soviet-inspired communist model that linked most closely with the Japanese program in the former Japanese imperial heartland, industrial northern China,
and the main industrial areas of Korea. Thus, Japanese colonial legacies are important, but communist-era legacies loom large, too.

Northeast Asia's socialist regional order, which took shape with the defeat of
Japan, is explored by Stephen Kotkin and Charles K. Armstrong. During the cold
war, the socialist bloc may have portrayed itself as monolithic—and been accepted
as such by its opponents—but the bloc's Asian incarnation was never as cohesive
as the interlocking system of American alliances. The Sino-Soviet rift was un-
matched within the U.S.-led regional order: Japan knew its place. In addition,
initiative from subordinated powers was not ipso facto a threat to the American
order (though it was sometimes perceived as such in Washington). For many reasons, then, from internal competition to external competition, the socialist regional
order did not long endure. Nonetheless, it had long-lasting consequences, among

them extensive aid and technology transfer, especially in the military sphere—even including transfer of atomic bomb capability to China. Even North Korea's relative autonomy (achieved by playing off China and the Soviet Union) took the form of a hyperextension of the heavy-industry-centered and military-based Soviet model. By contrast, Mongolia—the first Soviet satellite, long predating Eastern Europe—belatedly gained its independence, though it lost its central transit role for trade between the two giants, a role that is now coveted, in a wider vision, by proponents of Korean reunification.

Japan's Asian regionalism, which had a boom in the 1980s, is explored by Chung-in Moon and Seung-won Suh, largely from the point of view of its effects on South Korea. Elaborating upon a 1997 essay by Viktor Koschmann about Japan's "ambivalent Asianism," Moon and Suh detail the complexities of Japan's normalization in Asia. To be sure, having become the world's second largest economy, Japan could be expected to be a giant throughout Asia—and, of course, it is. But Moon and Suh argue that even as what they call "Japan's spontaneous economic regionalization" had established the basis for Japan's renewed regional consciousness and ambition, new regional political mechanisms were slow to take shape, partly because of Japan's struggle to come to grips with its place in Asia. The regional options debated within Japan—an open regionalism, preferential trade agreements—have not been able to trump a desire to sustain Japanese regional leadership. For South Korea, postwar Japan has been indispensable, yet, also a challenge, whether because of chronic trade deficits or patterns of investment. Moon and Suh conclude with brief mentions of what they call anti-Americanism in the regional calculus, and of how China and Russia affect Japan's role in the region and its relation to the Korean peninsula. Their suggestion that South Korean policy makers will be increasingly preoccupied with a free trade agreement with Japan, rather than a broader regional vision linked to the Asian mainland, remains to be seen.

Looking back through the competing regional configurations—the Japanese empire in both its prewar and wartime incarnations, the postwar U.S. alliance system (or hegemony), the socialist bloc and within it the Chinese challenge to Soviet leadership, and finally Japan's fraught reassertion within Asia—we can see that Korea appeared to constitute a periphery in every one. But did it? Inside the different Soviet and American regional orders during the cold war, which in varied ways subordinated even the big powers China and Japan, both Koreas deepened their national consciousness, playing off against each other. Indeed, small-nation nationalism has remained the exclusive story line for South Korea and North Korea, and this contemporary nationalism is often projected backward to time immemorial. But history can play tricks. With the sudden, surprise moves toward a transcendence of the cold war, nationalism has hardly disappeared, but the Korean peninsula's geographical centrality has reemerged in transnational possibilities for a broadly integrated future Northeast Asia. At the same time, imperial and cold-war legacies linger.

Japanese quarters in the Ch'ungmuro district of Seoul, called "Honmachi" by the Japanese. 1930. (Reproduced with permission of *Donga Ilbo*, Seoul, Korea.)

Korean guerrillas in the anti-Japanese movement in Manchuria, 1930s. Kim Il Sung is in the back row, middle. (*Shiho bunko,* Japan)

American soldiers ride the first test train across the newly reconstructed Han River Railroad Bridge in Seoul, Korea. June 12, 1951. (Reproduced with permission of the Fort Wood Engineer History Office.)

East German engineers and their families participate in a parade commemorating the tenth anniversary of the founding of the DPRK, 1958. (*Tongdok top'yonsu Resel ui Pukhan ch'uok* [Korean Reminiscences of East German Master Craftsman Ressel]. Photographs by Erich Robert Ressel; text by Paek Sung-jong. Hyohyong Publishing, Seoul, Korea)

Influence of the Soviet Union in Asia (New York: Nester House Publications, Inc., 1960)

5

From Japanese Imperium to American Hegemony

Korean-Centrism and the Transformation of the International System

Bruce Cumings

First as a colony, and then as a divided country, Korea became a site, and subsequently a highly unlikely fulcrum, for the transformation of the international system —from one of rapidly declining British leadership in the early 1930s, to a short period of regional Japanese hegemony in East and Southeast Asia, thence to a defining crisis in 1950–51 that became the global building block for American global predominance. Korea was Japan's most important colony and, later, a model for Manchukuo, and was the centerpiece of its regional strategy of political economy in the interwar period. Later on, the Korean conflict ushered in a transformation of American power in the world, and in the 1960s the Republic of Korea (ROK) became a key model for American-promoted export-led development as the remedy for underdevelopment in the "third world."

I will seek to distinguish four aspects of this transformation: (1) a model of industrializing political economy that began under Japanese auspices in Northeast Asia in the 1930s, forming a regional bloc that deeply shaped the postwar political economy in the region; (2) the contribution of that regional formation to hastening British manufacturing decline (in the 1930s) and assisting American manufacturing advance (in the 1940s), which was one important aspect of the shift from British to American hegemony that characterized the twenty years from 1930 to 1950; (3) the civil war in Korea which provided in 1950–51 the fulcrum for building the military sinews of the American global position abroad and a national security state at home, both of which have now long outlasted their ostensible cause, namely, the cold war that ensued from 1947 to 1989; (4) and the ROK's rapid industrial development from the mid-1960s onward, which ultimately led to a fully industrialized South Korea in the 1980s, and a key victory for the United States in the cold war competition with Moscow to fashion a viable model of development in the postcolonial or "third" world.

The Japanese empire in Northeast Asia embodied three countries that speak different languages, have different histories, different cultures (albeit all traditionally influenced by China), and, in Korea and Japan, two highly homogeneous but quite different ethnic constituencies. The dominant modes of inquiry in American economics, along with modernization theory, reinforced a tendency (at least since 1945) to view each country apart from the others and to examine single-country trajectories. Yet a country-by-country approach is incapable of accounting for the remarkably similar trajectories of Korea and Taiwan. Thus, specialists on Korea argue that its development success "is unique in world history."[1] Taiwan specialists make similar claims. Both groups of specialists omit the essential Japanese context of Korean and Taiwanese development.

Conventional neoclassical economists attribute growth in Taiwan or Korea to specific attributes of each nation: factor endowments, human capital in the form of a reasonably educated workforce, comparative advantage in labor cost, and so on. Modernization theorists offer a diffuse menu of explanations for Taiwan or Korea, ranging from the discipline or "rationality" of traditional Confucianism, through various cultural arguments, the passion for education, U.S. aid and advice, the presumed "natural" workings of the product cycle, and the diffusion of advanced education, science, and technology.[2] My position has been that an understanding of the Northeast Asian political economy can emerge only from an approach that posits the systemic interaction of each country with the others, and of the region with the world at large. Rapid upward mobility in the world economy has occurred, through the product cycle and other means, within the context of two hegemonic systems: the Japanese imperium to 1945, and intense, if diffuse, American hegemony since the late 1940s. Furthermore, only considerations of context can account for the similarities in the Taiwanese and South Korean political economies. Simultaneously, external hegemonic forces have interacted with different domestic societies in Korea and Taiwan to produce rather different political outcomes: This, too, has been characteristic throughout the century. Korea was more rebellious in 1910; it was more rebellious through much of the postwar period.

In the 1930s, Japan largely withdrew from the world system and pursued, with its colonies, a self-reliant, go-it-alone path to development that not only generated remarkably high industrial growth rates but changed the face of Northeast Asia. In this decade, what we might call the "natural economy" of the region was created; although it was not natural, its rational division of labor and set of possibilities have skewed East Asian development ever since. Furthermore, during this period, Japan elaborated many of the features of the neomercantile state still seen today. One prescient writer in the mid-1930s speculated that Japan's heavy industrialization spurt was so impressive that "if world trade were not restricted by tariff walls and import quotas . . . Japan might become the largest exporter in the world—and in a very short time." Guenther Stein saw in this spurt "the beginning of a new epoch in the industrialization of the world."[3] He was right on both counts. (This is not the usual dating: The watershed years of 1945–50 are presumed to have remade Japan, but, as we shall see, they did not.)

Furthermore, we can find in the work of the best neoclassical economists an acknowledgment, however indirect, of the advantages of contiguity in this region: In the middle of a highly technical article where he proposed to test all sorts of propositions about Taiwan's economic success, Simon Kuznets paused to note that

> given the expected economic flows among market economies, particularly those in geographical and historical proximity to each other, the fact that some of them experience a rapid rate of growth in total and per capita product makes it easier to explain a similar experience in other countries of the group. Thus Japan's spectacular economic growth from the early 1950s to the early 1970s is a significant factor in the high growth rates of Japan's trading neighbors, including Taiwan; reciprocally, the high growth rate in Japan's trading neighbors contributes to Japan's growth. In that sense, the growth experience of any single country is a function of the growth of others.[4]

At a later point in his monograph Kuznets also cites "the growth-stimulating effect" of "the backlog of unexploited production opportunities" provided by "the forward movement of technology and efficiency in other countries not affected by the conditions that retarded progress elsewhere." This effect occurs "even in LDCs" (less developed countries):

> Though a backlog is presumably continuously present in them, even in some less developed countries per capita product may have grown in the past (as in Taiwan under Japanese occupation), a process that may have been interrupted by war preparations and war (again as in Taiwan since the early or mid-1930s). If, as noted above, Taiwan managed, even with Japanese dominance and constraints on domestic industrialization, to attain a growth rate of between 1 and 2 percent per capita per year before war preparations began, the interruption added to the effective backlog of production opportunities. Once the institutional and political conditions had changed, a much higher growth rate could be attained.[5]

This is an interesting example of the reasoning of American economists, particularly their supposition that language—in this case tortured English prose—is transparent and meaning is self-evident after a certain level of literacy. For example, what does "historical proximity" mean beyond a redundancy for geographic proximity, since Japan, Korea, and Taiwan have not moved any closer since their human settlement a few tens of thousands of years ago. This might, however, signify Kuznets's recognition of a "historical proximity" known as Japanese imperialism, when Tokyo's Birnham Wood did indeed march to the hinterland's Dunsinane. Of course, these statements would seem to render impossible the scientific separation out and measurement of economic growth in Taiwan, Korea, and Japan, and instead would underline the influence of the history of economic interaction and the Northeast Asian regional economic effort, whether in the 1960s, the 1930s, or today.

The Level of the World

Since at least the turn of the past century, Japan has been acutely aware of its global position as a strong regional power, but a weak power vis-à-vis the hegemonic state. Thus, in 1902, it allied with the reigning power of the time, the United Kingdom, with the United States as a kind of hidden partner in the Anglo-Japanese Alliance.[6] After the Washington conference in 1922, the United States became the senior partner in this three-way arrangement, one that lasted into the late 1930s. After it lost the Pacific War, Japan reengaged with the new global regime as the junior partner of the United States, and remains so today—the second largest economy in the world, but with 100,000 American troops stationed in and around Japan. We can connote this longest-running position in the global system, and the preferences of Japan's leaders, with this metaphor: *Japan as Number Two*. Japan has prospered within a diffuse web of hegemony for the past century, with only one errant and disastrous attempt to escape.

Hegemony is a vexing term, no more so than now when neoconservatives like William Kristol use it to connote a unipolar and unilateral American role in the contemporary world. I mean something different by hegemony: the demarcation of outer limits in economics, politics, and international security relationships, the transgression of which carries grave risks for any nonhegemonic nation. In the postwar American case, hegemony meant the demarcation of a "grand area"[7] within which nations oriented themselves toward Washington rather than Moscow; nations were enmeshed in a hierarchy of economic and political preferences whose ideal goal was free trade, open systems, and liberal democracy but which also encompassed neomercantile states and authoritarian politics; nations were dealt with by the United States through methods ranging from classic negotiations and trade-offs (in regard to nations sharing Western traditions or approximating American levels of political and economic development) to wars and interventions (in the periphery or third world), to assure continuing orientation toward Washington.[8]

The hegemonic ideology, shared by most Americans but by few in the rest of the world, was the Tocquevillean or Hartzian ethos of liberalism and international-ism, assuming self-evident truths about human freedom generated in a born-free country that never knew serious (or European-style) class conflict. Not a colonial or neocolonial imperialism, this was a new system of empire begun with Wilson and consummated by Roosevelt and Acheson. Its very breadth—its nonterritoriality, its universalism, and its open systems (within the grand area)—made for a style of hegemony that was more open than previous imperialisms to competition from below. This form of hegemony establishes a hierarchy of nations, therefore, but not one that is frozen: It rendered obsolete the development of underdevelopment. Instead, far more than the German hegemony in Eastern Europe that Albert Hirschman analyzed or Japanese unilateral, colonial hegemony in East Asia, U.S. hegemony is open to rising talent from below and particularly to disparities of attention (what Burke, speaking of England and the American colonial revolution, called "wise and salutary neglect") that give leverage and room for maneuver to dependencies. As Hirschman put it in a classic study, the dependent country "is likely to pursue its escape from domination more actively and energetically than the dominant country will work on preventing this escape."[9] Finally, this form of hegemony also fused security and economic considerations so inextricably that the United States has never been sure whether economic competition from its allies is good or bad for grand-area security. American postwar hegemony grew less out of specific human design (although Dean Acheson as architect would come close) than out of the long-term reaction of hegemonic interests to the flow of events.

In East Asia we can identify an abstract schema representing the workings of this system over the past century. This schema will satisfy no one except practitioners of shorthand, but for purposes of strict brevity I want to present the structure of a world system in which modern Japan has been an important, but almost always subordinate part. An abstraction of Japan in the past century's international system unearths the following timelines:

(A) 1900–1922: Japan in British-American hegemony
(B) 1922–1941: Japan in American-British hegemony
(C) 1941–1945: Japan as regional hegemon in East Asia
(D) 1945–1970: Japan in American hegemony
(E) 1970–2000s: Japan in American-European (or "trilateral") hegemony

Highlighted is an interesting aspect of this structure: three of the periods (A, B, and E) are trilateral partnerships, and only one is colonial or necessarily imperial (C). A bilateral regime is predictable in the temporary phase of comprehensive predominance or hegemony (1945–70 for the United States), whereas a trilateral regime is predictable in the rising and falling phases of transitional hegemonies. Period C is perhaps the exception that proves the rule (at least for Japan).

This abstract pattern can be found readily in the oeuvre of the dean of diplomatic historians of East Asia, Akira Iriye, whose books dominate the field. Because Iriye's work has dwelt in the realm of culture, ideas, and imagery in international relations,[10] and perhaps because of his understated style, few recognize just how deeply revisionist his work is. Iriye has consistently argued through his career that:

(1) Japanese imperialism (conventionally dated from the Sino-Japanese War and the seizure of Taiwan in 1895) was subordinate to British imperialism, and coterminous with a similar American thrust toward formal empire in the 1890s, and no different in kind from the British or American variety;[11]

(2) Japan pursued a "cooperative" policy of integration with the international system at all times in the past century, except from the critical turning point of July 1941 and the resulting war;[12]

(3) Japan got the empire the British and Americans wanted it to have, and only sought to organize an exclusive regional sphere when the other powers did the same, after the collapse of the world economy in the 1930s (and even then their attempt was half-hearted, and their development program was "orthodoxly Western");[13]

(4) Japan's presumed neomercantilist political economy of protection at home and export to the free trade realm abroad, with corresponding trade surpluses, has been less important over the past century than an open market at home and a cooperative policy abroad.

On the critical 1941–45 period, Iriye noted that until the Japanese military's "turn south" in July 1941 (a decision deeply conditioned by Soviet power), Japan was still dependent on the United States, which he terms (in a nice summary of the dramatic change that came in the early 1920s) "the key to postwar international relations . . . its capital, technology, and commodities sustained the world economic system throughout the 1920s . . . as the financial, business, and political center of the world."[14] As conflict deepened in the late 1930s, the United States deployed a series of "slipknot" measures against Japanese expansion (to use Walter LaFeber's excellent metaphor),[15] finally invoking the outer limits of its hegemonic power by embargoing scrap iron and oil to Japan, which came as a tremendous psychological shock to Japan and made its leaders assume that the only alternative was war.

The U.S.-Japanese war moved quickly to its denouement, but even quicker was the American hand in pursuing Japan's restoration and its repositioning in the postwar international system. Within months of the attack on Pearl Harbor, a small cadre of internationalists in the U.S. State Department and in Japan began moving on remarkably parallel lines to reintegrate Japan into the postwar American hegemonic regime. According to Iriye, by early 1943, moderate Japanese and American leaders were coming back to "the framework of 1920s internationalism." In particular he cited a memo by Hugh Borton, a historian working for the State Department, which provided for "a framework for long-range planning for U.S.-Japanese relations" that would "reintegrate [Japan] into the world community of economic interdependence."[16]

The Great Crescent and the Kennan Restoration

The definition of Japan and Korea's place in the postwar world occurred in the period 1947 to 1951, and still governs the situation today. It was in that period that the tectonic plates of the international structure found their resting place after the earthquake of World War II. Dean Acheson, George Kennan, and John Foster Dulles—to take three of the most important American planners—wished to situate Japan structurally in a global system shaped by the United States, so that Japan would do what it should without having to be told—by remote control, as it were.

In so doing, they placed distinct outer limits on Japan's behavior, and these limits persist today.[17]

Japan was demilitarized and democratized during the early Occupation years, if with less thoroughness than the proponents of the policy had hoped for. It is thus proper to view the years 1945–47 as an exception to the general thrust of American policy toward Japan in the postwar period, a policy elaborated during the war years by Japanophiles in the State Department who looked forward to reforms that would quickly restore Japan's position in the world economy, and that would not penalize Japan's industrial leaders for their support of the war. It is also important to remember, however, that the twin goals of democratization and demilitarization were not antithetical to the subsequent strategy,[18] but in fact represent the extraordinary reach of American hegemony in the late 1940s: restructuring both the world system and the internal political economies of major industrial competitors Japan and Germany (something that England tried but failed to do in regard to Germany after World War I).

The United States was the one great power with the central economic, financial, and technical force to restore the health of the world economy. Although hegemony usually connotes "relative dominance" within the group of core states, by 1947 it was apparent that the United States would have to exercise unilateral dominance for some time, given the gross asymmetry between the robust American industrial system, then producing half of the entire world's output, and the poverty of nearly all the others. It was this critical problem of industrial revival, spanning Western Europe and Japan, that detonated basic shifts in 1947; the so-called reverse course in Japan was thus an outcome of global policy. The new goal was the reconstitution and flourishing of the German and Japanese industrial economies, but in ways that would not threaten hegemonic interests.[19] The revival of Axis industry also spelled out a new regional policy.

Soviet-American conflict in central Europe had erected barriers to almost any exchange, a great divide known to Americans after Churchill's 1946 speech in Missouri as the "Iron Curtain." This curtain sliced up marketing and exchange patterns that had underpinned important regional economies. The bulwarks dropped across the central front in Europe and the developing cold war in Asia cut the Western European and Japanese economies off from peripheral or colonial sources of food, markets, raw materials, and labor—in Europe, grain from Poland and Hungary, meat and potatoes from Poland, oil and coal from Romania and Silesia; in East Asia, rice and minerals from Korea, sugar from Taiwan, coking coal and soybeans from Manchuria, and tungsten from South China. With the European recovery so sluggish, Japan still dormant, and communist parties threatening in Italy and France, China and Korea, this structural problem was newly perceived and demanded action in 1947. The East Asian expression of this policy had an elegant metaphor.

By early 1947, George Kennan had elaborated plans for Japan's industrial revival, plans that called for a modified restoration of Japan's former colonial position in Northeast Asia. But the foundation of "containment" in East Asia was a world economy logic, captured by Undersecretary of State Dean Acheson's notion of a "great crescent" stretching from Japan through Southeast Asia and around India, ultimately to the oil fields of the Persian Gulf. Although containment was thought to be preeminently a security strategy against communist expansion, in East Asia it mingled power and plenty inextricably. To complement and to achieve their security goals, American planners envisioned a regional economy driven by revived Japanese industry, with assured continental access to markets and raw materials for its exports. This would kill several birds with one stone: It would link together nations threatened by socialist state-controlled economies (containment), make Japan self-supporting (not incontinent), weave sinews of economic interdependence with Japan and the United States (plenty), and help draw down the European colonies by getting a Japanese and American foot in the door of the pound and franc blocs in Asia (power and plenty). Peter Booth Wiley aptly summarized these changes as follows: "Japan, having emulated Perry in its first military expedition to the Asian mainland in 1876, was being invited to build a new economic empire under the guns of the modern equivalent of the black ships"; he referred to the Occupation as "the second opening of Japan."[20]

In South Korea, the "reverse course" started immediately, as the United States sought to contain both a strong left wing within the South, and North Korea, which was ruled by Kim Il Sung and his allies essentially from February 1946 onward. From 1945 to the 1980s the leading officers of the South Korean military came largely from those individuals who, in the 1940s, were trained in Manchurian and Japanese military academies.[21] The big central bureaucracy in Seoul not only was carried over virtually intact after 1945, but American Occupation authorities usually required that Koreans have experience in the colonial apparatus before employing them.[22] Such agencies as the Oriental Development Company simply had their names changed (in this case to the New Korea Company), and Americans found that they had to use Japanese systems of recruitment to staff the bureaucracy.

After the victory of the Chinese revolution, the search for Japan's Asian hinterland came to mean mostly Southeast Asia, but in 1947–48 Korea, Manchuria, and North China were all targets of potential reintegration with Japan. In a stunning intervention at the beginning of the famous "fifteen weeks" that inaugurated the Truman Doctrine and the Marshall Plan, Secretary of State George Marshall himself scribbled a note to Acheson that said, "Please have plan drafted of policy to organize a definite government of So. Korea and connect up [sic] its economy with that of Japan," a pearl that cannot be brought to the surface and examined without demolishing much of the diplomatic history on Korea in this period.[23] It captures with pith and foresight the future direction of U.S. policy toward Korea from 1947 through to the normalization with Japan in 1965, and the emergence of rapid export-led growth.

The irony, of course, is that Japan never really developed markets or intimate core-periphery linkages in East and Southeast Asia until the 1960s. It was the Korean War and its manifold procurements, not the "great crescent," that pushed Japan forward along its march toward world-beating industrial prowess (indeed, Chalmers Johnson has called the Korean War procurements "Japan's Marshall Plan"). A war that killed three million Koreans was described by Prime Minister Yoshida Shigeru as "a gift of the Gods,"[24] giving the critical boost to Japan's economy; the Tokyo stock market fluctuated for three years according to "peace scares" in Korea. Yet the logic of an Asian hinterland persisted through the Korean War; it is remarkable to see how vexed the Eisenhower administration still was with "the restoration of Japan's lost colonial empire."[25] Ultimately this logic explains the deep reinvolvement of Japanese economic influence in Korea and Taiwan from the 1960s onward.

Security and economic considerations were inextricably mixed. A revived Japan was both a bulwark against the Soviets and a critical element in a reformed and revived world economy. What is surprising, in the multitude of formerly classified American documents now available on early postwar Asian policy, is how powerful were the economic voices. In particular, a cluster of bankers and free traders, dubbed the "Japan Crowd," were instrumental in the ending of the postwar reforms in Japan and the revival of the regional political economy that persists.[26] Economics bulked so large because, as Charles Maier points out, the defeated Axis powers (Japan and West Germany) were to become world centers of capital accumulation and growth, not of political or military power.[27] Thus Japan's economy was reinforced, while its political and military power (beyond its borders) was shorn. The result is that in the postwar world economy Japan resembles a sector as much as a nation-state.

As thinking about a revived Japan evolved in 1948–50, two problems emerged: First, how could Japan's vital but second-rate status be assured; second, how could a prewar political economy that got raw materials and labor from the Northeast Asian periphery survive in the postwar world without a hinterland? George Kennan raised these problems in a 1949 Policy Planning Staff meeting:

> You have the terrific problem of how the Japanese are going to get along unless they again reopen some sort of empire toward the south. . . .
> If we really in the Western world could work out controls . . . foolproof enough and cleverly enough exercised really to have power over what Japan imports in the way of oil and other things . . . we could have veto power over what she does.[28]

Thus, once the decision to revive Japan was made, two questions predominated: the hegemonic problem and the hinterland problem. The U.S. Central Intelligence Agency (CIA) in May 1948 suggested Northeast Asia as the new (old) hinterland: "As in the past, Japan for normal economic functioning on an industrial basis, should have access to the Northeast Asiatic areas—notably North China, Manchuria, and Korea—now under direct, indirect, or potential control of the USSR."[29] A high official in the Economic Cooperation Administration, a few months later, suggested the same hinterland, and a drastic method of recovering it. Without North China and Manchuria, he argued, Japan would have "no hope of achieving a viable economy," it (and Korea) would be "doomed to military and industrial impotence except on Russian terms." Therefore, "Our first concern must be the liberation of Manchuria and North China from communist domination."[30] This rollback option, however, was delayed; the victory of Mao's forces throughout China and the possibility in 1949 that Washington might be able to split Moscow and Peking (Acheson's policy) combined to suggest a hinterland for Japan in Southeast Asia.

In July 1949, the CIA asserted that the United States had "an important interest" in "retaining access to Southeast Asia, for its own convenience and because of the great economic importance of that area to Western Europe and Japan." It argued that "the basic problem with respect to Japan is to recreate a viable economy. This in turn requires a stabilization of the situation in Southeast Asia and a *modus vivendi* with Communist China." The latter requirement might be satisfied if China could be drawn away from "vassalage toward the USSR."[31] Southeast Asia was the preferred candidate for Japan's hinterland. It would provide markets for Japan's textile and light industrial exports, in exchange for raw materials Japan badly needed. The problem was that France and Britain sought to hold the countries in the region exclusively, and nationalist movements resisted both the Europeans and a reintroduction of the Japanese. Thus, "Anglo-American consensus over Japan dissolved" as the United States played the hinterland option. Japan was a threat to sterling bloc trade and currency systems, and was "perforce in the dollar bloc"; the United States wanted Japan to earn dollars in the sterling bloc, which would have the dual virtue of supporting Japan's revival while encouraging Britain's retreat from empire.[32]

Particularly important is the triangular structure of this arrangement, a structure clearly articulated in the deliberations leading up to the adoption of NSC 48/1 in late December 1949, a document so important that it might be called the NSC 68 for Asia. (With this the United States made the decision to send military aid to the French and the Bao Dai regime in Vietnam, not after the Korean War began.) The first draft argued the virtues of a "triangular" trade between the United States, Japan, and Southeast Asia, giving "certain advantages in production costs of various commodities"—that is, comparative advantage in the product cycle. It also called for a positive policy toward communist-held territory in East Asia: The goal was "to commence the rollback of Soviet control and influence in the area." The final document changed this phrase to read, "to contain and where feasible to reduce the power and influence of the USSR in Asia."[33] The rollback contingency expressed both the fear of continuing communist encroachment, what with the fall of China in 1949, and the search for a Japanese hinterland.

Acheson came to understand Great Britain's inability to defend Greece and Turkey (and by implication, the Middle East) as the final death wriggle of British global leadership; after receiving the British Foreign Ministry's famous "blue note" in February 1947, he walked off to lunch with a friend, remarking that "there are only two powers in the world now," the United States and the Soviet Union. In a short five years since Roosevelt reached for global leadership after Pearl Harbor, events had delivered it into the American lap. It was also in those fifteen weeks that Acheson told a Senate committee in secret testimony that the United States had "drawn the line" in Korea, and sought funding for a major program to turn back communism there on the model of "Truman Doctrine" aid to Greece and Turkey.

Thus decisions made in early 1947 foreshadowed the American decision to enter the Korean War in June 1950; the initial decision was simply to defend South Korea, but by late August, Truman and Acheson had decided to attempt a "roll-back" of the North Korean regime (in the language of National Security Council document 81). Chinese and North Korean forces dealt a catastrophic defeat to American and South Korean soldiers in the depths of that frigid winter, but later on Secretary of State Dean Acheson remarked that "Korea came along and saved us," because it finally convinced Congress to fork over the massive defense budget that he and Paul Nitze had called for in the most important American cold-war strategy paper, National Security Council document number 68 (approved but not funded in April 1950). U.S. defense spending was pegged at $13.5 billion in June 1950, and nearly $55 billion six months later (or more than $500 billion in current dollars, a high point never reached again).

Two June visits symbolize both the abrupt change, and the desires for continuity, that the Korean War occasioned. A Toyota representative landed in San Francisco on a mission to interest Americans in his products. The war began during this visit, however, and he immediately returned to Japan—as Toyota's fortunes took off, selling trucks and other vehicles to the United States in Korea. That same month, the veteran industrialist Pak Hung-sik showed up in Japan and gave an interview to the *Oriental Economist*, published the day before the war began. Described as an adviser to the Korean Economic Mission (i.e., Korea's Marshall Plan organization), he was also said to have "a circle of friends and acquaintances among the Japanese" (a bit of an understatement). In the years after Liberation a lot of anti-Japanese feeling had welled up in Korea, Pak said, owing to the return of "numerous revolutionists and nationalists." Today, however, "there is hardly any trace of it." Instead, the ROK "is acting as a bulwark of peace" at the Thirty-eighth Parallel, and "the central figures in charge of national defense are mostly graduates of the former Military College of Japan." Korea and Japan "are destined to go hand in hand, to live and let live," and thus bad feelings should be "cast overboard."

The Japanese should buy Korean raw materials, he said, of which there was an "almost inexhaustible supply," including tungsten and graphite; the Koreans will then buy "as much as possible" of Japanese merchandise and machinery. They will also invite Japanese technical help with Korea's textile, glass, chemical, and machine industries. Pak himself owned a company that was an agent for Ford Motors: "we are scheduled to start producing cars jointly in Korea before long." The problem today, Pak said, was the unfortunate one that "an economic unity is lacking whereas in prewar days Japan, Manchuria, Korea and Formosa economically combined to make an organic whole."[34] If Karl Polanyi was right to call the Rothschilds the microcosm of the internationalist vision, Pak Hung-sik was the embodiment of the Japanese colonial idea—having been born a Korean his only unfortunate, but not insurmountable, fate.

After the crisis of 1950–51, American elites came to agree on a bipartisan strategy of containment, putting "liberation" or "rollback" on the back burner of covert action thereafter—useful only against new regimes or small countries that appeared to be going communist, like Cuba. But containment was very expensive, necessitating the building of military and economic bulwarks at various choke points around the Sino-Soviet perimeter. U.S. expeditionary forces remained in Korea and garrisoned Japan, keeping it on twin outer-limit dependencies: resources, primarily oil shipped from the Middle East along lines policed by the U.S. Navy; and a defense dependency that has rendered Japan a semisovereign state ever since. All this happened quickly, coterminous with the emergence of the cold war and the hot war in Korea, and it deepened as Japan benefited from America's wars to lock in an Asian hinterland, first in Korea and later in Vietnam. This dual structure of international relations and regional political economy remains in place to this day.

South Korea's Industrial Takeoff

In the fifteen years after World War II it was rare to find any American official who thought the ROK would find a way to become "economically viable," in the stock phrase, without unification or a very close connection to Japan. This was George Kennan's judgment right in the middle of the worst fighting at the Pusan Perimeter in August 1950. Japan, he told Acheson, was "the most important single factor in Asia," but at the moment it was "too weak to compete." However, "with the revival of her normal strength and prestige," Japan would be able to regain her influence in Korea:

> It is important that the nominal independence of Korea be preserved, for *it provides a flexible vehicle* through which Japanese influence may someday gradually replace Soviet influence without creating undue international repercussions.[35]

That is an unusually frank statement, but it is essentially what Acheson and many American officials after him believed; some thought the ROK useful as a "buffer between Japan and Communist Asia," but not for much else. One official reported that in 1960, "only one or two of the score of officials" in the Eisenhower administration involved in planning for Korea thought that South Korea could become "economically viable" short of reunification.[36] As late as the mid-1960s, even scholars of East Asia had trouble seeing South Korea's future as any different from its past, so wrapped up were they in the previous two decades' perception of economic stagnation and dislocation. Thus James W. Morley wrote in 1965 that South Korea had still not "taken off."

It has made little progress. It has remained politically unstable and economically prostrate. . . . The day when it can be more than a ward of the United States not only has not dawned but cannot now be foreseen.

American economic and military aid still accounted for about 75 percent of the South's military budget, 50 percent of the civil budget, and nearly 80 percent of available foreign exchange, Morley wrote; meanwhile North Korea was growing and industrializing rapidly, with its people better fed and housed than ever before.[37]

In spite of such pessimistic prognoses, the ROK found a way to combine its learning under Japan in the 1930s with its strong state and its wealth of human talent, to begin a long period of rapid industrial growth—helped along by a great deal of American advice and aid. Lacking much domestic capital, the Korean state found a way to use foreign capital and earnings both to reward its friends and promote efficient production. It fostered one rising industry after another, starting with simple assembly operations and ending with gigaflop microprocessors etched in infinitesimally small lines upon silicon wafers. It created from scratch octopus-like firms now known to the world as *chaebol* (the Korean pronunciation of the characters for *zaibatsu*). In conditions of often stunning political and social dislocation, it worked effectively to build support and slowly to legitimate its hell-bent-for-leather development program.

American policy also helped to redirect Korean development. Within weeks of the inauguration of John F. Kennedy, W.W. Rostow and his close associate, Robert Komer, had taken a close look at South Korea and argued that in spite of its truncated and isolated condition, it had strong human resources and was an ideal place to develop light industries for export. In a March 15, 1961, memo called "Action in Korea," Komer outlined "the major thrust of U.S. effort[s] over the next decade": (1) "crash economic development," (2) "creation of light labor-intensive industry," and vigorous U.S. action "in directing and supervising ROK economic development." Komer and Rostow thought Korea had one major, underutilized resource: its people.[38] A major revision of U.S.-Korean policy in 1965 embodied the new American judgments. Although it restated Korea's utility as a strategic backstop for Japan, it now also touted the ROK as an example, like Taiwan, that "the non-Communist approach to nation-building pays off." Among eight policy goals, number two was "economic growth averaging at least six percent per year" over the five years 1966–71. Nor was the United States unhappy with the strong role of the state in the Korean market: It wished to promote "whatever appears to be the most effective division between the public and private sectors."[39]

In the early 1960s the labor cost saving for firms in the United States willing to move to Korea was a factor of 25, since workers were paid one-tenth of American wages but were 2.5 times as productive. How is this possible? Let an expert explain:

In transistor assembly operations, for example, given wage rates 1/10 of those of equivalent operators in the U.S. (for the same firm), the machinery is run at physical full capacity, that is, 6 days, three shifts a day, which is 20 percent above the U.S.

equivalent. . . . In spite of the greater use of labor, productivity per worker seems to be higher partly due to the fast learning process . . . but mainly to the greater discipline and attentiveness on the assembly line throughout. For example, in one firm the difference in speed of assembly on identical equipment yields a 30 percent differential in output. . . . These greater speeds of operation, either due to faster machines or operator pacing, are once again accomplished by putting additional women into more intensive testing, inspection and repair efforts than in Japan or the U.S.[40]

Park Chung Hee was a stolid son of Korea's agrarian soil who had come of age in Manchuria in the midst of depression, war, and mind-spinning change. In this radicalized milieu he had witnessed a young group of military officers organize politics, and a young group of Japanese technocrats quickly build up many new industries—including Kishi Nobusuke, who later became prime minister of Japan.[41] In *Our Nation's Path*, Park's first book after his 1961 coup d'état, regime scribes lauded the 1868 Meiji Restoration as a great nation-building effort; but it was really the Manchurian model of military-backed forced-pace industrialization that concentrated Park's mind.

Economic planning was another wrinkle that Park borrowed either from the Japanese in Manchuria in the 1930s or the North Koreans thereafter; successive five-year plans (FYP) unfolded from the hallowed halls of the Economic Planning Board (EPB), known as "Korea's MITI" after Japan's Ministry of Trade and Industry. The first FYP was to run from 1963 through 1967, but Americans in the Agency for International Development (AID) mission did not like it, and refused to certify it for foreign lending. It never really got off the ground. The second FYP (1967–71) was more to their liking, but the Koreans had also learned how to counter American minds: When Joel Bernstein, director of the AID mission in Korea, complained that Korean future projections were much too optimistic, the Koreans quoted him back to his boss, Walt Rostow, who headed the State Department's Policy Planning Staff. As Bernstein wrote to Rostow,

> You are being quoted as saying that conventional economists always underestimate demand for the products needed in a growing economy, that Korea should not worry about overcapacity because demand is always underestimated, that estimates of requirements should be made in the ordinary way and then everything should be doubled, and that economic development is too serious a matter to leave to economists who do not understand it adequately.

The Koreans, Bernstein thought, had a "damn their torpedoes" attitude, and still lacked understanding of "the principle of marginal utility."[42] Rarely have we had a better example of conventional American economics confronting neomercantilism; Bernstein did not win, of course, because the Koreans were right: Rostow was just as neomercantilist as they were. Soon, every year Korea held "Export Day," a national celebration with President Park coming down to give guidance, laud a new overfulfilled export target, cut a ribbon on a Hyundai ship, try out some new slogans, and make a speech. None other than Kim Yon-su, founder with his brother of Kyongbang Textiles in the 1920s, got Park's "Gold Pagoda Industrial Medal" in 1971, as the nation's most successful exporter.[43] But South Korea also had other things in mind: a quick move into heavy industry.

At his New Year's Press Conference in January 1973, Park announced a program of "heavy and chemical industrialization," with steel, autos, ships, and machines projected to be 50 percent of 1980 export totals. The target was $10 billion in exports and $1,000 per capita income within a decade. This was the press conference Park had wanted to give a decade earlier but could not; it was always his dream to make steel the symbol of his industrialization drive, and not shoes or wigs. Steel meant national power, he often said; North Korea turned out thousands of tons of the stuff, an essential part of their armaments industry and just about everything else. The Pittsburgh of Korea was to be P'ohang, a small port city virtually erased during the Korean War because of its location along the shifting lines of the Pusan Perimeter. Steel, however, was just one of six great industries to be built virtually overnight; the others were chemicals, automobiles, shipbuilding, machine tools, and electronics.

American advisers and multilateral institutions like the International Monetary Fund were less than impressed. The world market had too much capacity in most of these industries, and the Korean domestic market was too small to absorb them. Their conduit of influence within the government was the EPB, which wanted to continue leading from Korea's comparative advantages in light-industrial exports. Park therefore centralized the third FYP team in the Blue House: The Economic Secretariat of the Presidential Palace was the brains, and the Corps for the Planning and Management of Heavy and Chemical Industries was the horse for this gallop, this end run around foreign and internal opposition on the Schumpeterian grounds that incremental, marginal utility was not the name of the game: How about a great leap forward, on the grounds that every future estimate of demand should at least be doubled—or tripled, or quadrupled? The Blue House became a hothouse for neomercantilists, of which the biggest was President Park himself. Much as the Manchukuo mafia industrialized Japan out of the world depression, the Blue House team industrialized Korea out of the 1970s miasma of stagflation and oil shocks.

Pohang Steel came onstream in 1973 at an annual capacity of 1 million tons; by 1976, 2.6 million tons of crude steel poured out of the mill, 5.5 million in 1978, and 8.5 million by 1981. In a decade Korea's steel capacity grew fourteenfold.[44] Who bought all this steel? Korean shipbuilders who had no factories in 1970, Korean automakers who were not supposed to be needed by the world market, American manufacturers who bought Korean steel delivered to the Midwest well below the posted price in Pittsburgh or Gary, Indiana. A steel and chemical industry is also, of course, a guarantee of independent capability for the manufacture of all sorts of weaponry and armaments. It was the Big Push that created Korea's big firms, now known by their names or logos all over the world. It is amazing to realize that this Korean business phenomenon is only as old as Park Chung Hee's early 1970s program: Daewoo did not exist until 1967, and the other big *chaebol* all went into heavy industry only from this formative period. Nor was this a matter of technocrats conducting market surveys and testing the waters: Park would call in the *chaebol* leaders and tell them what to do.

For any country lacking access to raw materials and energy sources, the chemical industry was always the sine qua non of self-reliance, putting synthetics in the place of absent natural resources. It had been for Germany and Japan, as it was for North Korea; and since Japanese chemical plants had been built in the North, South Korea was completely dependent on imported fertilizers in the 1950s. In the first fifteen years of the Park administration, this industry grew dramatically, however, with production expanding by a factor of 180. Still, almost all of this production had been in joint ventures—with Dow Chemical, Gulf, Bechtel, Mitsui, and other firms, and many of them had been acrimonious (Dow left in a huff in 1982).[45] By 1973, however, an independent Korean chemical complex emerged at Ulsan, making polyethylene, methanol, and other materials. Korea's dependence on imports of synthetic fibers for its textile industry nearly disappeared, plummeting to 10 percent by 1975.

The pièce de résistance for Park was his new machine-tool complex, the industry that builds the machines for all the others, and the heart of an autonomous defense industry.[46] He placed the Changwon Machine-Building Industrial Complex in the harbor of Masan on the southeast coast, as far from the demilitarized zone as you can get and still be on the peninsula. In 1970 Korea had a remarkable 86 percent rate of dependency on foreign imports in machine tools, much of it from American firms, at a time when President Richard Nixon was cutting back on troop commitments to Korea. In spite of its new economic prowess, Korea still could not manufacture an internal combustion engine for its own automobiles, and many of the 2,500-odd parts that make up a car still had to be imported.

Park herded all the big firms into Changwon to build more than one hundred factories, and required foreign construction firms to source out their components in Korea (if it had the domestic capability to make them). Changwon took off like a rocket, with machine building increasing an average of 36 percent a year during the years of the third FYP. By 1977, domestic parts made up 90 percent of Korean autos. Park and his successor also assured that as more Koreans bought family cars, they would be Korean cars. Today the market is so protected that it is as hard to find a foreign car in Seoul as it is to find someone walking at a measured pace (even the old people hustle through the markets now).

One big success piled on another, but no one would have expected Korea to rival Japan and the United States so quickly in high-technology electronics. By the mid-1980s, however, it became only the third country in the world to manufacture 286-bit silicon chips and it soon papered the walls of American discount houses with low-cost 286-chip home computers. If these 286 chips seem like the equivalent of Model T Fords today, this was a stunning success at the time, replicated many times over since. This simple fact must have dropped onto Kremlin fore-heads in the mid-1980s like the proverbial "Chinese" water torture: How can the best Soviet and East German technicians not do what South Korea can do, a coun-try that Soviet T-32 tanks rolled over so easily in 1950?

The "Korean model," generalized to Southeast Asia and then to China, broke the back of Stalinism as a model of development not just in North Korea, but all over the world: By 1990, only a fool would still believe that "socialism in one country" would one day catch up with East Asian capitalism as practiced in Japan and South Korea, or that "self-reliant" third world development was the way to go (as nearly every postcolonial leader had believed a generation earlier). It was no small irony that a South Korea long written off as a mere American dependency yanked industrial self-reliance from the jaws of the world economy. After this "Big Push," the ROK had the basis to go all the way and develop a comprehensive industrial structure. In spite of all the attendant costs, this was a grand success, and a declaration of Korean independence. Ever since, Koreans have straightened their backs and walked with confidence.

For half a century Koreans had to struggle with Japan, the United States, China, and the Soviet Union to grasp something for themselves amid a series of destruc-tive calamities: colonialism, civil war, national division, and four decades of au-thoritarian governments. The argument of this chapter has been that a focus on Korea as both a fulcrum for and a generator of transformation can tell us much about changes in the international system through much of the twentieth cen-tury. It might seem too much to credit the Korean model of industrial develop-ment with more than fashioning an industrial nation now rivaling any other in twenty-first century competition, but China's double-digit growth on a model of export-led development resembles the Korean pattern enough to argue that Ko-rea may not just be the focus, but the originator of a new way to achieve national wealth and power.

6

Japanese Colonial Infrastructure in Northeast Asia

Realities, Fantasies, Legacies

Daqing Yang

At their historic summit meeting in Pyongyang in June 2000, the leaders of the two Koreas reached an agreement to reconnect the trunk railway running through the demilitarized zone (DMZ) for the first time in half a century. On September 18, 2002, reconstruction was started simultaneously in the South and North Korean sectors. The date was auspicious: It coincided with the seventy-first anniversary of the Manchurian Incident, the beginning of Japan's invasion of Manchuria, which also changed the fate of colonial Korea. By early December, the de-mining of the two corridors, western and eastern, as well as track laying had been almost completed. The South Korean government reportedly set up a committee to look into the possibility of building an underwater tunnel under the Korean Strait, so that Japan would be linked with the continent for the first time. The idea of a trans-Korean railway based on a reintegrated and expanded railway network on the peninsula, in the meantime, has given rise to the vision of an "Iron Silk Road," which would link the entire Eurasian landmass together by a major railway network. In this sense, although Korea is now an economic powerhouse in its own right, the Korean peninsula will again serve its historic role as a land bridge—except this time, not just for the Northeast Asian region, but for a reconnected Eurasia in the age of the global economy.[1]

The preparation to reconnect the railway across the DMZ focuses world attention on part of Japan's colonial infrastructure in Northeast Asia. Similarly, the excitement over the potential of the trans-Korean railway serves as a reminder of the grand visions already present in the heyday of Japan's colonial empire more than half a century earlier. In present-day common usage, the term "infrastructure" has come to refer to basic facilities or institutions in support of long-term economic and social development.[2] In this chapter, I define colonial infrastructure as basic facilities in the colonies necessary for imperial control and development.

They include administrative, military, or industrial single-use facilities. In this sense, the colonial Government-General building in Seoul, fortifications along the Manchukuo-Soviet border built in the late 1930s, or hydroelectric power plants in northern Korea, all fall under this category. Infrastructure also includes dual-use facilities such as railway and harbors, as well as communication links that serve both military and economic needs.

There are numerous recent studies that address some aspects of infrastructure in the Japanese empire.[3] Instead of attempting to provide an exhaustive inventory of Japanese colonial infrastructure, I shall describe broad trends, paying particular attention to transportation networks. I am concerned above all with the following questions: What motivated the Japanese to embark on massive infrastructure building in its colonies? What types of infrastructure did the Japanese envision and succeed in building in Northeast Asia? What was the state of Japanese colonial infrastructure at the end of the war and what were its postwar legacies?

Two main factors justify such an approach. First, in assessing postcolonial legacies, social scientists—economists in particular—are fond of speaking about balance sheets.[4] Often lacking are historical case studies that examine specific sectors or even sites while taking into consideration the variety of changing conditions. Compared with the numerous aggregate studies, there is a need to disaggregate economic analysis of the legacies of Japanese colonialism and to question many existing generalizations. Second, studying Japan's colonial infrastructure, especially the transportation sector, compels us to look at the entire Northeast Asia region as a useful corrective to most of the existing works on Japan's colonial development that are country specific.[5] Given the widely assumed linkage between transportation infrastructure and economic or even political integration in a region, a historical study of Japan's colonial infrastructure helps bring into proper perspective the rhetoric and reality of the emerging concepts of economic regionalism in Northeast Asia today.

Prewar Japanese Infrastructure in Northeast Asia

The Janus Face of Colonial Transportation

If Rome was not built in a day, neither did the Japanese—government bureaucrats, military officers, private entrepreneurs, and engineers—conceptualize or construct the vast infrastructure of Northeast Asia overnight. The term "infrastructure" had no Japanese equivalent in the prewar era.[6] This in part reflects changing concepts and goals on the part of Japan's military and civilian planners. In order to assess the legacies of Japan's colonial infrastructure, it helps to understand how it came to be created. Even though they did not possess a definite vision of their imperium from the start, Japanese government and business leaders had given much weight to transportation and communication infrastructure because of their importance for political control, military strategy, and economic activities. This was largely based on their experience at home in building the national transportation and communication network in the early years of the Meiji.[7]

The railway had long been one of the most important instruments used by imperialist powers to advance their security and economic goals.[8] Japan was no exception, using the railway to advance its own commercial and military goals in neighboring Korea and China. Railway trunk lines in Manchuria (northeastern China) were not originally built by the Japanese but inherited from the Russians after the Russo-Japanese War. Established in 1906, Japan's South Manchurian Railway Company (SMR) not only greatly expanded the railway network, but grew into an industrial conglomerate managing mines, iron works, and harbors, among others. It quickly became one of the biggest "national policy" companies in prewar Japan. The dual mission of such infrastructure as the railway in the informal empire was best summarized by Goto Shimpei, medical doctor-turned colonial administrator and visionary. The South Manchurian Railway Company, according to Goto, was supposed to be "military preparation in civilian disguise."[9]

In Japan's formal colony, too, the railway was to serve a dual mission. As Japan competed to gain a foothold on the Korea peninsula, the railway concession took on strategic importance and Japan built the trunk railway before its annexation of the country. Because the Korean railway was to be linked with the railway in Manchuria and beyond, the Japanese adopted the wide gauge used in Manchuria instead of the narrow gauge used in Japan proper.[10] Total railway length in Korea increased after annexation in 1910, though not as rapidly as one might imagine. The Industrial Investigation Conference convened by the governor-general in 1921 produced an ambitious twelve-year expansion plan. Five new lines were proposed, totaling 1,400 km.[11]

The impact of Japan's colonial railway in Northeast Asia has been summarized well by Bruce Cumings:

> Railways in Korea and Manchuria had this same penetrative and integrative effect. . . . The rails symbolized permanence and integrity—the permanence of industry (if not of Japan), and the integrity of the Japanese empire, within which national boundaries were increasingly less relevant. But above all, railway development in Korea and Manchuria advanced the commercialization of agriculture and drew the two regions not just into market relations with the Japanese metropole but also into the world market system.[12]

Its economic import notwithstanding, the colonial railway always retained its military function. As a result, Japan continued to build new railways in frontier regions specifically as part of the military infrastructure. After Japan's occupation of Manchuria, military preparation for war against the Soviet Union came to have a significant effect on Japan's infrastructural developments in Northeast Asia. The "Northern Development" strategy stipulated by the Japanese authorities in the 1930s called for extensive infrastructure building in thinly populated northern Manchuria. The SMR expanded new railway links at an amazing pace: In 1937 the total length was just under 10,000 km; three years later, it reached 11,000, equivalent to half of the national railway within Japan. Much of this was primarily for military purposes: As much as 46 percent of all railways added in 1940 was considered "noneconomical lines."[13]

Colonial Industrialization

By the time World War I broke out, Japan's economy at home was already moving into new industries such as steel, shipbuilding, and especially chemicals. This change was not just economic. Japanese military planners learned from Germany's defeat that Japan must be prepared for a total war.[14] Consequently, a major feature of Japan's infrastructure development was power generation, in order to meet increasing energy demand. As the high-tech industry of its day, the chemical industry in particular required huge amounts of electricity, as did the gradual electrification of railway locomotives. Power generation via hydraulic works was a global phenomenon after World War I; the Tennessee Valley Authority and Hoover Dam in the United States were but two prominent examples that Japanese engineers studied intensely. Within Japan, whereas railways occupied the largest share of all civil engineering projects from 1868 to 1912, between 1912 and 1945, the largest share of civil engineering projects was devoted to electric power.[15]

Colonial Korea took the lead in large-scale hydroelectric projects, in part due to its abundant resources. Both the business and the government took an active part in this. In 1926, Noguchi Jun of Japan Nitrogen Company set up a Korea Hydroelectricity Company (*Chosen suiden*) and began constructing a major hydroelectric dam on a tributary of the Yalu River in Northern Korea. The Fusenko Dam was similar in size to the largest dam in Japan proper, but its output of 200,000 kW far outstripped the largest in Japan (45,000 kW). The abundant electricity enabled Noguchi to operate his chemical fertilizer plant in Hungnam.[16] From 1931, as Governor-General Ugaki Kazunari promoted industrialization in Korea, the colonial government drew up a Plan for Electricity Generation and Transmission Network. By offering a favorable infrastructure—setting aside 80 percent of electricity for industrial use—the Government-General of Korea (GGK) sought to entice Japanese industrial capital to Korea. Governor-General Minami Jiro's promotion of Korean integration with Manchukuo paved the way for joint harnessing of the Yalu River, which stretched between the two areas. A Yalu Hydroelectric Company was established in 1937, which drew up plans to build seven large dams on the river with a total of 193,800 kW capacity. The first stage was the Suiho (Sup'ung) Dam. At 106.4 meters in height and 899.8 meters in width, it was the largest dam in Asia and the second largest in the world. It was to be equipped with seven 100,000 kW generators—the largest of its kind in the world, with a total capacity of 700,000 kW. The Suiho Dam began generating electricity in 1941 and was completed in 1944.[17]

Within Manchukuo, the Japanese also built large-scale dams on several major rivers after the 1937 initiation of the five-year plan for industrial development.

Begun in 1937 and still incomplete in 1945, the Fengman Dam stood out as one of the largest in Asia, with an output of 700,000 kW. In addition to generating electricity, the dam also provided flood control, irrigation, and water supply to industries and residential areas.[18]

An Emerging Northeast Asian Regional Economy

Given Japan's growing presence in both areas after the Russo-Japanese War, connecting Manchuria with Korea had always been an important policy for the Japanese. The Japanese built the first bridge on the Yalu River in 1911, linking the railway in Manchuria and Korea. The Manchurian Incident of 1931, followed by the establishment of the state of Manchukuo the following year, changed the map of Northeast Asia and marked the beginning of a truly regional political and economic unit under Japanese control. Building an integrated regional transportation network became an even more urgent task.

Defense buildup, Japanese settlement, and economic activity became closely intertwined in northern Manchuria after 1931, in turn spurring infrastructure development in that area as well as northeastern Korea. Not long after the Japanese occupation of Manchuria, Japanese officials from Korea and Manchuria met in Shinkyo (Changchun) and signed an agreement on bridge building over the Yalu and Tumen rivers. The 1932 agreement stipulated that both sides would undertake to build half a dozen highway bridges over the two rivers within the next seven years at a cost of ¥7.5 million.[19] The SMR undertook to build a new port in Najin after 1933, eventually estimated to reach a shipment capacity of 15 million tons after its three-phase completion in 1948. With the completion of Harbin–Tumen and Tumen–Rajin railway lines, shipping service via Rajin was considered the shortest distance between the heart of Manchukuo and Japan. The joining of the two railways was heralded as "a revolution in the transportation system in East Asia."[20] With such integrated transportation infrastructure in northeast Manchuria and Korea, predicted one Japanese observer, the city of Harbin in northern Manchuria would become more prosperous than anyone can imagine.[21]

Given the increasing demand for large volumes of raw materials deemed essential for Japan's autarkic economy, harbor construction became an area of concentrated effort throughout Japan-dominated Northeast Asia in the 1930s.[22] Transportation also proved essential to the increasing movement of people within the empire, especially Japan's ambitious project of massive settlement in northern Manchuria. The Korean Strait, which separates Japan from the continent, had been connected with the Shimonoseki–Pusan ferry since 1905. By increasing the frequency of ferry transport and introducing larger and faster ships, the Japanese were able to increase ferry capacity remarkably. Annual passenger volume reached half a million in 1922, surpassed one million in 1937, and peaked at three million in 1942.[23]

As Japan expanded the scope of an integrated regional economy to include

China, harbor construction also proceeded on the China coast. Not long after the Manchurian Incident, the Japanese military came to the conclusion that natural resources in north China, such as coal, were indispensable to Japan's autarkic economy. While seeking to detach north China from the control of the central government by military and political means, the Japanese attempted to integrate north China with Japan economically. With cooperation from the North China Garrison Army, the Japanese government dispatched several engineers to conduct a survey of harbor facilities in the region even before the war broke out with China in 1937.[24] Unlike Manchuria, whose harbors had been developed over the preceding decade, north China urgently needed expanded harbor facilities in order to ship large amounts of resources to Japan. After 1937, the biggest effort of harbor construction took place in north China. Japan began constructing a new harbor near the mouth of the Hai River outside of Tianjin, the largest commercial center in north China, as the existing port was situated further inland and its capacity was severely limited due to silt. The annual capacity of the New Tanggu port was originally set at 27 million tons—20 million tons of coal and 7 million tons of other mineral resources. It was later scaled down to 8 million tons.

Elsewhere on the long coast of China, Japanese either expanded harbor facilities or built new ones. From north to south, harbors at Qinhuangdao, Qingdao, and Lianyuangang were all expanded in order to increase Japan's access to resources in north China. The Lianyuangang harbor was first built by the Nationalist government as the terminus of China's crucial east–west railway trunk line. After the Japanese navy occupied Hainan Island in southern China, mainly to cut off aid to the Chiang Kai-shek regime, large deposits of high-quality iron ores were discovered. This led to a flurry of construction there. The Japanese military and government engineers, working together with private companies, developed two mines and three ports, along with a railway linking the mines and Japan's military facilities. In 1943, the first shipment from Hainan began for Japan's Yawata Steel Mills.[25] Transportation infrastructure would play a central role in regional integration.

Means of Integration

How successful was Japan at integrating the existing infrastructure and launching a regional transportation network? Obviously, infrastructure alone could not integrate the region. As the Japanese came to realize, separate development was simply not sufficient. Due to the long presence of Japanese-controlled railway and shipping operations beyond its borders, the regional coordination of railways began in the 1920s. Beginning in 1924, the Japanese held annual meetings to coordinate railway transportation between Japan, Korea, and Japanese-operated railways in Manchuria. Shipping companies regularly entered into pooling arrangements. More emphasis was placed on coordination than construction, in view of the vast network of rail lines already in place. By 1940, a Japan-Manchukuo-China Forum was founded to discuss the coordination of railway expansion plans and the unification of operations. As the core of the new Greater East Asian Co-Prosperity Sphere, the forum's planners believed that the three countries involved must further strengthen the exchange of materials and guarantee mutual security.

Japanese Railway Ministry official Horiuchi Daihachi evoked the familiar comparison of transportation capacity to the distribution of blood vessels in the human body. Like blood vessels, he claimed, the flow of transportation demand (human beings, goods, and letters and printed materials) must be systematized in the proper distribution of transportation capacity in the Greater East Asian Co-Prosperity Sphere. As he explained it, systemic distribution consisted of three dimensions: (a) the consistency of capacity of land transportation, port facilities, and shipping; (b) a unified planning and strengthening of the main transportation routes and their capacities within the Greater East Asian capacity; and (c) organized trunk (main) line capacity with local capacity. Therefore, comprehensive planning and coordination was key to building an integrated East Asian transportation system.[26] Together with telecommunications and broadcasting, which formed the "nerve system," Horiuchi noted, transportation networks were to serve as the "artery" of the empire. As Horiuchi emphasized, the coordination of land, port, and maritime capacity was crucial.

> Just as all roads led to Rome in the past, now in East Asia all roads must lead to Tokyo, Shinkyo, and Nanjing. And the distance between these three capitals must be shortened. It is no longer a fantasy or old dream to turn the Sea of Japan into a lake, and to make the Yellow Sea and East China Sea into inland waters. These are the issues to be realized with the joint forces of Japan, Manchukuo, and China.[27]

Japan's control over Manchuria and the China coast meant that the Japan Sea and East China Sea had come to be effectively within the Japanese sphere. Increasing emphasis was put on integrating land and maritime transportation in Northeast Asia. By 1940, the Japan-Manchukuo-China Consultative Committee on Transportation had developed into an impressive umbrella organization. Headed by Japan's Railway Ministry, it included the colonial governments in Taiwan and Korea, three railway companies, five shipping companies, and three aviation companies (see Table 6.1).[28] In mid-1940, the fourteen members signed an agreement to connect transportation between Japan, Manchukuo, and China. With some 560 articles and numerous appending charts, graphs, and tables, the agreement was the result of a year-long deliberation. It stipulated tariffs, connection charges, customs clearance, and the purchase of connection tickets. It was now possible for a passenger to purchase a train ticket to Beijing at the Tokyo Station, or to have items shipped from Osaka to Shinkyo.

In addition to this umbrella organization, railway, shipping, and aviation were to have their own coordinated networks. As Nagasaki Sonosuke, director of the Transportation Bureau of Japan's Railway Ministry, pointed out in 1942, a railway conference would help formulate common plans between the three countries, and thus contribute to the "realization of their ideals."[29]

Table 6.1

Japan-Manchukuo-China Transportation Conference, 1940

	Land	Maritime	Air
Japan	Japan-Railway Ministry	Toa Kaiun	Dai-Nippon Airlines
	Taiwan-Transportation Bureau Korea-Railway Bureau	Nihonkai Kisen Nippon Yusen Osaka Shosen	
Manchukuo	South Manchurian Railway Co. (SMR)	Dairen Kisen	Manchurian Airlines
China Proper	North China Transport Co. Central China Railway Co.		China Airlines
Total	6	5	3

Source: Nichi-Man-Shi kōtsu Kondankai Dai-ichi Chōsakai Jimukyoku, comp., *Tōa kyōeiken nai kōtsuryō tōkei (1936–1940)* (Tokyo, 1942).

Even with this agreement, there were still many obstacles to full integration: Because the agreement was not a treaty with full legal power, there were still questions about the authority of certificates issued by members. As maritime transportation was indispensable to the regional transportation system in East Asia, Horiuchi argued, bodies of law regulating land and maritime transportation must be brought closer. "A major problem in East Asian transportation policy," he noted, was the issue of customs clearance. Even if abolition of customs in the three countries was not desirable, he argued, methods to unify the customs-clearance procedure could be found. For instance, customs clearance could be performed by officials belonging to another country, but he proposed at least moving clearing offices closer to each other and conducting clearance without a break, in order to strengthen trading power. And as a fundamental solution to the problem of integration, Horiuchi even proposed nationalization of the main shipping lanes in East Asia.[30]

Reordering the Space of Northeast Asia

Rise of the Japanese Raumordnung

Besides shifting military and economic imperatives, new ways of conceptualizing the relationship between economy and space also affected Japan's strategy of infrastructure development. To be sure, calls for the rational location of population and industry could also be heard within Japan. Urban congestion and over-concentration of industries in narrow areas in Japan due to rapid industrialization had raised considerable concern. Japanese urban planning could be traced to the late Meiji period, but got a strong boost with the reconstruction of Tokyo after the Great Kanto earthquake in 1923.[31] In addition to urban problems, the vulnerability of Japan's vital industries to air raids became increasingly worrisome as Japan moved toward a quasi-war economy at home.

The concept most important to Japanese thinking before and after World War II is National Land Planning (*kokudo keikaku*). This was the Japanese answer to what was called in German *Raumordnung* (literally, "spatial order"), a concept, introduced to Japan in 1938 by an engineer in the Home Ministry, for curbing the growth of large cities, distribution of industrial zones, and protection of rural areas. In the following year, both the Home Ministry and the Ministry of Commerce and Industry launched studies to deconcentrate heavy industries in Japan.

As Japan embarked on new continental expansion in the late 1930s, *Raumordnung* seemed to provide a scientific rationale for reordering the newly expanded imperium. Spatial planning became popular among policy makers in the early 1940s as a result of both changing strategic needs and the influence of geo-political-economic thinking from Germany.[32] Imperial spatial planning for Japan and its expanding overseas territories had already gained considerable momentum within Japan, thanks in part to the long-standing popularity of German geopolitical theories.[33]

In June 1940, the Manchukuo government announced its Outline of Comprehensive Location Planning, with three main objectives: industrial location, population distribution, and a transportation/communication network. In a radio broadcast, Japanese officials defined "comprehensive location planning" as follows: to distribute geographically production and population following the principle of suitability, and to "reconfigure space" (*kūkan kisei*) by shortening distances via the transportation network. Its purpose was "to utilize land—the basis of national life—most rationally and efficiently for the entire people.[34] As with many other economic policies, Manchukuo served as a testing ground for the government in Tokyo.[35]

In July 1940, the champion of the political New Order, Prince Konoe Fumimaro, became prime minister for the second time. His cabinet ushered in a plethora of blueprints for restructuring the domestic political and economic system as well as for giving greater substance to building the New Order in East Asia. As its first item of business, the new cabinet adopted an "Outline of Basic National Policies." Prepared under Hoshino Naoki, the architect of planning in Manchukuo who was now in charge of the Cabinet Planning Board, the outline called for a national defense economy based on a self-reliant economic reconstruction of Japan, Manchukuo, and China into one bloc. The following month, the Konoe cabinet adopted an "Outline of Economic Reconstruction of Japan, Manchukuo, and China." The reconstruction consisted of three processes: (1) reorganization of Japan's domestic economy, (2) strengthening of the self-sufficient sphere in Northeast Asia, and (3) expansion of the Greater East Asian Co-Prosperity Sphere. The achievement of the "organic unity" of the self-sufficient sphere on the basis of national defense and geopolitical status required the political, cultural, and economic integration of Japan, Manchukuo, North China, Inner Mongolia, and "certain protruding islands off the South China coast." The goal was that by 1950 Japan would achieve economic self-sufficiency, with Japan, Manchukuo, and China united as "one link." Central and South China, Southeast Asia, and other areas in the south would form the rest of the Greater East Asian Co-Prosperity Sphere, which would complete the national defense economy.[36]

In October 1940, the Cabinet Planning Board gathered a team of officials and academics for the task of national land planning. Headed by former Tokyo Imperial University professor Tanaka Tadao, the group worked over the next three years on a wide range of issues, both long- and short-term.[37] In the same month, the Government-General in Korea set up its own Committee for Korean National Land Planning. The age of comprehensive infrastructure planning had begun.

Envisioning Infrastructure for the Future

In September 1940, the cabinet adopted an "Outline of National Spatial Planning," which set out the broad and ambitious goals of coordinated, long-term development of the entire imperium in Northeast Asia.[38] Separated into the "central plan" and the "Japan-Manchukuo-China plan," the Outline called for further studies in the following areas: distribution of the economy among Japan, Manchuria, and China; industry and mining; transportation and communication; population distribution, agriculture, forestry, husbandry, and fishing; power generation; mountain and river management; and cultural and health facilities. Interestingly, the Central Plan covered the home islands and the formal colonies—areas that claimed to have blood relations with the Yamato race. Korea was defined as "the bond that ties together Japan and the continent as well as the important base of northern defense." Together with two other locations in Japan proper, the Keijo (Seoul) area was named a candidate for Japan's capital.[39]

By the end of 1941, spatial planning became more specific in its targets. "Opinion on Land Planning Concerning Economic Construction of Greater East Asian Co-Prosperity Sphere," issued soon after the outbreak of the Pacific War, emphasized the need for strengthening the geographical, historical, and ethnic bonds within the newly expanded Sphere. In October 1942, the Land Planning team under the Cabinet Planning Board drafted an Outline of Hwanghae/Bohai Zone Land Planning, which represents the most comprehensive spatial planning at a high level before 1945.[40]

First, the entire area spanning Korea, Manchuria, and North China was said to possess the character of a "singular geopolitical entity" given its history of political, commercial, and cultural exchange since ancient times. In the present stage of development of heavy and chemical industries in greater East Asia, this area was considered "relatively secure against threat from land or sea, with easy transportation access to Japan proper, rich in natural resources such as coal, iron, salt, and

Table 6.2

Production Target in 1947 (10,000 tons)

	Iron/ steel	Coal	Alum- inum	Synthetic petroleum	Ammonium sulfate	Soda
Korea	300	1,500	20	1	80	30
Manchuria	700	20,000	20	200	70	110
North China	700	23,000		500	70	130
Subtotal	1,700	44,500	40	700	350	270
Percent	57	74	50	88	58	60
Japan	1,000	11,300	20	100	230	170
Taiwan	100	700	10		20	10
Southeast Asia	200	3,500	10			
Total	3,000	60,000	80	600	150	300

Source: Sugai Shirō, comp., *Shiryō Kokudo Keikaku* (Tokyo: Taimeidō, 1975), p. 81.

great potential of hydroelectric power." Moreover, the region had "good industrial labor both qualitatively and quantitatively among the native population, and yet is also suitable for mass migration of the Yamato people." From a geopolitical perspective, the Outline pointed out, the Hwanghae and Bohai region constituted the "inland sea of the Japan–Manchuria–China Bloc." The plan projected the production of key resources in the entire region after fifteen years, as well as targets for labor (skilled and laborer), land, water, raw material, and power in each area.

An integrated economy meant, among other things, a vast quantity of goods to be moved between these areas. The 1943 Central Plan estimated that each year Japan would import 5 million metric tons of coal, 2.4 million metric tons of iron ore, and 8 million koku (about 1.4 million tons) of rice from Korea; 2 million metric tons of coal and 2 million tons of rice from Manchuria; and 34 million metric tons of coal and 2.55 million metric tons of industrial salt from North China. In addition, 16 million metric tons of iron ore would come from Central and South China. Korea would import 320,000 metric tons of coal from northern Manchuria, 1,480,000 metric tons of coal, 500,000 metric tons of industrial salt, and 120,000 tons of aluminum from North China, plus 500,000 metric tons of iron ore from South China. In addition, there would be millions of pounds of cotton to be shipped to Japan and Korea from North China.[41]

To accomplish this enormous task, the Outline called for a "giant leap forward" in the transportation and communications infrastructure that connected Japan, Manchukuo, and China in order to promote integration of the economies of the three countries and meet the demands of national defense. Means of transportation would be a focus of development. As there were few natural good harbors in newly occupied North China, efforts would be given to locate and create new ones. In addition to expanding the rail network, canals would be developed alongside river management and utilization. Finally, in recognition of Korea as a land bridge between Japan proper and the continent, consideration would be given to expanding connections across the Korea Strait. Railway expansion was a major component. The plan reiterated the project of a bullet train within Japan, in part due to consideration of the soon-to-be enhanced transport capacity on the continent. In addition to strengthening the existing railway system in Korea, the 1943 plan projected new railway lines: the second Seoul–Pusan line, second Seoul–Sinuiju Line, and the Sansenpo–Taejon line. Plans for the Manchukuo Railway Network consisted of three five-year plans beginning in 1945. During the first phase, emphasis would be placed on exploiting resources for heavy industry, connecting Manchuria, Korea, and North China—twenty-eight routes, totaling 3,033 km. When the second phase started in 1950, priority would be given to agriculture and forestry, especially in the Dongbiandao region, adding twenty-three lines totaling 3,814 km. Finally, the third phase would further strengthen defenses along borders, major cities, and connecting trunk lines, with twenty new lines of 3,545 km in length.[42] Though not primarily for freight, aviation also received due attention. The 1943 Central Plan called for building or expanding about sixty airports throughout the Northeast Asian region, thirteen in Korea alone.

Colonial infrastructure planning reached its peak in the year of 1943, when the tide of war began to turn against Japan. Many of the blueprints for empire produced during the early 1940s bordered on technological fantasy. The idea of a Transcontinental Trunk Railway (Jukan Tetsudo Kansen) in Asia received many endorsements. For instance, the Imperial Railway Association (Teikoku Tetsudo Kyōkai) floated the idea of a railway going from Manchukuo through China to the Strait of Sumatra. The South Manchurian Railway Company drew up a similar plan for an Asian continental railway network that would serve as the artery of the Greater East Asian Co-Prosperity Sphere under Japan's control. At the Greater East Asian Reconstruction Exposition held in Manchukuo in August 1942, the SMR unveiled this ambitious plan for a Trans-Greater East Asian Railway. The total distance of some 8,000 km between Manchukuo in the north and Singapore in the south would be covered in seven days. The entire railway would be managed by the SMR, whose total workforce had already reached three hundred thousand at the time.[43] In a proposal on transportation policy in Greater East Asia, Sato Ojiro, vice minister of the Ministry of Colonial Affairs, proposed a Transcontinental Railway linking Pusan, the gateway on the southern tip of the Korean peninsula, to as far away as Rangoon, Burma. Such a land-based transportation artery would be a strong political bond and military shield, Sato noted, because it would "enable Japan's political influence to penetrate all areas in the Co-Prosperity Sphere" and "connect northern Manchuria with Burma in the shortest and most efficient military route."[44] In 1939, Yumoto Noboru, a Japanese Railway official once posted in Berlin, proposed an underwater tunnel between Japan and Korea via Tsushima in his book on a trans-Eurasian railway from Japan to Germany. This underwater tunnel came to be seriously considered by 1941, when actual investigation began. Japan did succeed in building a 3.6 km underwater tunnel linking Kyushu and

Honshu in the early 1940s.[45] In 1942, Yumoto proposed extending the Trans-Greater East Asian Railway all the way across the Strait of Malacca to the island of Java. With fast trains and the elimination of railway gauge differences, Yumoto calculated that the 11,618 km between Tokyo and Batavia could be "overcome" within four and a half days.[46] With sea lanes under the threat of Allied naval and air attacks, this land-based transportation artery would be of crucial importance to Japan's war effort in Southeast Asia.

State of the Japanese Infrastructure

Not surprisingly, much of the ambitious wartime planning for future infrastructure in Northeast Asia existed only on paper. After 1943, when the war turned against Japan in the Pacific, Tokyo abandoned much of the *Raumordnung* plans aimed at reordering Northeast Asia for the future, and became increasingly preoccupied with defending the home islands. In 1943, the Land Planning team was disbanded, and a smaller staff was folded into the Home Ministry.

Even before then, various concrete construction plans fell behind schedule due to the increasingly serious shortage of material, manpower, and ironically, means of transportation itself. A leading example is the industrial coastal city Dadong. Situated near the mouth of the Yalu River on the Chinese side, the site was chosen because of its potential as an all-year harbor (to replace Andong, whose capacity decreased due to silt), inexpensive land suitable for further expansion, proximity to cheap power supply on the Yalu River (the Suiho Dam was to begin power generation in 1941, initially at 200,000 kW), mild climate, and proximity to Andong (population 200,000), the source of abundant labor. Encouraged by Kishi Nobusuke, then vice minister of industry in Manchukuo, preparation began in 1938 to build a major industrial-transportation hub. There was division of labor between SMR and Manchukuo: The former was to build port facilities and to extend the railway to the site, the latter was responsible for urban planning, water supply, and navigation. Many Japanese industrial enterprises indicated interest, including some forty-four factories by late 1939. The estimate had to be modified in 1940, with a population increase from 400,000 to 1 million. When complete, the Dadong-Andong area would become a giant industrial zone encompassing two million people. By 1941, 15 percent of the estimated ¥235 million was spent. The 13 km railway linking Andong began operating, as did the 1.7 km long, 20 meter wide highway. The war in the Pacific slowed down construction, however, and the project was still incomplete at the time of Japan's surrender.[47]

The U.S. strategic bombing of Japanese infrastructure in Manchuria and Korea was not as severe as that in the home islands; although wartime data are lacking, most of Japan's transportation network registered its highest volume in 1943.[48] Some of the facilities were damaged during the short but intense fighting in Manchuria. After the fighting ended, what remained of such infrastructure in Manchuria and North Korea faced extensive removal by the Soviet forces; many facilities in Manchuria were destroyed by the communists in the civil war, or simply by vandals; and the Korean War dealt the remaining facilities in Korea a heavy blow.

Assessing Postcolonial Legacies

In January 1946, four months into the Allied occupation, the Japanese government set up a Committee to Investigate Overseas Assets (Zaigai zaisan chōsakai).

Consisting mostly of officials and academics associated with Japan's colonial administration, the committee produced a massive report a year later. Under the title *Historical Studies of Overseas Activities of the Japanese People*, this internal report ran some thirty-five volumes and covered wide geographic and topical areas.[49] Eleven of these volumes were devoted to Korea. In the concluding chapter on Korea, its author noted:

> Japan's thirty-six-year rule over Korea came to a close on August 15, 1945. Even if the leaping forward of the Korean economy in this period was not aimed at benefiting all Koreans, it cannot be denied that it modernized Korea and laid the material basis for independent Korea as a nation-state.[50]

Ever since then, the legacy of Japanese colonialism in Asia has always been a highly contested issue, both politically and in terms of historiography. If former colonial subjects understandably tend to deny or downplay any positive impact of colonial domination, quite a few colonial administrators and their sympathizers readily point to the "positive contributions." Japanese Foreign Ministry official Kubota's remarks about the positive contributions of Japan's colonial rule once helped derail diplomatic negotiations for normalizing relations. Many old Japanese visitors embark on nostalgic trips to northeast China, where they photograph Manchukuo-era buildings or ride on the railway once operated by the South Manchurian Railway Company. On the other hand, the South Korean government under Kim Young Sam demolished the entire Government-General building in downtown Seoul, beginning on the fiftieth anniversary of liberation from colonial rule. The scholarly assessment has been equally divided. To this day, most Chinese historians still view Japanese economic activities in northeast China between 1931 and 1945 as nothing more than plunder. This view was shared by many academics in the West until the rise of the Asian economies of South Korea and Taiwan brought about a reexamination of Japanese colonial rule and its legacies.[51] Since then, the continuity thesis has gained dominance in the scholarship on East Asian development.

Although it has become popular to speak of the postwar legacy of Japanese colonialism, few have undertaken to examine how the Japanese colonial infrastructure actually fared in the postwar environment.[52] So far, most have focused on whether Japanese colonial infrastructure aided or hindered postwar economic development. In order to assess postwar performance, one must look at the postwar damage, recovery efforts, and new political and economic context in which they operate. Obviously, this is a huge task, made more difficult by the lack of primary evidence, the chaos of postwar transition, and complex political conditions.

First, to make use of the colonial infrastructure that remained, technical know-how was indispensable. While some of it was provided by the Japanese—both the local technicians trained by the Japanese and Japanese who stayed behind temporarily—in many key areas it was the newcomers that mattered. For China and North Korea, this absence would be partially filled by the arrival of Soviet advisers and technical help.[53] For South Korea, as Kobayashi Hideo reminds us, U.S. intervention was important. The degree of reliance on American technical know-how in South Korea remains to be investigated.[54] Second, we should explore how the remaining infrastructure came to be used. How sustainable was it in the postcolonial world? Was there structural dependency? Could it function independently of colonial metropole? If not, how was reorientation achieved? How important was the factor of location—once so crucial to imperial planning? An example, albeit on a smaller scale, was the remark in the Pauley Mission report that the industrial equipment in northern Korea and Manchuria had been built at the site of or near the natural resources, thus having its greatest value only where it was located.[55] To borrow the vocabulary of economic geographers, did Japan's colonial infrastructure system create path dependency after the war?

Whatever the intentions of Japanese architects, much of the colonial infrastructure continue to function, if sometimes for entirely different purposes. The Korean peninsula provides a dramatic demonstration of Japan's imperial legacy, as does the railway linkage between Japan and Manchuria. Since Japan had built the railroads in Korea during the colonial period, repair and replacement items could be obtained from the Japanese National Railways and quickly airlifted to Korea, an important advantage to the United Nations troops.[56] During the Chinese Civil War of 1946–49, the railway in the north transported remaining Japanese material to the Chinese Communist forces, contributing to their victory over the Nationalists in Manchuria. Thus, in ways no one could have predicted, what remained of Japan's imperial telecommunications and transportation network contributed to postcolonial Korea and China's transition to the world of the cold war.

If Japan's infrastructure played a crucial role in the geopolitical struggle, postwar economic development in Northeast Asia did not follow the trajectory laid out by the Japanese colonial planners. North Korea and northeast China followed the Soviet model in the early postwar era. As far as the overall path of industrial development is concerned, there seemed to be (initially at least) some happy *coincidence* between the Japanese-initiated industrialization in Manchuria and northern Korea and Stalin's preference for economic development led by heavy industry. Geographical proximity provided the further justification: Relatively well-developed infrastructure in northeastern China made it easier to further concentrate some of China's heavy, chemical, and military industries. It was not until the late 1960s, when Sino-Soviet relations soured and an armed conflict seemed imminent, that China began moving some of its industrial facilities away from northeastern China to the western part of the country. Still, given the need to move the industrial equipment from the Soviet Union and other socialist countries as well as the agricultural and mineral products for export to pay for them, the relative absence of new construction in the transportation infrastructure shows that the colonial infrastructure must have served both China and North Korea well.[57]

To be sure, there were areas where discontinuity seemed to be the rule, where Japan's colonial infrastructure remained unused or underutilized. Lack of fresh incentive as well as capital to complete all unfinished projects were important factors. When the regional economy is considered as a whole, however, the assessment seems to be quite different. Just as plausible was the lack of need. Designed and built for the purpose of serving a Japan-centered autarkic economy, many large infrastructure projects simply no longer made sense. Unlike most industrial facilities left by the Japanese in Manchuria, the unfinished Dadong Industrial Zone did not seem to be utilized by the People's Republic of China until the 1980s, when reconstruction resumed.[58] The port facilities in Hainan Island in south China, built during the war for shipping iron ore to steel works in Japan, were not fully used either.

One obvious factor contributing to this disconnection had to do with the drastically altered geopolitical situation in the region by the 1950s. A region once under the domination of a single imperial power—Japan—became four sovereign states, which, moreover, were on opposite sides in an ideological and military confrontation known as the cold war. At the heart of this cold war division was the partition of Korea into two separate and mutually antagonistic states. Economic embargo, coupled with the absence of diplomatic recognition, effectively broke down the scheme of regional integration actively promoted by the Japanese before 1945. Even economic relations within each camp, between China and North Korea on the one side and between South Korea and Japan on the other, were not always as close as they had been in the colonial era. There was probably a greater degree of reintegration between the latter—especially after diplomatic normalization in 1965—than between the former. Even so, it was not until 1970 that regular ferry service between western Japan and Pusan was resumed.[59] Furthermore, the geoeconomic landscape of the region also differed drastically from the prewar period, with the full industrialization of South Korea, together with the reemergence of Japan as the dominant economic power.

It should not be forgotten that Japan's colonial infrastructure had a dark legacy that continues to remind the world of the human cost of its development. The rush of infrastructure building in the colonies in the last decade of the Japanese empire required the mobilization of hundreds of thousands of native workers, and occasionally prisoners of war. The colonial condition afforded them less protection than construction workers in Japan proper, while the pressing needs of war often led to almost total disregard of human endurance. The result was a heavy toll on human lives. Even for those who survived, the experience of being forcibly uprooted and of abuse left bitterness that the passage of time has not washed away.[60]

Toward a Reintegrated Northeast Asia?

The projected reopening of the inter-Korean railway is only the latest episode in the historic drama in Northeast Asia that began unfolding in the early 1970s: the gradual reintegration of three socialist states into the capitalist world system and the intensification of regional economic ties. Since then, China has normalized diplomatic relations and gradually established close economic ties with Japan (1972) and the Republic of Korea (1992). As China ended its policy of "self-reliance" and embarked on the "four modernizations" in the late 1970s, some of the earlier in-frastructure from the Japanese period was given a new lease on life, sometimes receiving generous Japanese loans for upgrading and expansion. For instance, ports such as Dalian, Yingkou, Tianjin, and Lianyuangang now support major exports of coal and petroleum to Japan. In the early 1980s, China began building a new harbor with the capacity of 15 million tons on the Yellow Sea coast, not far from Lianyuangang. Shijou port on the Shandong Peninsula facing Japan, for instance, received ¥47 billion in the early 1980s in order to become a large port for exports of coal from southern Hebei and Shanxi, primarily to Japan, and imports of sundry goods for the hinterland. Together with the capacity of 15 million tons of coal facilities (after the First Phase), railway links were also added. A second phase began in the early 1990s. Lianyuangang, another port on the east coast and termi-nus of China's Xian–Xuzhou railway (the east–west artery), was first built during the Japanese Occupation period. In the 1980s, it also received yen loans to be upgraded, though primarily as a route connecting to China's vast hinterland.[61] The Japanese connection proved decisive.

In the mid-1980s, the Soviet Union under Gorbachev expressed greater interest in economic participation in the Asia-Pacific region. In some ways this move was equally historic, given the fact that Russia's economic role in the region had been very limited since the beginning of the century. The abundance of natural resources in Siberia and the Russian Far East, particularly natural gas and oil, has the poten-tial to tie the region closer than ever in history.[62] Finally, beginning from the 1990s, North Korea undertook some steps to open up its economy. The Najin-Sonbong economic zone was opened in the late 1990s. In late 2002, Pyongyang decided to establish a new special zone in Sinuiju on the Korean-Chinese border, itself his-torically a major nexus connecting Japan with the continent.[63]

At the present time, there are already indications that transportation infrastruc-ture has become an engine driving Northeast Asian regional cooperation. The Tumen River Area Development Project between Russia, China, and Korea reflects both the dilemma and opportunity of a partially reintegrated regional economy—an issue the Japanese were wrestling with in the days of the empire. It was China's Jilin Province that gave the initial push. Sandwiched between Heilongjiang and Liaoning, the province that once boasted the capital of Manchukuo is landlocked. The closest point to the ocean is 15 km from the mouth of the Tumen River, sepa-rating Russia and northern Korea. During the Manchukuo era, it was not so much a handicap, but now no longer part of an integrated transportation network, Jilin Province proposed to the United Nations to jointly develop the lower Tumen area with Russia and North Korea. Despite the initial promise, different priorities within each country, together with new environmental concerns, have slowed down the progress of the ambitious multilateral project.

Indeed, intensified regional economic ties have begun to change the ways that the region is viewed and given rise to a number of new concepts envisioning an integrated "large economic region" (*kōki keizaiken*). Historians exploring the "common historical image" of the Northeast Asian region have pointed out that historically Asia tended to integrated around a series of inland seas from north to south.[64] Within Northeast Asia, there are also competing visions of subregionalization. The idea of a "Japan Sea Rim" has an even longer history, but has been lagging behind in realization.[65] By contrast, the "Yellow Sea Rim Economic Zone" seems to have taken shape in the past two decades. Perhaps not surprisingly, this also comes closest to resembling the prewar Japanese blueprint. The recent designation of Sinuiju on the Sino-Korean border as a new economic zone, seems to fill the last piece in the jigsaw puzzle and lends hope to a fully revitalized corridor along the Yellow Sea.

More than anything else, infrastructure, especially the transportation network, gives concrete shape to the vision of spatial integration. The excitement over the potential of the trans-Korean railway in fact goes back to visions already present at the dawn of the railway age in Asia. A reconnected trans-Korean railway, as part of the "Iron Silk Road" reintegrating the vast Eurasian landmass, revives in new form the ideas of Japanese imperial planners, imagining Korea and the Northeast Asian railway system as channels of regional co-prosperity in the new global economy.

7

A Socialist Regional Order in Northeast Asia After World War II

Stephen Kotkin and Charles K. Armstrong

Japan's defeat in World War II might have allowed the Soviet Union to emerge as the dominant power in Northeast Asia. Instead, of course, the United States established an alliance system to contain the Soviet Union and, in the process, built up a powerful U.S.-led regional order. Even so, a Soviet-led socialist regional order *did* take shape in Northeast Asia, based on communist revolution and the planned economy model. It was, to be sure, brief. Communism in Asia collapsed in the Soviet Union and its satellite, Mongolia, in 1991, but well before then, China repudiated much of the Soviet model, which left North Korea as the sole remaining piece of the post–World War II socialist order in Northeast Asia. Though short-lived, this socialist variant of regionalism had multiple ramifications, and its legacies can still be felt.

Marxism-Leninism and the Layers of History

The long history of Russia in Asia is one of weakness, of promises unfulfilled, and wild exaggeration.[1] Russo-Chinese relations, from first contacts in the seventeenth century right through 1949, were often strained and have been almost continuously rivalrous.[2] By contrast, Russo-Japanese relations, though usually rendered as eternal enmity, have generally been closer and more cooperative, twentieth-century wars notwithstanding.[3] As for the Korean peninsula, it enjoyed only a brief moment in Russia's sights.[4] And Outer Mongolia, following the medieval period of Mongol rule over Russia, had long been within the Chinese sphere of influence, despite a reversal in the twentieth century to the Russian sphere. Thus, it was historically anomalous that a Northeast Asian regionalism incorporating Mongolia, part of the Korean peninsula, and China, would coalesce under Moscow's leadership. But it happened.

Whether the socialist camp in Northeast Asia, such as it was, resulted from inherent expansionism or opportunism, or both, can be debated. What seems evident is that a reversal of fortunes in the war against the Nazis in the West, and the American need in 1945 to continue fighting in the Pacific Theater, combined to open up Soviet vistas in the east, where Moscow had earlier established its first satellite (in Mongolia) and where it had territorial ambitions. In August 1945, Japan's former Northeast Asian empire in Manchuria (Northeast China) and on the Korean peninsula began to fall to the advancing Soviets. The Soviet army conquered Southern Sakhalin and the Southern Kurils (which Russia had once controlled), and the Soviet Union was poised to invade Hokkaido in the summer of 1945 until Stalin, after a communication with U.S. president Harry S Truman, reversed his invasion order.[5] The Soviet Union also refrained, again at the insistence of the United States, from attempting to take the entire Korean peninsula—even though the United States had no troops in Korea yet. The Soviet Union appears to have complied with U.S. instructions to stay out of South Korea largely because it hoped to be invited to participate in the occupation of Japan, but Washington managed to exclude Moscow from playing a role on the main Japanese islands. Still, the unexpected (from the Soviet viewpoint) communist victory in China expanded the socialist sphere well beyond Manchuria and the northern Korean peninsula. And so, by the late 1940s, China and North Korea, along with Mongolia and the Soviet Far East, were poised to form a socialist regional order.

Nominally, China, North Korea, Mongolia, and the Soviet Union were united by their having Marxist-Leninist regimes, which in the Soviet worldview were to be guided from Moscow. Substantial economic exchanges, borrowings of practices, and the training of personnel also strengthened the connections. But soon enough, a Sino-Soviet rift as well as the specificities of North Korean developments undermined the incipient socialist regional order. Later, Soviet-led regionalism was further undercut by the unprecedented economic booms in East Asian capitalist economies, communist China's turn toward market approaches, and Japanese ambitions to carve out their own Tokyo-led regional order, not to mention the distant revolts against Soviet rule in Eastern Europe and the overall stagnation of the Soviet model. What had looked promising in the 1950s and the early 1960s came to seem outdated by the 1970s and 1980s.

To be sure, communist victory in Vietnam seemed to portend the opposite of socialist decline—the possible spread of the communist bloc throughout Southeast Asia—but hostilities between communist Vietnam and communist China (not to mention communist Vietnam's invasion of communist Cambodia) revealed deep divisions within the ostensibly socialist bloc. Indicative of what was to come, even during the Korean War, with Stalin's full backing, China experienced immense difficulties trying to coax North Korea into a joint command, let alone a unified one.[6] Such divisions were largely absent from the U.S.-led camp in Northeast Asia, which encompassed Japan, South Korea, and Taiwan.[7] At a minimum, Japanese ambitions never matched those of China, which refused to remain a junior partner in someone else's hegemony. Of course, tensions among the capitalist countries were prevalent, too, especially between Japan and South Korea, but neither of the latter allowed their enmities or ambitions to destabilize the U.S. security umbrella upon which the political establishments in both South Korea and Japan were dependent. In the event, the Soviet threat, or more broadly the communist threat, served as a greater unifying factor in Northeast Asia than did socialist ideology or supposed socialist common interest.

Equally fateful for a socialist regional order in Northeast Asia was the contradiction between post-Stalin efforts at regional integration under Soviet leadership and the Soviet Union's own model of self-reliance, or "socialism in one country." It was Soviet developmental success—rapid industrialization through self-reliance, leading to an ability to stand up to so-called imperialist powers—that had attracted elites in the People's Republic of China (PRC) and Democratic People's Republic of Korea (DPRK), especially Mao Zedong and Kim Il Sung, to the Soviet orbit in the first place. But in both countries proponents of a Soviet-led "socialist division of labor," or fully integrated economy under Moscow, were sidelined, and in many cases purged. In the late 1950s, China and North Korea embarked instead on the path of what the Chinese called *zili gengsheng* (regeneration through one's own efforts), whose Chinese characters were pronounced *charyok kaengsaeng* in Korean, though commonly referred to in North Korea as *juche*. Such official "self-reliance" did not signify a refusal of Soviet subsidies—on the contrary—but it did entail a refusal of Soviet hegemony and thus of the systemic integration that was on offer, thereby exposing the limits of a socialist regional order.

Soviet Imperial Economy?

Korea was not central to Soviet concerns in Northeast Asia at the end of World War II, but Korea was the locale where a socialist regional order began to be seen. Economically, access to the natural resources and industrial plants of Manchuria constituted the principal Soviet goal in the region, and the Red Army's large-scale removal of Japanese-built equipment during its occupation, similar to Soviet actions in Eastern Europe (especially Germany), are well documented.[8] Strategically, the Soviet Union's main concern was preventing the reemergence of Japan as a military rival in the region. It was in that regard that Korea was important, because the peninsula had been a major battleground of the Russo-Japanese War of 1904–5 and the staging ground for Japanese incursions on the Asian continent afterward. A June 1945 report from the Far Eastern Department of the Soviet Foreign Ministry stated that "Japan must be forever excluded from Korea, since a Korea under Japanese rule would be a constant threat to the Far East of the USSR."[9]

Beyond this unmistakable desire to keep Japan down, the accessible historical record on Soviet postwar designs in East Asia is ambiguous. Any "plans," such as they were, could only have been very fluid. For example, little evidence has emerged that the Soviet occupation of North Korea was a "pre-conceived formula for a take-over," as trumpeted by a Korean War–era report of the U.S. State Department.[10] Events moved more quickly than anyone could have conceived. Certainly the rapacious behavior of Soviet occupation forces convinced the Americans in the South at the time that Moscow must not have been planning for a long-term occupation of the peninsula, though U.S. policy makers were not always well served by reading Soviet behavior through American eyes.[11] Nevertheless, by early 1946, after the breakdown of the December 1945 Moscow Agreement that had called for a four-power "trusteeship" government over Korea, both the United States and Soviet Union moved toward the creation of separate regimes under their respective patronage without relinquishing claims to rule in the name of the entire peninsula. Whatever the wartime discussions, the possibility of a Soviet-dominated, communist regime in North Korea presented itself to Moscow following the fall of Japan as well as a series of events having to do with U.S.-Soviet rivalries in Europe, political alignments among Koreans in both occupation zones, and the mutual hardening of U.S. and Soviet positions on the Korean issue.[12]

Just as the Kremlin's intentions remain difficult to establish, so the formation and actual status of North Korea have been subjected to divergent interpretations—something evident even before the controversy over responsibility for the onset of the Korean War in 1950.[13] Some American observers in the 1940s had speculated that Moscow intended to make North Korea into a republic of the Soviet Union—the same status that was rumored but never materialized for Poland.[14] Then, the September 1948 proclamation of the Democratic People's Republic of Korea was largely perceived as a Soviet initiative, making North Korea as much a "satellite" as the new Soviet-aligned states in Eastern Europe, if not more so.[15] By contrast, more recent historiography has highlighted a dominant Korean role, forged in Manchurian exile, in both the establishment and ongoing rule of North Korea. And yet, scholars who have made use of newly declassified Soviet materials continue to emphasize Moscow's role.[16] However we might interpret the precise nature of Soviet domination or influence and Korean agency, what stands out is the almost immediate integration of North Korea into the Soviet orbit.

In North Korea, the Soviet Union encouraged a political purge of officials deemed to have collaborated with the Japanese to a far greater degree than the Americans did in South Korea. Simultaneously, though, the Soviet forces—again, far more than the Americans in South Korea—built upon Japanese foundations in establishing a state-owned and state-run economy.[17] It was through this economic dimension, as much as on the ideological plane, that a socialist regional order in Northeast Asian was defined and attempted.

Economics was always "the base" in Marxist thinking, and even before the existence of a separate North Korean state, Moscow began to draw North Korea into an almost exclusive economic relationship through trade, aid, and the creation of joint-venture companies. On top of that came technical training. In 1946, for example, the Soviet Union and the North Korean Provisional People's Committee (the de facto central government in Pyongyang) initiated an exchange program to send Koreans to the Soviet Union for technical training. In 1947–48, 120 undergraduates and 20 postgraduates were said to be in Soviet institutions of higher education, according to archival documents. But those figures did not include the village of Nagornoe, outside Moscow, where there was a secret school for thirty-five North Koreans who were to become high-level functionaries. They studied Russian, Marxist-Leninist political economy, the history of the Communist Party, world history, and dialectical materialism. The North Korean students were also served by cooks, waitresses, kitchen hands, a plumber, a nurse, and other staff in almost a one-to-one ratio to the students at a time when the Soviet Union was flat on its back from wartime devastation.[18]

In addition, the Soviet Union had an unusual card to play in North Korea—Soviet ethnic Koreans, the largest and most assimilated group of East Asian immigrants, with a long history of living on Russian and then Soviet territory.[19] Back in 1937, during Stalin's purges, Korean ethnics in the Soviet Far East had been deported en masse to Central Asia. In 1940, a military intelligence school near Moscow began to train Soviet Koreans (there were six graduates in 1942). In late August 1945, a dozen Soviet Koreans were tasked with aiding Soviet forces in the Far East with political issues, and these were followed by many more Soviet Koreans in the fall. The new Kim Il Sung University in Pyongyang employed Soviet lecturers, many of whom were of Korean descent, and the local Soviet authorities lobbied for more such teachers to be sent.[20] Even more substantially, as of 1947 some two thousand Soviet-trained Koreans were said to be involved in running major North Korean industries.[21] This figure is phenomenal, especially in light of the fact that in 1947 there were said to be 470 Soviet "advisers" in North Korea, including just 60 in Pyongyang.[22]

By late December 1948, when the bulk of Soviet armed forces departed North Korea, some four hundred to five hundred Soviet Koreans remained behind as civilian administrators and schoolteachers, some of whom became professors or party officials. Only perhaps in the three small Baltic states, once part of the Russian empire and reconquered in World War II, or in Outer Mongolia, did Soviet inhabitants of the local ethnicity "return" to play as prominent a role as in North Korea. Whether the exchange on balance benefited North Korea or the once deported, undereducated Soviet Koreans, remains an open question. Between 1958 and 1961, most Soviet Koreans in North Korea returned to the Soviet Union, usually involuntarily, though one, Mikhail Pang, who was known as the Korean Beria, survived politically (he died peacefully in North Korea in 1992).

Total Soviet aid to North Korea has been estimated variously. The task is complicated by the absence of market prices in socialist economies, the challenges of ruble conversions into dollar terms, and political considerations.[23] Whatever the precise measurement of the aid, it was clearly substantial, though it came with innumerable strings attached. Indeed, the North Korean economy arose as a dependency of the Soviet Union and, secondarily, of China. Eastern Europe, too, was seen as an unguarded supply depot by the North Korean regime, and even indigent Mongolia sent what it could (mostly horses) for the war and reconstruction.[24]

Soviet policy toward North Korea favored the development of industry rather than pure extraction (as in Manchuria). The U.S. Presidential Commission sent to investigate economic conditions in North Korea in May–June 1946, led by Ambassador Edwin W. Pauley, found that most of the heavy industry was functioning and had not been stripped by the Soviet forces.[25] The Pauley Commission dismissed the widespread accounts of Soviet confiscation of physical plant and equipment from North Korea, surmising that these were in fact industrial goods from Manchuria being transported through Korea for shipment to the Soviet Far East.[26] One contemporary observer concluded that "every effort of the Soviet command appears to have been to rehabilitate rather than destroy the economy of North Korea."[27]

At the same time, forced labor and violence were integral methods of Soviet-style economies. Indeed, rather than merely dependency through the exchange of personnel and goods, the Soviet Union also provided a total model of how to organize the economy and politics, via nationalization of the so-called means of production and an emphasis on heavy industry. North Korea adopted a Soviet-style, two-year economic "plan" for industrialization as early as February 1947. By 1949, following the establishment of formal independence, the North had reached prewar levels of industrial production, according to official statistics. Its economy was tightly embedded in a network of trade and resource flows that included Manchuria and the Soviet Far East. And after the People's Republic of China was founded in October 1949, Moscow belatedly sought to develop more fully the Manchurian sector of the Northeast Asian regional economy alongside the North Korean. Formal agreements of economic "cooperation" followed.

Mongolia fills out our cursory overview of a regionalism that was rooted in planning, or anticapitalist modernization, of despotic regimes that relied to a considerable degree on coercion. Soviet involvement in Mongolia, especially the use of Soviet Mongols or Buryats, has been well studied. Certainly the substantial number of Mongols trained in the Soviet Union has long been known.[28] (One should also mention the fifteen thousand Japanese prisoners of war who labored to build the Mongolian government building, party school, national theater, and other edifices in Ulaanbaatar—that was socialist-style regionalism, too.[29]) Less well known, perhaps, is that China also provided mass assistance to Mongolia, from finances to labor power. In 1956, Chinese nationals outnumbered Soviets in Mongolia, though these numbers fluctuated with Sino-Soviet tensions. Despite the tensions, however, as a regional hub between the two giants, Mongolia received transit fees for much of the immense rail traffic going each way—monies that floated Mongolia's state budget.

In sum, although the national Northeast Asian economies were very far from being integrated together to the degree of the planned economy in the Soviet Union proper, they did all adopt the basic Soviet model, and they became interdependent upon one another. Here was a regional economy not unlike the Japanese imperial economy, with central directives and some regional division of labor, only without the Japanese.

Ultimate Technology Transfer?

Soviet economic cooperation with China is the most dramatic dimension of the Northeast Asian socialist regional economy. In early 1950, the Soviet Union offered China a low-interest loan valued at $300 million over the next five years, largely to reconstruct the industries of the Northeast, which had been China's most industrialized region before 1949. True, the outbreak of the Korean War delayed the reconstruction effort, and the PRC used much of its loan to pay for the war, a circumstance the Chinese leadership deemed unfair.[30] After the war, Beijing expected large-scale aid from the Soviet Union as compensation for China's sacrifice of blood to the war effort, a sacrifice the Soviet Union had conspicuously not made. In the event, Soviet assistance to China in the post–Korean War period did grow: New trade and aid agreements between China and the Soviet Union, and between China and various countries of Eastern Europe, brought a mass infusion of money, equipment, technology, and advice in the 1950s.

More than eight thousand Soviet and East European advisers came to China in this period, and some seven thousand Chinese students went to Soviet-bloc countries, mainly for technical training. In 1959, a year that saw the biggest increase in Sino-Soviet trade, nearly 50 percent of China's total trade was with the Soviet Union.[31] By this time, though, the political relations between China and the Soviet Union were fraying, and the following year Moscow famously removed its entire team of advisers from China and abrogated most of its economic agreements with Beijing—but not before the ultimate technology transfer in Northeast Asia had taken place.

China detonated a nuclear bomb in October 1964 (on the day the Soviet leader Nikita Khrushchev was removed in a palace coup) and a thermonuclear device less than three years later, joining the United States, Soviet Union, Britain, and France as the fifth avowed nuclear state.[32] The Chinese maintain that they developed the bomb through their own efforts. Adding weight to the Chinese claim, the Soviet Union always took the position that it had refused to give the bomb to China because transfer would have extended license to the imperialist camp to proliferate the technology (to West Germany and Japan)—a position enunciated by the high party official Mikhail Suslov at a February 1964 plenum of the Communist Party of the Soviet Union (CPSU).[33] But as the top expert of the subject has summarized, "the Soviet Union built all the essentials of China's fledgling nuclear infrastructure, based on six Sino-Soviet nuclear cooperation and assistance agreements between 1955 and 1958."[34] That assistance included weapons-design laboratories, experimental reactors, a cyclotron, uranium-enrichment facilities, joint prospecting for uranium throughout China, and significant on-site personnel.

During the Stalin-Mao meeting in Moscow in 1949, the topic of the atomic bomb had already come up, according to N.T. Fedorenko,[35] but Sergei Goncharenko, relying on Soviet Foreign Ministry documents, states that "large-scale Sino-Soviet cooperation in building military industries began in early 1955."[36] In fact, between 1955 and 1958, the Soviet and Chinese leaders signed a number of agreements regarding the Chinese nuclear program—something discussed by the Chinese and Westerners, never by Moscow. And yet, Goncharenko suggests, the second Taiwan crisis in 1958 precipitated a reevaluation by Moscow. Other scholars have also noted Soviet second thoughts. In this regard, the Khrushchev-Mao unofficial Beijing meeting of July–August 1958 has been singled out as the turning point, when Mao objected to a joint naval fleet, an idea that Khrushchev hastily withdrew. "If Mao Zedong was unwilling to cooperate in the naval sphere, suspecting Moscow of intending to violate China's sovereignty," one scholar has surmised, "what would happen when Khrushchev would have to bring up the problem of the command of joint nuclear forces?"[37]

By fall 1958, if not earlier, the Soviet Union began to delay its deliveries of military technology, including technology for nuclear weapons. But in what may have been a related move, it reaffirmed the Soviet nuclear umbrella's coverage of China.[38] Furthermore, Moscow's second thoughts had limits. Officials in the U.S. government, according to declassified documents, contemplated a preemptive knockout strike against Chinese nuclear facilities. There were strong advocates of such a move, perhaps in part because Khrushchev rebuffed a suggestion by President John Kennedy's envoy W. Averell Harriman even to discuss Chinese nuclear weapon facilities—something the Chinese nonetheless feared the Soviet leader would collude in.[39] The Soviet leaders stood up for the Chinese more than the Chinese seem to have expected.

Goncharenko deepens the mystery of the bomb transfer by indicating that the Soviet Union hesitated to lose its socialist-camp nuclear monopoly; that Mao's statements on nuclear war in 1956 had aroused grave concern in the Kremlin, as Chinese efforts had done in 1958 to leverage the Soviet nuclear capability to increase its own political weight; and that by 1960 Moscow even feared for its own security if the Chinese acquired the bomb. Pointedly asking "why Khrushchev and his leadership seemed willing to take the extraordinary risks involved in providing another country with nuclear weapons," Goncharenko points to "the enthusiasm for socialist construction and technological achievement in Moscow during the mid-1950s." In this reading, "Khrushchev and his close associates believed in the alliance with China in a way that their predecessors never did and in a way that Khrushchev himself later regretted bitterly. During these leaders' first enthusiastic years in power, providing China with nuclear weapons may have seemed a small price to pay for an alliance that would lead two continents into socialism." And yet, Goncharenko speculates that "the Soviet leaders never seem to have had a clear vision of why China needed nuclear weapons."[40]

The mystery of Soviet motivations has not been solved in what is probably the most comprehensive research to date, by Tatiana Zazerskaia, who scoured Foreign Ministry, Central Committee, and Council of Ministers archives as well as some Chinese memoirs and secondary sources. She suggests that "during all the years of cooperation, the Soviet side exerted vigilance, sharing secrets only within the allowed parameters, and carefully followed every step of its Chinese friend." She adds that none of this changed right after Stalin died, citing a Chinese official's complaints.[41] This gives weight to Goncharenko's assertion that actual cooperation commenced in 1955. But the question remains: why? What in the world was Moscow thinking when it transferred science and technology for the bomb to Beijing?

According to the Chinese, Khrushchev became more forthcoming with the most complex technology after the events in Poland and Hungary in 1956. By the second half of 1958, with more than a hundred Soviet nuclear specialists in China,[42] the Soviet Union helped the Chinese prepare a facility for modeling an explosion and to look for a test site. It may have been the case that the Soviet Union anticipated not just building but also controlling a combined Soviet Union-PRC nuclear force. In 1957, the Chinese signed a license agreement for the Tu-16 bombers, which could carry nuclear payloads, and a factory in Harbin turned out the first Chinese prototype (known as the H-6) in 1959 (a modified version of this aircraft dropped the Chinese bomb at the Lop Nor test site in May 1965).[43] Despite Mao's rebuff on a joint navy (and a joint long-distance radio facility on Chinese soil), Khrushchev withdrew his offer of a prototype bomb only well after his 1958 visit, when he saw the Chinese dragging the Soviet Union into a possible conflict with the United States over Taiwan.[44] At this point, however, the Soviet leaders were convinced that the Chinese were on the cusp of producing a bomb.

Sino-Soviet tensions curtailed cooperation, and the upshot was a denial of the Soviet role by both sides. Nonetheless, "Soviet assistance was considerable," according to David Holloway. "The Soviet Union supplied design information about nuclear weapons—in particular about its own 1951 design. It appears also to be the case that, when relations soured, the Soviet specialists supplied faulty information to try to sabotage the Chinese effort."[45] Whether Khrushchev fantasized about world revolution and joint Soviet-Chinese forces under Moscow's command or fretted about NATO and Japan, it seems that the Chinese communists played on Khrushchev's sentiments to press for ever-greater technology transfer. Khrushchev had tried to treat Mao and the Chinese better than Stalin had—withdrawing from Port Arthur, for example—engaging in the kind of accommodating behavior that, paradoxically, the Chinese saw as weakness.

Proliferation in Asia did not stop with China. India announced that it had developed its own bomb in 1974, after its scientists had begun visiting and cooperating with the Soviet Union.[46] In turn, China helped Pakistan with the development of a bomb in the early 1980s, providing blueprints as well as highly enriched uranium and key components for the engineering process. To be sure, the United States had trained Pakistani scientists in nuclear-reactor technology and supplied Pakistan's first nuclear reactor, while later turning an expedient blind eye to Pakistan's weapons development. The United States had also furnished China with the impetus and justification for acquiring nuclear capability with threats to use nuclear weapons against it.[47] Many of China's nuclear scientists trained in the United States during the 1950s. Still, directly or indirectly, it was the Soviet Union more than the

United States that is responsible for the proliferation of the bomb to Asia—China, India, and Pakistan. After the eruption of the second U.S.-DPRK nuclear crisis in 2002, U.S. and other intelligence agencies reported a lively and long-standing exchange of nuclear fuel, technology, and expertise among Pakistan, North Korea, Libya, and Iran,[48] a lasting legacy (in part) of the Soviet-Asian nuclear technology transfer.

Whether North Korea possessed nuclear weapons was a hotly disputed issue by the early 1990s, one that brought the United States and the DPRK to the brink of war in June 1994. A U.S.–North Korean agreement signed in Geneva in October 1994 seemed to freeze North Korea's nuclear program for several years, but American allegations of renewed North Korean nuclear weapons-related activity in October 2002 again brought the two nations to a crisis point.[49] Weapons or no weapons, North Korea had certainly benefited from Soviet nuclear largesse. According to Russian physicist Georgii Kaurov, formerly of the Russian Ministry of Atomic Energy, Soviet–North Korean cooperation in the peaceful use of nuclear energy was part of Moscow's "overall plan for promoting socialist economic integration in the Far East."[50]

Russian scientists and officials have insisted that Soviet policy forbade any exchange of nuclear weapons technology with the DPRK or any export of excessive supplies of nuclear fuel that could be used for weapons.[51] Nonetheless, the Soviet Union and North Korea signed their first agreement on atomic energy cooperation in September 1959 and established North Korea's first nuclear research center and reactor in Yongbyon, about 100 kilometers north of Pyongyang (the location of suspected weapons activity and target of a potential U.S. air strike in 1994). As a result of the agreement with Moscow, hundreds of North Korean nuclear specialists were trained in the Soviet Union, including many at the leading Soviet laboratories in Dubna. In the 1970s and 1980s, North Korea ramped up its program of nuclear energy development, helped not just by Soviet advice and assistance but also by substantial deposits of natural uranium. The fact that Japan and South Korea were similarly developing nuclear energy on a large scale was no doubt a factor in spurring DPRK actions. The further circumstance that South Korea was also trying to develop nuclear weapons—until it was stopped by the United States—may have magnified North Korea's desire to develop its own deterrent.

North Korea's nuclear ambitions could not have gotten off the ground without decades of Soviet assistance. That assistance ended abruptly. In December 1985, the Soviet Union had agreed to help the DPRK construct a nuclear power plant near Sinp'o on the east coast of North Korea, but in 1992, North Korea's failure to pay for construction led a destitute and no longer communist Russia to halt work on the Sinp'o project, leaving the DPRK $1.7 million in debt to Russia's atomic ministry. In April 1993, after North Korea announced its intention to withdraw from the Nuclear Nonproliferation Treaty (NPT), then-president Boris Yeltsin halted all remaining Russian–North Korean cooperation relating to nuclear technology.

By that time the genie, apparently, was out of the bottle.[52] The site near Sinp'o was precisely where a U.S.-led consortium would propose building two nuclear reactors as part of the 1994 Geneva Agreement. In 2003, when the Geneva Agreement broke down, with little more than holes in the ground where the reactors were to be built, the North Koreans could claim that they had been cheated out of nuclear power plants twice, first by the Russians and then by the Americans. Of course, North Korea's own cheating played no small part in the breakdown of both agreements. In any case, in 2003 North Korea again threatened to withdraw from the NPT, and this time it carried out the threat.

Dependency, Rivalry, Independence

In socialist Northeast Asia, undeniable economic dependency did not automatically become the basis for political dependency. Sergei Goncharenko estimates that, in 1959, Soviet exports to China of industrial technology and know-how reached an astonishing 7 percent of Soviet gross domestic product. With that money, he writes, the Soviet Union could have funded construction of 2.6 million apartments at home, overcoming its housing shortage. These figures may be fairly disputed, but no doubts should remain about the enormous significance of Moscow's role in China's development. Yet, despite the fact that China was itself dependent on Soviet assistance, Beijing attempted to compete with Moscow in providing economic assistance to both Mongolia and North Korea.

Contemporary Soviet sources divide foreign assistance to the DPRK between 1953 and 1960 roughly in thirds, no doubt a division of labor suggested by Moscow. Some 33.3 percent of reconstruction aid came from the Soviet Union, 29.4 percent from China, and 37.3 percent from other countries.[53] More specifically, the aid came from the sources shown in Table 7.1.

North Korea was dependent on fraternal assistance for more than 80 percent of its industrial reconstruction needs between 1954 and 1956, the period of the three-year plan.[54] By far the most important source of this assistance was the Soviet Union.

Among other projects, Soviet aid and technical assistance built or rebuilt the Sup'ung hydroelectric power plant (the largest in Asia at the end of World War II, destroyed by the United States in the Korean War); the chemical works in Hungnam (also destroyed in the war); the steelworks at Songjin (renamed Kimch'aek in 1957, after a DPRK hero killed in the Korean War); the port at Namp'o; and a textile factory in Pyongyang. Soviet aid was both extensive and diverse (see Table 7.2).

North Korea could not possibly have rebuilt its economy as quickly as it did without this massive inflow of aid into nearly every sector of production and consumption. But the DPRK did not remain aid-dependent for long. Partly this was out of necessity, as socialist-bloc aid was intended from the beginning to be phased out as reconstruction was completed. Still, it is interesting to note how quickly North Korea's aid dependency dropped. In other words, North Korea's declaration

Table 7.1

"Fraternal" Assistance to the Democratic People's Republic of Korea, 1953–1960 (million rubles)

Total	879.3
Soviet Union	292.5
Others	586.8
China	258.4
German Democratic Republic	122.7
Poland	81.9
Czechoslovakia	61.0
Romania	22.0
Hungary	21.0
Bulgaria	18.7
Albania	0.6
Mongolia	0.4
North Vietnam	0.1

Source: Natalia Bazhanova, *Kiroe son Puk Han kyongje* [North Korea Economy at the Crossroads], trans. Yang Chuyong. (Seoul: Hanguk kyongje sinmunsa, 1992).

Table 7.2

Soviet Aid to the Democratic People's Republic of Korea, 1953–1957

Type	Amount/unit	Quantity
Technical assistance and equipment	10 million rubles	601
Oil products	1,000 tons	113.6
Rolling metal	1,000 tons	134.8
Rope and steel cable	1,000 tons	4.9
Tubing	1,000 tons	22.8
Rolling nonferrous metals	1,000 tons	3.8
Fertilizer	1,000 tons	122.1
Tires	1,000 pieces	59.6
Lumber	1,000 cubic meters	113.3
Cotton weave	1 million meters	11.9
Cotton thread	1,000 tons	2.9
Livestock	1,000 head	16.9
Rice	1,000 tons	39.8
Cooking oil	1,000 tons	4.6
Sugar	1,000 tons	9.0
Medicine and medical equipment	1 million rubles	23.4

Source: SSSR i Koreia [The USSR and Korea] (Moscow: USSR Academy of Sciences, 1988), pp. 256–57.

of "self-reliance" by the end of the 1950s was not without substance. In 1954, 33.4 percent of North Korea's state revenue came from foreign aid; in 1960, the proportion had dropped, by official statistics, to 2.6 percent. By contrast, well over half of South Korea's government revenue had come from foreign assistance in 1956.[55]

To be sure, statistics on North Korea can be debated. But whatever the precise dimensions of North Korean self-sufficiency, it is beyond dispute that the period of postwar reconstruction in North Korea was the time that the Soviet Union, China, and the Soviet-aligned countries of Eastern Europe and Mongolia cooperated, at least economically, to the greatest degree. That economic interdependence, in turn, fostered, at least in North Korea, a push for economic independence.

The Soviet Union and China contributed such enormous resources to the reconstruction of North Korea partly out of solidarity and partly—especially in the case of China—out of rivalry. Besides assistance in cash and goods, China contributed several thousand "People's Volunteers," soldiers who remained after the Korean War to help with construction and other projects. North Korea was an area of crucial strategic importance to China and one place where the potential for Chinese influence, built on the "blood-cemented friendship" of the Korean War, was considerable. China's ambitions extended well beyond Korea. After Stalin's death, Mao tended to see himself as the leader of the world communist movement, and the Chinese revolution as the natural model for revolution in the third world, where communism would make its greatest advances in the third quarter of the twentieth century.[56]

Whatever the attractions of the Chinese model for North Korea, the latter, like Mongolia, remained utterly dependent on the Soviet Union for economic and military aid, and thus remained wary of alienating Moscow. Alone among smaller communist countries caught up in the Sino-Soviet split, the DPRK managed to maintain a rough balance between the two communist giants throughout the three decades of Sino-Soviet alienation. It is not so much that North Korea "leaned toward" one or the other of its patrons, although at times it did, but rather that the DPRK maintained a certain distance from both while gaining from each the benefits of its strategic position vis-à-vis the other. In this respect the DPRK was a practitioner of "the power of small states," playing off the competition between its two much larger neighbors to its own advantage.[57]

Sino-Soviet rivalries involved not just competition but a kind of division of labor in intracommunist economic relations. Kim Il Sung led a delegation to the Soviet Union and Eastern Europe in June 1956 to negotiate renewed assistance in economic reconstruction. As a result of this visit, the Soviet Union cancelled North Korea's debts and postponed repayment of debts amounting to over a billion rubles, and offered new aid in both money and goods.[58] China, at the time, did not renew its pledge of aid, although in September 1958 China did extend $25 million in credits to North Korea.[59] In July 1955, China had offered 800 million yuan in assistance to North Vietnam, roughly twice as much aid as Hanoi received at the time from the Soviet Union.[60] This seemed to reflect an understanding between the Soviet Union and China, in which the latter would take the lead in assisting revolutionary movements and regimes in Southeast Asia, while the Soviet Union and Eastern Europe would focus on the north Asian countries of Mongolia and

North Korea. In fact, however, Soviet and Chinese policies in East Asia were becoming more divergent than complementary by the late 1950s.[61]

The Unraveling and the Legacies

Developments internal to the Northeast Asian socialist regional order pulled it apart. Soviet economic support for the DPRK declined sharply after the end of the three-year plan, both because of Soviet parsimony and because of North Korean insistence on self-reliance. But the Soviet Union also wanted to maintain its influence in Pyongyang, partly as a counterweight to China and partly out of concern about centrifugal forces in the Soviet bloc after the 1956 Hungarian uprising. This resulted in a kind of negative policy toward the DPRK: The Soviet Union reduced the number of advisers and level of assistance to North Korea after 1956, but it also refrained from criticizing or interfering in North Korea's domestic affairs. The little Stalins were toppled in Eastern Europe with de-Stalinization, but Kim Il Sung endured.[62] Yet, as late as 1957, three-fifths of the films shown in North Korea were Soviet productions, and only one-tenth North Korean. A degree of dependency persisted, even in mass culture.[63]

The early 1960s were when North Korea ostensibly leaned closest to China,[64] but China had little to offer economically after the disaster of the Great Leap Forward in the late 1950s. On the contrary, famine in China pushed tens of thousands of ethnic Koreans across the border into North Korea.[65] (Even more of China's Korean minority would flee across the border later in the decade, as a result of political and ethnic persecution during the Chinese Cultural Revolution.) Despite official praise for China's achievements during the Great Leap Forward, internal statements of the Korean Workers' Party were critical of Chinese Communist Party's economic policies.[66] Chinese promises of economic assistance to North Korea after 1959 went mostly unfulfilled; literally, China could not deliver the goods, despite strenuous attempts on the part of the PRC to compete with the Soviet Union in offering North Korea equipment, technical assistance, and entire factories for light-industrial production.[67]

Still, although the economic benefits of relations with China showed limited returns, China was a military and political balance against the Soviet Union. On July 6, 1961, the DPRK signed a Treaty of Friendship, Cooperation and Mutual Assistance with the Soviet Union in Moscow, and then, four days later, signed an almost identical treaty with China.[68] The Soviet Union offered greater material support, but ideologically North Korea drew closer to China. After a brief rekindling of cultural exchange with the Soviet Union in 1959–60, North Korea again raised the walls against "revisionist" influences in the wake of the 1961 twenty-second congress of the CPSU and the renewed push for de-Stalinization, while Pyongyang made declarations of the desirability of unifying the peninsula, raising the prospect of war and exacerbating the tension with the Kremlin.

Radio Moscow's Korean programs were no longer broadcast in the DPRK after November 1961.[69] Issues of Soviet periodicals that covered sensitive subjects such as Stalinism and the Albanian question were withheld from circulation.[70] A major shake-up of the CPSU sent many mid-level cadres out to the provinces, and the East Europeans noted even greater restrictions on contact between Koreans and foreigners, and a tightening of political controls over the population as a whole.[71]

By contrast, the number of PRC official delegations visiting the DPRK went up sharply after the end of 1961, beginning with a trade delegation in early January 1962.[72] Events in China were covered extensively in the North Korean media, exceeding Soviet news in quantity and level of praise—circumstances watched closely by Soviet leaders.[73] In turn, Kim Il Sung's birthday was celebrated prominently in the PRC in April 1962, while in the Soviet Union, media coverage of North Korea was muted. Commenting on recent North Korean films, a Soviet diplomat in Pyongyang remarked to a Hungarian colleague in January 1962, "one cannot show films based on the personality cult when there is a fight against the remnants of the personality cult in the USSR."[74] Soviet–North Korean relations appeared to reach a nadir just as Sino–North Korean relations peaked in 1963–64.[75] In October 1963, the *Korean Workers Party Newspaper* published a lengthy editorial entitled "Let Us Defend the Socialist Camp," which put the DPRK squarely on the Chinese side in the Sino-Soviet conflict, attacking Soviet arrogance, chauvinism, and blatant interference in the affairs of sovereign socialist states. The editorial also attacked Khrushchev's "socialist division of labor," institutionalized in the Council for Mutual Economic Assistance (CMEA), as a direct threat to the independence of fellow socialist countries.

So much for a Northeast Asian socialist regional order!

Within North Korea, the late 1950s/early 1960s chill in DPRK-Soviet relations was expressed through increased harassment and monitoring of Soviet and East European technicians and diplomats. Foreign specialists in the DPRK were now required to be fingerprinted, and they had to report to the North Korean authorities all of their movements, contacts, and Korean friends.[76] The DPRK passed a law in 1963 forbidding marriages between Koreans and foreigners, meaning almost entirely marriages with East Europeans. Mixed-race couples were forced to move out of Pyongyang, and Koreans were pressured to divorce their European spouses. The German Democratic Republic (GDR) ambassador to North Korea denounced this law and the agenda of "racial purity" it implied as nothing short of "Göbbelsian."[77] In retaliation, the Soviet, Hungarian, East German, and other Soviet-bloc governments restricted the activities of the North Korean embassies in their countries, and refused to allow them to publicize the DPRK's anti-"revisionist" propaganda.[78] Soon, however, during the Great Proletarian Cultural Revolution, it was China's turn to be subjected to DPRK denunciation (albeit indirect) for ideological profanation. In the late 1960s, the Chinese and the North Koreans sent troops to their common border, where some clashes evidently took place.[79] The North Korean leadership swung back toward solicitation of the Soviet Union, as well as of Eastern Europe, conspicuously (perhaps in part desperately) stepping up ties to the GDR. The socialist bloc, like America's alliances, extended beyond Northeast Asia, but the geographic sweep invited recurring jockeying, not common-enemy solidarity.

Not long after it had taken shape, the socialist "community" in Northeast Asia was in shambles. For China and North Korea, nationalism trumped any potential benefits of integration into a Soviet-led economic amalgamation. Both China and North Korea embarked on Soviet-inspired programs of "self-reliance" in the late 1950s, a path China would abandon by the 1970s, but which North Korea would follow—with disastrous results—for decades to come. Of course, Sino–North Korean and Soviet–North Korean political and economic relations would continue, but by 1964 the Sino-Soviet alliance was dead, and trilateral cooperation—much less regional integration—was not possible again until the very end of the cold war. With the collapse of the Soviet Union and the normalization between South Korea and both China and Russia, hopes reappeared for an integration of the economies of Northeast China, the Russian Far East, and the Korean peninsula. One major impediment to realizing this new vision of regionalism, however, was the last living legacy of the old socialist regionalism, namely, North Korea. The contrast with the former satellite Mongolia—now a democracy with economic and foreign policies open to the world—could not have been starker.

The lesson that North Korea had learned all too well from the Soviet Union was not internationalism, which it firmly rejected in the late 1950s (external propaganda notwithstanding), but Stalin's "socialism in one country," which provided the model for the DPRK in the foundational 1940s. By the early 2000s, North Korea was quite literally a roadblock to Northeast Asian and trans-Eurasian integration, refusing to sign on to an "Asian Highway" agreement sponsored by the United Nations in April 2004, which would have built a 140,000-km highway between the Pacific and Europe, including a line through the Korean peninsula.[80] For all its rhetorical flourishes about fraternal cooperation, North Korea had never been an enthusiastic participant in Soviet-led socialist regionalism; one could hardly expect a defensive DPRK to subscribe to the open regionalism of the early twenty-first century that is promoted so heavily by its archenemies, South Korea and Japan. Needless to say, only a very different regional dynamic, or a very different North Korea, could overcome the remnants of cold war isolationism in Northeast Asia.

8

Japan's Asian Regionalism and South Korea

Chung-in Moon and Seung-won Suh

The geopolitical destiny of Korea as a peninsular state was always subject to the vortex of two contending powers, China and Japan. Whereas China had a rather pacified relationship with Korea through its tributary system, Japan's regional ambition since the late nineteenth century severely undermined Korea's domestic and international standing. Japan's annexation of Korea in 1910 and Korea's unwanted entanglement in the Pacific War were unfortunate results of Japan's rampant imperial expansionism in the region. Japanese regional moves, benign or malign, critically influenced the shaping of Korea's geopolitical and economic outlook.

Japan's defeat in the Pacific War and the hegemonic ascension of American power led to a profound transformation in the regional landscape of East Asia. The bipolar cold war structure, coupled with institutional constraints embodied in the Peace Constitution, fundamentally delimited the scope of Japan's regional security maneuvers. Under the American security umbrella, Japan pursued a passive and incremental foreign and security policy toward the Asian region.[1] Japan's foreign economic policy was also devoid of regional initiatives throughout the 1950s and 1960s since an odd mix of multilateralism and mercantilism governed its external economic behavior. Japan sought to maximize its mercantile interests within the framework of a liberal international economic order founded on American hegemonic power. This free riding was tolerated by the United States for security reasons. Thus, Japan was not in a position to seek its own regional policy, and its regional posture was by and large a reflection of American preference in the region in the 1950s and 1960s. Japan had limited influence over South Korea as Seoul-Tokyo security relations were mediated through the United States.

Beginning in the early 1970s, regional and international environments changed rapidly. The Nixon Doctrine in 1969, Nixon's surprising visit to China, and the advent of détente reshaped strategic perimeters in the region. Japan's growing confidence in its economic vitality and newly emerging trade frictions also strained Japanese-U.S. relations. Facing these changes, Japan began to pursue regional security and economic policies somewhat independently of the United States. Japan's new regional moves in turn affected South Korea's strategic positioning.

Japan's Asian Regionalism: Historical Overview

Japan has always been ambivalent toward its Asian identity, wavering between "Japan in Asia" and "Japan and Asia."[2] While the perspective of "Japan and Asia" reflected an internationalist orientation based on "*Datsua*" (away from Asia), "Japan in Asia" was manifested in the form of "Asianism," which was to be achieved through "*Nyua*" (reentering Asia). The first opening of Japan to the outside world in the 1850s mandated two national goals. One was to get away from its peripheral status in the China-centered regional order, and the other was to transform Japan into a modern, civilized state system. Fukuzawa Yukichi suggested the *Datsua* thesis as a viable answer to the two mandates. According to him, Japan could achieve its national goals by joining Western civilization, while discarding China and Korea. There was no hope in Asia.[3] As the chapter in this volume by Takashi Inoguchi explains, Meiji-era reforms were a reflection of this new thinking. Emulation of Western modernity and civilization served as the guiding ideology in the latter part of nineteenth-century Japan.

Fukuzawa's *Datsuaron* was not consummate, but instrumental. His *Datsua* was nothing but an instrument for *Nyua*. Obtained through the adoption of Western civilization and the doctrine of *fukoku kyohei* (rich nation, strong army), Japan's national power was to be utilized for the forced colonization of Asian countries that were fragile and underdeveloped.[4] Japan expanded under this logic, and its imperial order eventually replaced the Sino-centered tributary system. Japan defeated China in the Sino-Japanese War in 1894–95, and the Shimonoseki Treaty was signed, whereby China gave up suzerainty over the Korean peninsula, while recognizing the complete independence and autonomy of the Choson dynasty.[5] Japan's influence over East Asia grew phenomenally following the Sino-Japanese War. Japan paved the way to the annexation of the Korean peninsula by defeating Russia in the Russo-Japanese War in 1904–5. It also expelled Germany by forming an alliance with Great Britain in 1910.

Before long, Japanese colonial expansion encountered domestic challenges. The formation of the League of Nations and the advent of Taisho democracy in the early 1920s precipitated the rise of idealistic Asianism, which ranged from Asian Monroism and New Asianism to Great Asianism. They all called for the end of Japanese colonialism as well as for Asian solidarity and community, but these movements faded away as Western powers began to contain Japanese expansion in the name of the "Yellow Peril." Japan had "reentered Asia" by emphasizing its Asian identity, but the reentry took the form of an assertive militaristic expansion. Japan beautified its imperial conquest under the slogan of Pan-Asianism.[6] In the Japanese vision of Pan-Asia, all nations and peoples were not necessarily equal. As the only modernized and industrialized nation in the region, Japan was entitled to lead. Central to this Pan-Asianism was the concept of a New East Asian Order (*Toashinchitsujo*), which was designed to form an East Asian economic bloc under the leadership and guidance of Japan.

In 1940, the Konoe Fumimaro cabinet announced the Basic National Policy Outline (*kihon kokusaku yoko*), which formalized the doctrine of the Greater East Asian Co-Prosperity Sphere. This comprised five categories of states: a guiding state (Japan), independent states (Republic of China, Manchukuo, and Thailand), independent states under Japan's protection (Burma, the Philippines, and Java), colonial states under Japan's direct rule (Korea and Taiwan), and colonial states outside the sphere (French Indochina and Portuguese Timor).[7] These countries were incorporated into the sphere under the principle of "one extended Japanese imperial family" (*hakkoku Ichiu*).[8]

The Co-Prosperity Sphere had several important implications. First, it was predicated on imperial expansion through territorial conquest. Although the doctrine declared Japan as the guiding state, Japanese hegemonic leadership was more malign than benign. Second, the Co-Prosperity Sphere can be seen as a Japan's defensive move to counter Western economic penetration and domination as evidenced through the Yellow Peril. Thus, the sphere, which was based on intraregional division of labor (industrial production in the North and agricultural production in the South) took the form of closed regionalism that was mediated through the Japanese yen hegemony. Finally, as the notion of "one extended Japanese imperial family" illustrates, Japan attempted to develop a unified organic entity through acculturation. Thus, the Co-Prosperity Sphere emphasized the importance of cultural identity inasmuch as it was a political and economic instrument for Japanese domination.

Japan's Asian adventures imposed unbearable costs and humiliation on Korea and Koreans. Korea's sovereignty and wealth were taken away, and numerous Koreans lost their lives during the unwanted Pacific War. Indeed, an assertive Japanese regionalism is considered by Koreans to have been a curse on the peninsula.

The allies' victory in the Pacific War reshaped the contours of the East Asian regional order. The advent of the cold war led to a bipolar structure, dividing the region into two axes: the southern axis comprised of the United States, Japan, and South Korea, and the northern axis of the Soviet Union, China, and North Korea. Under this tight bipolar structure, the scope of Japan's security maneuvering was profoundly limited. Japan was placed under the American security umbrella, and its global and regional reach was mediated by the United States.[9] It was more so because Japan, a defeated nation, was deprived of its military sovereignty as mandated by the Peace Constitution, and was solely devoted to an exclusive defense strategy (*senshu boei senryaku*). The Yoshida Doctrine epitomized par excellence Japan's security posture in the 1950s and 1960s. Namely, Japan attempted to maximize its economic benefits under the American security umbrella. The alliance with the United States was given the highest priority, and the old patterns of expansionism and confrontation were rejected. Japan was a pacified state with an American security blessing. It did not pursue any regional economic policy, enjoying the benefits of free riding in the liberal international economic order that was founded and sustained by the United States. Although Japan resorted to neomercantile practices in the 1950s and 1960s, its external economic behavior was by and large governed by multilateral norms. Accordingly, its impact on Korea throughout the 1950s and 1960s was not pronounced.

Japan's Regional Security Policy and Implications for South Korea in the 1970s and 1980s

Beginning in the late 1960s, the American strategic posture in Asia underwent a major shift. The Nixon Doctrine in 1969 was the first prelude to the shift. As a way of getting away from the Vietnam debacle, President Nixon urged Asian defense in the hands of Asians, portending signs of gradual American disengagement from the region. Along with the doctrine, the United States transferred Okinawa to Japan, and pulled out twenty thousand U.S. troops from South Korea in 1970. But more shocking news was yet to come. That was President Nixon's visit to China in 1971, a shock to Japan because the United States never consulted it. The United States accelerated the process of détente, ultimately leading to President Carter's decision, soon to be retracted, to withdraw American forces from South Korea in 1977. The American disengagement and the collapse of South Vietnam in 1975 further heightened security concerns in Japan.

A series of changes in the regional security environment alarmed the Japanese leadership. In order to minimize damage from the changing American strategic posture, Japan tried to uphold the framework of the Japan-U.S. alliance. The Nixon-Sato meeting in 1969 exemplified Japan's efforts to retain the existing alliance system. Meanwhile, Japan began to take its own initiatives. One of the most notable responses was Japan's approach to China. Prime Minister Kakuei Tanaka paid a visit to China in September 1972, where he and Premier Zhou Enlai adopted the Shanghai joint communiqué, which led to diplomatic normalization between the two countries. Overriding strong opposition from the anti-China faction led by former Premier Nobusuke Kishi, Tanaka expedited a rush into China.

Japan's China initiative was justified on three accounts. First, the Japanese leadership regarded normalization with China as a strategic move to complement American efforts to contain the Soviet Union. After all, improved ties between Beijing and Washington resulting from Nixon's visit were perceived as being an American effort to form a common front with China against the Soviet Union. Second, diplomatic normalization with China was seen as a sign of Japan's complete return to Asia. Japan made an important step toward regaining its status as an Asian power by normalizing its relations with South Korea in 1965, but that was an incomplete return to the Asian world. Rapprochement with China completed the process of Japan's Asianization. Finally, economic motives mattered. Global recession, followed by the oil crisis in the mid-1970s, prompted Japan to diversify its export markets. China emerged as an alternate market for Japan.

Japan's China rush peaked with the signing of the China-Japan Peace and Friendship Treaty in August 1978. The Masayoshi Ohira cabinet not only offered full endorsement of China's economic opening and reforms, but also extended large-scale economic assistance. It pledged to provide China with $2 billion in long-term public loans to support seven major development projects, development loans amounting to ¥420 billion for coal and oil development, and short-term commercial bank loans worth $6 billion. Along with this, the Generalized System of Preference in tariffs was extended to China, while relaxation of the Coordinating Committee for Multilateral Exports (CoCom) regulations was assured.[10] These changes did not amount either to a strategy for regionalism or to a break with the United States. The Japanese leadership was well aware that new economic ties with China should be pursued within the boundary of the Japan-U.S. alliance.[11]

Even before the 1978 treaty divisions over China were exposed within the Japanese leadership. The Takeo Fukuda cabinet, which was inaugurated in December 1976, pursued a policy somewhat different from its predecessor. Prime Minister Fukuda placed more emphasis on strengthening Japan's diplomatic relationship with Southeast Asian countries. Since the 1960s, Japan had been expanding its export markets into Southeast Asia, but it was not perceived favorably. A bitter memory of Japanese atrocities during the Pacific War, coupled with aggressive market penetration, cultivated fierce anti-Japanese sentiments in much of the region. Massive anti-Japanese riots during Tanaka's visit to Thailand and Indonesia alarmed Japan, redirecting its diplomatic attention to Southeast Asia. While attending the Association of Southeast Asian Nations (ASEAN) Manila summit meeting in 1977, Fukuda delivered a speech that became known as the Fukuda Doctrine. It emphasized four points: First, Japan is an economic power, but it would not seek the status of military power; second, Japan and Southeast Asian countries are members of Asia, and they should seek "heart-to-heart" relations going beyond economic and material interests; third, exclusive economic blocs are tantamount to committing economic suicide and would be counterproductive to ASEAN interests; and finally, he welcomed improved ties between ASEAN and Indochinese countries based on mutual understanding. What Fukuda had in mind was to consolidate a new economic axis linking the United States, Japan, Taiwan, and ASEAN.[12] This position was reinforced through Prime Minister Zenko Suzuki's Bangkok Speech in 1981, reassuring Southeast Asians of Japan's resolve to retain its Peace Constitution while pledging to increase economic assistance to the region as well as to initiate a new project for training human resources.

Japan's policy on South Korea was shaped in a similar context. As Victor Cha aptly points out, fear of abandonment by the United States might have brought close security ties between Japan and South Korea.[13] Nixon's Guam Doctrine sent a mixed message to Japan and South Korea. On the one hand, it called for Japan and South Korea each to play a greater role in its own defense. On the other hand, the doctrine aimed to pave the way to a close security linkage between Japan and South Korea. This was well reflected through the Korean clause in the Nixon-Sato joint communiqué in 1969, which stipulated that the security of the Republic of Korea is essential to Japan's own security.[14] "If South Korea and Taiwan came under attack, Japan would regard it as a threat to the peace and security of the Far

East,"[15] and Japan would take prompt and positive measures such as allowing the United States to use its military base within Japan to respond to the armed attacks. The Korean clause allowed the United States to continue to have access to its military bases in Japan, which made up for the military vacuum caused by the reversion of Okinawa to Japan in 1972.[16]

The Korean clause, however, stirred a major policy debate in Japan. The Tanaka cabinet was pursuing a pragmatic diplomacy by taking advantage of the new détente mode. Japan's active rapprochement with China through the principle of the separation of politics and economy underscored this approach. Tanaka even wanted to undertake an equidistant diplomacy on the Korean peninsula, but the Korean clause, which stipulated a close security linkage between Japan and South Korea, was seen as a barrier to its diplomatic initiative to North Korea. Thus, the Tanaka cabinet reinterpreted the Korean clause in such a way that the entire Korean peninsula, not the Republic of Korea, is essential to Japan's security. Afraid of remaining a hostage to the Korean conflict, Japan wanted to detach itself from South Korean security, causing major diplomatic friction between the two countries.[17]

A series of events led to further deterioration in Japan–South Korean relations. The kidnapping of Kim Dae Jung, then a political dissident, from a Tokyo hotel in August 1973 seriously strained the bilateral relationship because the South Korea Central Intelligence Agency was suspected of being involved. The Mun Se-gwang incident made matters worse. Mun, a second-generation Korean resident in Japan, attempted to assassinate President Park Chung Hee on August 15, 1974, the Independence Day of the Republic of Korea. President Park narrowly escaped the assassination attempt, but lost his wife. Seoul-Tokyo ties hit rock bottom, overshadowing mutual security and economic cooperation.

The collapse of South Vietnam in the spring of 1975 precipitated major strategic rethinking in Japan. Japan feared the spread of a communist domino effect to the Korean peninsula because the collapse of South Korea at the hands of North Korea would pose a direct and grave threat to Japan. Departing from the previous position, the Takeo Miki cabinet reaffirmed the Korean clause and Japanese–South Korean bilateral relations became reactivated. Japan also resumed public loans to South Korea. More important, Premier Fukuda personally intervened and vigorously lobbied the Carter administration to suspend its decision to withdraw American forces from South Korea. Improved Japanese–South Korean ties were evidenced by an exchange of defense officials. The chief of staff of the Japanese Ground Self-Defense Forces and director of the Japanese Self-Defense Agency paid a visit to South Korea in 1979 for the first time.[18]

Entering the 1980s, the security landscape in East Asia was subject to another round of realignment. The Reagan administration's assertive pursuit of a new containment strategy fundamentally altered the security equation in the region. The cabinet of Yasuhiro Nakasone (1982–87) sought a dual strategy in coping with the new security environment. Nakasone endorsed and supported Reagan's new security posture and strengthened Japan's alliance with the United States through his personal ties with President Reagan. At the same time, he wanted to transform Japan from an economic into a political superpower, seeking to overcome the psychological barriers imposed by the Yoshida Doctrine, which portrayed Japan as a "follower" state. In order to prepare for global leadership, Nakasone argued, Japan needs to be remade into an international state and to assume a more proactive role in global strategic affairs.[19] He took some concrete measures to realize his vision, such as strengthening Japan's diplomatic foundation, increasing and actively utilizing overseas development assistance, and enhancing defense forces.[20]

The Nakasone initiative gave priority to East Asia. China drew his utmost attention. His preferential treatment of China exceeded that of the Ohira cabinet, which was regarded as being the most pro-China. On the occasion of his March 1984 visit to China, Nakasone pledged not only a second round of extensive public loans but also a long-term commitment to the modernization of China. His gifts to China were impressive: a $2.4 billion Export-Import Bank loan for energy development, a $2 billion commercial bank syndicate loan, joint development of nuclear energy, permission to raise Chinese public bonds in Japan, and implementation of overseas investment insurance to promote Japanese investment in China.[21] Nakasone wrote his impression of China in his diary immediately after the visit in the following way: "Conclusion of China visit. Reaffirmation of no war between China and Japan. China-Japan cooperation is vital to peace and stability in Asia and the world. Mutual promise not to allow war on the Korean peninsula. Need to strengthen ties with ASEAN, Europe, and China within the Japan-U.S. axis in order to counter the Soviet Union. Ready to accept frozen relationship with the Soviet Union."[22]

Nakasone's new Asian venture also included South Korea. He strongly believed that improved relations with South Korea are vital to Japan's national interests. Moreover, he realized the strategic value of a strengthened Japan-U.S.-South Korea axis in the context of the new cold war. On January 11, 1983, Nakasone paid the first official state visit of a Japanese prime minister to South Korea, agreeing on a $4 billion loan prior to his visit. The Chun Doo-hwan government in South Korea, which seized political power through a military coup in 1980, had requested that Japan provide a $6 billion loan for South Korea's economic recovery. South Korea linked economic recovery to its overall security in demanding the loan. Despite American pressure, however, the Suzuki cabinet refused to link the loan to Japanese and South Korean security ties, and the Seoul-Tokyo relationship had soured over the issue of loan negotiations. It was Nakasone who settled the issue, normalizing bilateral ties. In addition, Nakasone cultivated an intimate personal relationship with the new political leadership in South Korea.[23] Nakasone's pro-Korea moves were motivated by his strategic calculation to exercise Japan's political leadership in Asia as well as to consolidate the Japan-U.S.-ROK strategic triangle.[24] South Korea became a companion to Japan's new march toward Asian leadership through the 1980s.

The end of the cold war in the late 1980s triggered new discourse on the normalization of Japan.[25] Inspired by Ichiro Ozawa's proposal on a "normal state" (*futsu no kuni*), Japan's passive role in the first Gulf War, and domestic political debates on the dispatch of United Nations Peacekeeping Operation forces to Cambodia, a growing number of Japanese intellectuals argued that Japan should contribute to international security through the United Nations by going beyond the exclusive defense strategy, and such contributions would not violate the letter and spirit of the Peace Constitution as well as its security treaty with the United States.[26] Apart from the idea of Japan as a normal nation through active participation in UN-sponsored collective security, the mainstream policy makers and analysts favored the concept of collective defense by strengthening the existing alliance with the United States. Proponents of this line of strategic thinking soon were to argue that a strong bilateral alliance with the United States through Japan's own defense buildup and active support of U.S. military operations in the region are vital to coping with the rise of China as a regional and global power as well as ensuring strategic stability in the region.[27] Ultraconservatives such as Shintaro Ishihara went further by suggesting an independent strategy. They argued that Japan should pursue a strategy more independent of the United States and redefine its national security in more Asian terms. This position emphasizes a constitutional amendment so that Japan can become a normal military state and revision of the Japan-U.S. security treaty to reflect a more symmetric relationship. According to this approach, Japan's mission is to create a common peace and prosperity in East Asia by promoting Japan's political and economic leadership.[28]

Of these three contending visions, Japan's strategic thinking throughout the 1990s was framed around the second variant of continuing alliance with the United States. Japan's security relations with South Korea were also shaped by such strategic perimeters. Japan and South Korea did not have any institutionalized framework for security cooperation throughout the 1990s, and they maintained a quasi-alliance relationship through the American mediation. Beneath the status of quasi alliance lay sources of concern emanating from the collective memory of the historical past. The specter of Japanese militarism in the 1930s led some South Koreans to perceive Japan as a potential, if not actual, enemy, while some conservative elements in Japan envisage major potential threats coming from a unified Korea.[29] Moreover, both sides' territorial claims over Dokdo (or Takeshima) remained another source of mutual security concerns. Thus, security relations between Japan and South Korea in the 1990s can be seen as having been rather ambivalent. While the triangular security ties buttressed by American hegemonic leadership made Japan and South Korea quasi allies, historical memory of colonial domination and subjugation have became a constant source of tension and insecurity. The failure to overcome distrust through four decades of continued cold war, where the two sides shared allies and enemies, made it difficult to advance when enemies were no longer so clear.

Of course, a major improvement occurred during the Kim Dae Jung government (1998–2003), as evidenced by the 1998 Japan-ROK strategic partnership declaration between President Kim and Premier Keizo Obuchi. It included several significant elements for bilateral security cooperation. They were: (1) to prod North Korea to abide by the nonnuclear proliferation pact and to avoid the use of chemical weapons; (2) to hold regular consultative meetings on security policy as well as to strengthen the exchange of defense experts at various levels; (3) to jointly push for the establishment of a multilateral security forum; and (4) to strengthen policy consultation on North Korea in order to ensure peace and stability on the Korean peninsula (*Korea Times*, October 8, 1998). Security cooperation between the two countries had accelerated in part because of North Korea's test launching of Taepodong long-range missile on August 31, 1998. In September South Korean Defense Minister Chun Yong-taek met with his counterpart, Nukaga Fukushiro, in Tokyo to reach an agreement on joint efforts—in both policy and intelligence areas—to counter North Korea's missile program. With a commonly perceived threat from North Korea, the need for close security cooperation was one of the main topics discussed. Following Kim Dae Jung's visit to Japan in October 1998, the Korea-Japan Security Policy Coordination Council was put in place, and since 1999, the joint chiefs of staff of Japan and South Korea have held high-level staff meetings. The Japanese and South Korean navies also conducted a joint naval exercise for emergency relief in the southeastern part of Jeju Island (*Asahi shimbun*, August 6, 1999). In the maritime area where common interests intersect—sea-lines of communications, intelligence sharing, maritime interdiction, search and rescue —emphasis was placed on greater security cooperation, in spite of the existing limitations on operational exchanges. Maritime cooperation as such was in line with the new U.S.-Japanese Defense Guidelines that implicitly call for specific missions that require some degree of Japan–South Korea coordination.[30]

Security cooperation improvements notwithstanding, Japan and South Korea began to experience a major policy coordination problem on North Korea. The Kim Dae Jung government desperately needed Japan's assistance in accelerating its sunshine policy. Japan's steady support of the Korean Peninsula Energy Development Organization (KEDO) project, its economic assistance, especially through the official development assistance (ODA) framework, and ultimately diplomatic normalization with North Korea were integral parts to the success of the sunshine policy. Until August 1998, the Japanese government was also pursuing its own version of engagement policy aimed at inducing voluntary changes in the North through exchanges and cooperation.[31] But the test-launching of the Taepodong missile and suspicion of nuclear facilities in Kumchangri led Japan to suspended negotiations over diplomatic normalization with North Korea, freeze financial support to KEDO for light-water nuclear reactors in the North, and begin to restrict remittances to North Korea by Korean residents in Japan. Japan also decided to undertake joint research on Theater Missile Defense (TMD) with the United States and to acquire a spy satellite. Japan's shift to a hard-line posture on North Korea undercut South Korea's engagement policy. As Tsuneo Akaha discusses (chapter 11 of this volume), in 2000, when the sunshine policy was at its peak, and in 2003–4, when the nuclear crisis strained South Korean relations with Japan as well as the

United States, South Koreans and Japanese grew further apart in their reasoning on security. For a long time Japan did not have any coherent regional security policy of its own, and its security policy on South Korea was by and large influenced by the American factor. In the 1990s, however, North Korea emerged as another critical factor affecting Japan-ROK security relations.

Japan's Economic Regionalism and South Korea

Since the end of the Pacific War, Japan's regional economic maneuvering was fundamentally limited not only because of its reliance on multilateral economic order, but also because of the lingering memory of the Greater East Asian Co-Prosperity Sphere. Thus, Japan did not have any clearly defined regional economic policy until the late 1970s. Japan's reach into Asia was undertaken primarily through networks of trade, investment, and development assistance, which were by and large shaped by the complementarity of development strategies.[32] Japan was the pacesetter, whereas other Asian countries followed its lead, resulting in the flying geese formation of the intraregional division of labor. Emulation and replication of Japan's developmental experience and growing intraregional trade deepened the horizontal division of labor in the region, which moved steadily upward in levels of manufacturing sophistication.

Owing to the flying geese pattern of development strategy, intraregional trade has been on the rise, its share of trade in the Asian region having risen from 23 percent in 1980 to 40 percent in 1996. During this period, intra-Asian trade grew 9.49 times—much faster than Asian exports to the United States—while trade between East Asia and the United States increased by only 5.77 times. Meanwhile, during the same period, total Japanese trade with Asia grew from 31.3 percent to 42.4 percent, and, in 1991, the volume of Japanese exports to Asia for the first time surpassed that of exports to the United States. These flows can be expected to continue.

A similar trend can be found in Japan's foreign direct investment (FDI) in Asia, which increased dramatically due to the appreciation of the yen against the U.S. dollar since the Plaza Accord in 1985. The surging yen forced Japanese manufacturers to relocate their production lines to other Asian countries. Offshore production helped Japanese firms cope with protectionist barriers as well as ease the friction resulting from chronic bilateral trade surpluses with Asian countries. As a result, Japan's total investment in Asia rose from $2 billion in 1985 to $8.5 billion in 1995, putting Japan far ahead of the United States as the largest investor in Asia. The Heisei recession decreased Japan's overseas investments from $56.9 billion in 1990 to $36.2 billion in 2002, but the Asian share declined very slightly from $6.9 billion in 1990 to $5.1 billion in 2002. In the case of China, Japan's foreign direct investments grew from $349 million in 1990 to $1.95 billion in 2002.[33] Regionalization of Japanese firms has also been expedited since 1990. Japanese firms established 2,862 local corporate entities in Asian countries in 1990 (1,591 in East Asian newly industrialized economies [NIEs], 1,121 in ASEAN countries, and 150 in China). But the figure rose to 6,919 in 2000 (2,729 in East Asian NIES, 2,478 in ASEAN, and 1,712 in China).[34] Japan took advantage of the increased FDI in Asia to construct a regional division of labor that sustained Japan's business expansion and facilitated its domestic economic restructuring.

Japan has also been the number one donor of official development assistance in Asia. Although the recipient countries have increasingly spread throughout the world, Japanese aid is still concentrated in the Asian region. In 1994, $5.54 billion —equivalent to 57.3 percent of Japan's total ODA—went to Asia. Eight of Japan's ten largest recipients in 1996 were Asian countries—Indonesia, China, Thailand, India, the Philippines, Pakistan, Bangladesh, and Sri Lanka.[35]

Likewise, Japan actively pursued spontaneous regionalization through trade, investments, and overseas development assistance. Japan and South Korea had traditionally maintained complementary economic relations. While liberal international economic order created and sustained by the American hegemony allowed Japan and South Korea to enjoy the benefits of free riding, South Korea was deeply integrated into a horizontal division of labor. As an offshore production site, South Korea took huge advantage of Japan's export booms in the 1960s and early 1970s. But a major change came in the mid-1970s as South Korea ventured into heavy-chemical industrialization. The industrial structure in Japan and South Korea became almost identical, and both countries began to compete in similar market destinations with similar export items, entailing a situation of zero-sum competition.[36] The sensitivity of South Korean exports to the value of the Japanese yen underscores this relationship. Fluctuations of the yen have become the most reliable predictor of South Korean export performance. While a sharp appreciation in the yen leads to a South Korean export boom, its depreciation precipitates a drastic cut in South Korea's exports.

But the growing economic interdependence between Korea and Japan was not symmetric. It has entailed a structural dependency of the South Korean economy on Japan, which was manifested by chronic trade deficits. Thus, the South Korean government has been struggling to reduce these deficits. South Korea's trade deficits with Japan were $2.8 billion in 1980, but rose to $5.9 billion in 1990, $15.7 billion in 1996, and $13 billion in 2002, about a fivefold increase in twenty years. What is more troublesome is the disproportionate relationship between the volume of Japan-Korea trade and South Korea's trade deficits with Japan. While the ratio of South Korea's trade with Japan out of total trade decreased from 22.4 percent in 1980 to 15.2 percent in 1997 and 14 percent in 2002, its trade deficits with Japan have exponentially increased during the period.[37] The primary cause of the deficits lies in South Korea's excessive dependence on Japanese machinery and parts and components. Trade deficits with Japan in machinery including parts and components were $15.5 billion in 1996, accounting for 95 percent of the total deficits.[38] In addition, overall weakness in South Korea's competitive advantage, coupled with Japan's neomercantile trade practices, have been responsible for the deficits.[39]

South Korea–Japan trade friction resulting from the chronic trade deficits could have been eased or averted if there was a compensatory mechanism such as increased Japanese foreign direct investments in South Korea. But there has been a constant decrease in Japan's foreign direct investment in South Korea. Prior to 1980, Japan accounted for more than 35 percent of total foreign investment in South Korea. Since the late 1980s, Japanese investments have been sharply reduced not only because of the poor investment climate in South Korea (e.g., high wages and bureaucratic red tape), but also because of Japanese diversion into China and Southeast Asian countries. For example, Japan accounted for 27.4 percent of South Korea's total foreign investment in 1993, but it dropped to 7.9 percent in 1996 and 3.8 percent in 1997. Following the International Monetary Fund (IMF) crisis in 1998, there was a slight reversal of the trend, recording 14.9 percent. In the first half of 2002, Japanese investment in South Korea totaled $360 million, a share of 7.4 percent.[40] Compared with the size of trade deficits, the amount of Japan's foreign direct investment in South Korea has been rather insignificant since 1994.

It is the confluence of the competitive nature of industrial structure, chronic trade deficits, and poor investment relationships that has shaped the foundation of South Korea's economic calculus toward Japan. Forging a complementary bilateral industrial structure, coping with chronic trade deficits, and inducing Japanese foreign direct investment have become the primary policy concerns for the South Korean government. Thus, Japan's spontaneous economic regionalization through the market has been a rather mixed blessing to South Korea.

Japan has also deliberated on explicit forms of economic regionalism since the late 1980s. They are open regionalism, Japan's economic leadership in the region, and preferential trading arrangements (PTA). The idea of open regionalism first surfaced during the Ohira cabinet in the late 1970s. When Ohira took office as premier in December 1978, he commissioned Saburo Okita to form a study group on the Pan-Pacific Community,[41] and the idea was advanced to create a loose coalition among pan-Pacific countries in the economic and cultural areas. In advancing this idea, Japan formed a coalition with Australia. The Pan-Pacific Community idea helped Japan overcome its East Asian geographic boundary and project its reach across the entire Pacific Ocean. It can also be seen as a more independent economic diplomatic initiative.

The Reagan administration was skeptical of the Japanese proposal and suggested a rather informal approach. The Pacific Economic Cooperation Conference and the Pacific Basin Economic Council were formed and activated in this context. In the late 1980s, however, the Japanese government launched another initiative for open regionalism by officially declaring three principles. First, it should not exclude any other regions. Second, it should aim at forming open and interdependent economic relationships in the region. Third, it should be complementary to existing bilateral and multilateral relations. In order to implement these principles, several guidelines for policy engagement were suggested. The Japanese government should exercise leadership in forming an open regional organization, but its contribution should not be seen as pressure on other countries. It was also recommended that the Japanese government should present a clearly defined market-oriented development strategy that would enhance liberalization of trade, investments, and capital flow. Finally, it was also emphasized that any new regional cooperative organization should be more than a loose consultative framework. It needs to be institutionalized with its own secretariat and enforcement mechanism.[42]

In 1989, with Australia, Japan took the lead in initiating the Asia-Pacific Economic Cooperation (APEC) forum, which was designed to create open regionalism through the promotion of free trade, investment, and technology transfers within the Pacific basin. But Japan was reluctant to transform APEC into a more viable and formalized mechanism. Since the Seattle meeting in 1993, Japan has been treating it as a consultative body for regional trade and investment liberalization rather than as an institutionalized forum to evolve into a free trade area and customs union. Its emphasis on an Asian style of consensus building, relaxed discussion rather than tense negotiations, and gradual reduction of tariffs through discussion impeded the process of institutionalizing APEC.[43] Japan's efforts to protect its farm sector further undercut progress toward the formation of a free trade area in the region. Apparently, Japan was losing the will to pursue APEC as a way of enhancing intraregional economic cooperation.

South Korea shared sentiments similar to Japan. It, too, initially anticipated twin benefits from APEC: easy access to export markets and capital in the region's industrialized countries and a secure supply of raw materials from resource-rich countries such as Australia and the Southeast Asian countries. But slower progress in intraregional trade and investment liberalization, coupled with strengthening of the World Trade Organization, significantly diluted its strategic value. Interestingly, South Korea allied with Japan in resisting the American initiative to transform APEC into a more formalized free trade area. South Korea's protection of the agricultural sector as well as the rejection of the principle of early voluntary sectoral liberalization were testimonials to this. Japan and South Korea are likely to continue to favor gradualism, while opposing immediate implementation of a large-scale free trade area covering the entire Pacific Basin.

Since the early 1990s, the prewar ideology of a Greater Asia was resurrected, profoundly influencing the discourse on regional economic architecture.[44] It offers a tempting rationale for Japan's regional leadership in the economic and political arena. Okabe Tatsumi, for example, calls for a regional division of labor among Japan and Asian countries by arguing that the central task for Asia-Pacific cooperation is to carry out smoothly the adjustment of industrial structures, or the establishment of a division-of-labor structure, based on comparative superiority. He envisaged a Japan-centric regional economic structure based on the principal of comparative advantage.[45] In a similar vein, Kobayashi Yotaro, an influential business leader, has urged Japan's re-Asianization by asserting that Japan should find its identity and destiny in Asia because it cannot escape its cultural roots and geographical neighbors.[46] More provocative is Ishihara, who argues that Japan's future lies primarily in contributing to the creation of a dynamic and ever-growing Asian economic bloc, which can counterbalance the increasingly anti-Asian West.[47]

The resurgence of an Asian identity can be ascribed, in part, to the rise of anti-American sentiment, intensified by growing trade friction with the United States in the early 1990s, as well as to Japan's frustration over the disjuncture between its economic and political power in the international arena. However, the dynamic transformation of the East Asian economy and subsequently growing regional economic interdependence have played an equally important role in reviving Asian sentiment in Japan. It was in this context that despite the haunting memory of colonial domination and the Pacific War, some ASEAN countries were increasingly supportive of the idea. Malaysia's prime minister Mahathir Mohamad proposed the idea of the East Asia Economic Caucus, an exclusive East Asian trading bloc, to counter the emergence of protectionism and closed regionalism elsewhere in the world. The proposed idea was exclusive because it was supposed to be comprised of only the eleven Asian members of APEC—excluding the United States, Canada, Australia, and New Zealand.

South Korea was critical of the proposal, fearing Japan's economic dominance. Ironically, however, the Asian financial crisis in 1997 brought Japan and South Korea closer to the idea. As an extension of the new Asian awareness, Japan undertook a bolder regional economic initiative by proposing the formation of the Asian Monetary Fund (AMF). At a joint IMF/World Bank meeting held in Hong Kong in September 1997, the Japanese finance minister, Kubo Wataru, suggested the idea of forming the AMF in order to assist Southeast Asian countries under financial and foreign exchange crises through the provision of standby loans for current account deficits, extension of trade credits, and the facilitation of foreign exchange defense. The AMF was supposed to pool $100 billion of which $50 billion was to be drawn from Japan, and the remaining $50 billion from China, Hong Kong, South Korea, Taiwan, and Singapore. In parallel with the proposal, Japan was exercising its financial leadership. Since July 1997, Japan disbursed over $44 billion to Asian countries in financial crises through IMF-led bilateral cooperation, assistance for private investment activities, facilitation of trade financing and assistance for structural reforms, social safety nets, and human resources development.[48] As the financial crisis deepened, the Japanese government announced the Miyazawa Initiative in October 1998 through which Japan pledged to provide a package of support measures totaling $30 billion to assist Asian countries under financial crises.[49]

Despite such efforts, the idea of a Japan-centered AMF never materialized. Several factors explain this. The United States and IMF were rather critical of the AMF idea for the reasons of duplication, resource waste, and moral hazards associated with the relaxation of conditionalities. And the Japanese Ministry of Finance was rather cautious in steering the proposal primarily because of the enormous financial burden associated with the provision of collective goods. South Korea's responses to the AMF idea were mixed. The South Korean government initially opposed it for several reasons. First, as a recipient of IMF rescue financing, South Korea could not endorse what the United States and the IMF opposed. Second, South Korea realized its desirability, but was skeptical of its feasibility not only because of Japan's lukewarm commitment and leadership as well as its ailing economy, but also because of potential spillover effects on the creation of a yen bloc. Finally, national sentiments in South Korea would not tolerate Japan's hegemonic ascension in the region's economic sphere.

After having gone through the financial crisis in late 1997, however, South Korea gradually changed its attitude. Japan was the largest creditor nation, and it was most generous by extending $10 billion through the IMF rescue package and rolling over short-term loans. The Japanese government also turned one-third of the short-term loans (about $7.9 billion) into medium- to long-term loans. Crisis contributed to breeding new trust in Japan. As a result, both the government and the private sector began to make positive assessments of the AMF. The first positive signal came from the private sector. Delegates of the Federation of Korean Industries, the top organization representing big business in South Korea, made a quasi-public endorsement of the Miyazawa Initiative and the AMF on October 29, 1998, at its annual meeting with the Keidanren (Japanese Federation of Economic Organizations). They shared with Keidanren a view that there must be greater efforts toward internationalization of Japanese yen and that there is a need for official study of the AMF designed to stabilize the financial system in Asia (*Maegyung*, October 29, 1998). The South Korean government also began to endorse the idea cautiously.[50] Several factors facilitated this shift: the harsh IMF conditionalities, an expectation of a reduction of excessive dependence on the American dollar that deepened rigidity in foreign exchange operations, practical gains through reduced interest rate burden, and the increasing feasibility of AMF through an expanded credit pool of East Asian countries.[51]

Although the Japanese government did not have any immediate plan to establish the AMF (see Obuchi's interview with *Joongang Ilbo*, December 30, 1998), South Korea's endorsement of the AMF idea greatly enhanced mutual trust between the two countries. Given South Korea's deep-rooted distrust of Japan and blind catch-up race against it, this represented a profound development. Indeed, salience of economic gains made South Korea converge with Japan for economic survival and prosperity, gradually defying the old fear of Japanese domination and exploitation. Although the idea of the AMF was aborted by the lack of Japanese will, intention, and capability, this can be interpreted as one of the most remarkable positive externalities resulting from the 1997 financial crisis.

The most recent Japanese regional economic initiative took the form of a free trade agreement (FTA). Japan has been traditionally negative on bilateral or subregional preferential trading arrangements, while favoring the multilateral trading system. Since 1998, however, Japan has shifted its position by pushing for bilateral, subregional, and regional trading arrangements.[52] The spread of the Asian financial crisis, the consolidation of the European Union and the North American

Free Trade Agreement, and the stalemate of APEC forced Japan to venture into new policy alternatives such as a South Korea–Japan free trade area.[53] Japan believes that a Japan–South Korea FTA, along with one for Singapore, would produce positive spillover effects on its efforts toward ASEAN.

The South Korean government initially showed a positive response to Japan's proposal on an FTA. The first Japan–South Korea ministerial meeting under the Kim Dae Jung government, which was held in Kagoshima on November 28, 1998, recommended joint private and public research on the free trade area arrangement. The first official discussions on the Japanese-Korean FTA took place in 1999 within the framework of the Japan-Korea Economic Agenda 21, proposed by Prime Minister Obuchi. The Institute of Developing Economies (IDE) and JETRO of Japan and the Korea Institute for International Economic Policy (KIEP) of South Korea were officially commissioned to conduct research on the feasibility of the FTA. Their research findings were interesting. An analysis by IDE-JETRO shows that trade liberalization through the Japanese-Korean FTA would increase Japan's export to Korea by 16.3 percent, whereas South Korea's exports to Japan are expected to rise by 8.6 percent, leading to a 34.5 percent trade surplus for Japan. KIEP's research findings were very much congruent with those by IDE/JETRO: An FTA between Japan and South Korea would increase Japan's exports to Korea by 16 percent, resulting in an overall trade surplus of 37.1 percent for Japan.[54] Along with the short-term anticipated loss in trade, several other factors have made South Korea hesitant to pursue an FTA with Japan actively: political opposition from the agricultural sector, fear of Japan's economic domination over South Korea, and the legacy of mutual antagonism rooted in the historical past.[55]

Nevertheless, South Korea has been actively seeking its FTA with Japan under the Roh Moo-hyun government, precisely because of new strategic moves by China and Japan. China has shown a greater interest in establishing an FTA with ASEAN rather than with its Northeast Asian neighbors. In fact, China and ASEAN agreed to establish a bilateral FTA within a decade. In fear of China's initiative, Japan has also been expediting its FTA with ASEAN. South Korea's proposal to set up a Northeast Asian FTA has encountered a new challenge, with a widespread fear of being left out by China and Japan. In order to cope with this change, South Korea is giving more serious attention to its bilateral FTA with Japan. Given the structure of domestic opposition, its feasibility still seems remote. However, South Korean policy makers are increasingly realizing the strategic importance of an FTA with Japan.

Conclusion

Over the fifteen years since the end of the cold war, Japan has shown great interest in strengthening its regional position in East Asia, but it has had difficulty finding an effective strategy for dealing with the Korean peninsula. Looking back to the cold war era and its immediate aftermath, we can observe the seeds of Japan's

problems. The 1965 normalization of diplomatic relations with South Korea occurred without any effort to resolve sharply conflicting differences in views of
history. Three decades later the same issues troubled public opinion on both sides.
Although it was demonstrated in October 1998 that a bold Korean leader in the
right circumstances could agree to leave the history issue aside, public opinion
and leading politicians on each side had not accepted the logic of forward thinking. They failed to make substantial progress when they were thrown together in
the cold war as U.S. allies, when they drew closer as economic partners with few
other nearby partners in Asia, and even when South Korea joined Japan as a democratic state. Rising Japanese nationalism after the cold war would exacerbate the
perception in Korea of offensive justifications of the past and more outspoken
campaign rhetoric and parliamentary remarks in Korea would leave the Japanese
ill at ease. Japan's reentry into Asia has been rather reactive, gradual, and constrained. While the United States has fundamentally delimited the scope of its
regional leadership projection, Asian countries' collective memory of Japan as an
abrasive colonial power has impeded its full reentry into Asia. Despite its economic power and growing political influence, Japan's Asian regionalism can be
seen as an incomplete and uncertain venture.

Although the U.S.-Japan-ROK trilateral axis has facilitated a quasi alliance
between Tokyo and Seoul, the bilateral security ties have remained more formal
than substantive, and their cohesion is very much dependent upon the United States.
During the cold war a shared sense of threat led to some expansion of security ties,
mostly under U.S. pressure, but they did not deepen much or lead to a shared sense
of geopolitical challenges. Soon thereafter, different views of Russia became evident, as Japan refocused on its territorial dispute, along with sharply different assessments of a potential security threat from China. In addition, a divergent threat
perception of North Korea in recent years is posing a major barrier to shaping a
new frontier of common security between the two. Already in the cold war era,
coordination on North Korea at times was missing, and in 1990 Japan again showed
that it was prepared to act independently.

In contrast, on the economic front, Japan and South Korea have proved over
many years that they are interested in working hard to enhance bilateral relations.
The 1997 Asian financial crisis and recent FTA movements eloquently demonstrate that the two countries can cooperate closely in the face of common challenges such as American economic checks and balances, China's economic
ascension, and increasing cohesion among ASEAN members. If until the early
1990s the pattern of common responses was still mostly framed around protection
of domestic industries, later we observe more willingness to accept open, rather
than closed, regionalism, given their shifting economic orientation.

Unresolved legacies such as disputes over past history, the tribute to the Yasukuni
Shrine, and a clash of ultraconservative nationalist sentiments can still complicate
the Japanese–South Korean bilateral relations. They could literally wipe out trust
dividends resulting from cooperation in the security and economic areas, and,

recently as tourism has grown rapidly and Korea is relaxing its cultural barriers, in sociocultural areas. Thus, healing the fractured pains of the past and recognizing or adjusting to each other's national identity are as crucial as improving security and economic relations. Without addressing and resolving the issues of history and identity, the bilateral relationship may not be able to get away from the recurring pattern of suspicion and distrust, clouding the prospects for future cooperation. The cold war era started Japan along a path of reentering Asia without striving to make South Korea a close partner. Right after the cold war, Japan proceeded either by taking the Koreans for granted or by bypassing them. Only at the end of the 1990s did it shift direction; yet differences on China and North Korea have intensified just as economic agreement and bilateral cultural linkages have been growing. The legacy of Japan's relations with South Korea in the cold war is an important factor slowing the emergence of regionalism in East Asia.

Part III

Toward a Broad Regionalism?

Northeast Asia is on the move. In his inaugural address in February 2003, South Korean President Roh Moo Hyun said, "In this new age, our future can no longer be confined to the Korean peninsula. The Age of Northeast Asia is fast approaching. Northeast Asia, which used to be on the periphery of the modern world, is now emerging as a new source of energy in the global economy." Roh further noted,

> Koreans have lived through a series of challenges and have responded to them. Having to live among big powers, the people on the Korean Peninsula have had to cope with countless tribulations. . . . Within the half-century since liberation from colonial rule, and despite territorial division, war, and poverty, we have built a nation that is the twelfth-largest economic power in the world.

Referring to the divisions of the past as a point of contrast, Roh called for South Korea to embrace the growing regionalism in Northeast Asia, and to play a leading role in defining it. Korea should no longer be the shrimp caught between whales, he implied, but should become the hub of a wheel with collaborative spokes integrating all of its neighbors into a single unit, a wheel ready to roll on the road of a globalized economy.

Was Roh deluded? In some ways, South Korea is well placed to be this hub. Geographically, it is located at the center of the region, a position that has doomed it to be the arena of contest in the past but might now make it the meetinghouse of cooperation. Economically, it is increasingly integrated with both Japan and China, and Korean foreign direct investment (FDI) is serving as a mechanism for production technology transfer to China. Politically, the constant security question of North Korea has evolved into a regional question: Given North Korea's development of missiles and nuclear weapons, South Korea has become an essential component of regional security considerations. Culturally, South Korea has both relaxed its restrictions on foreign cultural imports and begun exporting its own culture to its neighbors. At the same time, however, there are limitations on the role South Korea could play in the Northeast Asian regional environment. While the Republic of Korea (ROK) is the world's twelfth largest economy, Japan is the second largest, China the sixth largest (with a far higher position in the offing). Japan, China, and Russia all have larger populations than South Korea, and the expanses of China and the Russian Far East contain greater natural resource endowments. North Korea can be as much a burden to South Korea's leadership as a facilitator. And South Korea lacks the history of regional leadership that China, Japan, and Russia can each claim, although these claims differ in degree and type.

Gilbert Rozman's chapter traces the recent history of ROK involvement in regional cooperation. Beginning with South Korea's successful manipulation of the changing conditions at the end of the cold war to normalize relations with both Moscow and Beijing, it has been able to launch a number of initiatives aimed at a broader cooperation among its neighbors. Since that time, however, the confrontation between the United States and North Korea over the latter's nuclear program has been a major stumbling block to further regional integration. Successful resolution of the nuclear standoff with North Korea would likely give a boost to the South's central role, helping it to minimize the costs of reintegration with the North, to stabilize security that reduces its dependency on the United States, and to achieve a four-power balance conducive to regionalism. Yet, given China's high expectations for regional leadership and continued suspicion of Japanese nationalism, Rozman offers some reasons why South Korea will not be able to step swiftly into the role of regional leader. In particular, it will be difficult for South Korea to balance use of the North Korean security issue as a means of facilitating regional interaction while assuaging U.S. distrust of regionalism in an area it considers vital to its interests and that it fears will before long fall under China's sway.

Samuel S. Kim points out that many of the questions of regional leadership have to do with the ongoing formation of national identity in Northeast Asia. Russia, having been distanced by its nonrole in the 1994 Agreed Framework between the United States and North Korea (DPRK, or Democratic People's Republic of Korea), has searched for alternative ways to assert its regional presence. President Vladimir Putin has done so in part by intensifying the quality of diplomatic relations with the DPRK. The North Korean threat, meanwhile, has contributed to the reemergence of a pronounced nationalism in Japan, which itself has spawned nationalist fervor in South Korea and China (PRC, or People's Republic of China). If this spreading nationalism is of a virulent strain, regional efforts will become much more difficult. The catalyst for regionalism in Northeast Asia seems to be China more than South Korea, according to Kim. Having abandoned its idiosyncratic global orientation at the end of the cold war, China's continued consciousness of acting the role of a responsible great power will have much to do with the success of future efforts toward regionalism.

Turning to Japan, Tsuneo Akaha argues that developments in Asia, particularly in its northeastern subregion, have encouraged Japan to "reenter Asia." The benefits of economic integration in Northeast Asia, the urgency of the North Korean nuclear crisis, and the need to develop a multilateral security framework in Northeast Asia beyond the nuclear crisis have both promoted and complicated Japan's efforts to balance its bilateral and multilateral interests in the region. Addressing the North Korea threat can serve as a facilitator for Northeast Asian regionalism. Japan's concerns about the DPRK are currently hindering regional efforts because of a Japanese preference for unilateral and bilateral approaches, particularly over the abduction issue, but trilateral coordination with the ROK and the United States might lead to a broader regionalism in the future. The clarity of Japan's regional orientation is hindered in part by the on-again, off-again pattern of inter-Korean talks and by the opaqueness of U.S. goals toward the DPRK. Japan and South Korea, according to Akaha, are increasingly coordinating their security positions, supporting a U.S. regional presence and also a U.S. nonaggression commitment toward North Korea. Akaha concludes that Japan should contribute to a multilateral solution to the nuclear crisis and seek diplomatic normalization with the DPRK, even if that means Japan may have to tone down its demands on the abduction issue.

Jae Ho Chung, employing Lowell Dittmer's theory of strategic triangles, describes the increasing cooperation between South Korea and China, to the point that ROK-PRC relations have become an independent variable in U.S. consideration of Northeast Asia. The triangular relations involving China and South Korea have evolved from stable marriages—when the ROK was the clear enemy of the PRC-DPRK marriage and the PRC was the clear enemy of the U.S.-ROK marriage—to romantic triangles. New bonds of friendship between the governments in Beijing and Seoul have alienated former partners—Pyongyang and Washington, respectively. The United States remains most enamored of Japan, meanwhile, with all other potential suitors casting a wary eye in its direction. In fact, Chung argues, the attraction of the United States and China to each is key for the region: If these unlikely partners can maintain cordial relations, it will facilitate Northeast Asian regionalism; if not, regional efforts are unlikely to come to fruition. For Korea, no less than for Japan or Russia, there is little to leverage U.S.-PRC relations.

Russia has had a singularly difficult time maintaining leverage in Northeast Asia. Using archival materials from the Russian State Archive of Contemporary History, Evgeny P. Bazhanov describes Moscow's frustration in first leaning entirely toward South Korea, and then again when it partially reversed itself and reembraced the North. One of Russia's specific goals in improving relations with Seoul was to guide Russian entrance into regional organizations, but South

Korean displeasure with Russia's faltering finances and political and economic instability drove Moscow back toward Pyongyang, leading to the 2001 Moscow summit between Kim Jong Il and Vladimir Putin. But Russian attitudes toward the DPRK again cooled after the September 11 terrorist attacks, George Bush's axis-of-evil speech, and the October 2002 emergence of the second nuclear stand-off. Bazhanov's chapter helps explain Russia's frustrations at trying to become involved in an integrated Northeast Asian regionalism.

To assess the patterns of regionalism and the prospects for future regional collaboration, Shin-wha Lee looks at the environmental arena. According to Lee, Northeast Asia is ripe for cooperation on environmental issues, given the number of transboundary pollution, natural-resource, and energy-security problems in the region. From the yellow dust that sweeps through Mongolia, China, and Korea to the rising use of nuclear energy in the face of oil scarcity, there are a number of issues around which regional collusion could grow. While a few small international regimes have developed or been active in Northeast Asia, Korea has made the most of its environmental suggestions in bilateral settings. Lee argues that current cooperation could evolve in sustained regional regimes and that this is more likely than action by extant international organizations or the explicit creation of an environmental regime. Environmental issues provide Korea with a space in which to consolidate its regional leadership.

Korea has also taken on a new leadership role in a somewhat unexpected domain: that of culture. One way that Northeast Asia has become a defined region is via the distinctions of international media conglomerates. Jung-Sun Park describes how this has led to the export of Korean television and film to hungry markets in Taiwan and China, where other sources have either dried up or have been found politically incompatible. Korean fashion styles have in turn become common on the streets of Shanghai and Taipei. The future status of Korean cultural production will depend on the growth of China's and Taiwan's own cultural production industries. Park offers the prediction that the prominence of the "Korean wave" will decline but the contents of Korean culture will become ingrained in the everyday life of those cultures where it is now popular. On a grander scale, we cannot discount the impact that growing cultural awareness and transculturation can have on regional conversation and cooperation.

The balance sheet? The centripetal forces of increasing economic interaction and multilateral security arrangements are meeting the centrifugal forces of nationalism and differing opinions on security management in Northeast Asia. Further, many of the countries of the region are in flux regarding their national identities and how these relate to the region as a whole. Clearly, much hinges on China. Should China decide to continue to act the role of responsible great power, and should this continue to coincide with U.S. goals in the region, the prospects of a successful broad regionalism seem strong. But the potential explosiveness of the North Korean security issue and the possible resurgence of national animosities dampen optimism. In terms of South Korea's role in this regionalism, the key evolution has already occurred: Korea is no longer the marginal shrimp, but a pivotal player in Northeast Asian economics, security, and culture. In continuing to spread its cultural production and in continuing to build the bilateral components of larger regional regimes, South Korea has a number of avenues by which it could play a leadership role. With this in mind, Roh's pledge to devote his "whole heart and efforts" to bringing the Age of Northeast Asia to fruition "at the earliest possible time" may seem neither a delusion nor an empty promise.

South Korean President Roh Tae Woo and Soviet President Mikhail Gorbachev complete normalization talks in Moscow, December 1990. (Reproduced with permission of the Office of the Secretary of the President, Republic of Korea.)

Russian President Vladimir Putin, right, and North Korean leader Kim Jong Il shake hands during their meeting at the Kremlin in Moscow, August 2001. (AP/ Wide World Photos)

Semiconductor plant in Cheonan, South Korea. (Reproduced with permission of Samsung Electronics.)

Incheon airport. (Reproduced with permission of Incheon International Airport.)

A large section of a container ship is hoisted into place in a Hyundai Heavy Industry Co. Ltd. Shipyard in Ulsan, South Korea on Thursday, August 12, 2004. (Seokyong Lee/Bloomberg News/Landov)

Marketing popular Korean soap operas abroad in Asia. (Reproduced with permission of the Korean National Tourism Organization.)

Website advertising the development of New Songdo City. (Reproduced with permission of KPF [The Masterplan Architect Company] and Gale International.)

Map of Northeast Asia today

9

Regionalism in Northeast Asia

Korea's Return to Center Stage

Gilbert Rozman

When one power dominates in Northeast Asia, Korea has little room to assert itself. Such was the case for most of a millennium when China's tributary state system operated, again for close to half a century when Japanese imperialism was ascendant, and most recently for nearly half a century as South Korea depended on the United States during the cold war. At times of relative balance in the region, however, Korea becomes the object of rivalry. In the 1590s, a newly unified Japan, with unprecedented mobilization of armed power and economic strength, tested its prowess by challenging China's hegemonic role in Korea. In the 1890s, as Japanese and Russian power grew, Korea became the proving grounds for their expansion. After World War II, a divided Korea again became engulfed in war as the Soviet Union, along with the newly established People's Republic of China, and the United States measured their strength in Northeast Asia. Finally, after the end of the cold war, a still-divided Korea drew the attention of four great powers. What makes the period since 1989 different is that South Korea is taking the initiative, seeking in the shadow of tensions over North Korea and in the glow of rising hopes for regionalism an opportunity to shape the balance of power and the pattern of economic integration in Northeast Asia.

In the late 1980s, Americans pointed to South Korea as the crowning achievement of their postwar strategy, combining cold war protection by troops that paid the greatest peacetime sacrifice of any U.S. forces, open-market modernization that tolerated the most protectionism of any U.S. trade partner, and, finally, democratization that set the most glaring contrast with a communist rival. If Japan had long been proclaimed the standard of U.S. success with an ally, and Taiwan, despite being shunted aside as a nonstate, was proving to a reforming China through its democratization that the U.S. model worked, South Korea captured the spotlight as the all-around tribute to American sacrifice. As defenders of freedom, an economic miracle, and a democracy, the Republic of Korea (ROK) presented few complications for U.S. foreign policy. This was as reliable an ally as the United States could have outside NATO: (1) dependent on the United States for its very survival; (2) drawing its economic lifeblood from the U.S. market; (3) caught in a secure web of triangular economic ties with its old nemesis Japan that only tightened the U.S. embrace; and (4) sharing fundamental American values, amid three continental neighbors whose values seemed to offer no appeal.

Who would have anticipated the story of how over fifteen years South Korea turned into the centerpiece of regional diplomatic balancing, often to the discomfort of the United States? It can be told in stages, as Seoul strengthened its standing in the midst of great-power strategic recalculations. In 1990 Moscow abandoned Pyongyang for Seoul, but in 1996 it started to woo Pyongyang again, and in early 2000 it positioned itself, with Seoul's blessing, to be the chief intermediary between the two. In 1992 Beijing recognized Seoul, and in 1994 its pivotal role rose in the first nuclear crisis between the North and the United States. Integrating economically with South Korea at an extraordinary pace while supplying the North with vital oil and foodstuffs, Beijing raised its profile as an indispensable force for the peninsula, a presence that would be confirmed in the nuclear crisis of 2003–5. In 1998, Tokyo and Seoul reached agreement on the highly sensitive history issue that had kept arousing the Korean public and creating a backlash among the Japanese public. In the fall of 2000, Tokyo made new overtures to Pyongyang that eventually resulted in the September 2002 summit. Supporting all of these initiatives, the South Korean government helped to create an environment that would position it adroitly to manage the fundamental antagonism between North Korea and the United States.

In contrast to the cold war era, South Korea's political outreach extended to all four of the remaining actors in peninsular affairs, beyond just the United States. Acceptance of Russia as a special partner, political and cultural reconciliation with Japan, economic integration with China, and the sunshine policy to North Korea formed the background for a Korea able to say "no" to the United States. South Koreans had come to trust multidirectional diplomacy no less than the U.S. military. They foresaw regional economic ties anchored in China to be more important for their future prosperity than American markets.[1] Still ambivalent about Japan, they rejected the Bush administration's early push for a strong triangular alliance, while also delaying agreement with Prime Minister Junichiro Koizumi's call for a bilateral free trade agreement (FTA) without China.[2] National unity, shared Confucian traditions, and regional interests all eclipsed democracy and U.S.-led globalization as guiding forces in Seoul's foreign policy.

In mid-2003, the insecurity of the standoff between Washington, which demanded a nuclear-free Korea, and Pyongyang, which insisted on developing nuclear weapons at least in the absence of security guarantees, left South Korea aware of its own limitations in exerting influence on either side. As Japan drew closer to the United States and global investors pulled back, the newly elected president, Roh Moo Hyun, had little option but to give his agreement to trilateral coordination. The absence of a news conference at a May summit with George W. Bush, the refusal to associate his country with the word "pressure" on the North at a June summit with Junichiro Koizumi, and the image of a meeting of the minds in a July summit with Hu Jintao revealed, as Roh made the rounds of the South's three main partners, that differences remained. When six-party talks convened in Beijing on August 27–29, the South shared the dismay of China and Russia that the United States did not address the North's security concerns and North Korea threatened to test a nuclear bomb. As long as the crisis intensified, Seoul could do little to shape regional relations.

As the nuclear crisis dragged along and Roh rapidly lost popularity at home for "amateur politics,"[3] the challenge of steering his country through the minefield of great-power relations grew more onerous. Yet Roh rebounded in 2004, gaining vindication in April National Assembly elections, seeing a U.S. offer at the June six-party talks as a step forward and claiming the role of "balancer" for his country. In early 2005 he was at odds with the United States and critical of Japan as he charted a new course.

Increasingly, three challenges became intertwined in Seoul's quest to place itself at the center. The first challenge was the difficulty of drawing Pyongyang into sustained summitry and security arrangements. The geopolitics of peninsular and great-power relations remained the centerpiece in diplomacy. Second, Seoul gave growing attention to the economics of overcoming the North's deteriorating situation and starting the process of reunification. Under President Kim Dae Jung, steps to develop economic ties advanced not only directly with the North but also indirectly with neighbors encouraged by Seoul. Third, beyond efforts linked to North Korea, Seoul was playing a leading role in boosting Northeast Asian regionalism. This chapter concentrates on regionalism, while suggesting linkages with the geopolitics involving North Korea and the economic strategy to draw the North closer to the South. Looking back at seven stages in the transition from cold war to war against terror and the spread of weapons of mass destruction (WMD), we can spotlight the growing South Korean confidence despite the financial crisis that hit in 1997 and the cycles of presidential politics as one leader after another started fast but eventually faded in the polls.

While all eyes are fixed in 2005 on the geopolitical struggle involving North Korea, a more compelling long-term question is how regionalism will evolve in Northeast Asia and what its relationship to globalization and the U.S.-shaped world order will be. China, Japan, Russia, and South Korea all keep regionalism in mind when they deal with North Korea and each other. As the dynamics of regionalism have changed over the past fifteen years, so too has South Korea's place in the strategies of the other great powers. In turn, the South keeps adjusting its own calculations about how it can best shape the course of regionalism while enlisting the powers in steps to integrate North Korea into the region, inducing economic reform as the key to its transformation.

South Korea's Place in Regionalism at the End of the Cold War

In the mid-1980s, as South Koreans prepared for the Seoul Olympics, Northeast Asia was being transformed. China's economic reforms accelerated, spreading the open door policy to cities looking across at South Korea. At the 1986 Asian Games in Seoul, a large group of Chinese athletes increased the visibility of bilateral contacts that had accelerated in 1983 with cooperation over the hijacking of a Chinese plane. Already in the presidential campaign of 1987, Roh Tae Woo stressed the goal of diplomatic relations with China along with development of the coastal areas facing it. Trade had risen from $120 million in 1983 to $3.087 billion by 1988.[4] No wonder South Koreans eyed China hopefully, both economically and politically, as a power that could influence the North.

Hopes for the Soviet Union were more muted, despite the fact that Moscow gave a higher priority to great power relations than to support for North Korea.[5] Yet, after "new thinking" drew the Kremlin into intensified talks with China and Japan as well as the United States and led to media praise for Korea's economic strategy, in July 1988, Roh Tae Woo announced his "northern strategy" to start with cultural exchanges and trade in order to achieve diplomatic ties, and, eventually, pressure North Korea to negotiate.[6] As the Soviet economy deteriorated, Seoul grew hopeful about the possibility of using economic assistance as a lever to reduce Moscow's military and economic support for Pyongyang.

A newly democratic South Korea did not overcome popular animosity to Japan. In 1983, Prime Minister Yasuhiro Nakasone made the first state visit since the 1965 normalization, and this was followed by a return visit of Korea's president Chun Doo Hwan. Yet, there was no progress on the treatment of Koreans in Japan, market opening to reduce South Korea's large trade deficits, technology transfers from Japan, or signs of engagement of North Korea by Japan.[7] When in 1985 Nakasone made the first official visit by a premier to the Yasukuni Shrine and then, in 1986, Japan's education minister raised the history issue by suggesting in an interview that Korea voluntarily united with Japan in 1910 about the same time that textbook revisions whitewashed occupational policies in Korea, Tokyo had forfeited its chance to earn the goodwill of the Korean people.[8]

The United States did not do enough to build goodwill either. Among the demonstrators who led the democracy movement were students who considered the United States complicit in the bloody repression in 1980 of the Kwangju student demonstrators and were riled by Ronald Reagan's later embrace of its perpetrator, President Chun, and his authoritarian rule. Although the United States eventually welcomed Korean democracy, it failed to take reassuring measures, such as relocating army bases, to address widespread anti-Americanism among some parts of the population. Shortsightedly, Americans took South Korea for granted.

As the 1980s ended, the United States triumphantly preached a more active globalization, accompanied by sharper criticisms of South Korean protectionism. Japan optimistically boasted of its great economic power that would now be converted into political power, especially through reentry into Asia.[9] Both of these developments left South Koreans uneasy. They feared that their leverage, already very low, would be reduced further.

In the year 1990, two developments offered promise that the momentum of the

Seoul Olympics would be sustained. First, China in the face of sanctions after its bloody repression of demonstrators in Tiananmen Square made regional diplomacy and economic ties its priority. This gave an opening to Seoul. Second, Russian leaders after failing to reach an understanding with Pyongyang decided to abandon its former ally. For a promise of $3 billion in loans and assistance, South Korea won diplomatic relations and an abrupt change in the geopolitics of the region.[10] Rather than relying on U.S. leadership in economic and security globalization or Japan's strategy for regionalism, Seoul could explore its own agenda.[11] Joint admission with North Korea into the United Nations was but the first of many steps anticipated on the path to multilateral diplomacy.

South Korea's Place in Decentralized Regionalism of the Early 1990s

From 1990 to 1993, Japan Sea coastal prefectures, led by Niigata and Ishikawa, pressed for grass-roots regionalism under the label "the Sea of Japan Rim Economic Sphere." At the same time, northeastern provinces of China, led by Heilongjiang and Jilin, championed Northeast Asian regionalism through "border fever" and the "Tumen River Area Delta Development Program." To the north, Russian regional administrations, with Primorskii Krai and Khabarovsk Krai in the forefront, seized the opportunity of Boris Yeltsin's advocacy of decentralization in his struggles for power against, first, Mikhail Gorbachev and, then, the Russian Supreme Soviet to gain control over exportable items and to open their borders to consumer goods and joint ventures. South Korea stood in the middle in this craze for "borderlessness" by forces that did not trust openness and were doubtful about their own competitiveness in a market environment.[12]

South Korea offered each of its three neighbors the promise of close partnership in cross-border networks without committing itself heavily. Korean scholars and officials attended conferences on the Sea of Japan Rim, urging a name change to the "East Sea Rim" without showing much enthusiasm for Japan's leadership ambitions.[13] Yet they did not object if Japan invested more in infrastructure along this sea with likely payoff for parts of South Korea that had been left behind as well as enticement for North Korea to reform and open its borders. Gradually, the Pusan-Fukuoka connection was developing, where the two countries were in closest proximity, even if it did not have much spillover to the rim of the sea. Taking South Koreans for granted without building trust by calming anger over historical issues, the Japanese could not have expected close ties in regionalism.[14]

South Korean support for Jilin's Korean autonomous region also proved to be superficial. Interest in the Tumen River area project depended on North Korea's approval for building an international city on its border and granting access to the sea to the Chinese and others, an outcome never approved. Seoul would have preferred to proceed with direct ties across the Thirty-eighth Parallel. While it invested in Korean communities on the Chinese side of the Tumen River, assisting the city of Hunchun and offering jobs to Korean Chinese who came to South Korea on temporary permits, most investments went to Shandong Province and the large cities of North China. They solidified bilateral economic ties with China under Seoul's firm leadership, but they did little for local networks further north. Economic success with China did not expand into regionalism.

In the Russian Far East, South Koreans showed more interest than anyone else in showcase projects, while keeping their eye on Moscow for geopolitical purposes. They would have liked to encourage Koreans who had been disbursed into Central Asia in the 1930s to return to the Primorskii Krai around Vladivostok, but Russians, fearful of their competition and of territorial claims for the Khasan area, permitted only small numbers to make their way back. If Seoul corporations promised to develop an industrial park in the promised free economic zone of Nakhodka, they were thwarted by reluctance in Moscow to pass the necessary legislation. When later firms did establish workplaces for as many as fifteen thousand textile workers in an effort to export to the United States, they found turnover to be high and productivity low, leading to the hiring of Chinese to work in Russia.[15] If economic linkages expanded for a time, South Koreans were no more successful than others in overcoming the arbitrariness and lawlessness of Russia's Far East.

Even within South Korea decentralization peaked in the first half of the 1990s only to lose vitality as it became clear that the fierce competition of globalization made reliance on the modern economic forces of the Seoul metropolitan area essential. If cross-border linkages were to succeed, they would need to draw primarily on the capital area. One suggestion called for an urban corridor called BESETO from Beijing to Tokyo with Seoul in the center.[16] Another linked the new metropolitan airport at Inchon across the Yellow Sea with a corner of Shandong Province. A third that eventually drew substantial attention pointed to three routes across the demilitarized zone (DMZ) linking the Seoul area to North Korea: (1) the Kumgang Mountain tourist route in the east; (2) the Kyesong city industrial zone in the west; and (3) the "iron silk road" railroad corridor near the middle. After "borderless" regionalism faded in the mid-1990s, more limited cross-border strategies persisted. Most successfully, South Koreans kept investing across the Yellow Sea, big firms following small ones and bilateral trade skyrocketing toward about $50 billion in 2004 on the verge of surpassing South Korean trade with its longstanding number one partner, the United States.

South Korea in Search of a Civilizational Path to Regionalism in the Mid-1990s

Before the Asian financial crisis, South Koreans took pride in the stunning success of their economic miracle, attributing it in part to cultural factors. In the heyday of the Asian-values debate, many argued that Korean Confucian values, the developmental state, and special social qualities accounted for the edge achieved in economic growth.[17] It did not hurt that in the first half of the 1990s, the Chinese showed keen interest in the South Korean model. After archrival Japan saw its bubble economy burst, Koreans took added satisfaction from their continued rapid growth to 1997. Crossing the threshold of $10,000 per capita income and entering the Organization for Economic Cooperation and Development club of developed states, South Korea yielded to pressures to open its financial markets without realizing that they would expose serious flaws in economic management and permit the contagion that would hit Southeast Asia to put an abrupt end to the claims of civilizational superiority popular through the mid-1990s.

It was Japan's strategy to become a cultural great power that boosted the theme of East Asian civilization through the 1980s. Although often narrowly linked to nationalist pride in Japan's uniqueness, gradually the theme became associated with the rise of an entire region. After the collapse of the socialist bloc and global condemnation of China in 1989, the Chinese embraced the theme of "Eastern civilization" too. In 1993–94, double-digit growth and World Bank recalculation of Chinese GDP on the basis of purchasing power parity boosted confidence. Beijing had managed to shift attention from its membership in the failed group of socialist states to an identity as a "dynamic" East Asian state.[18] While Japanese were still downplaying nationalism and accentuating a shared past imbibing the region's great tradition rather than the imperialist half-century as regional tormentor,[19] these were ideal circumstances for Koreans to seek advantage as the most Confucian of East Asian societies, the best judge of whether Japan could shed one historical mantle for another, and China's restored partner ready to reciprocate for its historic role as teacher.

Civilizational themes did not create a firm foundation for regionalism. They put a bulwark in the path of necessary adjustments to the onrushing forces of globalization, serving narrow vested interests. China's main objective was multipolarity, appealing to Russia to join in resisting the cultural as well as the geopolitical implications of U.S. global leadership. South Korea, as Japan, had modernized with unusually protected domestic markets and inward-looking citizens and sought to block the essential opening that was expected after the abnormal cold war atmosphere was ended. Appeals to values reinforced defensiveness in the face of mounting pressures, both regional and global.

Instead of shared memories of more than a millennium of Confucian traditions, the civilizational theme drew attention to divisive memories of Japan aiming to obliterate Korean culture and to conquer China. In 1995–96, the history theme inflamed passions. Instead of using the fiftieth anniversary of the war's end to offer a final reassurance to its victims worthy of a nation intent on rebuilding trust, the Japanese rallied around a reassertion of nationalism that whitewashed critical aspects of their nation's conduct. By 1996, the Liberal Democratic Party had regained political domination, dispensing with socialists such as Murayama Tomoichi, who as prime minister had tried in 1995 to make a far-reaching apology. From the perspective of Koreans, Japan's lack of trust and understanding in them made closer ties difficult.[20] A wave of books in the mid-1990s in Korea on Japan heightened the distrust.

South Korea in Great-Power Balancing in the Late 1990s

From 1996 to 1998 South Korea lost ground in Northeast Asia. Bilateral relations with Japan and Russia deteriorated for a time, while the Asian financial crisis left a bad aftertaste toward the United States. Relations with North Korea showed no sign of progress. When the four great powers in the region explored strategic partnerships and breakthroughs in relations, the South stayed in the shadows, lacking leverage to shape the process. Under International Monetary Fund (IMF) receivership, Seoul kept a low profile. Until Kim Dae Jung launched a sweeping revamping of relations with each power after the great-power jockeying had reached an impasse by early 1999, the South appeared sidelined in the jockeying to reshape a region.

China's assertiveness led in transforming the dynamics of regionalism. Although economic ties with South Korea kept expanding, China gave priority to geopolitics in forging strategic triangles and made Russia the prime target.[21] Seoul could not expect Beijing's help with Pyongyang or a multilateral security framework that would stabilize the region. Moscow reciprocated Beijing's interest, calculating that Seoul had little to offer strategically or even economically, and turned its attention increasingly to restoring ties with Pyongyang.[22] A spy scandal brought bilateral ties with the South to their nadir after normalization. An anxious South Korea grew more sensitive about relations with Japan, rallying not only against its growing nationalism but also from concern about expanded U.S.-Japanese military ties intended to check China and shape the balance of regional power. South Koreans were also nervous about Japanese efforts to open talks with the North, reflecting the poor state of triangular coordination with the United States on the North.[23] In the throes of economic crisis without a clear path forward in diplomacy with its four great-power partners, South Korea did not look like a prospective regional leader. Yet the decision to establish the Association of South East Asian Nations (ASEAN) +3 grouping in 1997 with China and Japan set in motion a pathway toward regionalism that would soon put the South at the center.

Great-power maneuvering proved ephemeral. Beijing overestimated its leverage with the United States, as indicated by growing negative sentiment after U.S. president Bill Clinton's visit in the summer of 1998. In 1997–98, ties with Russia were already proving difficult to solidify beyond rhetorical flourishes and arms imports, and after the Kosovo War, Yeltsin cut a deal with Washington that cast Beijing aside. The Japanese had turned so negative toward China after the public relations fiasco of President Jiang Zemin's visit in November 1998 that there was little point in repeating the illusion of a triangle that secured the region. Despite its steadfast support for North Korea's economy, Beijing found itself ever more frustrated with Pyongyang's mismanagement and recklessness, observed in the August 1998 provocation toward Japan through a missile launch over its territory. China's growing interest in economic regionalism as the great-power maneuvering was facing a dead end finally presented South Korea in 1999 with an opportunity to raise its profile.

Although North Korea may have raised its hopes that the rhetorical struggle by Beijing and Moscow against American hegemonism could have given it new breathing room to play off various powers jockeying for power, the South had to understand that only a process of regional integration and great-power cooperation makes its appeal to the North for a soft landing credible. It would take Kim Dae Jung two years to build a coalition of engagement before he would entice and bribe North Korean leader Kim Jong Il into a summit meeting. He would be helped by recalculations in China in favor of accommodation to the United States and "smile diplomacy" toward Japan, and by Vladimir Putin's rise to power in Russia not only as a pragmatist ready to work with the United States but also as an advocate of a new regional strategy raising the profile of the Korean peninsula. Seoul emerged from its diminished status in 1997–98 ready to take the initiative in the favorable environment of a region aware of the need to abandon jockeying for great-power advantage in order to boost regional security.

The Sunshine Policy and Its Meaning in the Search for Regionalism, 1999–2000

Kim Dae Jung turned weakness into a platform for activism after taking power in the midst of financial crisis and diminished regional impact. Instead of voicing national distress toward the United States, he championed structural reform in accord with IMF demands and presented his country as the most ardent regional supporter of globalization.[24] Through disarming U.S. doubters, he opened the way to energetic pursuit of regionalism. His breakthrough with Japan proved to be an even more stunning success. Building on growing acceptance of economic interdependence in the financial crisis, he agreed to put the history issue aside and open his country to Japanese culture in return for what Tokyo labeled the final apology. With Japanese opinion increasingly favorable, Kim had room for an active foreign policy on behalf of regionalism and a breakthrough with the North.

After William Perry, former U.S. secretary of defense, succeeded as the U.S. emissary in winning Pyongyang's agreement to suspend missile testing, the time was ripe for Kim to seek help from China and Russia in arranging for direct ties with North Korea. This gave Russia the opportunity to complete its efforts to reestablish firm ties with the North, while fixing on an appealing vision of regionalism with its axis along a vertical corridor from Khabarovsk to Pusan. It also served China's interest in cajoling the North to reform while increasing the momentum for regionalism. Nobody objected when Seoul in the first months of 2000 assumed leadership in appealing to Pyongyang, arranging for the firm Hyundai ASAN secretly to offer a bribe of about $500 million for Kim Jong Il to agree to a summit meeting as well as to secure development rights for projects in the North.

The sunshine policy raised expectations through the spring and summer of 2000 and reverberated strongly through the fall as the Clinton administration, until its last days, explored a summit in Pyongyang and Kim Dae Jung basked in the glory of the Nobel Prize ceremony. Taking credit for encouraging Kim Jong Il, Russians optimistically eyed the large-scale economic projects that were now on the table. The Chinese heartily welcomed the "evenhandedness" of the process without pressure on the North. By contrast, Japan anxiously watched from the sidelines, fearing reconciliation steps would leave it without a voice but with pressure to pay a large bill. Since the North placed first priority on a breakthrough with the United States, the election of George W. Bush as president interrupted Bill Clinton's dalliance with Pyongyang and reinforced Kim Jong Il's hesitation to proceed. Kim Dae Jung's strategy to put Korea at the center ran afoul of a new U.S. determination to keep regional relations under its firm control and the North's fierce obstinacy over WMD.

Northeast Asian Regionalism in the War Against Terror, 2001–2002

After attempting a difficult balancing act in 2000 through the sunshine policy, Seoul faced three different situations over the following three years: in 2001 in its wait for the Bush administration to set a direction for its policy toward the North, in 2002 after Bush had vilified the North as part of the "axis of evil," and in late 2002 into 2005 during the nuclear crisis caused by the North's defiant initiatives and Washington's delay in making assurances to the North's leadership on security. Through this period, Seoul's basic course remained to make use of multilateral diplomacy to entice Pyongyang into closer relations, but the global environment kept changing. Increasingly, Seoul appeared helplessly caught between the Bush administration's uncompromising opposition to the "axis of evil" and the Kim Jong Il regime's resolute refusal to conduct reform or dialogue that could undermine its domestic control or its capacity to brandish WMD and retain a conventional threat to the South should its goals not be realizable through negotiations.

In the year 2001, Kim Dae Jung waited in vain for a decision by Bush on how to resume talks with Kim Jong Il that had almost produced a decision by Clinton in the waning days of his term in office to go to Pyongyang in order to secure an agreement to put a stop to missile testing and exports. The South Korean president's options were also limited by the uproar at home over new middle school textbooks approved in Japan and then the promise of Prime Minister Koizumi to visit the Yasukuni Shrine on the war-ending date of August 15, a visit he later shifted to August 13 to lessen the impact. With Putin visiting Seoul early in 2001 and Kim Jong Il taking a long train ride across Russia in the summer, South Koreans naturally looked to Russia as an alternate key to unlock the North Korean mindset. Even more important, booming economic ties with China and broadening regional cooperation left many in the South optimistic of its positive role in relations with the North. When the Bush administration appeared to be moving toward containment of China in its first half year, public opinion in the South fixated on finding a multilateral strategy to escape from an apparent dead end. Anxious to revive his active diplomacy to place Seoul at the center of the region, Kim Dae Jung could only wait.

After September 11, 2001, two contradictory tendencies left South Korea further in doubt. On the one hand, the world rallied behind the United States in the war against terror. Putin led the way, and Jiang Zemin consented as well in the war against the Taliban in Afghanistan, while Koizumi scrambled to repair frayed relations with China, Russia, and South Korea even as he drew closer to the United States. In a new spirit of cooperation Seoul might forge a consensus on how to approach Pyongyang. Indeed, with Washington preoccupied elsewhere it might even welcome a regional solution that would keep one potential WMD threat quiet. Yet Kim Jong Il did not respond to September 11 with new moderation, and signs from Washington even before the war in Afghanistan had ended suggested a hardening position toward Pyongyang. Assertive U.S. leadership was ratcheted up another notch.

In January 2002, Bush's State of the Union address branding the North as part of the "axis of evil" left Kim Dae Jung at an even greater impasse than Bush's refusal a year earlier to sustain engagement with the North. Kim patiently proceeded, striving for progress with the North on reconnecting the railroad through the DMZ, on building a land route to the Mount Kumgang tourist site, on developing an industrial park at Kyesong, and on reuniting families.[25] Given North Korea's hesitant and often abortive cooperation, perhaps from fear of being overwhelmed by the South,[26] Kim Dae Jung had little choice but to maximize multilateral diplomacy. This is not easy because Japan, despite momentary hopes at the time of Koizumi's visit to Pyongyang in September 2002, is more concerned with abductees and deterrence, and China and Russia denied a need to press the North.[27]

As Kim Dae Jung left office in February 2003, South Koreans were split in their verdict on his tenure. On the one hand, he merited praise for overcoming the financial crisis and economic recovery, for raising the national image in the World Cup soccer finals, and for improving ties with North Korea. On the other, he was faulted for corruption, one-sided, surreptitious assistance to the North, and failed social welfare reforms. The public was sharply divided, ambivalent about the pros and cons of the sunshine policy.[28] If the North had failed to respond as desired, at least they could be satisfied with multilateral diplomacy as a mechanism for approaching it. Kim Dae Jung had put Korea at the center.

From the Iraq War to the Nuclear Crisis and South Korea's Aspirations

Okonogi Masao, a Korea specialist in Japan, calculated that within twenty-four hours a "second Korean War" that could be ignited by U.S. mishandling could leave Seoul a sea of flames, one million persons killed or wounded in Korea, the country's industry crippled, more than a million North Korean refugees fleeing the country, and tens of Nodong missiles flying at Japan. In the aftermath of the Iraq war, he estimated that Kim Jong Il would become more assertive in fighting a war of resistance, but also might respond if left with some face. This endgame allows room for Japan, with its large pockets, even more than China or Russia, to play a role as an intermediary between the United States and the North, reinvigorating the Pyongyang declaration of September 17, 2002, which had been undercut by the nuclear crisis. Instead of emotionally fixating on abductees as the entry point for diplomacy, he cautioned that the Japanese public must think strategically in preparation for flexible diplomacy with the nuclear question at the center.[29] Knowing that Seoul welcomed Tokyo's outreach to Pyongyang, some Japanese anticipated a boost in bilateral relations to act alongside South Korea in centering the new region.

Funabashi Yoichi, commentator for the newspaper *Asahi shimbun*, pointed more directly to China, as supplier of food and energy to the North, as the key to resolving the crisis. Noting forces there who do not stress relations with the North and various remarks by China's leaders distancing their country from the North, he suggested that the United States as well as Japan would rely on China, although it was already slow in cutting off supplies.[30] This notion associated Japan with China's emerging centrality in support of South Korea opening to the North. Although less appealing to conservatives than a two-way focus on the South, the outcome would also favor a regional solution.

Soon, however, the options were narrowing to ways to work with Washington for a solution. A comparison of the editorial positions of the six leading newspapers in Japan shows a range of responses, all dependent on the United States. At one extreme, the newspaper *Sankei shimbun* warned that weak diplomacy only invited a military attack; Japan must pressure the North and this could be done only in close coordination with the United States without regard for South Korea's reluctance. Less rightist papers also closed ranks with the United States: *Tokyo shimbun* called for consideration of sanctions against the North; *Nihon keizai shimbun* appealed to the Security Council to use the "stick," since the "carrot" does not suffice; and *Yomiuri shimbun* demanded that the Security Council act quickly as North Korea must recognize that it has isolated itself from international society. Only the two left-leaning national dailies disagreed: *Mainichi shimbun* insisted that it is not the United States but international society that faces the North, and *Asahi shimbun* argued that the four other countries all hoped that U.S.–North Korean dialogue would be realized.[31] Debate swirled around Japan siding with multilateral incentives under the initiative of South Korea or with unilateral pressure from the United States, in which a special partnership would raise Japan above the rest.

Even as Japanese nationalists were emboldened by the shift in public opinion in response to the North Korean threat and the growing inclination for "normalization" of Japan's armed forces and revision of its postwar constitution, hope rose that South Korea, as part of three-way coordination with the United States, would acquiesce. When the newly elected president of South Korea Roh Moo Hyun went to Tokyo in June 2003, the Japanese grew hopeful about accelerated negotiations for an FTA, the final steps in cultural opening to Japan, and a close partnership. In contrast, no matter how much Roh tried to convey a tone of solidarity with Japan at a time of national danger, the mood in South Korea was one of temporary conciliation but withholding final steps toward an FTA, cultural opening, and solidarity. To accept Tokyo's embrace along with U.S. pressure aimed at regime change in the North would deny Seoul its regional aspirations and the anticipated security of managed outreach to Pyongyang. Soon Roh acquiesced on the FTA talks and cultural opening, as nervousness about relations with the United States far outweighed concerns about Japan.[32]

With Russia having signaled that the Korean peninsula is now the centerpiece in its regional strategy and Japan increasingly focused on the Korean peninsula, observers are looking to see if China has a new diplomacy. Squeezed between North Korea and the United States, it nervously awaited further encirclement by the Bush administration. *Nihon keizai shimbun* in March 2003 suggested that Beijing indeed is redoubling efforts to strengthen relations with neighboring countries, but it concluded that despite receiving essential food and energy assistance Pyongyang was angering Beijing. After promising to consult on important questions in advance, Kim Jong Il proceeded in the fall of 2002 with the Koizumi summit, the Shinuiju Special Economic Zone, and restarting his nuclear program without such consultations. Now some Chinese talk of using the "economic card" against the North. Having raised its international prestige in 1997–98 by its handling of the Asian financial crisis, China has another opportunity to do so and to improve relations with the United States. The analysis suggests that some Japanese are counting on China, and, in the process, are anticipating a big boost to regionalism.[33] Even *Sankei shimbun*, despite its usually contemptuous attitude toward compromise with the Asian states, praised the idea of making oil supplies and railroad construction through cooperation among South Korea, China, and Russia the keystone of a regional approach to the North.[34] As warm as ties between Japan and the United States seemed during most of 2003, repeated warnings asserted that Japan cannot just follow the United States; it needs Asian diplomacy as a base and South Korea as the entry point, even more so with the continued rise of China's economy.[35]

As the nuclear crisis deepened following the six-party talks of August 27–29, 2003, the five countries opposed to North Korea's nuclear weapons development looked for common ground. The Japanese recognized that their aspirations, whether for resolution of the abduction issue or for deterrence of the North, depend on the U.S. government above all. The political right gained ground, rejecting politicians who had brought the opening in 2002 with the North and accepting, for the time being, U.S. leadership.[36] Sino-U.S. relations found new purpose after Jiang Zemin's visit to Bush's ranch in Crawford, Texas, on October 25, 2002, leading to a spirit of cooperation aimed especially at producing a nuclear-free Korea that would not damage the interests of either party.[37] A crisis was bringing the region together, but it could grow so dangerous that fissures would reopen. The United States had not made up its mind to guarantee the North's security in a way the other four parties saw as necessary, and North Korea had not committed itself to verified elimination of nuclear weapons as sought by the other five parties. Amid this impasse to regionalism, the South reaffirmed its optimism that the North would respond well to a reasonable offer, which, not incidentally, would allow the South to emerge from the crisis with a follow-up to the sunshine policy, centered now in a more multinational framework.

By the summer of 2005 a year-long lull in six-party talks had been marked by a spiral downward in U.S.–North Korean relations, a tightening bond between the United States and Japan, and a sharper divide between South Korea and the United States. The soft line of Roh toward North Korea clashed with the hard line demanded by Bush in the face of a declared nuclear power insistent on its right to these weapons. As tensions rose, Koizumi drew on intensifying nationalism while Chinese students marched against Japan and Roh gave voice to harsher criticisms of it. Although Roh called for the South to become a balancer between China and Japan, he managed mostly to irritate Japan and the United States without gaining through new relations with China. The three-year-old crisis was coming to a head. If at the same time preparations were under way for the first East Asian Summit to establish a regional community, the gap between China and Japan had widened too far for South Korea to have any hope of bridging it. Growing U.S. criticism of China also meant that the international environment would not be conducive to regionalism or to South Korea enjoying the kind of trust it had in 2000 when its diplomacy had become most active.

A new strategy for regionalism could get a big lift from a peaceful resolution of the nuclear crisis in which the threat from North Korea diminished sharply as it became the object of economic reconstruction enhancing ties among all of its neighbors. This would require, first, the United States and China to reach an overall agreement and, second, Japan to have a regional strategy, including a breakthrough with Russia and improved ties with China, into which Korea-centered regionalism could fit. Even fifteen years after the end of the cold war, it appeared that most of the coming decade might be needed to achieve these objectives.

A Snapshot of Korea-Centered Regionalism

The geography of North Korean integration may offer an opportunity to advance many ideas raised over the past fifteen years in proposals for regionalism in Northeast Asia. In the north at the Russian border five themes may reappear: (1) a transportation corridor from Northeast China to the Rajin-Sonbong port area onto the Sea of Japan (East Sea); (2) an international city at the Tumen River combining Chinese, Russian, and Korean urban areas into one development zone; (3) an upgraded railroad corridor joining the Korean peninsula to Vladivostok and the Trans-Siberian line; (4) an energy corridor of pipelines for oil and gas fueling industrial development; and (5) a program of labor allocation into the Russian Far East, expanding on the growing number of North Koreans sent there for construction and other jobs and incorporating also Koreans returning from Central Asia to the

Vladivostok area. If Russians remain wary of the Tumen River development and returning Koreans, they may be reassured through an overall package that would at last overcome the crisis atmosphere in the Far East. Since 2000, Vladimir Putin's coziness with Kim Jong Il and strong support for the "sunshine policy" have placed the Korean peninsula at the center in efforts to protect the Russian Far East while pursuing regional integration that would not be dominated by either China or Japan.

China could benefit greatly from development centered on North Korea. It would have at least five goals in mind: (1) to recuperate the investment already made in the Hunchun area of Jilin Province, where a Korean autonomous area has been awaiting the investment that seemed promising during the first half of the 1990s; (2) to find an engine to power the rebuilding of much of the rest of Northeast China, where the closing of state-owned enterprises has left rampant unemployment, and access to the sea through a short corridor is viewed hopefully as a means to convert two inland provinces into coastal ones; (3) to reestablish the Northeast as the energy reservoir of China, replacing the depleted oil fields of Daqing with, first, a direct pipeline from Russia already under study and then a network of pipelines linked to Korean development; (4) to sustain the momentum of South Korean–Chinese economic ties by adding North Korea's economy to North China's belt of maximum prosperity in the Liaodong Peninsula and around the Yellow Sea; and (5) to reduce the inflow of migrants from North Korea as well as the burden of relief for a country on the verge of economic collapse. Increasingly enthusiastic about regionalism to balance globalization and assertive U.S. unilateralism, China needs the Korean peninsula in the face of Japanese and Russian nervousness about China's rapid ascent.

Japan has a critical role to play if this vision of regionalism is to advance. It must determine not only that its immediate concerns are satisfied, but also that the long-range prospects for North Korea and regionalism serve its national interests. At least four issues figure in its economic calculations: (1) expanding trade across the Sea of Japan to revive its coastal cities left behind in the postwar boom that favored the Pacific coast and further in the stagnation era; (2) boosting energy security through supplies of Russian oil and gas from both Sakhalin in northeast and southeast Korea near Japan's southwest; (3) making sure that the Korean peninsula will not become so one-sidedly joined to China that Japan will lack clout in shaping its evolution; and (4) forging a process of regional integration that gives proper return to Japanese capital in order to give life to economic growth and to give meaning to the slogan "reentering Asia." Enthusiasm for an FTA with South Korea and an energy initiative to Russia gave impetus to regionalism, although measures to keep the alliance with the United States in readiness gained the most attention.

South Korea eyes, above all, direct ties across the DMZ. It hopes to minimize the costs of reintegration through at least five steps: (1) building industrial parks that employ large numbers of North Korean workers; (2) developing a north–south corridor that will become an axis of economic growth favored by transportation and energy access; (3) encouraging firms to lead in the establishment of service sector and light industrial jobs that ease the transition of North Korea from a command economy; (4) raising the place of its economy in production networks through a division of labor that draws on different economic stages in the region; and (5) orchestrating joint efforts with others in support of regionalism, in which the South becomes the indispensable partner of each of the four great powers. Seoul supports regionalism, and it envisions the North becoming linked also to China, Russia, and Japan as it emerges from its prolonged isolation.

Washington has to make up its mind where it stands on the subject of North Korean economic integration that could get started in stages as part of the realization of a Northeast Asian regional community. Unilateralists are likely to be dubious about the effects of a regional grouping that could widen its scope into matters of security, and, even in the context of the World Trade Organization, pose some barriers to globalization. Many also object to a soft landing for the North that leaves in place, through a transitional period, elements of totalitarianism and military threat. At stake is not just the danger of WMD, but also the uncertainty of regionalism in a world order that the Bush administration is intent on shaping according to its own tastes. The United States must be given a large role in a regional community, but most are also seeking a venue that keeps that role within limits.

For the moment, the image of North Korean belligerence serves the Bush team's ideology of a world divided between good and evil, enabling the United States to stay on the offensive, to draw Japan closer, and to keep the pressure on China. Although the South Korean public is suspicious of U.S. intentions, for the time being only radicals dare to question a U.S. troop presence. A deal with North Korea that would start the wheels of reintegration going could challenge the U.S. commitment to multilateralism, perhaps opening the way to some reconciliation between China and Japan that would require a very different U.S. strategy to manage. Recent divisions between South Korea and the United States may herald the Korean peninsula becoming the center of an entire region in search of a community that the United States may not easily accept. North Korea's threatening posture delays regionalism, while reinforcing awareness of the need for regionalism that the United States may find difficult to manage once integration of North Korea becomes a shared theme across Northeast Asia.

10

Inter-Korean Relations in Northeast Asian Geopolitics

Samuel S. Kim

A glance at the map and the geopolitical smoke spewing out of the latest U.S.–North Korean nuclear standoff suggests why Northeast Asia (NEA) is among the world's most important yet volatile regions. For over a century, geography and history have combined to turn the Korean peninsula into a highly contested terrain that has absorbed and reflected wider geopolitical struggles and even sanguinary wars involving, to varying degrees, tsarist Russia, Meiji Japan, the Soviet Union, Qing China, the People's Republic of China, imperial Japan, and the United States. Each of the Big Four of Northeast Asia (China, Japan, Russia, and the United States, hereafter the NEA-4) has come to regard the Korean peninsula as the strategic pivot point of Northeast Asia security and therefore as falling within its own geostrategic ambit.[1] Complicating matters is the fact that the Korean peninsula is divided, meaning that the NEA-4 cannot address the threats and opportunities inherent on the peninsula without paying heed to inter-Korean relations, and also that the seemingly local and bilateral relations between the two Korean states are, in reality, part of the nexus of great-power politics.

Out of this fact emerges the greatest irony of the region: that North Korea, the weakest of the six main actors, seems positioned to be a primary driver of NEA's regional geopolitics. Defying all the gloomy collapsist scenarios and predictions, as well as the classical realist axiom that "the strong do what they have the power to do and the weak accept what they have to accept,"[2] Pyongyang has demonstrated its uncanny resilience and stunning ability to withstand seemingly fatal internal woes and external pressures. As it did in the nuclear crisis of 1993–94, Pyongyang has catapulted itself into the center stage of regional geopolitics with its BBB (brinksmanship/breakdown/breakthrough) diplomacy.[3] How then do the events on the Korean peninsula and between the two Korean states translate into the region at large? And in what ways have the NEA-4 chosen to involve themselves in inter-Korean affairs?

To follow these lines of inquiry, this chapter is organized in four sections. The first section depicts sui generis regional characteristics based on three theoretical perspectives. This provides context for the analysis of the dynamics of inter-Korean relations that follows in the second section. The third section examines the complex interplay of global, regional, and national forces shaping the changing patterns of relationships between the two Koreas—especially North Korea—and the NEA-4, with special attention to the shifting identities and roles of the NEA-4 as manifested in their evolving Korea policies. The concluding section assesses the future prospects for establishing a more peaceful and prosperous regional order.

The Northeast Asian Geopolitical Environment, Old and New

The Northeast Asian strategic environment in the post–cold war era defies neat characterization or confident prognostication; it is more amenable than ever to diverse interpretations. Three competing perspectives on international relations offer insight into NEA as an international region: realism, liberalism, and globalization.

By the logic of realist power-transition theory, belligerent preemptive or preventive actions are motivated by fear and by a fundamental dissatisfaction with the status quo, largely as a result of closing windows of opportunity and increasing vulnerability brought on by relative power shifts.[4] The realist image of the region is that NEA is ripe for the revival of classical great-power rivalry.[5] The rises and declines of China (People's Republic of China, PRC), post-Soviet Russia, South Korea (Republic of Korea, ROK), and North Korea (Democratic People's Republic of Korea, DPRK) created the greatest regional swings in power in the last two decades of the twentieth century. The "back to the future" correlation between rapid internal growth and external expansionism has troubling implications for the Northeast Asian regional security order in the future.

Geography is important in the shaping of any state's foreign policy, to be sure, but this is especially true and enduring in NEA. The Korean peninsula as a whole shares land and maritime borders with China, Russia, and Japan, uniquely occupying and situating itself at the geostrategic vortex of the region. Today North Korea is the one and only country in the post–cold war world that is surrounded by so many large powers (the NEA-4 plus South Korea). From its location, Pyongyang has the "negative power" to destabilize the region with brinkmanship, the instigation of hostility or instability, or the mere threat of collapse, potentially entrapping China or all other regional powers in a spiral of conflict escalation. The threat of a North Korean collapse and the costs of regional spillover in the form of refugees or escalating armed conflict have become a nightmare scenario for Beijing and Seoul, if not for Washington.[6]

Many liberals see the momentous changes in the international system at the end of the twentieth century as overturning mainstream realist theories. The received wisdom about the traditional Korean security predicament—that Korea is a weak country in a region of the strong—is no longer believed to be a reliable guide to the peace process on the Korean peninsula. For the first time in many years, the Korean peninsula is increasingly a site of great-power cooperation rather than rivalry.

The NEA-4 have expressed their shared interest in seeking peace and stability on the Korean peninsula.

However, NEA has traditionally been defined by a poverty of regionalism, especially in terms of security. Unlike in Europe, the primary threat after World War II remained intraregional, not extraregional. The comfort level that exists in security dialogue in Southeast Asia does not exist in Northeast Asia. Moscow has been virtually alone in showing continued interest in collective or cooperative schemes for the region, and even then its motive is to enhance its geopolitical and geoeconomic interests in the region.

Despite this lack of regionalism, NEA has recently been relatively peaceful. The reason for this lies in part in the rise of China as a responsible regional power that has transformed the geopolitical and geoeconomic landscape of Asia.[7] Within the wheel of emerging East Asian regionalism, China serves as the hub power, and China's successful settlement of territorial disputes, the corresponding sense of enhanced state sovereignty, the demise of ideological conflict, and the substantial accomplishment of China's status drive to become a great power have had a tremendous impact on the NEA geopolitical landscape.

In contrast to the clarity, simplicity, and apparent discipline of bipolarity that characterized the geopolitical character of NEA in the past, a new Northeast Asian regional order is emerging, one with multiple complexities and uncertainties, of indeterminate shape and content. Northeast Asian states must now worry not only about their military power but, more important, about the economic, cultural, and knowledge power required to survive and prosper in an increasingly globalized and competitive world.[8]

A rather unique and complex cocktail of regional characteristics—high capability, abiding animus, deep, albeit differentiated, entanglement of the NEA-4 in Korean affairs, North Korea's recent emergence as a nuclear loose cannon, the absence of multilateral security institutions, the rise of America's unilateral triumphalism (or "new imperialism"), growing economic integration and regionalization, and the resulting uncertainties and unpredictability in the international politics of Northeast Asia—challenges scholars and policy makers alike to divine the shape of things to come in the emerging regional order. In short, the parameters of post–cold war NEA international relations are still in a state of flux.

Back to the Future of Inter-Korean Cooperation

Of all the major events in the history of inter-Korean relations, the three-day summit meeting in Pyongyang between President Kim Dae Jung and Chairman Kim Jong Il on June 13–15, 2000, easily stands out as the single greatest moment. The Pyongyang summit, the first of its kind in the half-century history of politics of competitive legitimation and delegitimation on the divided peninsula, generated opportunities and challenges for the NEA-4 as they stepped back to reassess the likely future of inter-Korean affairs and the implications for their own national interests. The dramatic summit also led to some paradoxical expectations and consequences.

The Pyongyang summit is most remarkable because it was an internal rather than an external undertaking, a truly inter-Korean affair lacking outside impetus or sponsorship. Previous inter-Korean accords had been responses to major structural changes external to the Korean peninsula, such as the 1972 joint communiqué after Nixon's visit to China or the 1992 agreements following the demise of the cold war system. The chief catalyst for the Pyongyang summit was President Kim Dae Jung's consistent and single-minded pursuit of his pro-engagement "sunshine policy."

More than anything else, the offer of substantial if unspecified governmental aid to refurbish North Korea's decrepit infrastructure was the causal force behind Kim Jong Il's decision to agree to the summit. Until Kim Dae Jung's Berlin Declaration in March 2000 offering aid to the DPRK,[9] Pyongyang had taken a two-handed approach, attacking the sunshine policy as a "sunburn policy" on ideological grounds while simultaneously pursuing a mendicant strategy to extract maximum economic concessions. Before the official unveiling of the statement in Berlin, Seoul delivered an advance text to Pyongyang, Beijing, Moscow, Tokyo, and Washington, demonstrating that the NEA-4 had little to do with the initiation of the summit.

One result of the 2000 inter-Korean summit was enhanced prestige throughout the world for the DPRK and for Kim Jong Il. The North Koreans viewed and framed the summit, although native in origin, as a major concession to the United States, and the latter was therefore expected to make major economic and strategic concessions. Pyongyang did its best to exploit the new connection with Seoul in order to speed up normalization talks with the United States and to gain access to bilateral and multilateral aid and foreign direct investment.

In addition to the summit with Kim Dae Jung, the infamously reclusive Kim Jong Il also met with China's president Jiang Zemin in a secret visit to Beijing in May 2000 and then with Russia's president Vladimir Putin that July, after which he received a flurry of diplomatic missions to Pyongyang, including U.S. secretary of state Madeleine Albright, China's defense minister Chi Haotian, and a European Union delegation. The apparent thaw on the Korean peninsula intensified the desires and efforts of the NEA-4 to readjust their respective Korea policies to the rapidly changing realities on the ground.

The Joint Declaration produced during the June 2000 summit glossed over the absence of a common formula for reunification, with Kim Dae Jung repeating that he did not expect Korean reunification on his watch or in his lifetime. Furthermore, while the document speaks of economic cooperation and indeed has fostered some growth in that area, it fails to address military and security matters, lacking even a general statement about working together for tension reduction and confidence building. Pyongyang clearly desires to discuss security issues last, if at all, and then only with the United States. Tellingly, Pyongyang has held the new hard-line administration in Washington hostage to the resumption of inter-Korean dialogue and engagement, breaching not only the letter and the spirit of the North-South Joint Declaration but also its own longstanding party line that Korean affairs should be handled without foreign intervention or interference. From Pyongyang's own realpolitik perspective, the failure of the summit to accelerate DPRK-U.S. normalization may provide a logic for refusing to carry out Kim Jong Il's "promised" visit to Seoul for a second inter-Korean summit.[10]

Kim Jong Il's potential southern visit aside, something not so funny happened on the way to George W. Bush's accidental presidency in early 2001. The "shrimp among whales" metaphor returned with a vengeance, this time with Kim Dae Jung becoming a shrimp caught or almost crushed in the fight between George W. Bush (the next leader in the American political dynasty) and Kim Jong Il (the next leader in the North Korean political dynasty). The first half of 2001 saw inter-Korean relations hardly moving: Inter-Korean dialogue was suspended. The Bush administration's mindless hard-line policy instead inspired Kim Jong Il in June 2001 to resume coercive diplomacy. Pyongyang's cargo ships violated South Korean territorial waters, including crossing the Northern Limit Line, prompting an outcry from the ROK opposition and mass media. In many ways, however, the ROK chose to ignore these DPRK pinpricks, as did the NEA-4. Pyongyang upped the ante in 2002 with the revelations that sparked the second U.S.-DPRK nuclear standoff.

The Shifting Identities, Roles, and Policies of the NEA-4

These inter-Korean developments have forced the NEA-4 to reconsider their identities as actors on the Korean peninsula and in Northeast Asia in general. Regarding national identity, the state defines itself not only essentially, by what it *is*, but also behaviorally, by what it *does*. The net effect of state behavior in relation to other states over a given period of time may be characterized as a role played by the state; a national identity enacts itself as the state assumes various national roles. These roles perform the functions of mobilizing, testing, and validating an identity through interactions with other players in the same arena. A particular foreign-policy line is best conceived of as a form of implementation, specifying and ordering national roles emanating from a given national identity.[11] This section considers the construction of national identities and then discusses the Korea policies of China, Russia, Japan, and the United States.

Mainstream structural realists and the vast majority of neoliberals have neglected the impact of ideational variables (norms, culture, and identity) in international relations. They have assumed that state identities and interests are either permanently fixed or merely derivative of the perennial struggle for power and plenty. The end of the cold war and the collapse of the Soviet Union created considerable opportunity for cultural and sociological perspectives in international relations scholarship.[12]

National-identity enactment is often quite salient in the military and security domain.[13] National security and national identity are mutually complementary and interdependent; a stable, congealed national identity makes for the internal coherence and unity of the nation-state. This promotes effective national-identity mobilization and facilitates responses to external threats. Identities attributed to other states are assumed to facilitate recognition of and response to external threats. Successful nationalism—that is, effective national-identity mobilization—may also serve as a necessary, if not sufficient, condition for coping with domestic legitimation deficits.

Viewed in this social constructivist light, the shifting roles of the NEA-4 in the region have much to do with the difficulties of adjusting national identities to the new environment. With the stark bipolarity of the cold war removed, Northeast Asia reemerged as the site of civilizational divides and of historical and national-identity animus.

The Role of China

China is concerned with economic development, a threat-free regional security environment, and the cultivation of its status as a responsible great power in world politics. With these goals motivating policy in the post-Mao era, China's Korea policy has shifted incrementally from the familiar one-Korea (pro-Pyongyang) policy, through a policy of one Korea de jure and two Koreas de facto, and finally to a policy of two Koreas de facto and de jure. The decision in 1992 to normalize relations with South Korea was the culmination of this gradual process of balancing and adjusting foreign policy. Of necessity, China's two-Korea policy has had to reflect and effect its basic principles and interests as well as its simultaneous participation in multiple games at the bilateral, regional, and global levels.[14]

Pyongyang's growing siege mentality has remained the single greatest challenge to the smooth implementation of China's two-Korea policy. China's foreign-policy wish list with respect to its "communist" neighbor includes at least five "no's": no instability, no collapse, no nukes, no refugees or defectors, and no conflict escalation. Because of these concerns and given Pyongyang's political and geographical isolation, Beijing has been serving as the gateway to North Korea and as an indispensable venue for the DPRK's negotiations with South Korea, Japan, and the United States.

Beijing views its two-Korea policy as projecting its newly refurbished national identity as a responsible great power. Beijing's decision in August 1992 to recognize and establish full diplomatic relations with the ROK underscores the extent to which post–cold war Chinese foreign policy has shifted from ideology to a more material notion of national interest. During much of the cold war, China's regional policy remained a stepchild of its global superpower policy, driven by the U.S.-Chinese-Soviet geostrategic triangle. China was a regional power without a regional policy or identity. In the post-Tiananmen period and especially since the collapse of the Soviet Union in 1991, Chinese foreign policy has become increasingly Asia-centric.[15]

But the two-Korea policy is not unidirectional, and Kim Jong Il's choice of Beijing for his first-ever unofficial state visit (May 29–31, 2000) highlights China's place in Pyongyang's diplomatic outreach. With the visit occurring only two weeks before the June 2000 inter-Korean summit, Beijing was recognized as being back at the center of peninsular affairs. In October 2000 the PRC dispatched two high-powered delegations: a military delegation to Pyongyang headed by Defense Minister Chi Haotian, to reaffirm Sino-DPRK military ties, and a civilian delegation to Seoul headed by Prime Minister Zhu Rongji, to elevate Sino-ROK relations from "cooperative partnership" to "full-scale cooperative partnership." Then in September 2001 President Jiang Zemin made an official visit to Pyongyang—the first in eleven years. However, in a realpolitik policy reversal on the day before the visit was to begin, North Korea launched a unilateral diplomatic strike, proposing resumption of the stalled inter-Korean talks as soon as possible. The message was clear: North Korea makes such decisions without China's advice or pressure. Furthermore, the Jiang-Kim summit lacked a joint communiqué or declaration, whereas a month earlier the Moscow Declaration had capped a Putin-Kim summit with a compact denunciation of U.S. hegemony and unilateralism.

As China has provided more aid in a wider variety of forms—direct government-to-government aid, subsidized trade, and private barter transactions—it has become more deeply involved in the politics of regime survival in the DPRK. Paradoxically, Pyongyang's growing dependence on Beijing for its economic and political survival has led to mutual distrust and resentment. Indeed, Pyongyang's fundamentalism and its seeming inability to rework its national identity and national roles in the face of a changing geopolitical context has engendered intense bargaining amid an atmosphere of mutual suspicion. In every high-level meeting between the two governments, according to one Chinese scholar, North Korean requests for aid dominate the agenda.[16] Beijing, out of fear of refugee flows and regime collapse and in order to enhance Chinese leverage in both Pyongyang and Seoul, continues to provide "humanitarian aid." However, since the North Koreans realize that China's aid is given as a result of Beijing's own self-interest, the aid has not actually increased China's leverage with Pyongyang, to Beijing's growing frustration.

Central to Beijing's two-Korea realpolitik is growing concern about the possibility of Korean reunification by Southern absorption. China fears that North Korea could come to feel cornered and see no choice but to fight back. Even if the system in the North were simply to collapse, the likely result would be a bloody civil war rather than immediate absorption by the South, in which case China would face an equally great threat of refugee flows and contagious violence. A united Korea would add more fuel to China's ethnonational conflict, especially in the Yanbian Korean Autonomous Prefecture (Yanbian Chaoxian Zizhiqu) in Jilin Province, which holds Korea's largest diaspora population. Ultimately, China is not opposed to Korean reunification, we are told, provided that it comes about as a gradual, peaceful, negotiated unification producing a unified Korea that does not harm or threaten China's security or national interests.[17]

Beijing's uncharacteristically proactive conflict-management role in the latest U.S.-DPRK nuclear standoff suggests a Chinese reprioritization of competing interests and goals. In the 1993–94 U.S.-DPRK nuclear standoff, Beijing stayed away from the front lines for fear it might get burned if something went wrong. During the second nuclear crisis, since January 2003, Beijing was busy at long-distance telephone diplomacy, passing messages back and forth between Pyongyang and Washington. Beijing then successfully initiated and hosted a round of trilateral talks involving the United States, the DPRK, and China in Beijing (April 23–25, 2003). Despite or perhaps because of the inconclusive ending of the three-party Beijing talks, China's jet-setting preventive diplomacy then accelerated. In July 2003, Beijing dispatched its top troubleshooter—Deputy Foreign Minister Dai Bingguo—to Moscow, Pyongyang, and Washington to seek ways of "finding common ground while preserving differences" (*qiutong cunyi*).

The six-party talks in Beijing (August 27–29, 2003) were the hard-earned outcome of PRC president Hu Jintao's diplomatic efforts. Hu is said to have selected Dai to carry a letter to Kim Jong Il in Pyongyang. The letter promised to help resolve the crisis by mediating and facilitating negotiations, offered the DPRK greater economic aid than in previous years, and expressed a willingness to try to persuade the United States to make a promise of nonaggression against the DPRK. Kim Jong Il told Dai that he was willing to accept China's proposal and reopen talks with the United States in a multilateral setting while at the same time insisting that one-on-one negotiation would be his bottom line.[18] Thanks to President Hu's diplomacy, Pyongyang was persuaded at least to put in abeyance its principled stand of holding only bilateral talks, restrained from walking out halfway through the six-party talks, and convinced to advance a "package of solutions."

The major catalyst for Beijing's hands-on preventive diplomacy is growing security concerns about possible U.S. recklessness in trying to resolve the North Korean nuclear crisis through military means. The Chinese leadership, faced with such a possibility, opted to give the crisis the highest priority. China remains opposed to any coercive sanctioning measures because they only lead to more provocative and potentially destabilizing countermeasures. China seems more committed to the immediate challenge of maintaining stability than it is to pursuing its long-term objective of nuclear disarmament on the Korean peninsula.

Yet China's leverage is constrained in three ways. First, China does not have as much influence over North Korea's security behavior as Washington believes. Bargaining over food and oil aid is a double-edged sword because of Beijing's fear of provoking or causing collapse in the North. Second, China's leverage in reshaping the Bush administration's rogue-state strategy ranges from very modest to virtually nil. Third is the often-overlooked question of nuclear fairness and justice. If nuclear weapons are necessary for China's security, or if Israel, India, and Pakistan can get away with building a weapons program by dint of not signing the Nuclear Nonproliferation Treaty, why is the same not true for North Korea? As the world's third-largest nuclear power, China hardly can capture the high moral ground on this issue.

The Role of Russia

With the end of the cold war and the disintegration of the Soviet Union, post-Soviet Russia has become a minor player concerned largely with domestic and "near abroad" issues. Further, Russia has experienced the traumatic unraveling of its national identity as the socialist superpower, and the quest for a post-Soviet national identity has been difficult, at times seemingly futile. The precipitous and traumatic decline of Russia from superpower to poor and powerless state and the lack of a widely accepted national identity go a long way in explaining the turbulence of Russia's Korea policy.

Given the end of cold war bipolarity (1989–90), Sino-Soviet renormalization (1989), and Soviet-ROK normalization (1990), the Soviet Union under Mikhail Gorbachev was the single greatest factor in reshaping the strategic environment surrounding the Korean peninsula. The 1990 Soviet-ROK normalization decision had some paradoxical consequences for North-South dialogue and for Pyongyang's international conduct. Despite Pyongyang's initial accusations of "socialist betrayal," the event proved to be a major catalyst for the resumption of inter-Korean dialogue, leading to historic accords in 1991 and 1992. Rapid progress in Moscow-Seoul relations, coupled with an equally rapid decompression of Moscow-Pyongyang relations, quickly took the sting out of the longstanding Sino-Soviet ideological and geopolitical rivalry over North Korea and in fact catalyzed China's shift to a two-Korea policy.

By the end of 1994, however, Moscow's tilted Korea policy was in deep trouble at home. Attacks came from many domestic quarters, not just from communists, calling for a major restructuring. Despite its solidarity with the United States in the management of the first nuclear crisis of 1993–94, Moscow found itself sidelined from the actual negotiations that culminated in the Agreed Framework of October 1994. To add insult to injury, Moscow was not permitted to participate in the light-water reactor (LWR) deal; it watched helplessly as the new U.S.-ROK-Japan trilateral regime—the Korean Peninsula Energy Development Organization (KEDO)—replaced Russia as the supplier of LWRs to North Korea.

From Moscow's perspective, the Korean peninsula is an important region where it fought two and a half wars during the past century to protect its security interests (two Russo-Japanese wars in 1904–5 and 1945 and the Korean War in 1950–53), and yet post-Soviet Russia found itself pushed off the Korean peninsula both politically and economically. As Russia's domestic politics have become more nationalist, the DPRK has become a focal point for various Russian opposition parties. With these factors coalescing, Moscow retreated significantly from its tilted policy to a more balanced one after mid-1994, as a way of reassuring Pyongyang and thereby enhancing its leverage in the North, an emulation of Beijing's well-calibrated equidistant policy.

Only since 1999 has the downward spiral of Russia-DPRK relations really been reversed. The renormalization process gained momentum when Vladimir Putin's vigorous pursuit of realpolitik intersected with Kim Jong Il's new diplomatic opening to the outside world. Putin, upon assuming office as president of Russia in May 2000, reaffirmed his pledge to restore Russia as a great power. His state visit to Pyongyang in July 2000 coincided with the completion and ratification of new national security, military, and foreign-policy concepts. Together, these blueprints stressed safeguarding Russia's "national" interests, defined in terms of Russian exceptionalism and economic interests. They also express Moscow's inability and unwillingness to define its identity as anything but a great power, and "great powers seldom operate under the same rules and constraints as lesser powers."[19]

Putin's July 2000 visit to the DPRK was the first official state visit by a member of the NEA-4. A year later, Kim made a twenty-four-day train journey through Russia's vast expanse for a two-day summit meeting in Moscow, the longest and strangest trip made by any head of state in our times.[20] This personal diplomacy was a dramatic step not only toward bringing Moscow back into the equation in order to reassert Russia's great-power identity but also toward countering troublesome American unilateral policies. The DPRK-Russia Moscow Declaration of August 4, 2001,[21] called for "a just new world order," recognition of the 1972 Antiballistic Missile Treaty as a cornerstone of global strategic stability, a Korean reunification process by independent means and without foreign interference, and "understanding" regarding the "pressing issue" of the pullout of the U.S. forces from South Korea. The remaining points have to do with the promotion of political and economic cooperation, especially "the plan for building railways linking the north and the south of the Korean peninsula, Russia, and Europe." The summit also captured global prime time and headlines when Putin revealed that the North Korean leader had pledged to eliminate the missile program—a key U.S. rationale for National Missile Defense—if Western countries (i.e., the United States) would provide access to rocket boosters for peaceful space research.

During the second U.S.-DPRK nuclear standoff, Russia has seen the multilateral talks as a means of restoring part of its great power identity, and therefore it has worked to make sure that they do not stall or collapse. The North Korean issue has received attention in Russia's interactions with the other three members of the NEA-4, serving as a focal point around which Russia can interact with them on other policy matters. Yet, beyond joint policy announcements with Japan, it is unclear what Russian participation has added to the nuclear talks or how much leverage Moscow has.

Russia's Koreanists are always quick to point out that only Russia among the NEA-4 is an unequivocal supporter of reunification, since the status quo gives China more influence in the politics of divided Korea than would a strongly nationalist reunified Korea, especially one friendly to the United States. Russia would reap a huge economic reward from a successful unification, linking transport networks from Korea's Pacific ports to Russia and Europe while opening the Korean market for Russian natural gas. Russia also would like North Korea's huge foreign debt to be repaid by a unified Korea. However, Moscow's belated equidistant role playing appears to be too little, too late; by any measure Moscow has the least influence in Korean affairs among the NEA-4.

The Role of Japan

Although Japan looms large in NEA's international relations, the difficulty of assessing Japan's leadership role is vastly compounded by the long shadow of its imperial past. China and Korea remain deeply ambivalent about Japan's possible leadership role in Northeast Asia, making Japan's Asian identity no less awkward and problematic than China's. Even within Japan there is abiding doubt about its capacity for self-restraint should it assume leadership of East Asia.[22] Anti-Japanese demonstrations are common in South Korea, and the Japanese government seems congenitally unable or unwilling to put an end to old historical enmities, leading to historical controversies plaguing Japanese-Korean and Sino-Japanese relations.

Since the late 1990s, Japan's assertive rising-sun nationalism has been growing, reviving the problem of its "Asian identity." Right-wing nationalism in Japan can only spawn right-wing and left-wing nationalism in Seoul, Beijing, and Moscow, let alone in Pyongyang. Its official acceptance, evidenced by the August 1999 designation of the rising-sun flag and national anthem as official symbols of the nation, signals a shift toward a more hawkish stance that is likely to rattle the entire region.

North Korea is often said to be one of the major external factors in this recent rise of Japanese nationalism. North Korea's test firing of the Taepodong-I missile over Japan in August 1998 was at once a surprise, a crisis, and perhaps even a geopolitical blessing in disguise for Japan's born-again nationalism. Indeed, no single event is said to have impacted and reshaped Japanese public opinion as much as that missile launch. The widely expected test launch of a new long-range missile in August 1999, the Taepodong-II, is said to have supplied the necessary justification for the passage of the legislation on the rising-sun flag and anthem.

In the "identity war" between Tokyo and Pyongyang, a central pivot point has been the issue of alleged abductions of Japanese nationals by North Korean security agents in the 1970s and 1980s. The abduction issue has excited national identity politics in both countries in a zero-sum manner. Japanese Diet approval of a normalization treaty will not be forthcoming without public support, which in turn hinges upon resolution of the abduction issue. From Junichiro Koizumi and Kim Jong Il's summit in Pyongyang on September 17, 2002, came a joint declaration addressing a range of issues, including an exchange of apologies. The biggest surprise was Kim Jong Il's confession not only to Pyongyang's responsibility for the abductions but also that a substantial number of the abductees were dead. What Kim Jong Il received in return was neither diplomatic breakthrough nor a huge aid package but a Japanese backlash. Thanks to Japanese "yellow journalism," the abduction issue returned with a vengeance, blowing away any silver linings in the on-again, off-again normalization talks.

When it comes to the six-party talks on the North Korean nuclear program, Japan seems in many ways to be just along for the ride. Whereas China has been the most active in pushing the talks forward, Russia has sought to use the talks to bolster its own international political image, and the United States is of course the key element of any negotiating framework, Japan has played second fiddle to whichever of the other three members of the NEA-4 is taking the lead. Given that Japan is the second most proximate target for a North Korean nuclear strike, one might expect a little more eagerness on the part of the Japanese to settle the nuclear issue.

For the near future, Japanese policy makers seem to have quietly concluded that their best course is to maintain the status quo as long as possible. The possibility of Korean reunification poses a dilemma for Japan. While a strong, united, and nationalistic Korea could pose a formidable challenge or even threat to Japan, the continuation of a divided Korea with an unpredictable North Korea is no less threatening to Japan's security.[23] The challenge, therefore, is to navigate between the possibility of a unified Korea, with all its uncertainties, potential instability, and new challenges, and the current challenges of a divided Korea, with the continuing danger of implosion or explosion in the North.

The Role of the United States

As the most powerful external power in inter-Korean affairs as well as in NEA geopolitics, the United States has come to play the rather unusual role of the "honest broker" in negotiations toward the resolution of the Korean conflict. It has taken on this role, remarkably enough, without first dismantling the cold war U.S.-ROK alliance system, without addressing the presence of American troops in South Korea, and without normalizing its relations with North Korea. None of the three neighboring powers has a military presence on the peninsula, while the United States, the metaphorical neighbor, maintains some 37,000 troops on South Korean soil.

The American post–cold war strategy of the mid-1990s halted planned troop reductions in the Asia-Pacific region, keeping the existing level of about 100,000 troops; reinforced the U.S. bilateral alliance with Japan as the linchpin of the region; and called for the development of regional multilateral security dialogues and mechanisms as a supplement to, but not a substitute for, "American alliance leadership" in the region. All of this was justified as financially cost effective. According to Assistant Defense Secretary Joseph S. Nye, Jr., "because of the host-nation support provided by Japan and South Korea, it is cheaper to base the forces in Asia than in the United States."[24]

Paradoxically, North Korea's growing weakness and instability, combined with the dangerous asymmetry of power on the Korean peninsula, had set in motion an agonizing reappraisal of U.S. policy toward North Korea. It became increasingly clear that America's deterrence policy alone was no longer sufficient for coping with the threat of a North Korean "hard landing" (i.e., reunification via collapse leading to an absorption by South Korea). North Korea policy under the Clinton administration shifted in the late 1990s from deterrence to William Perry's concept of "deterrence-plus," intended neither to prop up the North Korean system nor to seek its collapse but to promote dialogue and confidence-building measures that move beyond deterrence.[25] A clear and continuing attack from right-wing Republicans, however, made the policy difficult to implement.[26]

Indeed, in Pyongyang's foreign-policy thinking and behavior, the United States is at once a strategic lifeboat, a mortal threat, and a Rorschach test, as the former employs an ever larger array and variety of threats as bargaining chips, as well as for existential deterrence.[27] Yet this America-centric survival strategy has encountered a host of problems, all stemming from the different priorities and incentive structures that drive each party's respective policies toward the other. For Washington, the central concern has remained how to deal with Pyongyang's asymmetrical threats in an alliance-friendly and cost-effective way. The North Korea policy of the United States is shaped by global concerns (such as maintenance of the integrity of the Nonproliferation Treaty regime) but also by East Asian regional and U.S.-ROK bilateral concerns and by fractious partisan politics at home. In the process of arriving at the 1994 U.S.-DPRK Agreed Framework, the Clinton administration learned the hard way that the United States had no viable (nonviolent) alternative but to retreat by accepting North Korea's package deal proposal.[28] Given the constraints on America's issue-specific power, the need for a cost-effective foreign policy, and the collapse of a bipartisan foreign policy consensus, the Agreed Framework could be said to be the worst deal, except that there was no better alternative.

At the same time, Pyongyang's normalization efforts are best seen as part of a cold war habit of manipulating major powers to gain maximum security and economic benefits. Kim Jong Il's agreement to hold the historic inter-Korean summit in June 2000 seems to have been a concession not only to Seoul but also to Washington, as Pyongyang sought to facilitate normalization talks with the United States and to gain access to bilateral and multilateral aid and foreign direct investment. The second half of 2000 witnessed a flurry of Pyongyang-Washington interactions, including two quasi-summit meetings—one between President Bill Clinton and Vice Marshal Jo Myong-Rok in Washington and another between Secretary of State Madeleine Albright and Chairman Kim Jong Il in Pyongyang. Despite significant progress toward a U.S.-DPRK missile accord, at the end of the year Pyongyang stopped short of diplomatic success, due to issues with on-site verification and rapidly changing American political circumstances.

With the coming of the hard-line Bush administration, it was Clinton's North Korea policy rather than North Korea itself that first experienced a hard landing, with the paradoxical consequences of a remarkable role reversal in the U.S.-ROK alliance relationship. To an unprecedented extent, the North Korea policies of Washington and Seoul are out of sync with each other. The Bush administration has initiated a major paradigm shift in its military and strategic doctrine, moving from a "threat-based" to a "capabilities-based" model.[29] The "evil-state strategy" of the Bush administration has had perverse consequences for North Korea, South Korea, American foreign policy itself, and the entire geostrategic landscape of Northeast Asia. Buttressed by the Bush doctrine of preemption, this approach can be said to have aided and abetted hard-liners in Pyongyang, reviving Pyongyang's BBB strategy that first came to the fore in the nuclear crisis of 1993–94. Faced with such a clear threat, along with the U.S. decision to stop sending monthly heavy fuel supplies as stipulated by the Agreed Framework, Pyongyang's alleged revival of its nuclear program can hardly be surprising. From the perspective of Pyongyang's siege mentality, going nuclear is an essential move in its survival strategy.

The DPRK did not create a crisis in October 2002 when confronted by U.S. evidence of a continuing nuclear program; rather, an extant simmering crisis, fed by the failure of U.S. policy since the signing of the Agreed Framework, simply came to light. Since 1994, the United States has ignored the need for common security and failed to acknowledge the necessity of living up to its parts of the agreement (i.e., normalization of political and economic relations, reduction of barriers against trade and investment, delivery of a light-water reactor by a target date of 2003, and the provision of formal no-nuclear-threat and no-first-use assurances). The hard-line rhetoric of the Bush administration stirred the simmering crisis and forced it out into the open.

Based on the Bush administration's behavior so far, the end result would seem to be the United States coming to loggerheads with the DPRK rather than conceding any ground. The non-sequitur diplomacy of talking but not negotiating directly and the persistence of the evil-state theology mean that the United States will act far more recklessly than it did under the Clinton administration, which is frightening since in 1994 there was serious consideration of surgical air strikes and a clear possibility of outright war. The DPRK's asymmetric negotiating tactics bolster the Bush administration's Manichean image of North Korea as an evil regime bent on destruction, a perception that hinders the possibility of serious negotiation and precludes an end to the enmity, both of which the DPRK persistently demands. The American evil-state strategy has also damaged the U.S.-ROK alliance and fueled anti-American sentiment in South Korea.

As for America's stand on Korean reunification, there is a double paradox. On the one hand, many blame the United States as the principal cause of the Korean division.[30] On the other hand, as shown in most public opinion surveys, U.S. opinion stands at the extreme of expressing "strong support" for Korean reunification.[31]

This support originates in three key assumptions: that Korea occupies a critical strategic location at the vortex of Northeast Asian geopolitics; that a unified Korea would be democratic and pro-American; and that the U.S.-ROK alliance would be maintained as the anchor of stability, not only for the Korean peninsula but also for the Northeast Asian region.

Conclusion

The preceding analysis leads to several obvious and not so surprising conclusions. First, the three theoretical perspectives briefly reviewed above and the constructivist notion of state identity all offer insights into the various dimensions and their interactive effects on different issue areas in the geopolitics of Northeast Asia, but none provides a completely satisfactory explanation of the geopolitical dynamics of Northeast Asia as a whole. Regional and country-specific variations cannot be explained adequately without reference to material, institutional, and historical/ideational factors. To fully capture the dynamic interplay of local, regional, and global forces at work in various issue areas requires more synthetic and interactive explanations. In considering the vexing question of Pyongyang's uncanny resilience and "the power of the weak," for example, there is no single monocausal theory.

Second, regionalism in post–cold war East Asia in general and NEA in particular is mixed at best, with some economic regionalization occurring but little political or security regionalism of note. Northeast Asia has spawned all kinds of strategic triangles over the years, but there has been no virtuous cooperative triangulation of Beijing, Moscow, and Tokyo on most regional or global issues. A handful of regional or subregional bimultilateral or minilateral forums and arrangements have emerged to deal with regional security and economic issues in an ad hoc and situation-specific manner. With the exception of the ASEAN (Association of South East Asian Nations) Regional Forum and the Asia-Pacific Economic Cooperation forum, which remain more Southeast Asian and Asia-Pacific than Northeast Asian in structure and orientation, none of the regional or subregional groups has all four Northeast Asian powers in membership. Therefore, the security challenge of Northeast Asia in the post–cold war era is being met not by a multilateral security dialogue but by shifting and unstable bilateral relations.

Third, in the absence of superpower conflict, the foreign policies of the United States, China, Russia, Japan, and South Korea have become increasingly mired in turbulent domestic politics. Foreign-policy decision makers are not preprogrammed to be constrained by the structure of the international system as they choose competing strategies from a set of feasible and desirable alternatives. More and more scholars have been shifting their attention away from conventional concerns about great-power rivalry toward domestic and societal sources of international conflict. Our understanding of the shape of things to come in inter-Korean relations is complicated by the fact that the countries involved have become moving targets on turbulent trajectories of highly charged domestic politics, subject to competing and often contradictory pressures.

Finally, as a result of the uneasy juxtaposition of continuities and changes, a new Northeast Asian regional order is emerging, with multiple pathways, complexities, and uncertainties, and of indeterminate shape and content. The challenge for the uncertain years ahead is therefore not to make a false choice between regionalization and globalization, nor to seek an alternative supranational regional or global organization, but rather to find greater synergy among the many types of state and nonstate actors in order to create a "working peace system."[32] The working-peace-system approach is premised on the belief that no single perspective or pathway is sufficient. The synergistic interplay of the multiple pieces of the peace process will expand the possibilities of enhancing inter-Korean reconciliation and cooperation in the coming years.

11

Japan's Multilevel Approach Toward the Korean Peninsula After the Cold War

Tsuneo Akaha

A divided Korea and a South Korea isolated until the end of the 1980s from its mainland neighbors opened the door to Japan to revive its Korean diplomacy and make plans to turn this peninsula into an entryway for regional leverage and cooperation. Until the final days of the cold war, the lone option was to forge closer ties with the South in preparation for a time when barriers would fall. Japan did not win the confidence of the South Korean people, however, and the path to regionalism looked long and winding. In the 1990s, new options at last could be contemplated: (1) Japan and South Korea together could lead in liberalizing economic ties with the nearby three states emerging from the traditional socialist model, finding common cause in their capitalist and democratic systems; (2) Japan could give priority to ties with China or Russia and press South Korea to avoid being left behind; and (3) Japan could directly approach North Korea and look for a breakthrough, which would support South Korea's effort at reconciliation with the North. Examples of all three of these approaches can be found over the fifteen years since the cold war ended. In 2004, negotiations for a free trade agreement (FTA) with South Korea were the latest sign of the first approach. Despite efforts in the first half of the 1990s to form a bridge with China and to create an economic zone around the Sea of Japan that would draw the Russian Far East closer, prospects of bypassing the Koreas had faded by 2004. The third approach to appeal directly to North Korea last drew attention in September 2002 when Prime Minister Junichiro Koizumi visited Pyongyang, and even in the ensuing dark days when the North epitomized all that the Japanese despised there were still rumblings of a turnabout through six-party talks in Beijing that could lead the way to regionalism.

Japan turned its attention anew to the Asian mainland in the 1990s, but its options to "reenter Asia" were limited by growing rivalry with a resurgent China and lingering distrust due to a territorial dispute with a despondent Russia. Sandwiched between these two continental powers are South Korea, heavily dependent on Japan's larger economy and on a virtual triangular alliance including Japan as well as the United States, and North Korea, seen as requiring massive economic assistance that may draw it to Japan. Unsuccessful in making a break-through in alleviating tensions with their large continental neighbors, the Japanese leadership and media intermittently rested new hopes on the Koreas. After a brief upsurge in relations early in the 1990s, in 1998 and 2003 newly elected presidents of South Korea visited Japan amid a whirlwind of expectations for a break-through able to raise relations to a new level. In 1990 and 2002, high-level visits to Pyongyang aroused hope, if only for a short time, that a milestone had been reached transforming a vitriolic foe into, at least, a partner in negotiations. More than bilateral relations were at stake in these overtures and accompanying discussions: To many, the peninsula represented the gateway to "Asia" or even to "normalcy" in international relations. A century after asserting control over Korea in 1905 as the opening wedge in its rise and fall on the mainland, the Japanese sought to secure a new, if different, foothold there in order to solidify a longstanding role in the emergent Northeast Asian regionalism.

Koreans pose a difficult challenge for the increasingly nationalist governments in Japan insistent not only on suppressing further criticisms of their country's conduct in the first half of the twentieth century but also on finding a measure of justification of the past that would revive national pride. To the consternation of many, South Koreans brandish the "history card" prominently when Japan crosses a well-understood line by tinkering with its textbooks or publicizing visits by the prime minister to Yasukuni Shrine, while North Korea uses the harshest language accusing Japan of reviving its imperialist past. Even when the Japanese media at times grew optimistic that a turning point had been reached, negative Korean perceptions were not long diminished. In spite of recurrent public skepticism, Japanese leaders kept looking to the Koreas to jump-start regionalism.

Foreign policy after the cold war became a more important means for politicians to boost their popularity. This could occur either by becoming identified with a possible breakthrough through what passed as "bold diplomacy" or by standing tall against what was deemed to be "pressure" from their Northeast Asian neighbors or against the now familiar *gaiatsu* (foreign pressure) from the United States. While the latter approach increasingly characterized the leadership's handling of ties to China and remained the most common treatment of North Korea, efforts to create the image of achieving a breakthrough offer the best evidence of Japan's aspirations for regionalism. Three objectives stand in the forefront: (1) economic regionalism, which beginning in 2000 fixed on reaching an FTA with South Korea as the critical goal; (2) security stabilization, which in 2002–4 concentrated on resolving the North Korean nuclear crisis and proceeding to regional cooperation to prevent any repetition; and (3) cultural understanding, which combines putting the history issue to rest, as Kim Dae Jung agreed in 1998, and ending cultural barriers to mutual respect and trust as appeared within reach when newly elected president Roh Moo Hyun agreed in 2003 to complete Korea's cultural opening to Japan. The Korean peninsula became the main venue for some foreign policy success.

South Korea as the Gateway to Regionalism?

The economic foundation for regionalism has been developing at an accelerated pace. By 2003, trade among the Northeast Asian countries had reached more than 31 percent, almost 55 percent, and over 42 percent, respectively, of Japanese, South Korean, and Chinese trade worldwide. The three countries together accounted for nearly 67 percent of total trade within the region. Even though the United States remained the most important trade partner of Japan and South Korea and the second most important for China, there was no doubt that the Japanese, South Korean, and Chinese economies formed the core of growing economic integration in Northeast Asia.

For decades Japanese–South Korean economic ties outpaced other aspects of relations, and in the 1990s the rise of China added the impetus of a triangular dimension within Asia and reduced U.S. economic influence. Having balked at U.S. pressure to reduce trade deficits in the first half of the 1990s, Japan and South Korea were each looking for balance. The Asian financial crisis renewed concern over U.S. pressure, now through the International Monetary Fund (IMF), giving Japan an opportunity to take advantage of growing interest in regionalism. Yet, Japanese ambitions to capitalize on integration of the two economies were met with suspicion. Koreans objected to the label "Sea of Japan Economic Rim" for Japan's early goal of a decentralized region, insisting on calling the body of water between the two countries the "East Sea" and fearing vertical regionalism that would keep their nation dependent. Even after agreeing to talks toward forging a bilateral FTA, the Korean side, galvanized by suspicious media, cautioned against proceeding quickly for fear that Japan's global corporations would in many vital sectors swallow up their smaller Korean counterparts. Willingness to advance at all rested on expectations of growing balance from ties to the Chinese economy and that an FTA with China would soon follow. Koreans were less comfortable than Japanese with bilateralism. Indeed, they suspected that Japan's objective was more to draw them away from China than to establish a region.

Political and security issues were still proving divisive. In 1994 the first nuclear crisis over North Korea found the two states drawn together in the Korean Energy Development Organization (KEDO) to pay for the nuclear reactors promised to the North, but this was an arrangement acceptable to the United States and China that was not well received by Japan, or, at the time, even by South Korea. In 1995, the Japanese undercut their own hopes for a special Korean connection when instead of joint resolutions to resolve the past on the occasion of the fiftieth anniversary of the end of the war and occupation era came a new spate of tensions, including strong Korean protests against unilateral resolutions of the Japanese Diet and prefectural assemblies and a renewed border dispute over the rocky island Dokdo/Takeshima. Insensitive to concerns widely articulated in newly democratic Korea, Japan faced renewed suspicions and even aggressive reactions that brought deteriorating relations during the mid-1990s under Kim Young Sam's presidency. In the summer of 2002, co-hosting of the World Cup soccer championship also failed to lead to full reconciliation highlighted by the emperor's much anticipated visit to the opening ceremony; instead, it unfolded in the shadow of a textbook controversy and the visit was scuttled. Hopes for concluding an FTA in 2005 also hung perilously as Koreans, after stalling talks, faced political turmoil, heightened by a vote to impeach Roh, that left relations with Japan rife with partisanship. While in the long run Korean firms are expected to become competitive and the trade imbalance to decline, the specter loomed of vital industries such as autos and home appliances unable to resist the former colonial power. The South sought to become a bridge to China and achieve reconciliation with the North, but Japan did not recognize it as the "hub of Northeast Asia" while, by contrast, it feared a rising China and a North Korea teetering toward collapse and then bent on brinkmanship.

From 2002 to 2004, coordination on North Korea proved to be the most glaring challenge facing the bilateral relationship. The Japanese vilified the North Koreans not only for their nuclear missile threat but also for their long delay in allowing reunification in Japan of the family members of abducted Japanese who had been allowed to return home after the September 2002 Koizumi trip to Pyongyang, and for the lack of reliable and full accounting for the other Japanese abductees who reportedly died in the North. From this perspective, the Japanese generally accepted the hard line taken by the United States in six-party negotiations, with public support for economic sanctions against Pyongyang steadily growing. In contrast, South Koreans, led by the Roh administration, mostly opposed U.S. tactics and reliance on pressure. Although far more South Koreans were assumed to have been kidnapped and held in the North, South Koreans preferred to concentrate on other matters. Not far in the background were different strategies for advancing the reunification of Korea and linking it to regionalism. Although neither Seoul nor Tokyo wanted South Korea's costly absorption of a collapsing North Korea, Seoul placed a much higher priority on peaceful reunification than did Tokyo, which remained ambivalent about the implications of Korean reunification for its relative position in Northeast Asia. The bilateral relationship between Tokyo and Pyongyang masked the high stakes for Japan's future.

Despite sharp differences, many Japanese and some Koreans looked back on a decade of considerable achievement in bilateral relations and anticipated over the next decade much greater success in forging the building blocks for regionalism. As evidence for such optimism, they pointed to the Kim Dae Jung visit of October 1998 that changed the tone, greatly reducing Korean political rhetoric at the top that could unsettle relations. They likewise recalled approvingly the co-hosting of the World Cup, when both the great success of the host soccer teams and the warm glow of Japanese rooting for Koreans left an enduring image. Finally, both sides were satisfied that cultural barriers had fallen.

Tourism, including Japanese shoppers descending on Seoul, had skyrocketed. Korean chic had led to a series of fads across Japan, ranging from food to musical groups. South Korean visitors to Japanese tourist and shopping spots were also growing fast. When Japan successfully concluded an FTA with Mexico in March 2004, it boosted hopes that other agreements were not far behind—most important, one with South Korea. As anti-Americanism lingered in the South, fueled by the unresolved status of the North's nuclear programs and the negotiations over them, the imperative for close ties to Japan became more obvious. Momentum was growing for a bilateral core within emerging regionalism

Japanese reasoning about regionalism was shifting toward a Korea-centered approach. For a long time Southeast Asia figured prominently in Japan's expectations, the most prominent examples found in its facilitation of the formation of the Association of Southeast Asian Nations (ASEAN) Regional Forum and its active participation in the ASEAN+3 forum. After the Asian financial crisis, however, Japan kept scrambling to match China's growing role in this area and also faced the instability of Indonesian resistance to globalization. The "Sea of Japan Economic Rim" strategy had floundered due to the failure of decentralized networks in a region where centralization long has dominated, including in Japan itself. From the second half of the 1990s China appeared more as a rival to balance than as a bridge to enhance Japan's influence. Despite the fact that South Korean relations were growing ever closer to China, Japanese fixed on that country as critical to their regional interests. When the South was optimistic, as about its economic model from 1995–97, its ties with the North in 2000, and its ability to forge a great-power coalition in 2002, then Japan did not make much headway. When the Japanese most offended South Korean sensibilities, as in dealing with the war legacy in 1995 and 2001, there was a setback in relations. Yet, the long-run trend raised Japanese expectations of a special relationship critical for a new regional framework. With nationalism on the rise, the Japanese were not ready to pay a price.

Pursuit of regionalism did not directly challenge two long-standing priorities that gained new life in the post–cold war years: protection of interest groups supportive of Liberal Democratic Party (LDP) power and alliance with the United States. The former complicated Japanese appeal to the South, since it included agricultural interests fearful of imports from Korea, narrow national interests reluctant to grant Zainichi Koreans full rights in Japan, and vocal patriotic forces that insisted on reasserting the legality of Japan's annexation of Korea and even the voluntary nature of Korean assimilation such as adopting Japanese names around 1940. The right wing intensified its warnings against extreme nationalism in South Korea, despite accepting some steps toward economic regionalism. The biggest change occurred on the political left, where its sympathy for North Korea had become a political liability in the eyes of the increasingly anti-North public and rapidly lost ground. Under the leadership of Kim Dae Jung and Roh Moo Hyun, South Korea became a beacon for Japan's left, diminished as it was. Having more fully embraced regionalism since the 1980s, the opposition parties found a common language with South Korea.

Unlike interest expressed in regionalism in the period 1988–95, Japan's views to 2004 increasingly upgraded the role of the United States. This followed from:

the 1997 agreement on defense guidelines; new nervousness after North Korea tested a missile over northern Japan in 1998; a sense of isolation as Kim Dae Jung's sunshine policy advanced in 2000; and especially from 2002 to 2004 as the showdown between the United States and North Korea left a nuclear weapons program in place. Washington had long encouraged Japan to cooperate more closely with South Korea; closer cross-Pacific ties did not hamper ties to the South.

Indeed, U.S. pressure on South Korea often allowed Japan to gain leverage. In 1997–98, Japan benefited from the accelerated opening of the South, turning intense globalization to the advantage of regionalism that also required more open economies while deflecting most of the blame to the United States. Again, from 2002 to 2004, Japan sided mostly with the United States in repeated trilateral meetings to coordinate policies for talks with North Korea; yet it had the benefit of South Koreans directing their frustration primarily against American pressure. If for most of the postwar era the United States brought two suspicious neighbors closer by its positive contribution to collective security and a shared division of labor, the U.S. impact now included a negative impact on the South that made it more susceptible to Japan. Although both the right and the left would have preferred a Korea policy that was more independent of the United States, North Korea's nuclear and missile development and refusal to fully account for the Japanese abductees boosted Tokyo's support for the U.S. policy toward North Korea.

Toward a Breakthrough with North Korea?

Japan had multiple objectives in relations with North Korea.[1] Some were quite separate from regional goals, centering on the maintenance of a peaceful international environment and a close alliance with the United States. Yet, others related to rising regional aspirations, aiming to shape the future of the Korean peninsula, to expand Japan's regional security role, to channel the rise of China as a regional power, and to resolve lingering bilateral issues with North Korea. Japan could hope to achieve the last of these goals only by normalizing relations with the North. In contrast, the other goals could have been facilitated by the development of political, economic, and security institutions for regional cooperation, as well as by the growth of a regional identity encompassing Japan and its neighbors. The road to building multilateral institutions continues to be formidable, but the normalization agenda vis-à-vis North Korea also was not advancing in 2003–4. It appeared that as long as Japan could not normalize its relations with North Korea and the North remained pitted against the United States in a nuclear weapons standoff, there was little hope for laying the groundwork for regional institution building.

Measured along many dimensions, Northeast Asia lags in developing regionalism. There are no regional institutions founded on a common identity upon which Japan could rely in pursuing its other foreign policy goals. Nor can it be said that Japan has eagerly sought the laying of ideational and material foundations for multilateral institutions designed to promote regionwide cooperation. It has been an important facilitator of regional cooperation in the Asia-Pacific region, playing a key role in the formation of Asia-Pacific Economic Cooperation (APEC) forum and the ASEAN Regional Forum. However, neither is set up to deal with such critical security issues as the tension on the Korean peninsula and nuclear proliferation dangers. Japan's immediate security concerns surrounding the Korean peninsula are being addressed, albeit with very mixed results, through unilateral, bilateral, and multilateral processes that do not involve, as yet, efforts to establish a permanent regional framework.

In the post–cold war environment of the 1990s, the overwhelming importance of Japan's alliance with the United States for its security and for the peace and stability of Northeast Asia rendered bilateralism vis-à-vis Washington the most prominent element of Japan's foreign policy.[2] Bilateral relations with the fast-growing China were also an important element of Tokyo's foreign policy, but those relations were subordinated to the Japan-U.S. alliance, with only economic considerations in Japan's China policy enjoying a degree of independence from the Pacific alliance. On matters concerning the Korean peninsula, the Japan-U.S. alliance remained pivotal for Tokyo. With regard to North Korea, Tokyo took steps to ensure that its bilateral relations with Seoul and Washington were supportive of each other.[3] Fundamentally, Japan's behavior was as Rozman described it: "When in danger, Japan reverts to the alliance [with the United States] that has protected it for more than half a century."[4]

Japan preferred incremental, evolutionary changes in North Korea to other scenarios, such as a military confrontation between North and South Korea, a collapse of North Korea, U.S. military intervention in North Korea, and rapid unification that could enhance China's influence or Korean nationalism. To the extent that Bill Clinton's selective engagement and Kim Dae Jung's sunshine policy could induce a less hostile and more open North Korea, Tokyo supported those policies. Japanese basically believed that improvement in U.S. and South Korean relations with North Korea would have a favorable impact on its normalization with North Korea. Yet, it was nervous about being excluded from the critical decisions or a process that advanced too fast for it to be confident of the consequences, as appeared to be the case in 2000. Tokyo hoped that its own normalization efforts would also contribute to the opening of North Korea, but it realized that pushing ahead with the normalization talks could risk damaging its more important relations with the United States and South Korea. In 1990 and 2002 this risk was apparent, but the North Koreans failed to resolve critical issues that might have led Japan to proceed anyway. From Japan's perspective, an ideal scenario would be one in which the United States, South Korea, and Japan simultaneously engaged North Korea. Such prospects existed prior to the 1994 nuclear crisis and even during the postcrisis Clinton administration, but not under George W. Bush. North Korea remained preoccupied with the United States and security, leaving normalization with Japan for the future.

The 1994 nuclear crisis in North Korea directly threatened Japan's overall goal of maintaining a stable and peaceful environment. Fortunately, Clinton responded by engaging Pyongyang and producing an Agreed Framework requiring North Korea to suspend its nuclear weapons development in exchange for construction of two light-water nuclear reactors and shipment of heavy oil to compensate for lost electric power. Following some initial grumbling about lack of prior consultations, Tokyo decided to support the Agreed Framework and joined the new organization KEDO to implement the agreement. Japan believed that the U.S.–North Korean accord would neutralize a major threat to stability in Northeast Asia and support the purpose of Japan's alliance with the United States.

Tokyo also endorsed South Korea's sunshine policy toward North Korea, although with some nervousness about where it was leading. The on-again, off-again talks between the two Koreas had long complicated Tokyo's own approach to Pyongyang, with periods of North-South impasse preventing any major initiatives from Tokyo. Tokyo waited until after the first round of high-level Seoul-Pyongyang talks in September 1990 before seriously exploring normalization with Pyongyang. Japan welcomed the simultaneous admission of North and South Korea into the United Nations in September 1991 and the North-South basic agreement and joint declaration on a nuclear-free Korean peninsula in December. The South Korean–Chinese rapprochement in 1992 also indicated to Japan an improving regional environment. Yet, when Japanese efforts to gain a large say on peninsular matters through accelerated talks with the North repeatedly floundered, there was ambivalence about becoming marginalized in regional decision making.

The normalization talks proved difficult, starting with some legal and jurisdictional disagreements. First, Japan wanted to establish that North Korea's jurisdiction did not extend beyond the Thirty-eighth Parallel, whereas Pyongyang apparently feared that such an interpretation would justify the division of the Korean Peninsula. Second, Tokyo argued the 1910 treaty of annexation of Korea was legally concluded and was therefore a legitimate treaty, but Pyongyang insisted the treaty was null and void from the very beginning. Third, Japan asserted that the San Francisco Peace Treaty (concluding the Pacific War in 1945) was an important consideration in the restoration of diplomatic relations, but Pyongyang rejected Japan's assertion because it was not a party to the treaty. A more tangible issue related to North Korea's demand for Japanese compensation for the latter's colonial rule in Korea until 1945 and for the losses it claimed to have suffered as a consequence of the Japanese–South Korean diplomatic recognition in 1965. Tokyo rejected Pyongyang's demand for postwar responsibility. Pyongyang pressed for war reparations and compensations, but Tokyo asserted that it had no obligation because Japan and North Korea were never officially at war. Tokyo also rejected Pyongyang's demand for damages due to what the North termed Japan's complicity in the Korean War. Normalization talks were suspended in 1992, when the North Korean side walked out.

Lack of progress on the normalization front was not of critical concern to Tokyo as long as it did not negatively affect its diplomatic agendas vis-à-vis the other major powers, and it did not until 1998, when North Korea launched a Taepodong missile over Japan on August 31, 1998. The incident promoted a quick response in Tokyo including unilateral sanctions against Pyongyang. Tokyo also halted chartered flights, humanitarian assistance, financial contributions to the KEDO, and negotiations for diplomatic normalization. It was not until December 1999 that a delegation representing all major political parties visited Pyongyang and the two sides agreed to resume talks.[5] The June 2000 summit of the Koreas was followed by a flurry of diplomatic meetings between Seoul and Tokyo designed to inform each other of their progress with Pyongyang and to impress on North Korea the close Japanese–South Korean cooperation. At the normalization talks in Tokyo in August 2000, the North Korean side repeated its demand for Japanese apologies and reparations, while the Japanese side raised the issue of ten Japanese citizens believed to have been abducted by North Korean agents in the 1970s and 1980s. The next, round of talks, the eleventh, in Beijing in October saw both sides reiterate their positions. Japan proposed to normalize relations on the model of the Japan–South Korea normalization, including Japanese economic assistance to North Korea, but the Democratic People's Republic of Korea side rejected the proposal.[6] The North Korean side expressed appreciation for Japan's decision to extend food aid, but there was no progress on the abduction issue. Despite advances in North Korean talks with all other states in 2000, Japan was left on the periphery.

In the first decade after the cold war North Korea played a smaller role in Japan's efforts to boost regionalism than in those of China, Russia, and South Korea. All along China sought to balance its ties in Korea in order to shape the evolution of the peninsula and regional security. In the case of Russia, an initial, abrupt shift from alliance with the North to one-sided reliance on the South yielded to increasingly successful efforts to rebuild ties to the North. In 2000, as Vladimir Putin was forging a personal connection to Kim Jong Il, Kim Dae Jung was doing so as well. Meanwhile, the Clinton administration was also making the Japanese nervous with its support for the sunshine policy and exploration of the possibility of a presidential visit to Pyongyang. Unexpectedly, North Korea had become the focus of attention in the region, and Japan was being sidelined. It had concentrated on economic regionalism, relying on the United States for security, without expecting that multipower diplomacy centered on security and the state of the Korean peninsula would shift the focus of the region. Japan had let first historical issues and then the abduction question decide its approach to the North, while others turned their attention to future-oriented matters. If delay in cultivating trust and partnership with South Korea in the first half of the 1990s had set back the schedule for realizing economic regionalism that bypassed North Korea, then disregard in the second half of the 1990s for the North's ability to energize multipower maneuvering left Japan ill-equipped to play an active role as security rose to the fore in regionalism.

Japanese diplomacy was being pulled in competing directions by developments in the United States and South Korea. The inauguration of George W. Bush in January 2001 dramatically changed the dynamics of international relations surrounding North Korea. The new administration systematically distanced itself from Clinton's policy of selective engagement with North Korea and the 1994 Agreed Framework and was openly skeptical about South Korea's sunshine policy. The terrorist attacks on the United States on September 11, 2001, and Bush's "war on terrorism" all but dashed any hope of U.S.–North Korean engagement. In his State of the Union address on February 1, 2002, Bush labeled North Korea, Iran, and Iraq an "axis of evil," having on September 20 already released a new strategic doctrine declaring U.S. willingness to launch a preemptive attack on terrorist groups and rogue states.

When Roh Moo Hyun became South Korea's president in 2003, adamantly committed to continuing engagement with North Korea and widely supported by a public that demanded a policy independent of the United States, the gap between Washington and Seoul widened, complicating Tokyo's policy. It was increasingly untenable for Japan to pursue normalization with North Korea when the United States and South Korea were at odds with each other over North Korea policy. Moreover, the Japanese people had become so obsessed with the issue of abductions and lingering family separations that leaders lacked flexibility to pursue a bilateral track.

Not to be left out of the evolving international politics surrounding North Korea, Prime Minister Koizumi decided to gamble on a breakthrough with North Korea by traveling to Pyongyang. Koizumi and Kim Jong Il met on September 17, 2002, and agreed on the Pyongyang Declaration, stating agreement to resume normalization talks in October 2002 and to discuss outstanding bilateral issues even before diplomatic normalization. The Japanese side apologized for the damage and suffering its colonial rule of Korea had inflicted upon the Korean people and agreed that upon restoration of diplomatic ties it would extend economic assistance to North Korea. The two sides agreed to "waive all their property and claims and those of their nationals that had arisen from causes which occurred before August 15, 1945." They also agreed to discuss the status of Korean residents in Japan and the issue of cultural property through normalization talks, concurring that they would "comply with international law and would not commit conduct that would threaten the other side." With regard to the "outstanding issues of concern related to the lives and security of Japanese citizens"—a reference to the abduction issue—the North said that it would take appropriate measures to prevent the recurrence of "these regrettable incidents," that had taken place "under the abnormal relations between the two countries."[7] To the surprise of the Japanese side, Kim personally apologized for the North Korean kidnapping of Japanese citizens.

The declaration stated further that the two sides would cooperate in maintaining and strengthening the peace and stability of Northeast Asia and confirmed the "importance of establishing cooperative relationships based upon mutual trust among countries concerned in this region" and the importance of building a framework for confidence building among the regional powers as part of the process of normalizing relations. The two parties agreed, "For an overall resolution of the nuclear issues on the Korean peninsula, they would comply with all related international agreements." Pyongyang stated it would extend its moratorium on missile launching beyond 2003, as the two parties agreed to consult each other on security issues.[8] Japan also told the North Korean side that it was important for North–South Korean dialogue to move forward and for U.S.–North Korean discussions to reopen.[9]

The most immediate impact of the Pyongyang Declaration was seen on the abduction issue, but not in the way Koizumi had hoped. On the contrary, the issue quickly hijacked the normalization agenda and caused the suspension of all diplomatic efforts toward normalization with Pyongyang. Japan had insisted on settlement of the kidnapping issue as a prerequisite for the resumption of normalization talks. The North agreed, admitting that thirteen Japanese nationals had been taken from Japan and eight of them had died in North Korea. In early October, Pyongyang announced that the five surviving Japanese abductees would be allowed temporarily to return to Japan. Soon they arrived to a thunderous welcome. At first, it was reported that they would stay for two weeks, but their families and some politicians pressed for their permanent resettlement in Japan. When the government made this official, North Korea was quick to accuse Japan of breaking its agreement. A new element of mistrust bedeviled efforts to engage in talks.

Media frenzy over the kidnapping issue continued, with only limited discussion of the other agreements at the Pyongyang summit. The revelation of the deaths of eight Japanese abductees and North Korea's less-than-full accounting of the circumstances of their demise angered the Japanese public. Deputy Cabinet Minister Shinzo Abe publicly demanded that the family members of the five returnees who had been left behind be allowed to come to Japan. Right-wing LDP members pressed for a tougher policy toward North Korea. A nonpartisan Diet Members' League on the Abduction Issue demanded that the government not enter normalization talks until the issue was satisfactorily resolved. Talks in Kuala Lumpur in late October 2002 floundered over the issue. Normalization had become a hostage to the abduction issue, as Tokyo insisted that resolution of the abduction issue was a precondition for resuming talks.[10]

With respect to other issues, Japanese observers heralded the Pyongyang Declaration as an important diplomatic achievement. One academic stressed that Koizumi's initiative exhibited an unusual degree of independence from the United States.[11] Another echoed this sentiment, stating that the Pyongyang Declaration was "an epoch-making" document in that it represented Japan's "first step toward 'a new Northeast Asian' regionalism, after 57 years of hiding behind bilateral relations with the United States following the miserable failure of its 'Greater East Asia Co-Prosperity Sphere' scheme."[12] A third professor offered an equally favorable assessment that the declaration opened up a possibility of multilateral talks on the Korean peninsula and that the document stressed the importance of solving the nuclear, missile, and other security problems through multilateral dialogues involving Northeast Asian countries.[13] A senior researcher of the National Institute for Defense Studies concurred and wrote that Japan succeeded in obtaining North Korea's acknowledgment of the need to develop a multilateral framework for confidence building and dialogue for peace and stability in the region.[14]

Japan later explored the possibility of bringing the abduction issue to the multilateral talks in Beijing, but China let it be known that it did not want to include the issue on the agenda, in apparent deference to North Korea.[15] Japan sought the endorsement of other countries for a compromise—if not to raise the issue during the six-party talks, at least to discuss it in a bilateral meeting with the North on the sidelines. Japan obtained U.S. and South Korean support as it took steps to impress on the international community how much importance it attached to the issue.[16] Thus, Japan "internationalized" the abduction issue but obviously did not want the issue to scuttle the multilateral agenda. For the LDP a tough stance on this emotional issue produced a positive political payoff, and there was no price to pay as long as the standoff between the United States and North Korea left other matters in abeyance. Yet Koizumi's second visit to Pyongyang in May 2004, as he urged the United States to be more compromising at the June six-party talks, suggests that some were looking beyond the standoff.

In 2004, the Japanese parliament approved legislation requiring all foreign ships coming to Japan to carry liability insurance against environmental damage they might cause while in Japanese waters. The law, which went into effect on March 1, 2005, applied to vessels of any nationality, but it was understood that the new requirement was aimed primarily at North Korean ships, most of which had no such insurance. Behind this action was the growing public support for economic sanctions against North Korea over the abduction issue. A *Kyodo News* poll in December 2004 showed that 75.1 percent of respondents wanted the Japanese government to "invoke economic sanctions and take a stern posture" against North Korea.[17] Similarly, in a *Yomiuri Shimbun* public opinion poll taken shortly after the North Korean declaration that it had nuclear weapons, 71 percent of the respondents stated Japan should set a deadline for resolving the abduction issue and impose economic sanctions.[18] In February 2005, Prime Minister Koizumi received a petition, signed by five million people, demanding economic sanctions against North Korea.[19]

In the spring of 2005, Pyongyang announced that it had completed the withdrawal of 8,000 fuel rods from its nuclear facilities in Yongbyon and continued to refuse to return to the six-party talks until "a proper time arrived." Talk was growing in the United States and elsewhere about a nuclear-capable North Korea. With the nuclear crisis deepening, some influential Japanese politicians openly began to advocate taking the nuclear issue to the United Nations Security Council.

In the crisis environment it was clear that Japan shares a number of other interests with its regional neighbors: the desire for a nuclear-free Korean peninsula and a negotiated settlement; and willingness to offer North Korea some form of security guarantee.[20] However, as long as the North demands a legally binding treaty with the United States but the latter rejects it, Japan has no viable alternative to offer. Japan also shares with China, South Korea, and Russia the concern that a regime collapse in North Korea or a major military conflict on the Korean peninsula, provoked or unprovoked by outside powers, would result in the outflow of tens of thousands of refugees and raise serious economic, humanitarian, and security issues for nearby countries.

Additionally, Japan shares a common interest with China, South Korea, Russia, and the United States in wanting North Korea to reform its economy and stop its threatening military posture. However, these countries are not agreed on what kind of economic reform North Korea should undertake and what role if any, each of them should play in support of reform. Furthermore, Japan and Russia share the view that their participation in the multilateral forum establishes their importance to the peace and stability of Northeast Asia generally, and, more specifically, guarantees them a role in the eventual resolution of the North Korean problem, in which Japan is likely to bear a substantially larger share of the burden than Russia.

Japan differs from the other regional powers in three important respects: it has distinct bilateral issues outstanding with North Korea; its security is fundamentally tied to U.S. policy, setting it apart even from South Korea, where there is a strong sense of ethnic or nationalist bond with North Korea, which tends to defuse perception of a North Korean threat; and all regional powers have varying degrees of suspicion about Japan's long-term interests, some based on the history of Japanese aggression and some on its alliance with the United States, which has encouraged Japanese rearmament over the years. These facts constrain Japan's ability to play a leading role in forging cooperation in the region and also limit bilateral cooperation, particularly with China. In the region, Japan and South Korea share the most immediate security concern with respect to North Korea, and largely due to this, the two countries have stepped up their security consultations and defense cooperation. Of course, their mutual security is intimately tied to U.S. policy in the region, placing a burden on the three, collectively, to coordinate on the North Korean challenge.

Japan and South Korea are closely watching the U.S. debate on North Korea. Japan's cautious approach to North Korea resonates with former secretary of defense William Perry's warning to the Bush administration that without engagement with Pyongyang, North Korea's nuclear weapons development might pass a point of no return, which would be a major blow to the Nuclear Non-proliferation Treaty.[21] South Korea, more than Japan, prefers engagement to confrontation with North Korea. Seoul believes that it should offer carrots to induce Pyongyang to give concessions. Roh Moo Hyun insists that the common bond as a nation between the North and South Koreans should be the basis of Seoul's policy. Although soon after his inauguration Roh's statements toward the United States had dramatically softened, the resulting efforts to coordinate trilateral policy left the initiative in Washington's hands and scarcely smooth over differences between Japan and South Korea.

Japan and South Korea share a number of common interests with respect to the peace and security of Northeast Asia in general and North Korea in particular. At the most general level, both countries desire a stable security environment in which they can concentrate on their pressing domestic problems, particularly on the economic front, and also pursue their foreign policy interests, especially in advancing the cause of regional economic integration and dealing with both traditional and nontraditional security challenges. To both, the end of the cold war meant the disappearance of the Soviet Union as a security threat. The two countries are now peacefully engaged with Russia and developing cooperation politically, economically, and in the security field. Both are keen on the development of oil and gas reserves in Siberia and the Russian Far East to reduce their heavy dependence on Middle East oil, sharing an interest in the development of railroad and pipeline links from Russia to their markets that would require North Korea's participation. A peaceful settlement of the current nuclear crisis would offer an economic bonus to Japan and South Korea, even though security remains their utmost concern.

China's burgeoning power is generating conflicting interpretations and responses in both Japan and South Korea. Some analysts in both countries view China's economic growth and concomitant integration with the international community as a positive influence on the region's stability inasmuch as China's expanded international presence increases the transparency of its international policy and its incentives for international cooperation. Others emphasize the current lack of transparency in China's defense policy and its authoritarian political system and fear its possible use of force over the Taiwan issue. With respect to China's policy toward North Korea, both Japan and South Korea welcome Beijing's more activist engagement in recent years but would be concerned if China were to become the most dominant architect of the future political landscape on the Korean peninsula.

Japan and South Korea also share some interests regarding U.S. policy in the region. They both recognize the crucial role that the U.S. military presence plays in preventing possible Chinese dominance in the region and in deterring North Korean aggression, agreeing that close consultation with Washington is crucial in dealing with Pyongyang. The United States serves as an indirect channel of defense cooperation between Tokyo and Seoul and ameliorates tension between them.[22] Since 1969, Japan has acknowledged the critical importance of the defense of South Korea to its own security.[23] In 1981, President Chun Doo Hwan stated, "The strengthening of Japan's navy and air force will reinforce our (South Korea's) territorial security system."[24] This results in a "virtual alliance."[25] In addition, in the event of a North Korean attack on South Korea, the U.S. bases in Japan would play a critical role in supporting South Korean forces and U.S. forces in South Korea. Japan is also expected to provide rear support for U.S. forces in such an eventuality.[26]

Beyond the Korean peninsula, Japan and South Korea also share some security interests. Access to Middle East oil and foreign markets for their exports is of critical importance to their economies. Japan and South Korea conduct 27 percent and 39 percent of their respective international trade with the other Northeast Asian countries. They are also heavily dependent on the United States as an economic partner, conducting nearly one-half and more than one-third of their respective world trade with the United States. Therefore, a peaceful and stable regional environment is very important to the two countries and securing maritime shipping in Southeast Asia, Northeast Asia, and across the Pacific is a matter of great strategic importance to them.

Japanese–South Korean relations remain strained, however. Contemporary bilateral ties remain hostage to the lingering animosity and suspicion among South Koreans regarding Japanese wartime atrocities against them and other Asian peoples. The history issue flared up again in 2004 and 2005 over the long-standing territorial dispute over Dokdo/Takeshima Island, Japanese history textbooks' treatment of Japanese colonialism and militarism in the previous centuries, and Japanese leaders' visits to Yasukuni Shrine, where war criminals and other war dead are buried. As tension mounted over these issues, in May 2005, Roh Moo Hyun stated his opposition to Japan's bid for a permanent seat on the UN Security Council.

It is North Korea and the security threats it poses that are the most pressing concerns in Japan–South Korea security and defense cooperation.[27] In 1969, Japan's Defense Agency and South Korea's Ministry of National Defense began exchanging personnel, but it was the 1994 nuclear crisis in North Korea that prompted Tokyo and Seoul to engage in genuine defense cooperation. During the crisis, Washington encouraged and mediated defense interaction between Tokyo and Seoul. Through this experience, Tokyo and Seoul came to realize the importance of strengthening their respective alliances with Washington and improving communication between themselves. Since then, defense officials of the two countries have been meeting every year. A series of incidents involving North Korea in 1996–99 further highlighted the importance of Japan–South Korea defense cooperation. In September 1996, a North Korean submarine ran aground on South Korea's eastern coast; in June 1998, the South Korean navy captured a North Korean submarine; and in August 1998, North Korea launched a Taepodong missile over Japan. The South Korean navy sank a North Korean submarine in its southern waters in December 1998, and in March 1999, two ships suspected to be of North Korean origin invaded Japanese territorial waters before returning to North Korea. These incidents led to the establishment of a hotline and an emergency communication system between Japan and South Korea and the start of joint search-and-rescue exercises on the high seas. Moreover, in 1999, Japan, South Korea, and the United States forged a trilateral consultation mechanism (the Trilateral Coordination and Oversight Group) to coordinate their approaches to North Korea.

The improving political relations between the two countries have made expansion of bilateral defense cooperation possible. The 1998 Partnership Declaration between Keizo Obuchi and Kim Dae Jung referred to the two countries' mutual security concerns, including missile development in North Korea. The declaration also formalized the meetings between the defense ministers of the two countries, which had begun in 1996. Today, in addition to defense personnel exchanges, bilateral security cooperation between Japan and Korea includes confidence-building measures between the Japan Maritime Self-Defense Force and the Republic of Korea (ROK) Navy, agreements on managing airspace between the Japan Air Self-Defense Force and the ROK Air Force.

Conclusion

Circumstances largely beyond Japan's control have forced the nation to pursue both bilateral and multilateral approaches toward Korea in recent decades. The bilateral initiatives, although they did not proceed far enough to be well tested, were generally compatible with the development of multilateralism over the evolving North Korean situation. The complicated multilateral scene, especially over the current nuclear crisis, is replete with immediate difficulties and longer-term complications, over which Japan has little or no control. Tokyo, therefore, has little option but to continue trilateral coordination with the United States and South Korea, while pressing each side, urging the United States to find a nonmilitary solution to the conflict, and appealing to the South to accept the need for pressure on the North. Because Tokyo is encouraging Beijing to stay actively engaged with Pyongyang to ensure the latter's constructive role in the six-party talks, the Japanese are becoming more aware of their dependency on a regional solution. They must also demonstrate a willingness to forgo immediate resolution of the abduction issue if doing so would enhance the probability of success in the multilateral talks. However, domestic pressure is pushing Tokyo in the opposite direction. A coalition of conservative politicians and nationalist critics of North Korea is supporting the five former abductees' campaign to be reunited in Japan with their family members left behind in North Korea. They are insisting that until then Tokyo should not resume normalization talks with Pyongyang.

The outcome of the six-party talks would have far-reaching implications for Japan's policies toward North and South Korea, for the Korean peninsula, and for the entire Northeast Asian region. The bilateralism of the Koizumi-Kim summit in Pyongyang envisaged a yet-to-be-defined multilateralism, in which Japan would have a big stake. Japan's trilateral coordination with South Korea and the United States has been an important means of balancing its policy with that of its partners, and since the beginning of the six-party talks, it has become an essential requirement for securing Japan's place in the multilateral talks. These talks will continue to test Japan's ability to pursue its own interests, find a commonality of interests with the other powers, and lay the groundwork for a multilateral framework for peace and stability in Northeast Asia. A successful conclusion would also facilitate Japan's goal of normalizing relations with North Korea and removing one of the last vestiges of its tumultuous history.[28]

In Japan's multilevel approach to Korea, in short, we see a possible building block toward multilateral regionalism. Japan must coordinate with the United States, whose views of security have recently put great pressure on the region and whose notions of economic globalization and political cooperation may impede regional initiatives. Japan must also sustain the momentum of recent improvements in relations with South Korea against recurrent challenges from nationalists on both sides. Finally, it will need to calibrate its timing in new initiatives toward North Korea to take advantage of any advances in the six-party talks and other venues without allowing the process of normalization to complicate relations with South Korea and the United States. The biggest challenges for Japan in using the Korean peninsula for regionalism lie ahead.

12

Korea and China in Northeast Asia

From Stable Bifurcation to Complicated Interdependence

Jae Ho Chung

As it did during the late nineteenth century, Korea—or two Koreas this time—have again emerged as the "center" of diplomatic attention, strategic importance, and security concern in Northeast Asia at the dawn of the new millennium. No elaboration seems necessary on the kind and level of attention the Democratic People's Republic of Korea (hereafter, North Korea) has received since the early 1990s for its nuclear brinkmanship, missile programs, dire economic conditions, illicit trafficking, and human rights violations. Irrespective of normative judgments, Pyongyang has indeed become a "center" of policy attention from all the major players in Northeast Asia.[1]

The Republic of Korea (hereafter, South Korea) has also been recently assigned a "center" status in terms of attracting economic, diplomatic, and strategic attention from both the United States and China. The curious relationship between Seoul and Beijing has come a long way from being antagonistic enemies to "comprehensive cooperative partners" for the future.[2] While South Korea has been highly successful in engaging China, the very success of Seoul's rapprochement with Beijing is now coming back to haunt it.

South Korea's decision in 1999 not to join the U.S.-led scheme for Theater Missile Defense and its sensitivity to discussing China-related issues at the Trilateral Coordination and Oversight Group displeased the United States. South Korea's emerging bilateralism with China has thus constituted a new variable in America's strategic design for Northeast Asia.[3] Whereas South Korea wishes to maintain amicable and beneficial relationships with both the United States and China, from America's perspective, Seoul's unprecedented efforts to maintain a strategic balance between Washington and Beijing have been viewed with grave concern.[4]

As the "Korean issue"—both North and South—has become paramount to regional peace and stability, Washington and Beijing each wish to pull Seoul toward their respective sides of the fence. It was even suggested that "China has moved to cultivate close relations with the government in Seoul—perhaps in anticipation of an eventual United States withdrawal. . . . The United States must make *special efforts* to sustain its close alliance ties to South Korea" (emphasis added).[5] South Korea is once again poised at the "center" between two competing—continental versus maritime—great powers.[6]

The quote above is highly reminiscent of the prescription that Huang Zunxian—a Qing diplomat based in Tokyo—offered to the Yi dynasty of Choson in 1880, namely, "[T]he priority order of Choson's external strategy should first be to side with China, second to align with Japan, and then to connect with America" (*qinzhong jieri lianmei*).[7] Will history repeat itself, imposing a choice between the forces of regionalism and globalization, this time with a reversed order of preference?

The contemporary conundrum, however, differs significantly from the earlier dilemma of the late nineteenth century in that the abnormalcy of the cold war created a bifurcation, and two pairs of Sino-Korean relationships were produced. With the two Koreas once again situated at the "center" of international attention, both positive and negative, the role of China—and its "rise"—becomes an increasingly important variable in determining the regional dynamics of Northeast Asia. And Sino-Korean relations have risen to the status of independent variable following the disintegration of the larger cold-war structure.

This chapter, tracing China's relations with two Koreas during the second half of the twentieth century (1948–2002), takes the position that China's relations with the two Koreas from the 1950s through the 1970s were principally the derivative of great-power relations, most notably of the strategic triangle among the United States, the Soviet Union, and China. In addition, it also suggests, Beijing's relations with Pyongyang and Seoul since the 1980s have become increasingly independent of the U.S.-Soviet power dynamics, thereby creating the space for the bilateral ties in their own rights. That is to say, in recent years, Sino-Korean relations have become more proactive than reactive, at the same time, making the modus operandi of these relationships more interest based than norm driven.

The remainder of the chapter consists of three sections. The first discusses the parameters within which China's relations with the two Koreas had been defined and confined by ideological norms and great-power relations during the three distinct periods of the 1950s, 1960s, and 1970s. The second section examines China-Korea relations during the 1980s and 1990s, as they became increasingly independent of great-power dynamics and based more on tangible interests than ideological norms. The third section offers some concluding observations concerning future relations between China and the two Koreas in connections with strategic contingencies involving the United States, Japan, and North Korea.

Sino-Korean Relations as Derivatives of Great-Power Dynamics

During the three decades from the Korean War to the late 1970s, Sino-Korean relations were predominantly circumscribed by great-power relations founded initially on ideological norms and later on strategic rationales. As with cases elsewhere, the cold-war structure—that is, U.S.-Soviet bipolarity—had defined the general parameter of strategic alignment for medium-size (China) and small powers (South Korea and North Korea). Room for independent maneuvering had been minimized for all three states during the 1950s, increased considerably for China and somewhat for North Korea during the 1960s, and expanded further for China and incrementally for South Korea during the 1970s. Sino-Korean relations remained largely the derivative of U.S.-Soviet dynamics in these three decades, during which the relative composition of ideological and strategic constraints gradually changed.

The "Stable Marriage" During the 1950s

If ideological and strategic factors facilitated the bifurcation of Korean-Chinese ties into South Korean–Taiwan and North Korean–Chinese relations, the Korean War (1950–53) solidified the cold war structure in Northeast Asia. In the post–Korean War years, military tensions across the Taiwan Strait, as well as between Seoul and Pyongyang, were constantly reinforced by intermittent conflict within the overall structure of the U.S.-Soviet rivalry.[8] These two pairs of Sino-Korean relations were thus the inevitable derivatives of the ideological war between Washington and Moscow during the decade of the 1950s.

The realist paradigm posits that the international environment is inherently anarchic and therefore military-strategic concerns always dominate the policy agenda, as the dictum of "conquer thy neighbor or be conquered by it" aptly describes. So long as survival is the ultimate priority, strategic concerns carry the most weight in any country's foreign policy formulation.[9] The borderline between survival and perishing was for most states ideologically drawn during the 1950s.

Survival was certainly the top priority for China, a new state with many painful wounds inflicted by foreign imperialism since the Opium War.[10] The same goes for the two Koreas as well: Neither was allowed to choose at will whether and with whom to ally. Alignment with either the Soviet Union (in the cases of China and North Korea) or with the United States (in the cases of South Korea and Taiwan) was never a choice but simply given.[11]

Whether the determinant for their respective alignment was wholly ideological is, of course, debatable. Perhaps strategic, historical, cultural, and even personal factors were all involved to varying degrees to augment the "northern" alliance of the Soviet Union, China, and North Korea vis-à-vis the "southern" counterpart of the United States, Taiwan, and South Korea. China's painstaking decision to enter the Korean War is perhaps the best example of the multitude of factors in operation. With the civil war continuing in Sichuan, Guizhou, and Tibet; with Taiwan pledging reunification by force; and with unbearable levels of inflation, China nevertheless chose to stand on the other side of the nuclear superpower, the United States, backed by the United Nations. Certainly, there was much more to its decision to support North Korea than ideological solidarity although ideology was no doubt a key determinant.[12]

The relationship among China and the two Koreas during the 1950s can thus be labeled as a "stable marriage"—a relationship of amity between two (China and North Korea) and of enmity between each and the third player (South Korea).[13] Yet these relationships were embedded in a larger global strategic confrontation between the U.S.-led capitalist bloc and the Soviet-led socialist bloc. Ideology played a crucial, if not exclusive, role, allowing little room for benign perceptions and improved relations between China and North Korea, on the one hand, and South Korea and Taiwan, on the other.[14]

The Emergence of a "Small Strategic Triangle" During the 1960s

The decade of the 1960s began with the Sino-Soviet split, which had fermented since the mid-1950s only to erupt in 1960. The Sino-Soviet schism and subsequent conflicts were due in significant part to China's unwillingness to swallow Soviet directing. China's "self-reliance" (zili gengsheng) tenet pronounced during the Great Leap Forward antagonized the Soviet Union, facilitating an eventual breakup of the Moscow-led socialist bloc. The Soviet Union's pursuit of "peaceful coexistence" with the United States further reduced room for a possible rapprochement between Moscow and Beijing.[15] China's subsequent adoption of the "anti-U.S. imperialist, anti-Soviet revisionist and anti-reactionary" (fandui dixiufan) stance created a radically different soil for Sino-Korean relations compared to that of the 1950s.[16]

The breakup of the socialist bloc, or the emergence of the "third" camp, generated a very different context for Sino-Korean relations. China was determined to stand against both the United States and the Soviet Union, even to the point of engaging in several military skirmishes with the Soviet Union in Xinjiang and Heilongjiang. The successful detonation of Chinese-made atomic and hydrogen bombs in 1964 and 1967 significantly boosted Beijing's confidence in dealing with Washington and Moscow. Nevertheless, ideology continued to define China's foreign relations; however this culminated in xenophobic extremism during the Cultural Revolution (1966–69).

North Korea's relations with China witnessed ebbs and flows during the 1960s. While Pyongyang more often sided with Beijing in ideological terms, it nevertheless had to seek considerable economic and military assistance from Moscow.[17] North Korea sincerely emulated several radical policies from China while actively increasing trade with and aid from the Soviet Union.[18] Over time, during this era of Sino-Soviet schism, a "small strategic triangle" formed among Moscow, Beijing, and Pyongyang, and North Korea managed to develop its own modus operandi in dealing with both the Soviet Union and China. In fact, it was in this period that Pyongyang learned the intricate tactics of tough bargaining vis-à-vis its stronger neighbors and counterparts.[19]

Throughout the 1960s, South Korea's relations with China remained deeply antagonistic due to the enmity generated during the Korean War and perpetuated by the radicalization of ideology within China as well as by South Korea's staunch anticommunist stance. China stressed a special amicable relationship with North Korea—except during 1967–69—one that was often dubbed an "alliance sealed in blood" (*xiemeng*). On the other hand, South Korea sustained a very amicable relationship with Taiwan, China's archenemy, not only through their firm commitment to alliance with the United States, but also via close personal ties between Chiang Kai-shek and Syngman Rhee and Park Chung Hee.[20]

The highly antagonistic relationship between China and South Korea continued throughout the 1960s. Occasional armistice meetings at Panmunjom provided the only venue for close encounters between Seoul and Beijing. A few fortuitous incidents could have served as useful pretexts for initiating official contact between China and South Korea, but did not. For instance, when two Chinese military pilots defected to South Korea with their AN-2 reconnaissance plane in 1961, Seoul simply chose not to communicate with Beijing at all and immediately sent the pilots and even the plane to Taiwan, which Seoul then recognized as the sole legitimate government of China. On the other hand, China often detained South Korean fishing vessels and their crew for periods up to fifteen years, charging that the boats had intruded on Chinese territorial waters. South Korea, however, had no channel or means to negotiate with China for their return.[21]

Worse yet, North Korea's intermittent military provocations—such as the *Pueblo* Incident and commando attack on the Blue House in 1968, and the EC-121 Incident in 1969—made it impossible for South Korea to imagine trying to improve relations with China. In sum, ideology remained a defining factor throughout the 1960s. The Moscow-Beijing-Pyongyang triangle became as—if not more—strategic as it was ideological, while the solidarity of the Washington-Tokyo-Seoul trilateral linkage remained mostly intact.

Pragmatic Realpolitik During the 1970s

During this period, China's perennial preoccupation with survival necessitated a radical break with its "isolationist" policy of the late 1960s and subsequently led to its strategic "alignment with the (capitalist) United States against the (socialist) Soviet Union" (*fansu lianmei*), or a "united front" (*yitiaoxian*) against Moscow. In hindsight, China had since 1969 been meticulously preparing for its new diplomacy and, to the surprise of many, succeeded in attaining America's tacit endorsement for replacing Taiwan at the United Nations Security Council in 1971. A series of shocking events thereafter—Kissinger's and Nixon's visits to China and the resulting Shanghai communiqué—were sufficient enough to demonstrate China's new strategic thinking in which ideology became increasingly irrelevant as far as foreign policy was concerned.[22]

The global strategic environment drastically changed during the 1970s, illustrated by the rapprochement between China and the United States, and China's diplomatic normalization with Japan and many West European countries. Washington, in response, relaxed export restrictions against China. These crucial measures were soon responded to by Premier Zhou Enlai's "Four Modernizations" drive in 1975, which stressed peace and stability in Asia. Motivated by the communist victory in Vietnam, Kim Il Sung allegedly proposed to Mao Zedong in 1975 that North Korea and China undertake joint military action to regain South Korea and Taiwan. Beijing quietly turned down Pyongyang's proposal.[23] If this was indeed true, China must have differed significantly from North Korea in its strategic assessment. Despite a curious interregnum during 1976–78 after Mao's death, perhaps due to China's succession politics and Taiwan's lobbying efforts, Beijing's alignment with Washington, based on strategic pragmatism, remained largely intact.[24]

North Korea responded in three different ways to China's more pragmatic stance. First, Pyongyang fine-tuned its "equidistance" policy vis-à-vis Beijing and Moscow. To maximize its chances of attaining military and economic assistance from both, North Korea meticulously refrained from criticizing China for its border war with Vietnam and from supporting the Soviet invasion of Afghanistan in 1979. Second, Pyongyang actively sought to elevate the *juche* (self-reliance) ideology to the level of Marxism and Maoism. At the same time, Pyongyang responded positively to Seoul's overture for reduction of tension on the peninsula by supporting family reunions via the Red Cross and exchanging high-level secret envoys.[25] Third, North Korea also sought to expand its trade with Japan and, by the late 1970s, Japan had become North Korea's third-largest trade partner. Pragmatism was clearly evident in Pyongyang's policy during this period.[26]

What merits our attention is South Korea's proactive diplomacy toward China. Keenly aware of China's influence over North Korea, Seoul concluded that improving relations with Beijing would help to reduce tension and maintain peace on the peninsula. In 1971, Kim Yong-Sik, South Korea's foreign minister, commented: "[I]t is the policy of my government to approach the question of normalizing diplomatic relations with the Soviet Union and the People's Republic of China with flexibility and seriousness."[27] In 1972, South Korea amended Article 2 of its Foreign Trade Laws so as to permit trading with communist countries.[28] After the Sino-American Shanghai communiqué was announced in 1972, China also began to refer to the Republic of Korea as the "South Korean authorities" (*nanchaoxian dangju*) instead of the "Park Chung Hee puppet regime" or the "South Korean running dog of American imperialism."

In 1973, Seoul issued the "June 23 Announcement" that fundamentally altered South Korea's foreign policy by abandoning the long-held "Hallstein Doctrine." The announcement in effect seeded the "northern policy" (*nordpolitik: bukbang jongchaek*) by opening South Korea's door to China and the Soviet Union. In 1974, South Korea lifted the ban on postal exchanges with communist countries, and China promptly responded by allowing ethnic Koreans living there to exchange letters with their relatives in South Korea through the International Red Cross.[29]

Given the previously mentioned interregnum, little overt development occurred in Sino–South Korean relations during 1975–77. After the dust of succession politics settled in Beijing, the two sides resumed the minuet of 1972–74. In November 1978, Kim Kyung-Won, the special assistant to President Park for security affairs, remarked that South Korea hoped to improve its relations with China. That same month, Foreign Minister Park Dong-Jin made it clear that "the government will not prohibit any commercial activities with Communist countries with which it does not have diplomatic relations." One month later, China's minister of foreign trade, Li Qiang, replied that China might consider having trade with South Korea.[30]

Although indirect trade between Seoul and Beijing started in 1979, official contact was strictly prohibited even in third countries. Yet significant changes had been under way, although they were mostly invisible at the time. The eye-catching success of the East Asian newly industrialized countries (NICs) had attracted the full attention of China's post-Mao leadership.[31] In late 1978, the Chinese Academy of Social Sciences (CASS) established a small research group to study South Korea's developmental model.[32] Furthermore, crucial remarks were made by high-level officials, such as Hu Yaobang and Zhao Ziyang. Zhao, China's premier, said in an interview that China was indeed studying South Korea's experiences in economic development.[33] Successful emulations required close contact and, as expected, paved the way for China's rapprochement with South Korea.

Sino-Korean Relations as a Key Independent Variable

During the 1980s and 1990s, Sino-Korean relations were significantly "de-ideologized" and, at the same time, gradually decoupled from the great-power dynamics. During the 1980s, while the cold-war structure remained, China and South Korea joined to create new trading networks.[34] As dogmatism faded, the room for flexible diplomacy expanded considerably for both China and South Korea, in contrast to North Korea, which stuck with its *juche* beliefs. During the 1990s, the cold-war structure was mostly dismantled and Sino–South Korean diplomatic normalization further reduced the space for North Korea's maneuvering. With U.S.-Soviet/Russian relations no longer constituting the critical variable for Sino-Korean relations, the "rise" of China as a great power itself has gradually elevated the Seoul-Beijing relationship to a key independent variable status.

Trade Precedes the Flag: The Seoul-Beijing Rapprochement of the 1980s

Having allied initially with the Soviet Union and later aligned with the United States, China was acutely aware of the systemic constraints imposed by strategic dependence on any superpower alone. China's hypersensitivity to issues pertaining to sovereignty also played a key role in hammering out a new direction for its foreign relations during the 1980s.[35] It was in 1982 that China formally adopted an "independent route of diplomacy" (*zizhu duli waijiao*). This new line of strategic reasoning, one analyst aptly noted, "represents a retreat from its single-minded efforts of the late 1970s to build a matrix of strategic relations focused on confrontation with the Soviet Union . . . and a determination to deal with each country on its own merits and not to allow either to use China as a pawn in some geopolitical game."[36]

Freed from constant preoccupation with Soviet hegemonism and American imperialism, Chinese foreign policy fundamentally shifted from emphasizing vulnerability, contention, and ideological rigidity to demonstrating confidence, reconciliation, and diplomatic flexibility.[37] By minimizing the systemic constraints imposed by the superpower triangle, China became ready to maximize practical benefits with the world at large.[38] Changes were clearly visible in China's relations with the Soviet Union as well as in its dealing with countries with which it had hitherto maintained highly antagonistic relationships, most notably Israel, Indonesia, South Africa, and South Korea.[39]

China's policy toward South Korea also changed from a "nonpolicy" to de facto trade diplomacy, heralding the rise of a new bilateral relationship in East Asia. Despite a calculated silence maintained out of its concern for North Korea, China was determined to learn more about South Korea's developmental experiences.[40] China was especially interested in emulating the export-oriented strategy of the East Asian NICs, and South Korea in particular.[41] China even copied some of South Korea's targets of economic development: Deng Xiaoping's projection of reaching the per capita gross national product of $1,000 by 2000 was allegedly modeled after Park Chung Hee's figure by 1980.[42] In fact, Deng Pufang, the eldest son of Deng Xiaoping, reportedly confirmed to South Korea's ambassador to China that his father had indeed been paying special attention to President Park's development strategies.[43]

Compared to the military-security realm, economic cooperation generally involves less risk and is potentially more mutually beneficial due to heightened willingness to reciprocate and relatively low cost involved in the event of betrayal.[44] During the 1980s, China became increasingly more receptive to various patterns of international economic exchange, as highlighted by its rapidly growing volume of foreign trade and its ever-expanding foreign direct investment.[45]

South Korea's relentless search for profitable overseas markets coincided with China's will to join the international trading regime under the slogan of "opening" (kaifang).[46] China hoped that its search for foreign capital and technology would be realized in significant part by South Korea, since it, unlike the United States and Japan, was much more forthcoming in offering both—especially intermediate-level technology—with few political strings attached.[47] Seoul's assessment of Beijing's strategic role in Northeast Asia, and vis-à-vis Pyongyang in particular, was also well matched by China's growing confidence that Pyongyang would never tilt too heavily toward the Soviet Union.[48]

Indeed, China reaped considerable benefits by engaging in foreign trade with South Korea during this period.[49] Initial successes in turn reinforced Beijing's confidence in the path of development it had chosen. While China initially had to be highly sensitive to North Korea's opinion about its clandestine economic dealings with the South, so far as it generated considerable economic benefits, China became increasingly willing to focus on tangible interests while giving some "face" to the North.[50]

Several events—the hijacking incident in 1983 and the Kunsan torpedo boat incident in 1985—facilitated direct contact between Seoul and Beijing. The 1988 Seoul Olympic Games also provided a convenient opportunity for South Korea and China to further expand their economic cooperation.[51] Since 1984, trade between China and South Korea far surpassed that between China and North Korea. Trade with South Korea comprised 2.3 percent of China's total trade in 1986, with Seoul becoming Beijing's seventh-largest trade partner. Expanding economic ties prompted the crucial decision in 1990 to open trade representative offices in Seoul and Beijing.

During the 1980s, China became increasingly convinced that North Korea was highly reluctant to tilt decisively toward the Soviet Union. Furthermore, to the surprise of many, Kim Il Sung was allegedly asked by a Chinese official to give serious thought to the option of cross-recognition during a visit to China in 1987.[52] This was a very different position from China's previous stance, which had been merely to repeat North Korea's position on reunification. One may even speculate that, by then, China had already come to the conclusion that inter-Korean relations were qualitatively different from cross-strait relations.[53]

China's confident foreign policy was reflected in its changing perception of South Korea as well. As one Chinese analyst has put it, "China no longer views the United States as wanting to use Korea as a springboard to attack her . . . [and] the Korean contradiction is now less one between the East and the West than one between rival political forces in Korea."[54] To China, the Korean issue thus became a more maneuverable game than it used to be under the circumstances where it had been directly linked to ideological dogmatism and superpower rivalry. This improved Seoul-Beijing relationship fundamentally transformed the trilateral dynamics between China, North Korea, and South Korea from a "stable marriage" to a sort of "romantic triangle."[55]

The 1992 Normalization and Beyond: Toward a Ménage à Trois?

The normalization of relations between South Korea and the Soviet Union in September 1990 clearly distinguished Moscow from Beijing in terms of their respective approaches to Pyongyang. That is, the pace with which the Soviet Union and East European countries had normalized their relations with South Korea created enormous pressure for Beijing to reach a rapprochement with Seoul, even at Pyongyang's expense. The special relationship between Beijing and Pyongyang, often dubbed as "brotherhood" (*xiongdi zhi bang*) based on historical solidarity, cultural affinity, and ideological similarity, faced a daunting challenge.[56]

Table 12.1

China's Trade with Two Koreas, 1980–2004 (US$ millions)

Year	With North Korea	With South Korea	Share in China's total (%)	Share in South Korea's total (%)
1980	678	188	0.5	0.5
1985	473	1,161	1.9	1.9
1990	483	3,821	3.3	2.8
1995	550	16,540	5.9	6.4
2000	488	31,250	6.6	9.4
2001	737	31,490	6.2	10.8
2002	738	41,152	6.6	13.1
2003	1,023	57,019	6.7	15.3
2004	1,385	76,460	6.6	16.6

Sources: www.stats.gov.cn; and www.kotis.or.kr.

Whereas the post-Mao Chinese leadership might have reached a consensus on the need to normalize relations with South Korea by the late 1980s, it nevertheless had to be convinced that the Korean problem could be clearly distinguished from the China conundrum. The accession of two Koreas to the United Nations in September 1991 finally and formally disentangled the issue of "two Koreas" from the cross-strait problem. This watershed change lifted the last hurdle for Beijing's diplomatic normalization with Seoul, and seven months later, Qian Qichen, China's foreign minister, proposed secret negotiations for normalization. The normalization took effect on August 24, 1992.[57]

During the postnormalization period of 1992–2004, China has been "rising" significantly over South Korea. Bilateral trade increased twelvefold in twelve years, from US$6.38 billion in 1992 to US$76.4 billion in 2004. In 2003, China became the largest export market for South Korea. Despite the popular expectation that the United States would remain South Korea's largest trade partner until 2008, Beijing surged as Seoul's top trade partner in 2004. In 2003, South Korea was China's fourth-largest trade partner, after Japan, the United States, and Hong Kong. Whereas bilateral trade had constituted a tiny fraction—0.5 percent—of each country's total trade in 1980, the respective share reached 6.6 percent for China and 16.6 percent for South Korea by 2004 (see Table 12.1). North Korea is no match so long as economic complementarity is concerned.[58]

With the deepening of economic interdependence between South Korea and China, their "special" relationship founded on mutual tolerance and benign accommodation has gradually given way to a "normal" relationship. Frictions accumulated over the years concerning trade and maritime and environmental cooperation culminated in the "Garlic War" of 2000–2001, signaling the demise of the honeymoon phase of Sino–South Korean bilateralism. China's harsh position suggested that Beijing was no longer willing to accept a "special" relationship with South Korea in the realm of foreign economic relations. The pace, magnitude, and aftershock of the trade dispute were felt so intensely that many observers in Seoul and Beijing shared the assessment that the "special" Seoul-Beijing relationship had finally given way to a more pragmatic and realistic relationship based on profits and reciprocity.[59]

Many in Seoul are concerned that a stronger China could increasingly impose its views on South Korea as the Ming and Qing courts did on Chosun. Given, in particular, that China is carrying out the "Northeast Project" (*dongbei gongcheng*) in an effort to incorporate much of Korea's ancient history into China's "local histories" (*difang zhengquanshi*), South Korea's concern over China's "imperial" aspirations is not totally ungrounded. The Kokuryo history controversy, in particular, left deep wounds in the minds of South Korean intellectuals as far as China is concerned.[60]

While Beijing no longer considers Pyongyang an "ally sealed in blood," it has nevertheless repeatedly stressed the ties with North Korea. Informal and private contempt notwithstanding, China officially continues to display sincere concern for North Korea.[61] One could argue that the North Korean state could not have survived without the economic assistance and energy supplied by China since the mid-1990s. Despite South Korea's high hopes for China's constructive role in dealing with North Korea and its program of weapons of mass destruction, China has demonstrated that it will not sacrifice Pyongyang for the sake of Seoul. The intricate process in which the high-level North Korean defector, Hwang Chang Yop, was eventually sent to Seoul via Manila in 1997 highlights China's modus operandi in dealing with both Koreas.[62]

In the South Korea–China–North Korea triangle, each wing thus represents a very different type of relationship. The Seoul-Beijing wing represents a relationship of deepening interdependence, based on the norms of globalization and embedded in pragmatic and reciprocal cooperation. The Beijing-Pyongyang relationship is characterized more by traditional factors such as historical solidarity and political sympathy. The emerging Seoul-Pyongyang connection, facilitated largely by the "sunshine policy," reflects both nationalistic compassion and a growing need for economic exchange. Whether this relationship will continue as a "romantic triangle" (with China as the pivot) or possibly evolve into a ménage à trois (i.e., all three players maintain amity among themselves) remains to be seen.[63]

The Two Koreas Between China and the United States

The extent to which regionalism and multilateralism will capture the Northeast Asian dynamic in this era of globalization seems uncertain. Northeast Asia is still devoid of a meaningful equivalent to Southeast Asia's Association of Southeast Asian Nations and South Asia's South Asian Association for Regional Cooperation. In the absence of a common threat perception or a well-defined platform of shared strategic interest, the Northeast Asian system will most likely remain a complex network of bilateral ties, its sporadic search for regional identities notwithstanding.[64] While establishing a multilateral forum that includes both the United States and China as members and at the same time confines its focus to Northeast Asia appears to be a daunting challenge, whether the most recent experiment with the "six-party" format can serve as a useful model remains to be seen.[65]

Given these conditions, South Korea's efforts for diplomatic pluralization, especially the rapprochement with China, have introduced an additional key variable, especially since it was pursued fairly independently of American direction. As one analyst put it: "Leaders in Seoul display a new appreciation that security means more than perpetuating the U.S. connection. . . . [I]t still remains vital, but so are Seoul's new-found diplomatic levers."[66]

In hindsight, the controversial comments by Hwang Byung-Tae, South Korea's ambassador to China, who remarked during President Kim Young-Sam's 1994 visit to China that "South Korea's diplomacy should go beyond the exclusive reliance on the United States" were evidently the harbinger of a long-term trend that South Korea might seek a certain balance of its own vis-à-vis the United States and China.[67] Beijing's surprising agreement in 1997 to participate in the four-party talks, along with its rapidly expanding economic role in both Koreas, as well as yet another unexpected effort to host trilateral and six-party talks in 2003–5, have significantly enhanced China's influence over the Korean peninsula at large.[68]

With more power, wealth, prestige, and influence than ever before, China has gradually become an indispensable regional presence to be reckoned with where the Korean question is concerned.[69] Yet few South Koreans talk publicly and negatively about the security implications of the "rise of China." Strategic ambiguity more aptly describes Seoul's view.[70] Moreover, it is widely believed that the economic interdependence between South Korea and China will surpass that between the United States and South Korea as rapidly as within five years. By 1997, Chinese residents in South Korea already outnumbered their American counterparts. In 1999, the number of South Korean visitors to China also surpassed that of South Korean visitors to the United States.[71]

In perceptual terms, too, the South Korean view of China has become increasingly favorable in recent years, while that of the United States has deteriorated considerably. This perceptual shift can be attributed in large part to generational changes.[72] This posits a crucial question as to whether the election of Roh Moo Hyun as South Korea's president in late 2002—engineered primarily by the voters in their twenties and thirties—will generate and accelerate changes in South Korea's foreign policy vis-à-vis the United States and China. The certain "rise of China" over the Korean peninsula indeed holds the key to the future strategic environment in Northeast Asia.[73]

Regarding perceptions of Japan, there seems to exist a huge gap between the United States, on one hand, and China and South Korea (and North Korea for that matter), on the other. According to two nationwide surveys conducted in South

Korea in 1995 and 1997, Japan was viewed as most threatening to South Korean security interests.[74] According to a 1996 cross-national survey, only 10 percent of South Korean respondents and 23 percent of Chinese respondents believed that Japan sincerely repented of its past military atrocities. Furthermore, 78 percent of South Korean and 63 percent of Chinese respondents were very hopeful that South Korean–Chinese strategic relations would improve in the future.[75]

In stark contrast, Americans have maintained highly favorable perceptions of Japan, which they generally consider quite unique among Asian countries.[76] According to a survey conducted in the United States in 1999, for instance, 46 percent of the general public and 62 percent of the elite (represented by the Luce Foundation Fellows) were in favor of Japan's rearmament.[77] According to two nationwide surveys done in 1997 and 2000, however, over 90 percent of the South Korean general public believed that preventing a resurgence in Japan's militarism should be Seoul's top foreign policy priority.[78] Of fifty-six American experts interviewed by the author during 2002–3, thirty-five (63 percent) projected that an enhanced strategic role for Japan in Asia would push South Korea closer toward China and away from the United States.[79]

The Sino–South Korean normalization and dramatic expansion of bilateralism thereafter, along with Russia's sober dealings with North Korea, heightened Pyongyang's acute sense of insufficient support and protection from Beijing. This in turn led Kim Il Sung and, later, Kim Jong Il to pursue a nuclear alternative for national security at the expense of economic hardship and international isolation.

If North Korea should collapse or should reunification occur on South Korea's terms, the great-power game over Korea will go into dormancy.[80] While the South Korea–U.S. alliance may persist, it will surely be significantly readjusted.[81] China, for its part, will pay special attention to its "traditional" sphere of influence with the confidence that, in the longer run, time will be on its side. As the "rise of China" will certainly be an extended process of at least twenty years, the status of the United States as primus inter pares will remain unchanged until 2020 at the earliest.[82] Hence, South Korea's bandwagoning with China appears highly unlikely, if not impossible, until then. Furthermore, many of Seoul's elites are afraid that a stronger China may become increasingly imposing and audacious vis-à-vis South Korea as the Ming and Qing rulers were on Choson. Prudent hedging is most likely Seoul's optimal strategy because it avoids making a specific choice prematurely.[83] This situation, however, does not favor constructive regionalism.

If North Korea should muddle through, we can conceive of two possible contingencies. If it becomes a nonnuclear, open state, which perhaps hinges upon some sort of leadership or regime change, then trade, investment, development assistance, and tourism may pour into Pyongyang. North Korea's joining the "trading world" may then lead to a significant reduction of tension on the Korean peninsula, which will in turn enhance the likelihood of more trade and investment. While the prospect of national reunification depends on a multitude of factors, the overall outcome in this case would be an expanded Northeast Asian regionalism based on an increasing level of interdependence.

Alternatively, as a worst-case scenario, the rise of a nuclear and aggressive North Korea may augment traditional alliance ties among South Korea, the United States, and Japan, leaving China's position to be determined and specified.[84] It is possible that China may gradually conform its position to that of the United States and South Korea, although behavioral inertia may continue to push Beijing to offer minimum-security assurance for Pyongyang.[85] If North Korea remains such a painful headache for all and Beijing stays behind Pyongyang, the overall outcome would be an extended "cold war" environment and stagnant regionalism in Northeast Asia.[86]

Above all—and particularly with regard to the last contingency—the evolution of U.S.-Chinese relations will constitute the ultimate variable. Sino-American relations are far beyond any independent control by South Korea or North Korea. If future Washington-Beijing ties are generally characterized by amity and accommodation, certain room for constructive regionalism may become available.[87] If, however, U.S.-Chinese relations become bumpy and even antagonistic, China will continue to consider Northeast Asia a "semiregion" (ci quyu) and focus primarily on bilateral ties. Consequently, both Seoul and Pyongyang will have only limited breathing space and "indiscriminate regionalism" will be at a premium.[88]

In conclusion, Northeast Asian interactions, and Sino-Korean relations in particular, are full of uncertainties. The interests of the major actors in the region are not necessarily coinciding or well aligned across the board. Quite the contrary is the case.[89] As a matter of fact, crosscutting interests necessitate diverse groupings or lineups depending on the policy issue concerned. Viewed in this light, increasing the level of interdependence in the region, though skewed and asymmetrical, seems most crucial, as it is the only way to transform these actors' major mode of behavior from norm based to interest driven. After all, interests are transparent and predictable, while norms are time consuming to share and internalize. Let the interests first lead the way toward constructive regionalism.

13

Korea in Russia's Post–Cold War Regional Political Context

Evgeny P. Bazhanov

In the 1990s Russia faced Northeast Asia anew, obliged to reconsider Soviet policies due to different domestic considerations and transformed regional conditions. In the early cold war years when China was the obvious priority and Japan was still recalled as the enemy, Korea suddenly assumed a large role in the struggle to reshape the region. The same evolution occurred a half-century later. After downplaying Korea's significance for most of the 1990s, Russia recognized its pivotal role as the "sunshine policy" started in 1999–2000 and, even more, when a crisis over nuclear weapons began in 2002–3. Caught between rapidly rising Chinese power and Japanese power still obsessed with four islands over which Moscow claimed sovereignty, Russians perceived an opening in the flux around both of the Koreas. This chapter traces the evolution of Russian approaches from traditional Soviet policies to the initial orientations of the new Russian state, and finally to Vladimir Putin's initial strategy both to the region and to the Korean peninsula.

The Korean War and the North Korean nuclear crisis stand as bookends on opposite sides of five decades of limited leverage but active involvement by Moscow in Korean affairs. Leaning completely to the North, Moscow often found that rivalry with Beijing deprived it of the clout necessary to have its way. In the 1990s when Moscow reversed direction and leaned heavily to the South, it again was frustrated by loss of leverage. Because policies toward Korea fit into a broader regional strategy, loss of influence became a factor in relations with all three of the other powers active in Northeast Asia. By the end of the 1990s, Russian leaders were again focusing on ways to become more involved in the struggles over the Korean peninsula in order to shape the evolution of a region.

Traditional Soviet Policies in Northeast Asia and Korea

Three important elements formed the foundation of Stalin's foreign policy after World War II: (1) assurance of the Soviet Union's national security; (2) expansion of communism's influence; and (3) great-power ambition to augment the territory of the Russian Empire. Combined, these elements provided the driving force behind

Moscow's very active, tough, and rigid policy. The Moscow-Washington rivalry led to the division of Korea into two states, and the Soviet Union spared no effort to build and strengthen a loyal regime in the North, materially, militarily, politically, and morally.[1] The attitude toward the South, however, was hostile from the beginning, seeing it as a product of "U.S. imperialism," detrimental to the aspirations of the Korean people, and dangerous for socialism, the Soviet Union, and peace in Asia. In 1950, Stalin approved the North's military attack against the South.

After Stalin's death, a new Soviet leadership adjusted its strategy. While adhering to a vision based on a two-dimensional conflict between socialism and capitalism and the notion of unavoidable ideological struggle in international relations, Nikita Khrushchev also emphasized peaceful coexistence with the West. In Korea, this translated into a desire to maintain the status quo. By the start of the 1960s, Soviet policy was becoming even more restrained as ideological and political contradictions developed with the North, which eventually sided with China in the growing Sino-Soviet dispute. Khrushchev came to disfavor Kim Il Sung, concerned that leftist fever that infested Beijing and Pyongyang at the time would set the Far East afire in war.[2] Yet he continued to demonstrate a completely hostile attitude toward Seoul in spite of cooling relations with Pyongyang.[3]

The Brezhnev leadership brought another change in foreign policy. To avoid a second war in Korea, they deemed it important to bring Pyongyang back from its newfound relationship with the People's Republic of China (PRC). North Korea was perceived as a strategic ally, a Far Eastern outpost in the overall picture of the Soviet Union's confrontation with the United States. Military and material aid increased. To win Pyongyang back, Moscow spared no effort to praise all that Kim Il Sung was doing. The leadership, in reality, did not admire Kim's personality cult, Pyongyang's *juche* (self-reliance) policy, and its behavior in economic relations.[4]

Gradually an understanding that Seoul was winning the economic competition grew among Soviet experts, and South Korea began to be viewed differently from how it was normally portrayed in North Korean propaganda. Still, the South continued to be perceived as an anticommunist state, a strategic springboard of the Pentagon, and a threat to the vital interests of the Soviet Union, "world socialism, and all progressive forces" of the world.[5] Moscow's fear of further harming its relations with Pyongyang posed an additional obstacle to major readjustments in its policy toward South Korea.[6]

No substantial changes in policy toward the South followed Brezhnev's death under either Yuri Andropov or Konstantin Chernenko. At the same time, Moscow and Beijing continued their rivalry for relations with Pyongyang.[7] Meanwhile, a subdued but growing understanding of the need to rectify policies regarding Korean affairs began to be detected in academic and political circles of Soviet society.[8] It is difficult to determine how successful this lobbying would have been were it not for Mikhail Gorbachev's advent to power in the spring of 1985 and his determination to reconstruct Soviet foreign policy.

Gorbachev's Strategy in the World and on the Korean Peninsula

At the twenty-seventh Communist Party congress in 1986, Gorbachev continued to promote the standard thesis on division of the world into two confronting camps, but his speech differed from what had been said on such occasions by his predecessors. He advocated urgently moving international relations from confrontation to cooperation.[9] Soon "new thinking" sought to overcome the international system of confrontational blocs while emphasizing human over class interests, across-the-board disarmament as an urgent goal, the construction of a common European community to include former socialist countries, and the creation of a global security system.[10] Moscow withdrew its troops from Afghanistan, agreed to liquidate all medium-range missiles deployed in Asia, and unilaterally reduced armed forces in the eastern part of the country by 200,000, while achieving a degree of normalization in relations with Beijing.[11] Korea did not yet draw the attention of the new leaders in the Kremlin. Previous approaches to the Korean problem continued.[12]

The process of realistically assessing Soviet policy toward Korea finally began in 1987–88. Officials became acutely aware that the Korean problem posed a major obstacle to superpower cooperation in the region, establishment of an Asian security system, and Moscow's participation in international economic cooperation.

Settlement of the Korean Issue and Far Eastern Security

The Soviet Union for decades had limited itself solely to open and voracious support for Pyongyang's positions on Korean issues.[13] In 1987–88, policy makers finally began serious analysis of the South Korean position and its proposals, finding that they had quite a number of rational elements.[14] A shift also occurred in attitudes toward the U.S. military presence in South Korea. Some politicians even argued that U.S. troops played a deterrent role against a flare-up of an uncontrollable conflict between North and South while helping to limit Japanese military expenditures.[15] Unlike in the past, the Soviet Union started to advance its own ideas for a settlement.[16] Untying the Korean knot became an important foreign policy goal.[17]

Officials expressed a desire to expand political dialogue with the North, and intensify bilateral military cooperation, while increasing the scope of economic aid and contacts in the scientific, cultural, and sports fields.[18] In response to this approach by the Soviet Union, North Korea's leadership took reciprocal measures. Pyongyang cooperated with Moscow on its foreign policy initiatives and was receptive to a number of requests made by the Soviets in the military arena. As rapprochement progressed, some cooling occurred in North Korean–Chinese relations.[19]

Although publicly reticent, Beijing was trying through private channels to pass a message to both Moscow and Pyongyang suggesting that they should be careful not to damage Chinese interests. The PRC switched its tactics and position, however, as a result of steadily improving Sino-Soviet relations in 1987–88, a progressive reappraisal of the Far East strategic-military picture, and its own unwillingness to carry on the burden of aiding Pyongyang. All attempts to torpedo improving Soviet-North Korean ties ceased.[20]

By the time Gorbachev went to China in May 1989 to fully normalize relations, there were virtually no traces of competition between the Soviet Union and the PRC over North Korea. Kim Il Sung contemplated adjustments in response to improved ties between Moscow and Beijing, and new problems cropped up in Soviet–North Korean relations as a result of growing differences in the ideological, political, and economic spheres. In 1988, the Soviet Union reduced the level of military aid to the North and, after that, rejected all attempts by Pyongyang at reinforcing military cooperation. In addition, the Kremlin pressured North Korea to accept international controls over its nuclear reactors. Because of ideological differences, it was increasingly difficult for the two countries to cooperate in such spheres as culture, education, and mass media. Another problem was critical articles in the Soviet press about the Democratic People's Republic of Korea's (DPRK) domestic situation. Pyongyang demanded that an end be put to such practices, but Moscow neither could act nor wanted to act.[21] Both Moscow and Pyongyang were unhappy with the results of their failed economic cooperation and talked of a need for change.[22] Moscow stressed that no matter how hard the Soviet Union tried to help its neighbor, it would be difficult for the DPRK to solve its problems until the confrontation and arms race under way on the Korean peninsula ceased and until the North shed its semi-isolation from business contacts with the majority of the developed countries.[23]

Evolution of Gorbachev's Policy Toward South Korea

A Politburo document dated May 11, 1986, called for weakening the position of the United States in Korea and elevating the Soviet role in settling the Korean issue. This meant changes in Moscow's approach to South Korea, "which was becoming a factor of global, military-strategic balance."[24] The real breakthrough came as a result of the Seoul Olympic Games of 1988. Moscow's perceptions of South Korea underwent a complete turnaround due to Seoul's adroit conduct of the Olympic Games in South Korea.

After the fall of the East European Stalinist regimes, both the Soviet government and the public underwent a profound ideological transformation. North Korea was no longer considered to be an ideologically close country. At the same time, the economic situation severely deteriorated, and Moscow urgently needed and sought South Korean capital, technology, goods, and credits. Yet, the Soviet military opposed any drastic alterations in Moscow's strategy in the Far East. General V. Lobov, a top planner on the General Staff, wrote in the summer of 1988 of the continued and growing threat from the United States in the Pacific. He mentioned South Korea as one of the principal "springboards" for potential aggression against the "socialist commonwealth." North Korea was identified as "an important bastion" obstructing "Pentagon schemes."[25] Soviet Armed Forces Chief of Staff M. Moiseev almost a year later talked of the necessity to strengthen the Soviet Union-DPRK alliance for the sake of promoting peace and security in the Far East.[26] Gorbachev listened to the proponents of establishing diplomatic relations, and he agreed to meet Roh Tae Woo in San Francisco on June 3, 1990, following a visit to Washington.

The San Francisco summit was a complete success from Moscow's point of view.[27] Roh promised vast economic aid to the faltering Soviet economy, and Koreans urged the Soviet Union to declare official relations quickly as a prerequisite for extending the aid. On September 30, Foreign Minister Eduard Shevardnadze met his South Korean counterpart in New York. After agreeing to establish official relations, he went out of his way to express his good feelings toward Pyongyang. This, however, could not prevent a strong negative reaction.

Relations with South Korea immediately became a priority in the Soviet Union's Asian-Pacific foreign policy. In December 1990, President Roh paid an official visit to the Soviet Union. Negotiations went smoothly, resulting in a "Declaration on General Principles of Relations between the USSR and Republic of Korea" as well as a number of economic agreements and conventions. Gorbachev called the declaration "an outstanding piece of goodwill and friendship between two sovereign nations," arguing that it opened new vistas for overcoming confrontational mind-sets and liquidating the cold war in the Asia-Pacific region.[28] At a meeting with close associates Gorbachev stressed that South Korea was the most promising partner in the East and opportunities there should not be lost.[29] Relevant to him was the fact that the Soviet Union and the Republic of Korea (ROK) were both leaving behind totalitarian practices and trying to introduce democracy to their societies.[30]

Initial Post-Soviet Russia's Policies and Korea

Though Gorbachev's legacy had a strong impact on the foreign policy of new Russia, its leaders nevertheless tried hard to disassociate themselves from the recent past. Yeltsin's right-hand man State Secretary Gennady Burbulis and Foreign Minister Andrei Kozyrev in their first appearance before the staff of the former Soviet Ministry of Foreign Affairs in December 1991 categorically denied any connection with Gorbachev.[31] Kozyrev argued that democratic Russia was about to initiate "a completely fresh policy of unrestrained partnership and integration with the West."[32] Russia conducted a clearly pro-Western policy.[33] The communist states—North Korea, Cuba, and Vietnam—were shocked by the anticommunism of the new Russian leaders and feared that the "democratic fever" could penetrate their own turf. Moscow in its turn consciously stopped all ideological links as well as special relations with these regimes, expecting their early demise. The Kremlin joined Western nations in condemning human rights violations in Cuba and the DPRK. The beginning of relations between the new Russian state and China was not particularly auspicious either.[34] At the same time, the new Russian state worked hard to advance political and economic relations with "stable, moderate and economically successful states" of the third world,[35] including South Korea, Taiwan, and the member countries of the Association of Southeast Asian Nations.[36]

By the second half of 1992, South Korea looked like a bright spot in Russia's interactions in the Asia-Pacific region. Its companies, interested in Russia's natural resources and its military and space technology, kept a high profile in the Russian market. Some explored opportunities for major investment, and Moscow in turn solicited Korean capital and pressed for resumption of the $3 billion loan that had been frozen by Seoul after the collapse of the Soviet Union. Finally, Yeltsin succeeded in regaining the loan.[37] Moreover, the two sides needed each other politically. The Kremlin played the "Korean card" to put pressure on Japan, and it generally displayed an interest in a greater political role for South Korea in East Asia and, for the future, an interest in unification of the Korean nation. South Korea looked to the Russian connection as a counterbalance to American and Japanese influence in the region and as an instrument for deterring the North.

Yet, bilateral relations soon deteriorated to a certain degree. After Moscow's decision to postpone the payments due on the $3 billion loan, Seoul newspapers called it "an act of arrogance beyond our understanding and patience." Seoul froze the remaining half of the loan, and the opposition used this opportunity to attack the ruling party for grave mistakes in foreign and economic policy. Russians, in turn, showed displeasure at fluctuations in Seoul's behavior in the economic sphere, unreliability, and the dishonesty of some Korean businessmen. Contention grew over the Russian moratorium on fishing in the central part of the Sea of Okhotsk and its demands to get compensation for the grounds of the old diplomatic mission in Seoul.[38]

In political relations, the Russian Foreign Ministry in 1993 denounced demands by certain South Korean officials that Moscow renounce military clauses in the Soviet–North Korean alliance treaty of 1961. South Koreans were also bitterly disappointed by the conclusion of a special state committee in Russia that Moscow could not be held responsible for the shooting down of the Korean Air 007 passenger plane over Sakhalin in 1983. The overall image of Russia in the ROK was further tarnished by the political instability and miserable socioeconomic conditions in the Russian Federation, Moscow's weakening international position, and its inability to influence North Korean behavior.[39]

Bilateral problems seemed minor compared to the stormy Moscow-Pyongyang "alliance." The advent of an anticommunist regime in Moscow worsened a deteriorating relationship, as leaders of the democratic movement felt nothing but contempt for communists both inside and outside of Russia, and the DPRK, with its pure Stalinist-type dictatorship, seemed the worst possible case.[40] No desire existed in the Kremlin to bolster the DPRK economically.[41]

The new Russian ideological and political order was not merely alien to North Korean communists but was seen as a source of subversive influence on their own people. Negative feelings were reinforced by a disastrous economic situation caused in part by the cessation of Russian assistance. While continuing to develop ties with the ROK, Moscow ignored political contacts with the DPRK. The Russian foreign minister declared that Moscow would stop all military cooperation with the North and put pressure on it to drop its nuclear plans. Yeltsin described the Soviet–North Korean security treaty as existing only on paper, and Information Minister Mikhail Poltoranin, while in Tokyo, advised the Japanese not to pay war reparations to the DPRK to prevent prolongation of this repressive, obsolete regime.

Pyongyang initially responded in kind, but over time it decided to keep channels open with a big neighboring state upon which it still depended in many ways (half of the DPRK's trade volume remained connected to Russia). Besides, the Russian Federation continued to experience internal upheavals, and hopes were rekindled in Pyongyang that the former friend could still come back to its senses. Pyongyang chose to refrain from denouncing or refuting anticommunist tendencies. Moscow agreed to restore a working relationship, accepting arguments that expansion of links with Pyongyang was advantageous to everyone, including South Korea. The ability to influence Kim Il Sung in the right direction would be welcomed by all.[42]

By late summer 1992, the Russian Foreign Ministry advocated seeking balanced relations with the South and the North, and the concept that it was important for Russians and Americans to maintain their security arrangements on the peninsula to ensure stability. But these attempts to patch up differences with Pyongyang and overcome the government's South Korean "tilt" did not succeed. By 1993, Russo–North Korean relations had reassumed an almost hostile character. In mid-1994, Yeltsin further infuriated Kim Il Sung by threatening to support international sanctions against North Korea if it persisted in its attempts to acquire a nuclear weapons capability.[43]

Factors of Change

Russia's relations with the two Koreas began to change in the mid-1990s due mainly to modifications in policies toward both the region and the world at large. Reforms were encountering ever-greater difficulties. The public naturally grew bitterly disappointed with liberal democrats and their slogans. More than half of the voters in 1993 and 1995 supported communists and ultranationalists in parliamentary elections. Under pressure, Yeltsin had to become more conservative in foreign policy.[44]

Conservative forces were helped by developments in the near vicinity of Russia as well as elsewhere.[45] In Asia security concerns came to the forefront. Awareness of the potential of renewed hostilities on the Korean peninsula led Moscow to seek to resume an active role in mediating differences between Seoul and Pyongyang. Such an approach required an improvement of relations with the DPRK and a more balanced policy on the peninsula.[46]

Economic considerations were a second motive for Russia's activities in the Asia-Pacific region. Moscow realized that the success of its modernization program, especially in its less developed eastern provinces, depended on cooperation with neighbors. South Korea continued to figure prominently among prospective partners, and Russia also tried to rely on the ROK in efforts to enter regional economic organizations.[47] In comparison to South Korea, the DPRK was certainly the loser economically in the eyes of Russians.

Still, Moscow recognized that the only way to get North Korean debts was to smooth tensions with the DPRK. It was deemed profitable to continue employing North Korean woodcutters and other workers in the Russian Far East. Deliveries of nuclear reactors to the North and involvement in the development of free economic zones in the border areas were other economic aims. Another argument was that only together with the DPRK would it be possible to realize some large-scale Russian–South Korean projects, such as a gas pipeline from Yakutia to the ROK via the northern part of the Korean peninsula.[48]

Great-power ambitions pushed Moscow toward both South and North Korea. It increasingly tried to regain influence and prestige throughout the region. It hoped to forge closer ties with new partners while returning, when possible, to former allies recklessly abandoned earlier.[49] The ruling elite of Russia no longer abhorred North Korea as it did in the early 1990s. There were even deputies in the Russian Parliament who welcomed the prospect of a nuclear-armed North Korea, seeing in it a contributing factor in the defense of Russia. Kim Dae Jung's election as president of South Korea helped to cement Russia's balanced approach to Korean affairs. Instead of reproaching Moscow for overtures toward Pyongyang, he encouraged rapprochement of the big powers, Russia included, with the DPRK.

Korea's Place in Putin's International Strategy

President Putin in his first year in the Kremlin approved a number of policy documents that confirmed recent foreign policy changes, while pursuing a strategy of open, multidirectional and balanced relations.[50] Foreign Minister Igor Ivanov said, "The balanced attitude derives from Russia's geopolitical position as the largest Eurasian power, a position which requires an adequate combination of its efforts on all fronts. This approach imposes a responsibility on Russia for guaranteeing world security on both global and regional levels, and it presupposes that it pursue complementary foreign-policy activities in bilateral and multilateral arrangements."[51] The goal remains to secure a prominent role for Russia in the emerging multipolar world.[52] The Asia-Pacific region is identified in Putin's doctrine as equally important with the West in the pursuit of Russia's goals on the home and the external fronts. Moscow places special importance on the development of close ties with China and Japan as well as on a settlement on the Korean peninsula by becoming an active and equal participant in the solution through evenhandedly cooperating with both Korean states and with world powers there.[53]

Initially, the balanced quality of Putin's strategy was not easily detected. The misgivings and wide skepticism of the West toward Russia coupled with growing assertiveness and aggressiveness of the Western alliance, especially of the United States, alienated Moscow and induced it to compensate with achievements in the East. Putin tried to lure the Bush administration to intensify cooperation on arms control, security arrangements in Europe, and antiterrorism (concerning Chechnya), but to no avail.

At the same time China and to a lesser degree Japan were responsive to Moscow's overtures. Security as well as economic concerns in Northeast Asia led the Kremlin to more vigorous diplomacy on the Korean peninsula with the following goals: (1) to ease military confrontation and tensions in Korea, making sure that a new war does not erupt there;[54] (2) to prevent the spread of weapons of mass destruction on the peninsula, which will almost certainly undermine stability and produce a nuclear arms race in the Asia-Pacific region;[55] (3) to activate the Korean factor for the benefit of Russia's economy, especially modernization of its Far East;[56] and (4) to restore Russian influence on the peninsula and strengthen Moscow's position in Northeast Asia as a whole. One feature of the new drive was a radical improvement of damaged Russo–North Korean relations with the expectation that it would help Pyongyang to feel more secure and subsequently to become less obnoxious and more flexible and forthcoming in dealings with Seoul and the outside world. It would allow Russia to further influence North Korea's national security policies, including its activities in the nuclear field.[57]

With regard to economic issues, Russia became disillusioned by the mediocre results of cooperation with South Korea. Trade and especially investment were much lower than originally anticipated. The idea was advanced that if Russia could induce the DPRK to restore transportation links with the ROK and extend them into the Russian Far East, it could bring Russia rich economic benefits. Russian companies, it was believed, might also fit into other multinational economic projects involving both Koreas and others in the region.[58] Of interest, too, were recovery of the debt accumulated in the Soviet era and the greater participation of North Korean workers in Russia's economy.[59]

Many argued that loss of leverage over the DPRK had led to loss of prestige in South Korea, weakening Moscow's position in a settlement on the Korean peninsula and in Northeast Asia as a whole. Losing the North Korean connection, it was claimed that Russia ceased to be a major player in the region and was pushed aside by the United States and China.[60] A real rapprochement between Russia and North Korea began in 2000. The two sides finally concluded the new treaty, which replaced the 1961 treaty and laid a basis for a normal state-to-state relationship between Moscow and Pyongyang. On July 19–20, 2000, Putin made an official visit to the DPRK, the first ever by a Russian or Soviet leader and coming just as Kim Jong Il chose to open up his country to a certain extent.

The DPRK had plunged into a chronic economic and social crisis, which could be solved only through an open door policy and internal reforms. Rapprochement with the ROK promised to give the North access to finances, technologies, and goods and to help in obtaining diplomatic recognition and various concessions from the United States as well as attract large-scale economic aid from the entire West. The accommodation on the peninsula had to strengthen the DPRK's security, which was increasingly difficult to maintain because of economic weakness and expanding military preparations by Washington and its allies.

The inter-Korean détente was very important to Kim Jong Il's regime internally. The decision to reverse the passive foreign policy and to take the bold step of meeting the ROK president at once woke up the North Korean establishment and the entire society. A long-forgotten air of excitement reappeared in the DPRK. Such expectations were reinforced by other fresh initiatives on the part of the supreme leader: his first foreign trip to the PRC and the resumption of active exchanges with Russia.[61]

While in the North Korean capital Putin and Kim signed a joint declaration. The Russian side agreed to believe that North Korea's missile programs were purely peaceful and subsequently not threatening to anyone.[62] The visit put an end to the remaining tensions in Moscow-Pyongyang relations. The two sides showed readiness to open a new chapter in their interactions erasing mutual complaints and offenses. Russia and the DPRK agreed to actively promote exchanges in commercial, economic, scientific, and technological fields. Moscow declared its eagerness to become a principal mediator between the North and the South, helping political détente and agitating for economic cooperation including both Koreas as well as Russia. Putin energetically championed three-way economic projects, especially modernization and utilization of the inter-Korean railway connecting it with the Russian Far East and the Trans-Siberian Railroad.[63]

Putin's visit to the DPRK sent a signal to the United States and other players in Northeast Asia politics of Moscow's intention to be present in Korea, to influence the course of political and military events there, and to compete with others in the economic sphere. "Russia showed that it was getting serious about developing its eastern lands and that with the help of the Korean connection it could score first practical results."[64]

Improvement in bilateral ties was solidified by a return visit of Kim to Russia in August 2001, which brought concrete results, although Russian media and society as a whole were disgusted with the pomp, security arrangements, and other oddities connected with Kim's prolonged train travel across Russia.[65] A declaration, signed by Putin and "the great leader," confirmed the convergence in their positions on preservation of the 1972 Antiballistic Missile (ABM) Treaty and promotion of global security. Kim reiterated the peaceful nature of the North Korean missile program and a moratorium to 2003 on ballistic missile tests.[66]

Unhappy at that time with Bush's policies, Moscow bent under Pyongyang's pressure and accepted in the declaration. "The DPRK explained its position that withdrawal of American troops from South Korea presents a pressing important problem in the interest of providing peace and security on the Korean peninsula and in Northeast Asia."[67]

While courting Pyongyang, Moscow continued to cooperate with Seoul in political, military, and economic areas. On May 27–30, 1999, South Korea's president Kim Dae Jung paid a state visit to Russia. During negotiations Yeltsin agreed to express support for the sunshine policy toward the DPRK.[68] A serious spy scandal between the two countries was also settled. Emphasis was, however, placed on promoting economic ties.

The next year at the United Nations Millennium Summit, Putin enthusiastically supported the inter-Korean dialogue and, as a way to achieve its success, economic cooperation among the two Koreas and Russia. This clearly showed that he was interested in both stability on the Korean peninsula and a Korean role in economic development in Russia's Far East.

The Moscow-Seoul top-level dialogue continued during Putin's visit to the ROK in February 2001. While repeating previous positions on the sunshine policy and triangle economic cooperation, Putin emphasized security concerns provoked by Washington's National Missile Defense (NMD) plans and convinced Kim Dae Jung to subscribe to the Russian view that the ABM treaty was a cornerstone of strategic stability.[69] After all, NMD jeopardized Kim's sunshine policy. If Kim later backpedaled, the fact remained that Moscow-Seoul mutual relations were marked by growing military cooperation: exchange of high-level visits, joint exercises, defense policy consultations, arms sales, and so on.[70]

Important too were joint economic plans of the two countries. On many occasions, representatives of Russia and South Korea discussed and finally agreed to establish a Korean industrial complex in the Nakhodka Free Economic Zone. Moscow hoped to speed up economic revival of the entire Far Eastern region, and for Seoul it could become a base for economic ties to the rest of Russia as well as the Central Asian states.[71]

Russia was very active as a mediator. Putin on a number of occasions conveyed Pyongyang's messages to the West and Seoul, adding his own positive appraisals of Kim Jong Il and North Korea's intentions.[72] Russia was clearly aiming at raising its regional prestige and influence by becoming the most valuable intermediary between the North and the South. Emphasis was placed not only on warm personal relations of Putin and Kim Jong Il but also on the potential for regional economic cooperation with a valuable Russian contribution. Moscow advocated trilateral cooperation combining Russian technologies, North Korean workers, and South Korean investments, but the reconstruction of Soviet-built factories in the DPRK did not meet with a positive response from South Korea. Seoul argued that products of these factories would not be competitive in the world market and that the factories themselves had to be demolished as totally obsolete.[73]

Another Russian idea had a much better reception—the one concerning restoration of the inter-Korean railway and its link with the Trans-Siberian Railroad. Following intense Russian lobbying on this account, two schemes came under scrutiny: the first regarding a line via China and Mongolia, and the second a line via Siberia. Russia obviously championed the second route, describing it as a great contribution to the economic development of the entire Northeast Asia.[74] Russian experts estimated that the opening of the new transportation route, would allow all regional states to save tremendous amounts of money and time while shipping goods to Europe.[75]

Detailed negotiations were devoted to gas pipelines from Russia to the two Koreas. Early in the 1990s an agreement was reached to build a 6,600 km natural gas pipeline from Yakutia to the Korean peninsula before Seoul decided the project would be unprofitable. The focus of attention switched to the Kovyktinskoye gas field in the Irkutsk region. As estimated, the gas field will be able to supply up to 20 million tons of gas to Russia, the two Koreas, and China for thirty years after its completion, covering half of all energy requirements of the DPRK and the ROK at a price one-quarter lower than today.[76]

It should be noted, however, that certain political constraints on multinational projects in the Far East exist from the Russian side. In the early 1990s, Moscow and Beijing began intensive preparations for the establishment of a special economic zone on the Tumen River with the participation of Russia, China, two Koreas, and Japan. Hopes were expressed that the zone would grow into a "new Hong Kong" relying on Russian natural resources, Chinese and North Korean labor, and Japanese and South Korean finances and technology.[77] While economists in Moscow energetically lobbied for the project, representatives of Primorskii Krai passionately opposed it, fearing the presence of large numbers of Chinese on Russian territory and suspecting that Beijing was deliberately causing a demographic expansion with the ultimate purpose of annexing these lands.[78] It was argued that the Tumen River zone "would drastically change the ethnic composition, undermine the economic and political interests of the Russian Federation, inevitably leading to chaos and loss of Primorskii Krai's Russian essence."[79]

As a result of such vehement resistance, Moscow put the Tumen project aside. Another project, the Japan sea ring, is equally controversial. Though it opens possibilities for attracting large-scale investments and integrating the Russian Far East into regional economic systems, residents of the Far East reject the idea. They claim that the project will "stimulate an influx of Chinese nationals, conserve the irrational structure of local industries (with an emphasis on raw materials), destroy ecology, and decrease cargo lines through Siberia to the European part of Russia."[80]

Escalation of the Chinese presence in the sparsely populated, economically weak regions of eastern Russia will continue to be resisted. At the same time, Korean participation in economic activities in Russia does not raise any doubts, creating a sense of optimism about prospects especially after the unification of Korea.

The September 11, 2001, terrorist attack on the United States led to significant changes in Russo-American relations, which influenced Moscow's overall international strategy. North Korea as well as regional politics in Northeast Asia as a whole went momentarily to the sidelines of Moscow's priorities. Russia concentrated on promotion of a renewed partnership with the United States, especially in the antiterrorist field, and paid less attention to pleasing Pyongyang. Toughening of the U.S. attitude toward the "axis of evil" member the DPRK further cooled Moscow's attitude toward the North.

A new crisis between Pyongyang and Washington in 2003 again put the Korean peninsula at the center of attention in the Kremlin. In its view, the crisis was due to blunders and intransigence on both sides, intensified by the war in Iraq. North Korean leadership became really fearful that their country would be the next target of the United States and decided to protect itself by both real and propagandistic moves in the nuclear field. Washington responded harshly, and the situation deteriorated to a dangerous degree.

The Korean peninsula turned, in Russian eyes, into a source threatening imminent war in the Far Eastern region. In July 2003, the Kremlin ordered local authorities in areas adjacent to North Korea to check civil defense facilities "in connection with the worsening situation on the Korean peninsula."[81] In August, war games were conducted by the ministries of Defense, Interior, and Emergency Situations as well as the Federal Security Service.[82] It was estimated that if the United States attacked the DPRK, Russia's Far East might be hit by a radioactive cloud or by a large influx of North Korean refugees.[83]

Officials became deeply concerned that a military operation against the North would lead to uncontrollable and unpredictable developments. Prolonged warfare with the use of nuclear weapons and participation of the great powers was not ruled out. It was argued that "there is plenty of evidence in the history of mankind when theoretically quick, easy military campaigns turned into nightmares for everyone, even for those who initially did not have anything to do with the conflict."[84] This argument against a war was advanced by the Kremlin in addition to such arguments as an absence of aggressive designs on the part of Kim Jung Il's leadership and the necessity to observe international law. Instead, Russia championed a peaceful solution to the crisis: North Korea's strict compliance with the nonproliferation regime in exchange for explicit U.S. security guarantees. Moscow feels that it would be rather difficult to convince the two sides to agree to such an outcome, but it does not see any alternative to this course. Achieving a positive resolution of the crisis has for now become the sole regional goal of Russia in Korea.[85] Only when peace is strengthened will Moscow be anxious to return to promising multinational economic projects, especially restoration of the inter-Korean railway and its link with the Trans-Siberian Railroad.

14

Environmental Regime-Building in Northeast Asia

Korea's Pursuit of Leadership

Shin-wha Lee

The Issue

Northeast Asia (NEA) is characterized by the absence of a comprehensive regional institution comparable to that of the European Union (EU), the Association of Southeast Asian Nations (ASEAN), and the South Asian Association for Regional Cooperation. Despite the prevalence of common challenges to the peace and security of the region during the cold-war era, political rivalries, historical animosities, economic disparities, and diverging systems among the countries in the region have acted as obstacles to the formation of a centralized coordinating mechanism that would address such challenges. This in turn has produced a spillover effect to regional environmentalism, where interstate cooperation has mainly remained insignificant with the exception of certain bilateral arrangements.

However, the post–cold war climate has more or less facilitated collective efforts at establishing a regional environmental management regime by alleviating the effects of existing political, economic, and social differences between NEA countries. For instance, a number of cooperative programs, projects, and forums have been developed through bilateral and multilateral dialogues and networks, especially since the United Nations Conference on Environment and Development (also known as the "Earth Summit" or "Rio Summit") in 1992. Japan and South Korea (Korea) have been the most active in initiating and engaging in such bilateral and multilateral cooperative efforts to address common environmental issues in East Asia in general and in NEA in particular.

While greater regional environmental cooperation could be accountable to the increased demand for cooperative environmental governance that was created by basic ecological needs, the national competition between Japan and Korea to take the initiative has also been the driving force to greater cooperation. Being equipped with everything but military might, Japan's aspiration to become the regional superpower has been translated into its eagerness to play a leading role in regional institution-building and agenda-setting. On the other hand, Korea, whose history has been marred by the power politics of colonial and cold war powers, has also aspired to secure and enhance its regional influence and dignity by actively addressing relatively neutral and politically less-sensitive problems, such as environmental issues, and in turn taking the initiative in various regional cooperative processes.

In view of this, this chapter intends to explore how transboundary ecological issues have rendered strong incentives for Northeast Asian regionalism in the domain of environmental cooperation. The chapter will also examine whether environmental institution-building in the region could be regarded as signifying the emergence of a more cooperative regional politics. While the NEA region includes China, Japan, South Korea, North Korea, the Russian Far East, Mongolia, Taiwan, and Hong Kong, the first three countries are the main focus of this chapter, insofar as they have been the most active in transboundary environmental cooperation efforts in the region.

Environmental Regionalism in Northeast Asia

There has been a growing worldwide consensus on the need for greater interstate cooperation in dealing with *global* environmental problems such as global warming, ozone depletion, tropical deforestation, and so on. In addition, interstate environmental cooperation has increasingly dealt with *localized* environmental issues because of their potential to influence the environments of neighboring countries and thus function as destabilizers to the peace and security of the region. Addressing such problems (global or regional) would require not only the establishment of practices promoting sustainable development under the auspices of the government but also interstate cooperation and policy coordination at the regional and global levels.

In Northeast Asia, growing concerns over cross-border environmental problems have also led countries in the region to engage in interstate negotiations that have aimed to establish a collective and systematic mechanism for environmental cooperation. Still, environmental regime-building in NEA has remained both elusive and ineffective due to the general skepticism that exists in the region on the role and capacity of institutions to facilitate regional environmental cooperation. Such skepticism may be largely derived from the preexisting belief that the region has evidenced a poor history of institutional frameworks (formal or informal) that would address relevant issues at the regional level. The tendency for policy makers to prioritize the political, military, and economic agendas is also a major impediment to environmental regime-building in the region.

Here, the main question that remains is whether environmental institution-building in the NEA region can signify the emergence of a more integrated regional cooperation. In regard to this puzzle, there are two contending perspectives on the causal relations between environmental regime-building and broader regionalism in NEA.

The first view observes that the success of regional environmental cooperation is vitally contingent upon the progress of regionalism. Proponents of this view argue that traditional security and economic issues rather than environmental issues are more determinant in enhancing regionalism and various forms of cooperation even in the post–cold war era. For instance, the history textbook issue, along with Japan's prime minister Junichiro Koizumi's continued visits to the Yasukuni Shrine, which honors Japan's war dead who include fourteen of the country's top convicted war criminals, have unsettled Japan's political and diplomatic relations with Korea and China over the past few years. A series of disputes on the Diaoyutai/Senkaku Islands, including the most recent incident where Japanese authorities arrested and then forcibly expelled seven Chinese activists, who had insisted that the Diaoyutai Islands were part of Chinese territory, reflects the growing tensions between Beijing and Tokyo in recent years.[1] These tensions have in turn led to several setbacks in regional cooperation. For instance, the Chinese government denied Prime Minister Koizumi's request to visit China in 2003 and warned that Japan would be excluded from participating in the express train construction project that would link Beijing and Shanghai. Proponents of this first view argue that the spillover of these setbacks into the sphere of environmentalism has been clear, and that further environmental cooperation efforts have risked being postponed until regionalism regains its past momentum. Therefore, in order to convince decision makers to place the same priority on environmental issues as they do on the traditional security agenda, it has been suggested that meticulous strategies that would clarify the linkages between the former and the latter (e.g., energy security) should be developed.[2]

The contrary view maintains that environmental cooperation is the independent variable to sustained and broader-based regionalism. That is, the relatively neutral character of the issue is conducive to relieving tensions between states and thus can contribute to bringing about regular intergovernmental dialogues and exchanges that would deal with more intransigent issues where conflicting national interests are more acute.[3] Even if this correlation is questionable to some, governments seem to have recognized the necessity for closer environmental collaboration due to the high level of environmental interdependence in the region. This can be verified by the fact that despite the aforementioned political setbacks during the second half of the 1990s, bilateral environmental dialogues between Korea, Japan, and China, have been very active, along with the annual Tripartite Environment Ministers Meeting (TEMM) between the three countries.

Regardless of which view proves in the end to be correct, close environmental interdependence in the region makes it imperative to create a framework that would, at least in the sphere of environmentalism, promote greater regional cooperation.[4] In this context, closer regional cooperation in addressing environmental issues in the region would clearly be a key linkage factor to promoting regionalism at the broader level, given the fact that "[t]he literature on new regionalism underscores several key linkage factors as necessary conditions under which regionalism or regional integration can take place among a group of states, including linkage by geographical proximity and by various forms of shared political, economic, social, cultural, or institutional affinities."[5]

Common Environmental Problems in Northeast Asia

The geographical proximity of countries in the NEA region explains why they are classified within a single ecological region.[6] As a result, these countries can serve either as the source or the recipient of cross-border environmental threats depending on the time of year or type of issue. Therefore, collectively managing "common pool resources" such as air systems, oceans, watersheds, fisheries, and communal forests should be central to Northeast Asian politics.[7] These common resources cannot be exclusively claimed and appropriated by any single state because such a claim would leave the exploitation of such resources under the free disposal of self-interested actors (states), thus bringing about what Garrett Harding called the "tragedy of the commons."[8]

While some common environmental problems have originated from natural disasters such as hurricanes and earthquakes, man-made disasters have become much more prevalent in the region as a result of development-driven pressures on the environment. Damages to the ecosystem have been aggravated by high population density, weak environmental legislation, the inequitable access to resources, and the lack of popular participation in the decision-making process. These conditions are all present in NEA. The following are brief portraits of common environmental challenges in NEA, particularly those shared by Korea, China, and Japan, which have the potential to produce conflict between the three, but at the same time present the opportunity for further regional cooperation.

The region's dramatic economic development coupled with overpopulation and rapid urbanization, which has massively increased the consumption of resources and energy as well as the production of industrial pollution and wastes during the past few decades, have been the cause of various environmental problems. In particular, China's remarkable economic development and continued growth-oriented policies have created some serious domestic and regional environmental threats. As a prominent example, given that two-thirds of China's energy consumption is currently from coal, high sulfur dioxide (SO_2) and nitrogen oxide emissions from power plants in the country have become primary sources of transboundary air pollution. Indeed, emissions from Northeast China are emerging as a cause of major regional concern as Korea and Japan have suffered the most from the acid rain coming from pollutants emitted by Chinese factories. Several islands in the western part of Korea, which includes Baekryung Island, are directly exposed to the polluted air blown across the Yellow Sea from China. The acid rain is also believed to cause a decrease in biomass productivity and to aggravate the effects of deforestation, which in turn increases the rate of carbon dioxide in the atmosphere of the recipient countries.[9]

The "yellow dust" phenomenon, also known as *Hwangsa*, which plagues the NEA region every spring, originates from the inner regions of Mongolia and sweeps through Western China en route to the Korean peninsula. However, the levels and frequency of these dust storms have increased since 1998. While cases of "yellow dust" had been reported on an average of 3.9 days per year during the 1980s, the frequency had increased to an average of 7.7 days per year during the 1990s and to an average of 18 days per year since 2000.[10] Such an increase in the sand and dust blown by strong winds, which are caused by the atmospheric stratum of high temperature and dry weather in the northwestern part of China and the Yellow River (Huang He) areas, seems to have resulted from decades of tree-cutting, overgrazing, and rapid industrialization, which in turn have generated desertification. Northern China's yellow dust has increasingly meant trouble for its own people and regional neighbors, such as Korea and Japan, by causing health problems, for example, respiratory difficulties and eye infections. Limited visibility that has brought about an increase in flight delays,[11] along with recent reports that the dust from China contains dioxin, a toxic chemical that causes cancer,[12] have become a matter of grave concern to the affected regions.

Marine pollution is another transboundary environmental ill that plagues the NEA region. The Yellow Sea, which is surrounded by China and the Korean peninsula and whose coastal areas are scattered with industrial facilities, has suffered the most from industrial waste, domestic sewage, and oil spills. The Yellow Sea is already known as one of the seven "dying seas" of the world (Black Sea, Yellow Sea, North Sea, Barents Sea, Red Sea, Arabian Sea, and Caspian Sea), and is the second worst case after the Black Sea.[13] The East Sea, shared by the two Koreas, China, Japan, and the Russian Far East, is relatively less polluted than the Yellow Sea, but still suffers from industrial waste dumping, oil spills, and radioactive wastes, mainly from Japan.[14] Furthermore, in the marine and coastal areas of NEA, that is, the Northwest Pacific area, the eutrophication of the coast brought about by excessive nutrient inputs has increased the frequency of red-tide incidents.[15] Still, the level of government activities and public attention, as well as interstate agreements on transfrontier marine pollution issues, remain at a much lower level compared to those of air pollution issues, not to mention that they remain local and fragmented.[16]

In addition to marine pollution issues, the depletion of fishery resources is a problem in the NEA region. According to the World Resource Institute, Northwest Pacific area fisheries were fully depleted by 1998, while many other species such as sea grass, corals, mollusks, shrimp, and lobsters have become endangered.[17] In addition, the boundary delimitation of the overlapping exclusive economic zones (EEZs) between Korea, China, and Japan is a highly controversial maritime issue. The 1982 United Nations Convention on the Law of the Sea, to which all are signatories, has legitimized the 200-nautical-mile EEZ. However, as the distance from one coast to another in the region's seas nowhere exceeds 400 miles, the regulation of shared waters and fishing arrangements has been problematic because each state is interested in maximizing its access to the resources of the disputed areas. As observed in the disputes between South Korea and Japan over Dokdo (Takeshima in Japanese) Island and between Japan and China over the Diaoyutai Islands, fishing disputes are related not only to the economic concerns of the fishing industry but also to the identification of territorial boundaries and political sovereignty.

Securing energy supplies is another major environmental issue in NEA, where rapid economic development has generated a shortage of energy resources of coal, oil, and natural gas. Korea, Japan, and Taiwan are heavily dependent on overseas sources of energy and natural resources for their industrial and economic activities. Despite an abundant amount of untapped energy resources in China and the Russian Far East, these countries lack the ability to effectively develop and utilize these resources due to exorbitant development costs, technological difficulties, and poor transportation infrastructure. The region's overreliance on the politically precarious Middle East for oil could also have serious implications for the security of energy supplies. Such vulnerabilities in securing energy resources have pushed NEA countries to seriously consider nuclear energy as an alternative source. The steady growth in nuclear power usage has been under way in order to accommodate the region's expanding populations and economies.[18] However, the development of nuclear power production capacities has raised the problem of nuclear safety and waste disposal. The lack of storage space for nuclear wastes is also a serious problem for many of the overpopulated countries in the region.

In summary, environmental degradation both in terms of quality (e.g., transboundary pollution) and quantity (e.g., the scarcity of common resources) has given rise to trouble in NEA. These common environmental issues have produced divergent responses among NEA countries. For instance, in addressing the issue of transboundary air pollution, China has had the tendency to adopt a defensive posture when it has been suggested, if not blamed, to be a primary source of regional environmental degradation, while Japan and Korea have shared the common interest of responding as victims. Yet, it should be noted that there is a significant difference in the Korean and Japanese cases, considering that Korea, while being a victim of pollution originating from China, is also the potential source of pollution in Japan. Meanwhile, the scarce nature of common pool resources has caused their overexploitation by individual states. Since resources such as watersheds, land, and the atmosphere are most often held or used in common, the competitive abuses of shared ecological resources have taken the form of zero-sum games, which would ultimately result in further scarcity and conflict. This can be seen in the diminishing size of fisheries in the Pacific Ocean, where more than half of the world's fishing is conducted by East Asian countries like China, Korea, Japan, Thailand, and Taiwan. Unless coordinated efforts are taken, the competition to secure the dwindling stock of fish might well increase tensions among these countries.

Progress and Prospects for Environmental Regime-Building in Northeast Asia

Opportunities have ripened for regional discussion on the establishment of a cooperative environmental management system in NEA since the late 1980s, when regional awareness on pressing environmental issues had coincided with the relaxation of East-West relations brought about by the demise of the cold war. Since then, Korea, Japan, and China have been engaged in various bilateral and multilateral dialogues in order to promote regional environmental regime-building. Bilateral environmental cooperation between China, Korea, and Japan was really a product of the 1990s. For instance, bilateral environmental cooperation agreements between these countries were established during 1993–94, respectively, with the objective of establishing a cooperative environmental governance regime.

Several regional initiatives for environmental cooperation at the multilateral level had also emerged during the 1990s. The establishment of the annual Northeast Asian Conference on Environmental Cooperation (NEAC), the Northeast Asian Subregional Program of Environmental Cooperation (NEASPEC), and the Northwest Pacific Action Plan (NOWPAP) has been noteworthy. For instance, the NEASPEC, launched in 1993 under the supervision of the Economic and Social Commission for Asia and the Pacific (ESCAP),[19] was the first official attempt to develop a comprehensive mechanism for regional environmental cooperation in NEA, which included the participation of the two Koreas, China, Japan, Russia, and Mongolia.

In addition, the aforementioned TEMM, launched in 1999, has grown into a very useful forum for the environmental ministers of Korea, Japan, and China to collectively develop an implementation plan to address the long-distance movement of pollutants such as the yellow dust from China. Considering the importance of these three countries in Northeast Asian environmental cooperation, the three-party ministerial meeting might be able to play a role in guiding environmental cooperation in NEA. International organizations such as the United Nations Development Programme (UNDP) and the Global Environmental Fund (GEF) have also been instrumental in facilitating multilateral cooperation in NEA, as evidenced by the two-year Environmental Preservation Project of the Tumen River region (2000–2002), jointly pursued by South Korea, China, and Mongolia with the support of the GEF.[20]

Governmental efforts on regional environmental cooperation have also expanded beyond the NEA region. There are several examples of multilateral, intergovernmental environmental cooperation, which include East Asia, Asia, and even the Asia-Pacific region. For instance, the Acid Deposition Monitoring Network in East Asia was created in 1998 in order to promote cooperation among its member states on conducting research and monitoring the deposition of acid in East Asia. The Japan-initiated Environment Congress for Asia and the Pacific has also played an important role in enhancing environmental policy dialogues in Asia and the Pacific region. The Asia-Pacific Economic Cooperation (APEC) forum and the Asia-Europe Meeting have also been instrumental in providing important opportunities to address common environmental issues in Asia and the Pacific region.

Despite all these attempts to address common environmental issues, regional environmental cooperation in East Asia in general and NEA in particular is still in its embryonic stage compared to the level of cooperation in Europe, where multilateral environmental institution-building had already begun in the early 1970s. Just as regional cooperation resulting in the creation of formal institutions in the fields of security and economy has remained trivial, there have been hardly any signs of any formal environmental institution-building in NEA. As seen from the European experience, the transformation of state postures concerning environmental issues in the Asian region would require not only a growing normative awareness but also the political will of the countries involved. This is particularly true of the case in NEA. Although common environmental imperatives have provided some opportunities for promoting regional cooperation among NEA countries, their cooperation has so far lacked any concrete cooperative project or action plan, not to mention a legally binding agreement.

In fact, there is much skepticism about establishing a sustained, cooperative institution for regional environmental protection because of preexisting confrontations and distrust in the region, which go back to the colonial period and have continued throughout World War II, the Korean War, and the cold war. Despite the end of the cold war, several potential risk spots stand out according to traditional (military) security terms: the longstanding confrontation between the two Koreas; the China-Taiwan conflict; growing concerns over Japan's major rearmament; and the possible struggle for regional hegemony between China and Japan.

A further weakness that has prevented the development of regional cooperation lies in the lack of evidence concerning which state should assume the responsibility for transfrontier environmental damage. For instance, only occasional reports, which have estimated the level of ecological deterioration of some coastal areas, are available. This explains why no single NEA country has officially acknowledged its own responsibility for any of the transnational environmental damages in the region. Furthermore, the level of public awareness and political motivation to address the region's environmental issues still remain low, compared to traditional political agendas that are given more priority in setting the national agendas.

The great difference in economic development among countries in NEA has also prevented regional environmental cooperation efforts from galvanizing. Furthermore, despite growing environmental dialogues among NEA countries, none of them are willing to put their national welfare and interests at stake. Concerns over possible infringements to state sovereignty, even with respect to such relatively peripheral areas as environmental policy, have also acted as obstacles to further regional environmental cooperation. For example, notwithstanding diplomatic pressures from Korea and Japan, the Chinese government has shown few signs of incorporating environmentally sustainable development measures into its growth-oriented economy plan. Currently facing a shortage of other energy sources, China continues to rely heavily on coal as its main resource, although greater coal consumption would surely increase the scale and impact of cross-border acid rain deposition. Although China has begun to pay increasing attention to the issue of environmental degradation since the mid-1990s, as demonstrated by its publication of "China's Agenda 21—White Paper on China's Population, Environment, and Development in the 21st Century,"[21] it still remains to be seen how much the Chinese government will coordinate its economic development policies with those dealing with its resources and environment.

Furthermore, there are problems of duplication and unnecessary competition between environmental institutions within, between, and across the NEA region because governmental initiatives are often driven by national interests, and because of government aspiration to exert more political and diplomatic influence in the region rather than the honest hope for regional environmental protection.

In brief, it can be said that at least five factors are required for the establishment of an institutional mechanism for promoting regional environmental cooperation: (1) national leadership; (2) the involvement of international institutions; (3) the involvement of transnational scientific networks; (4) the active presence of nongovernmental organizations; and (5) significant public concern.[22] Unfortunately, none of these factors has been apparent in the NEA region, at least for the time being, in facilitating the formation of a formal regional environmental institution. Therefore, current developments on environmental cooperation in NEA can be compared to what occurred in Europe during the early 1970s. It is thus too early to assess the impact of such efforts to effectively address common environmental issues in the region.

In assessing the prospects for the establishment of a formal environmental cooperation regime in the region, the two diverging views that were introduced in the earlier section need to be revisited.[23] The first regarded environmental cooperation as a dependent variable in the development of regionalism, while the second regarded cooperative approaches in addressing environmental issues to be an essentially independent variable to sustainable and broader regionalism. Based on these two contending views, there are three foreseeable scenarios on how regionalism in NEA could evolve in the future.

The first prospect is that NEA environmental cooperation, as it now stands, will remain as it is, though it would not be in an institutionalized form. There is even the possibility that ongoing regional environmental dialogues will become inactive or break down if countries in the region hold fast to their respective national interests and issues of priority and are unable to compromise conflicting or competitive national interests. This first scenario would be probable if environmental goals are treated as secondary issues in multilateral approaches to regional cooperation. Given the clear potential for political-military rivalry and confrontations, plus for economic regional uncertainties to take the upper hand, this pessimistic view would seem justified. However, the ongoing and fruitful progress of environmental dialogues in NEA throughout the 1990s should be sufficient in dispelling concerns on the possible stagnation or collapse of current regional cooperative processes. The most optimistic interpretation, although not probable, is that regional frameworks such as APEC, the ASEAN Regional Forum (ARF), or ASEAN+3 (consisting of the ten ASEAN members plus China, South Korea, and Japan), will become effective and instrumental in addressing common environmental challenges in the Asia-Pacific region, including NEA.

The second prospect is that efforts toward environmental regime-building in NEA could eventually develop into a cohesive and formalized regional environmental organization equipped with its own charter and secretariat. If things turn out as they should, a strong regional organization specializing in environmental issues could effectively facilitate intergovernmental cooperation. Advocates of this second scenario argue that if a government in the region finds it difficult or politically unacceptable to engage in traditional security dialogues, either bilaterally or multilaterally with other governments, this government would have no other choice but to form a cohesive regional body that would deal with less sensitive issues such as those that deal with the environment so as to maintain its positive interaction with other countries. In this sense, the establishment of a regional environmental organization can be an important driving force for building up various forms of regional confidence and broader-based cooperation.

However, critics of this scenario warn that it is likely to be realized only when the need to institutionalize regional environmental cooperation expands through high-level governmental meetings (e.g., summits) between NEA countries. Critics also argue that this optimistic prospect is subject to many uncertainties because it depends on many variables like the long-term relationship between China and Japan, the potential for major changes on the Korean peninsula, and the future role of the United States and its relations with NEA countries. In particular, the U.S. government has retained its strong will to remain a major player in NEA, not only in the political, military, and economic realms, but also with respect to nontraditional issues such as human rights and the environment. Mindful of the strategic importance of the U.S. presence in the region, NEA governments are hesitant to create a regional body, regardless of its purpose, without the direct participation of the United States.

The third prospect is a "flexible" derivative of the second one. That is, regional environmental cooperation will continue to evolve into an ultimately Northeast Asia-specific regime, which would include a dispute settlement mechanism (for disputed regional environmental issues) and crisis prevention and management mechanism (for natural and man-made ecological disasters), while remaining at the same time consistent with existing regional cooperative mechanisms (e.g., APEC) and international organizations (e.g., the United Nations Environmental Programme, UNEP).

This third scenario seems the most realistic and least fragile in terms of sustaining current developments, and more ideally, advancing the momentum of regional environmental cooperation, insofar as this scenario would be the result of a combination of at least the following three situations. The first situation would be one in which governments in the region see a need to resolve bilateral security problems, and would in turn attempt to organize a multilateral cooperative initiative in order to engage one another in a more comprehensive security discussion (including nontraditional security concerns) that might otherwise be difficult to achieve. Even if the creation of such a multiple setting is hampered by financial and diplomatic constraints, existing broad-based institutionalized multilateral forums such as the ARF could be utilized for such a purpose. The second situation would be one in which it is no longer possible for NEA countries to disregard international environmental debates. Therefore, governments in the region would increase their efforts to promote a greater sense of common responsibility for environmental protection and to establish more channels of institutionalized regional cooperation. Usually, these efforts not only enhance a closer partnership between NEA countries, but also add a new dimension to existing regional frameworks. The third situation would be one in which NEA countries are fully aware of the reality that any regional cooperation should be flexibly pursued on the basis of open regionalism so as to comply with the reality of diversity within and beyond the region. In line with the current status of regional and international institutions, NEA cooperation would also abide by the international norms of nonexclusiveness. However, this prospect would be the case only if NEA governments find the necessity to collaborate on environmental issues by incorporating additional functions into existing regional and global institutions, as well as by institutionalizing an NEA environmental cooperative body that would function as a comprehensive organization. This comprehensive organization would not only deal with all relevant regional environmental issues, but also coordinate all regional environment-related activities, both governmental and informal, under the auspices of existing legally binding agreements.

No matter which prospect becomes the future for NEA regional cooperation, the formation of an effective regional environmental regime in the region would no doubt be a long-term process. Although environmental issues may not always enjoy the same degree of attention in regional cooperative frameworks, the process itself is pivotal as it would increase interstate dialogue and exchanges in the region, and would ultimately lead to the formation of a regime. Once this has been accomplished, the regime would contribute to reinforcing its own authority, which in turn would coordinate and bolster interstate endeavors on various issues, regardless of its success in addressing environmental issues.

Korea's Role in Regional Environmental Cooperation

The main objective of the Korean government's environmental diplomacy has been to participate in the global effort to protect the global environment and at the same time improve the quality of its internal environment. However, the development of Korean environmental diplomacy was not endogenous, since its birth was not the result of environmental movements led by civil society or the government's initiatives to promote environmental cooperation with its neighbors and within the international society. Rather, it was exogenous given that the government adopted a defensive and reactive posture to the global trend.[24] That is, the purpose of establishing the Environmental Cooperative Division within the Ministry of Foreign Affairs and Trade in 1991 was to efficiently deal with the need to represent Korea's official position on environmental issues, at a time when environmental debates and discussions on relevant policies increased in number with the occasion of the Rio Summit in 1992.

Despite Korea's passive approach at the beginning of the 1990s, its environmental diplomacy has evolved into one that has become active in its participation in environmental debates and international environmental conventions by representing its position and interests in international forums such as the United Nations, the World Trade Organization, and the Organization for Economic Cooperation and Development (OECD). The Korean government has signed many of the major environmental conventions, such as the Framework Convention on Climate Change, the Convention on Biological Diversity, and the Montreal Protocol on Substances That Deplete the Ozone Layer, and has engaged in their subsequent implementation action plans in order to actively participate in the global effort to protect the environment. Korea has also continuously provided its support to major international organizations such as the Committee for Sustainable Development and the UNEP.[25] Furthermore, as one of the newly industrialized countries, Korea has made the most of its position as a mediator between developed and underdeveloped countries on issues where respective interests have collided. For instance, during the Rio Summit, Korea succeeded in adding a provision that prohibits the application of trade regulations on the grounds of environmental protection.[26]

At the regional level, Korea has also attempted to take the initiative in promoting environmental protection and cooperation through bilateral environmental cooperation agreements with Japan, China, and Russia, as well as through regular multilateral intergovernmental meetings dealing with regional environmental cooperation. For instance, the Korean government took the initiative in establishing the NEASPEC in 1993, the first intergovernmental, high-level ministerial meeting on the regional environment in NEA,[27] while it has actively engaged in the Tumen River Area Development Program, a jointly pursued project with China, Russia, Mongolia, and North Korea that is supported by the UNDP.

Nevertheless, there are some improvements that should be incorporated into Korea's environmental diplomacy if it is to carry out a more active and leading role in future international environmental negotiations, which are likely to be larger in scope and more complicated in content.

First, it goes without saying that many of the international environmental treaties that have been concluded pose many direct or indirect limitations on the economic activities of a country. Like many other countries around the world, Korea's countermeasures to these treaties have mostly aimed at minimizing the negative effects that the domestic implementation measures of the treaties might possibly bring to its own industries and trade. Environmental negotiations are also part of a country's diplomatic policies, which have the objective of maximizing a country's national interests. While effectively coping with the issues that could limit its economic activities, Korea's environmental diplomacy therefore should observe its duty as a member of the international society and participate in the global effort to protect the environment, not only in order to escape international criticism, but also for the sake of enhancing Korea's role in the international community.

Given that Korea's own economy-first policies, which in turn weaken the country's environmental diplomacy, could be not only appropriated to the principle of realpolitik, but also to the lack of environmental awareness among the public, it is important to increase the level of environmental awareness within the Korean society. For this, it is necessary to publicize the significant interaction between mankind and the environment and, ultimately, the importance of global environmental politics and sustainable development. While the role of the government is to represent the country in international environmental negotiations, the role of an environmentally aware Korean society is to act as a surveillance mechanism so that politicians who struggle to win popularity would not neglect the environmental preferences of the electorate. Therefore, environmentally insightful citizens could play a crucial role in guiding their government leaders to be more balanced on development and the environment.

Second, at the domestic level, it is essential to improve the quality of Korea's environment by means of public and private efforts to adopt a more environment-friendly industrial structure. These measures would not only provide the solutions to Korea's domestic environmental issues, but also give more leverage to the Korean government in intergovernmental environmental negotiations. For instance, the United Nations Framework Convention on Climate Change requires that all OECD members adopt policies and measures with the aim of reducing greenhouse gas emissions by the year 2010. Though the Korean government has submitted a proposal asking for an adjustment in implementing this commitment, which would delay the deadline by ten to twenty years, it does not seem likely that the international society would accept this proposal. On the one hand, this is because developed countries are worried that if Korea, a developing country, were exempted from this commitment, it would be difficult to induce China to reduce its greenhouse gas emissions. On the other hand, underdeveloped countries do not want Korea to implement its commitment as an OECD member so that they would be able to include Korea in their negotiation strategies. Moreover, the urgency of reducing greenhouse gas emissions has greatly increased in the face of damages caused by increasingly precarious natural disasters and growing international concerns over global warming. Domestically, if Korea were required to reduce its greenhouse gas emissions by 2010, Korean industries would be hard-hit by the effects of these policies and measures because of its high dependence on fossil fuels. Moreover, such policies and measures would also weaken the competitive power of the Korean economy, which is still suffering from the aftereffects of the 1997 Asian financial crisis.

Therefore, the development of substitute energy resources, such as solar energy and the reorganization of Korea's industrial structure into one that is more energy-efficient, is a task that must be immediately addressed under the close cooperation of the government, businesses, and research laboratories. Korean enterprises in particular should consider the future economic profits that such energy-efficient reorganization policies would bring and increase their investment in developing environmental technology that contributes to preventing pollution and saving energy. Meanwhile, the government should provide incentives to enterprises that integrate such energy-efficient policies into their management plans along with strategies inducing energy-consuming enterprises to adopt more energy-efficient policies. While promoting cooperation efforts between China and Russia in the process of implementing its shared commitment to reduce the emission of greenhouse gases, the South Korean government should also integrate into domestic policies the use of such incentives as the Emission Trading System and the Clean Development Mechanism, which was suggested at the Third Conference of the Parties to the UN Framework Convention on Climate Change in 1997 in Kyoto.

Third, the Korean government does not generally place as much priority on environmental problems as it does on economic development or military security. Although there is a plausible reason for this relative neglect of environmental issues from the government when considering the present security situation of the Korean peninsula or the economic situation after the Asian financial crisis, environmental issues also are security issues that demand high-level negotiations between Korea's neighbors. As seen from the Convention on Climate Change, which requires Korea to reduce its greenhouse gas emissions and consequently might bring about large economic losses to Korean industries, the convention is as much an economic as an environmental convention. Therefore, it is essential for the government, academia, and businesses to train specialists in negotiation, law, and relevant technologies as well as to provide concrete action plans addressing specific issues. In order to achieve this objective, the government must make an active effort to place more importance on environmental issues.

Fourth, efforts to acquire more accurate scientific evidence and statistics need to be strengthened. For example, the serious impact of acid rain on the ecological conditions in Korea and Japan from China's coal burning has yet to be reported. Despite the serious impacts of yellow sandstorms mostly blown from Northeast China to the Korean peninsula, it is impractical to place the responsibility on China without providing any explicit scientific evidence. The first step should be to collect data on the amount of pollution produced by each country, and in turn conduct long-term observation and analysis of the effects of these sandstorms on neighboring countries. The fact is that there is no long-term research project in Korea on how many pollutants are carried by these sandstorms. In addition, there is no consistent solution to the effects that the "yellow dust" has on Korea. Notwithstanding the fact that the occurrence of "yellow dust" is rare in Japan, Japan has conducted in-depth research on the phenomenon since the early 1980s and has, as a result, collected data for over twenty years.

In summary, environmental conventions are concluded under the assumption of close cooperation and participation of many states, but cooperation is often undermined because of conflicting interests between states. That is, international environmental negotiations encompass both the situation of conflicting national interests and the situation of interstate cooperation, which aims to prevent global environmental disasters. In order to sufficiently understand this process and bring about a successful outcome, Korea's environmental diplomacy strategy must thus be developed by closely linking it with domestic environmental policies. That is to say, the government should develop domestic environmental policies aiming to promote sustainable development in accordance with the spirit of "Agenda 21," which was adopted at the Rio Summit, while at the same time understanding the possible barriers that might exist to their implementation, and thus ensure that measures are effectively implemented. This would not only narrow the dilemma between development and environmental protection that Korea is currently faced with, but also strengthen the country's leverage in international environmental negotiations.

Conclusion

Growing concerns over cross-border environmental problems have led many states to engage in regional and international negotiations that have resulted in the establishment of multilateral mechanisms aimed toward collectively addressing and tackling these threats. In short, while transnational environmental issues have been the source of interstate conflict, they have also provided the motivation for states to cooperate with each other. Northeast Asia has not been an exception, as such global trends have also increased cooperation in the region.

Although the need for cooperative environmental management has been motivated by ecological imperatives, national competition to take the initiative in promoting environmental cooperation in the NEA region has also been an important driving force for countries like Japan and Korea. Nevertheless, regardless of which has played a greater role in promoting regional environmental partnership, it can be claimed that stronger collective action would facilitate the process of environmental confidence-building, which would eventually accelerate the momentum for further regional cooperation in other issues.

Yet, critics argue that such claims are an example of what is called "naive environmentalism"[28] because Northeast Asian efforts for regional cooperation in the post–cold war era have remained somewhat scattered, making some progress in economic cooperation, while accomplishing close to nothing in political or security cooperation. Though some may maintain that some regional bilateral or multilateral arrangements have emerged to address common challenges present in the NEA, it is also important to remember that these have been mostly arranged on an ad hoc and situation- or issue-specific basis.[29] This has mainly been due to large national disparities in economic development and the priority given to environmental issues at the national level, not to mention existing tensions from the region's history of colonial rule, interstate wars, and the cold war, which have continued to hamper efforts to improve interstate relations and attempts to redefine security in more comprehensive terms.

Consequently, the creation and implementation of practical plans of action and legal agreements, the prerequisites for establishing a formal regional institution, have not been easy in the NEA region. The lack of an organizational and financial structure in many of the regional environmental initiatives that have been undertaken, has prevented regional environmental cooperation efforts from developing beyond their early stages because of the tendency for negotiations to deal with overlapping issues. Furthermore, different domestic views toward environmental issues among countries in the region, which have been influenced by what issues (domestic and international) are prevalent in the national agenda, have also precluded the development of regional environmental cooperation.

It should be noted, however, that NEA has been increasingly confronted with various environmental problems. At the national level, the negative impact of rapid economic growth and urbanization in several parts of NEA has manifested not only in ecological threats but also in human security threats, which in turn are related to population, health, food, water, and energy security issues. At the interstate level, the transnational nature of environmental pollution as demonstrated by the effects of cross-border air and marine pollution in the region increases the potential for increased interstate conflict if these issues are not properly addressed as well as the need for interstate cooperation in solving these issues.

Presented with such a mixed picture of threats and opportunities for the region, it is imperative for scholars, decision makers, and the public to share the view that environmental degradation is a serious regional problem that can be solved only through collective action. Thus, new strategies that closely examine the causal relations between security and the environment should be developed in order to convince policy makers, who are preoccupied with other priorities, to engage in environmentalism.[30] Meanwhile, considering that several environmental initiatives made at the subregional level have been stagnant due to institutional and financial difficulties, it is also important to integrate current intergovernmental efforts on promoting environmental cooperation in the NEA into one consolidated institution. This could be realized by reinforcing ongoing bilateral and multilateral cooperation efforts in the region through the establishment of a comprehensive Northeast Asian Environmental Regime (NAER), including legal and regulatory measures that effectively handle environmental crises and disputes.[31]

As for Korea, its limited discretion in handling security and diplomatic issues has been brought about by its modern history, which was tainted by Japanese co-lonial rule, a civil war, and the cold-war standoff between the United States and the former Soviet Union on the divided peninsula. Although the end of the cold war has called for a different security paradigm worldwide, inter-Korean relations have not yet emerged from their state of hostility. That is to say, in the midst of continuing rivalries and tensions among the United States, China, Japan, and Rus-sia, Korea's position in the region remains rather weak. Therefore, considering this particular diplomatic situation, where division, war, hostile confrontation, and alliances have prevailed, Korea's diplomacy would be capable of displaying more autonomy if it pursued its interests with a clear philosophy on issues that are less politically sensitive, such as those related to the environment. In other words, it is not only necessary for Korea to consolidate its alliance with the United States and cooperate with countries within and outside the NEA region on security issues, it is also imperative for the country to make an effort to assume a leading role in "soft diplomacy" issues such as technological development and environmental protection, which would contribute to reestablishing Korea's active diplomatic posture. For this, the Korean government must unify the divided tasks of the Min-istry of Environment and the environmental section under the Economic Coopera-tion Division of the Ministry of Foreign Affairs and Trade into a permanent governmental body that would undertake all the tasks and responsibilities of envi-ronmental diplomacy. It is also important to train professionals and develop a hu-man resource pool that would effectively execute these responsibilities.

On a final note, the position of many Northeast Asian states on the environment has largely remained passive and ex post facto. Unless a dramatic environmental catastrophe within one country spills over to affect the entire region, different interpretations and emphases on environmental standards and values are likely to remain as obstacles to regional regime-building. Given that the region currently lacks the institutions for regionwide dialogue and cooperation, the formation of an effective regional environmental regime would be a long-term process. Yet, as argued above, the process itself is pivotal in that it would increase dialogue and exchange from which a regional environmental regime could evolve. In a more promising way, environmental security could be defined by considering its most positive effects, that is, environmental confidence-building, which would provide the political opportunity to further security and peace in the region.

15

The Korean Wave

Transnational Cultural Flows in East Asia

Jung-Sun Park

At the beginning of the new millennium, the news about a new trend called *hanryu* (the Korean wave) caught many South Koreans by surprise. The term refers to the growing popularity of South Korean popular culture, especially music, TV dramas, movies, and fashion styles, in East/Southeast Asia, including China, Taiwan, and Vietnam. It began in the late 1990s and, by the early twenty-first century, it had become a widely visible phenomenon in the region. Shaken national pride and confidence caused by the economic crisis in the late 1990s were alleviated by the surprising yet delightful story, and many heated discussions about the meaning and significance of popular culture as well as the phenomenon itself were inculcated. Since then, *munwha* (culture), represented by popular culture, has become a key word in South Korean social discourse.[1]

Hanryu is indeed a quite interesting and puzzling phenomenon. Many have argued that cultural power is correlated with economic and political power.[2] If we follow this line of argument, South Korea's economic and political stance in Asia cannot easily explain its lately gained transnational cultural influence through *hanryu*. For example, Korea's economic status is not necessarily a notch above that of, say, Taiwan, and Korea's political instability, epitomized by division, makes it more a subject of outside intervention than a source of political influence. Moreover, until recently, its cultural industry did not necessarily have transnational competitive power in terms of resources and creativity. Then, what happened? What generated *hanryu*? Or, as some have argued, is *hanryu* merely media hype without substance or a temporary trend that will quickly disappear? This chapter is an inquiry into these questions. Based on research conducted in Korea, Japan, Taiwan, Hong Kong, and China in the summer and fall of 2003, I will examine the complex interplays of multiple factors embedded in the emergence of *hanryu* and the implications of *hanryu* for the transformation of global cultural flows.[3]

Transforming Global Cultural Landscapes: Changing Directions and Multiple Routes of Transnational Cultural Flows

As many have argued, global capitalism, the development of technology, and the fading of the cold war have profoundly transformed the global landscape.[4] The border-crossing experiences (both physical and cognitive) of people have increased tremendously, and the world is interconnected through new logic and media such as the Internet. In this context, transnational cultural flows have become easier and more extensive than ever before, and their directions have taken more complex routes. While the cultural hegemony of the West, symbolized by Hollywood, still lingers, new trends and attempts that challenge the unidirectional cultural flows from the West to the rest have emerged over the years.[5]

One such new trend is the increasing influence of non-Western, especially Asian, cultures on Western popular cultures. For example, African, Caribbean, and South American influences on U.S. and European popular culture have been noticeable.[6] Yet, until recently, Asian culture's influence on Western popular cultures had been minor. Moreover, Asian pop culture's presence beyond the geographical location of Asia had long been minimal, although the traditional cultures of Asia have been relatively well known. Considering Asia's increasing economic and, to a lesser degree, political power and the attention it has received from the West, it is puzzling why Asian popular culture has so long been underrepresented in the West.[7] In the past decade or so, however, Asian popular culture has gradually gained some saliency and visibility in the West, as exemplified by the growing popularity of Japanese animation, Hong Kong–style films, Zen-inspired fashion, and Indian-style body decoration and exercise.[8] Besides selective appropriations and consumption of Asian pop culture by the general public, more direct and indiscriminate importation and circulation of Asian popular culture is also easily found in metropolitan cities in the West, mainly through diaspora Asian populations. For example, in most major U.S. cities, Asian American communities' ethnic TV channels broadcast the latest TV dramas, entertainment programs and news from their countries of origin, and their ethnic spaces are filled with goods and information from the "homeland." And these information and goods are not only consumed by particular ethnic or immigrant groups but also by the general public, who have access to and interest in such things.[9] Moreover, nowadays information is transmitted almost concomitantly across borders through media such as the Internet and satellite, compressing time and spatial gaps to the minimum.[10] Thus, contemporary audiences in Western metropolises can be exposed to Asian pop culture in "real time" and the immediacy of cultural contact may intensify the impact of Asian popular culture on the West.

Another trend that challenges Western cultural hegemony is regionalized, such as inter-Asian, transnational cultural flows. In the face of globalization, regionalization also emerged, which was most clearly observed in the political and economic realms as exemplified by the European Union and the North American Free Trade Area (NAFTA). With the expansion of media globalization, this trend also appeared in the cultural realm partly because the national/regional sectors tried to maintain and reconstruct their cultures and identities in response to the homogenizing forces of globalization.[11] Ironically, such regionalization of cultural flows was further facilitated by the global media, a key player in cultural globalization, as they were interested in marketing cultural products based on region as well as globally.[12] In addition, the development and maturation of some local media industries enabled them to create and distribute attractive popular cultural products that appeal to the consumers in a region. For instance, the popularity of Hong Kong films in the 1980s and the success of Japanese TV dramas and music in the 1990s in East/Southeast Asia indicate this type of regionally bound cultural circulation.[13] With the growth of youth culture and economic development, Asian audiences' tastes and desires have increasingly become diversified and intensified and they have needed some fresh alternatives to the already too-familiar and too-dominant Western pop culture. Supported by the state and the business sector, the Japanese pop cultural industry was most successful at penetrating these new niches open in Asia and has exerted dominant cultural influence in many parts of the region, competing against Western cultural hegemony.[14] In the late 1990s, *hanryu* joined this trend of regionally based transnational circulation of pop culture, further diversifying the directions and routes of cultural flows and influence.

Born in this transformative time and context, *hanryu* is both a product and a symbol of the new directions, characteristics, and power relations of cultural encounters in the contemporary world. While the above-mentioned transformation of the global cultural landscape provides one layer of context, the birth and trajectories of the phenomenon are further intertwined with complex and multifaceted interplays of various socioeconomic, historical, and cultural factors. I discuss these in detail in the following sections.

The Market, the State, and Globalization of the Media

With the rapid expansion of global capitalism, the media industry has also quickly become globalized. Backed by advanced communications technologies, the emergent global media industries began to exert greater influence all over the world to an unprecedented degree. According to David Morley and Kevin Robins, "As part of their strategy for global hegemony, media corporations have sectioned the world into large geo-economic regions."[15] The Asian market, in particular, allured them with the number of consumers and their growing buying power; in the 1990s, it became "the hottest battlefield for transnational media corporations." The idea of "the actual and simultaneous reach of the same media products and popular culture in many parts of Asia" interested "Western global players such as News Corp., CNN, BBC, MTV, ESPN, HBO, and Disney"; consequently, "the idea of pan-Asian-mega-broadcasting" materialized. While this new marketing strategy further intensified the West's cultural hegemony, it also unwittingly contributed to and facilitated the more complex inter-Asian flows of Asian popular cultures that I mentioned earlier. Moreover, the (Western) global media industries' powerful presence and aggressive marketing raised concerns about the "foreign (mostly American) invasion from the sky" in a few Asian countries such as Malaysia,

Singapore, and China. In reaction, they "have advocated for the protection of 'Asian' values from the decadent Western morality transmitted through the media."[16] This enabled the creation of a new niche where other non-Western, especially Asian, media industries could enter. Equipped with marketable products and accumulated know-how as well as long economic and political ties rooted in the colonial times, the Japanese media industry, which has the second largest TV and music markets in the world, had effectively tapped into the new niche and expanded its market share in Asia in the 1990s, without much challenge from other Asian media industries.[17] Consequently, throughout the 1990s, Japanese popular culture has exerted dominant cultural influence in the East/Southeast Asian region along with Western pop culture.[18]

Moreover, media globalization, economic development, and the growth of a consumer culture (especially among the youth) led to the mushrooming of cable and satellite TV stations in Asia. Naturally, it brought about urgent demands for more programs to air, including TV dramas, news, and entertainment programs. Yet, not many local Asian media industries could produce sufficient, good-quality programs to satisfy ever-growing and fickle consumer needs; thus, new markets were generated for increased importation of foreign programs, which has reshaped the cultural landscapes in many Asian countries. In Taiwan, for example, since the government permitted the establishment of cable channels in 1993, cable TV channels have sprouted, once reaching more than a hundred in number.[19] However, the local Taiwanese TV industry could not produce enough (as well as good enough) programs to serve the skyrocketing demands of the new and many cable TV stations. Importing foreign (including Hong Kong and Chinese) programs and repeated rerunning of the same programs were the Taiwanese cable TV stations' ways of coping with this problem. Besides Hong Kong, Chinese, and Western programs, Japanese programs, especially, were imported in bulk.[20] The frequent airing of Japanese TV programs, along with the Taiwanese people's long familiarity with Japanese consumer goods and (popular) culture in general, had facilitated a phenomenon called *hari* (Japan fever), craziness for Japanese pop culture and its products. In the beginning, *hari* was a distinctive phenomenon such as *hanryu*, yet over the years, it has become almost an integrated part of Taiwanese youth culture, indicating the hegemonic influence of Japanese pop culture in the country.

By the late 1990s, ever-changing and capricious consumer tastes and needs demanded something different from the already too-familiar and too-abundant Western and Japanese programs in Taiwan. Moreover, the cost of importing Japanese programs had become too high, compelling cable TV companies to look for an alternative. In this context, some cable TV companies turned to Korean dramas, which had not done well in the mid-1990s, when few programs aired experimentally. To many people's surprise, however, this time, Korean dramas became big hits one after another. It almost coincided with the unexpected success of a Korean dance duo, Clone, and some other Korean singers in the country.[21] Rather quickly, fan clubs of Korean dramas and movies as well as actors, actresses, and singers were formed and interest not only in Korean dramas but also in Korean pop culture in general has rapidly grown. For the media industry, the success of Korean dramas has been encouraging enough that some cable TV companies began to specialize in Korean dramas. As my Taiwanese informants pointed out, Taiwan and Hong Kong are the testing grounds for the greater Chinese region and neighboring Southeast Asia for pop cultural products. Thus, *hanryu*, as a regional phenomenon, emerged as the popularity of Korean pop culture, most visibly manifested in Taiwan, soon spread to China and Southeast Asian countries.[22]

While pop cultural trends are often shared in the greater Chinese region and, to a large extent, in many parts of Southeast Asia, local contexts provide different patterns of reception and circulation. For instance, in China, importation and distribution of foreign pop culture are under close state scrutiny and regulations.[23] The country's economic growth and the innovation/open-door policy (begun in 1978) have brought about new demands for diverse cultural contents and information, especially suited to the taste of young people.[24] However, the existing Chinese cultural industry could not yet effectively cater to these needs. Fearing the "decadent" Western (or any foreign) cultures' harmful influence on its people, the Chinese government screens foreign TV programs before airing them, allocates a quota for the number of foreign movies to be shown annually, and regulates foreign entertainers' performance through a permission system. In other words, foreign pop cultural contents that are outside of the acceptable parameters of the state ideology and policies are, in theory, not allowed to cross Chinese borders. Of course, the increasing usage of the Internet (although this is still subject to state censorship), the proliferation of pirate copies of foreign music, film, and TV dramas, physical border-crossing, and so on make the borders porous and difficult to guard.[25] However, state censorship and regulations, at least, slow the indiscriminate inundation of foreign pop culture into the Chinese market. Given this situation, it is not surprising to find that a large number of Hong Kong and Taiwanese dramas and music have been imported to meet consumer needs. However, they alone could not satisfy the diverse and ever-growing needs of the audience. Consequently, a limited number of Hollywood and European films and Japanese dramas were also imported. But they have not gained the degree and kind of popularity that they had in many other parts of Asia or in the world, not only because of state censorship but also because of historical legacy (imperialism) and cultural distance. In this regard, Korean pop culture was suited for the Chinese market because it is relatively free from historical, political, and cultural burdens compared to many other foreign pop cultures such as American and Japanese.[26] Thus, at least in the beginning, Korean pop culture could enter the Chinese market without much sanction or difficulty.[27]

While the Chinese government has tried to protect its cultural borders by imposing censorship and regulations, the South Korean government has made an effort to aid its media industry to cross foreign borders by implementing policies and establishing organizations that support the export of Korean pop culture. The

South Korean government's growing attention to the genre of pop culture is largely motivated by nationalistic intention, that is, the expansion of South Korean cultural and economic influence in the Asian region.[28] This outward-bound, expansionist new nation-building effort in the globalizing era was first vocalized in the early 1990s in the name of *segyehwa* (globalization) discourse.[29] However, before its maturation and implementation, Korea had to face the bitter side of imposed globalization during the economic crisis in the late 1990s as it had to go through the major "restructuring processes" of its economy and society imposed by the International Monetary Fund. Having recovered from the economic crisis, the South Korean government in the early 2000s was ready to reposition Korea in the world and *hanryu* appeared to be a timely symbol for a new position.

The internal competition in the Korean media industry also contributed to *hanryu*. Until recently, Korean popular cultural products had been for domestic consumption only. Few people thought that Korean music, TV dramas, and movies had a competitive edge overseas and even a few attempts to sell those products in the Asian market in the early- to mid-1990s virtually failed.[30] Yet gradually the domestic competition grew strong, forcing companies and individuals to come up with commercially appealing products or to find a new market. For example, in the late 1990s, the cut-throat competition in the music industry in Korea urged a few small-scale production companies to explore overseas markets, especially in Taiwan and China, for "sheer survival." It is ironic that such an attempt for survival became successful and ignited what is later called *hanryu*. An owner of a Korean music production company told me that the success of Korean musicians in the greater Chinese market is not merely "luck" as some may think. He said that the Korean music industry disproportionately concentrates on dance music to the extent that anyone who survives in the intensely competitive Korean dance music market surely possesses the talent and quality that can elicit success overseas. Furthermore, the proliferation of "idol stars" created by the "star system" method expanded the pool of marketable entertainers and the adoption of more systematic management and promotion styles helped their overseas success.

In addition, certain marketing strategies enhanced the export of Korean cultural products. Although Korean TV companies have tried to export their programs overseas since the 1980s, it was not until the mid-1990s that the export of Korean dramas took off.[31] The long-term effort and investment as well as some flexibility in copyright and formatting issues may have contributed to the increasing sales of Korean programs. To illustrate, Korean TV companies allowed editing or reformatting of their products according to the format of overseas media industries. Asian countries have different formats for TV programs. For example, Korean TV dramas (miniseries) are generally composed of sixteen episodes whereas the Chinese format prefers twenty or forty episodes. In addition, the length and frequency of commercial breaks vary. Therefore, editing imported TV dramas is almost inevitable. While Japanese TV companies, in principle, do not allow reformatting of their dramas overseas as they are bound by complicated domestic copyright regulations, Korean TV companies, which usually possess the copyright of an entire drama, can have more leeway in exporting their products.[32]

Moreover, Korean TV companies sell their copyright as a whole instead of itemizing the rights. For example, in the Japanese industry's case, they sell video rights, CD rights, and so on separately, while Korean companies tend to sell all of those rights as a package, which is much more convenient for the foreign buyer. Thus, overall, Korean companies' "flexible" take on the format and copyright make the products more attractive, as they are "hassle-free."

Modernity, Desire, and Nostalgia

The emergence of *hanryu* is also closely related to the economic development of Asian countries and their similar degrees of modernity. Acquisition of a certain degree of modernity has generated new consumer tastes and desires for goods, including pop cultural products, all over Asia. Indeed, East/Southeast Asian consumers' tastes and desires tend to share some commonalities, and their constantly changing quests for diversity, freshness, and uniqueness were some of the main factors behind the success of *hanryu*.[33] But other than merely being fresh and different, *hanryu*'s success also relies on the high quality and sophistication of Korean pop cultural products. For example, besides the interesting storylines, many Asian audiences of Korean dramas are fascinated by the beautiful scenes of luxurious urban life, stylish clothes, and hairstyles depicted in TV dramas, movies, and music videos.[34] Oftentimes, these images trigger desires to imitate the styles depicted in them. On the streets of Taipei or Shanghai, my informants told me that they could easily spot "Korean-style dressing and hairstyles." If they do not visibly imitate, some audience members dream or fantasize about the life that they saw on screen. Some make this fantasy about a particular actor, actress, or protagonist a reality by visiting Korea to meet the actor or actress or the locations where the memorable scenes were shot. Through physical or imaginary visits to Korea, familiarity with and understanding of Korea and Korean culture increase and new kinds of transnational social relationships seem to be formed.

Some of my Korean informants who work in the media industry told me that other Asians' perception of Korea's economic success and its highly modern urban lifestyle has laid the groundwork for *hanryu*. Some even claimed outright that without a strong enough economic foundation, Korean cultural products would not have been alluring to overseas consumers. To some extent, this claim seems to have validity. Yet, what I find interesting is that the appeal of Korean cultural products to other Asian consumers seems to be related to the country's "in-between" level of economic development, which is neither too advanced nor too behind. This observation is particularly relevant to the Chinese context. For example, in my Chinese informants' perception, Korea is not as postindustrial as Japan, which creates distance as well as admiration. Korea's economic development is better than that of China, but, in their view, it is still within reach. So it simultaneously creates desire and familiarity. In other words, the Chinese audience fantasizes about Korean urban life depicted in dramas, yet it is either not completely far away from their own reality or it is very close to what may become available to them relatively soon. So they can "relate to" what they see without much mental reservation or distance.

This logic, however, may not be applicable to the cases of Hong Kong, Taiwan, and Japan, whose economic status and degree of familiarity with Western cultures are similar to or higher than those of Korea. In Hong Kong, for instance, it is the freshness of Korean popular culture that attracted them most. My informants claimed that while Hong Kong people are very open to foreign cultural influence, trends come and go very fast. Korean movies and TV dramas were well received in the late 1990s and early 2000s because they were different from the existing Hong Kong, Taiwanese, Western, and Japanese movies and dramas. In particular, Korean dramas' and movies' unique storytelling, good-looking protagonists, and visually pleasing scenes caught the Hong Kong audience's attention as a fresh new alternative.[35]

In Taiwan, besides the freshness, economic and cultural factors seem to play a part. While Taiwanese show ambivalent attitudes toward Korea's relative economic stance vis-à-vis that of Taiwan (some acknowledged that Korea is a well-to-do country on a par with their own, while some think that Korea is economically inferior to them), most of them seem to be impressed by Korean cultural products and the images of Korean urban life depicted in TV dramas and movies. Indeed, my informants expressed a desire for sophisticated Korean fashion, hairstyles, and urban lifestyles they have seen on TV and some have actually visited Korea to see and experience the images. Moreover, perceived cultural relatedness seems to ease Taiwanese emotional and personal-level acceptance of Korean popular culture. For example, my Taiwanese informants told me that one reason they like Korean dramas is because of the emotional proximity they find in them. In a way, the similar degree of modernity of the two countries makes it feasible to experience similar social phenomena at almost the same time, thus, issues and dilemmas portrayed in Korean dramas can actually be found in contemporary Taiwanese society. Even when the social relations and expressions of emotion depicted in Korean dramas are not relevant to Taiwanese society, my informants told me that they could still understand them because of the cultural traditions shared by the two countries.

Even in the whirlwind of *hanryu* in East/Southeast Asia, Japan remained largely untouched until lately. However, as illustrated by the recent success of some Korean dramas, especially *Kyoul yonga* (Winter Sonata), movies, and entertainers, Japanese interest in Korean pop cultural products has been rapidly growing. Some of my Japanese informants insisted that the attraction of Korean popular culture is based on emotional elements, especially nostalgia. For example, Japanese audience members seem to feel "nostalgia" when they watch Korean dramas because they depict things such as close, caring human relations and pure, long-lasting love, all elements Japan once had but lost. This explanation, which implies a time lag between Korea and Japan and Korea's backwardness in terms of development, seems to constitute a significant part of Japanese social analysis of the Korean wave. However, some Japanese informants, particularly those who work in the media industry, suggest other reasons. For example, the success of *Winter Sonata,* which became a social phenomenon in Japan, has to do with its main audience, that is, middle-aged women. Japanese middle-aged women have long been neglected by Japanese TV, which has focused on the young viewers, and their need for their husbands' attention and love has often been unmet. Thus it is said that when the Korean drama tapped an unserved market and touched the hearts of female viewers because of the warmth of the caring, handsome male protagonist, they immediately fell for the main character and the drama. With their strong purchasing power and unsatisfied emotional needs, these middle-aged women eagerly consumed anything related to the drama and, to some extent, Korea. This, in turn, greatly contributed to the rapid expansion of the Korean wave in Japan. In addition, my informants told me that the vibrant energy and creativity of Korean pop culture appeal to the Japanese consumers because that is what Japan lacks nowadays. Referring to the famous nationwide festive cheering for the Korean soccer team during the 2002 World Cup competition, a Japanese informant told me that some Korean pop cultural products exude such energy, and that may be what attracts Japanese to Korean pop culture.[36]

In this vein, Korean pop culture seems to be desirable and interesting to other Asians for multiple and sometimes contradictory reasons. On the one hand, it is alluring because it seems to embody what one wants to become or relates to. On the other hand, it touches an emotional chord, as it possesses what one lost. In this sense, Korean pop cultural products seem to embrace emotions and views of the past, present, and future of neighboring countries, which, in turn, enable their successful transnational flows.

Historical, Political, and Cultural Legacies in East and Southeast Asia

Hanryu is also interrelated with the historical legacy and geopolitics of East/Southeast Asia. As I mentioned earlier, Japan's strong political and economic influence in the Asia region, which traces its roots to the colonial times, on the one hand, has facilitated the wide circulation and ready acceptance of its popular culture. On the other hand, however, the colonial past hinders its penetration into some Asian countries. For example, in China, Japanese popular culture has not been successful, although Japanese media have long tried to expand their market in China. Most of my Chinese informants, both young and old, declared that they still remembered what Japan had done to the Chinese people during wartime and, because of the bitter memories, the Chinese people have reservations about Japan and, to some extent, Japanese products. This kind of sentiment partially explains why Japanese TV dramas have not received the kind of high ratings they have in Taiwan or Hong Kong, although they have been aired in China since the 1980s and had a small segment of enthusiastic followers. Even Chinese teenagers, the main target consumers of Japanese pop culture, were not hesitant to express their negative feelings toward Japanese wartime atrocities, although they are often forgetful when it comes to actual consumption of Japanese consumer goods. Given this situation, some argue that the historical legacy leaves room for Korean pop cultural products to find a niche in the Chinese market because Korea is free of past bad memories and Korea's traditional relationship with China has been "nonthreatening," to say the least.

Yet Korea is not completely free from historical or political burdens. In Taiwan, for example, the memory of the Korean government's abrupt severance of diplomatic relations with Taiwan in 1992 still leaves a bitter taste in people's mouths. The broken ties were partially mended when South Korea sent rescue forces to Taiwan at the time it was struck by a severe earthquake in 1999. The media's airing of the selfless and heroic efforts of the Korean rescuers left strong positive images in Taiwanese minds, attenuating the bitter feelings.[37] Yet I was told that the memory still lingers and that may be part of the reason Taiwanese occasionally show ambivalent attitudes toward Korea and its cultural products. In addition, the ambivalence is sometimes intensified by the competition between Korea and Taiwan for the same economic markets and niches.[38]

On a positive note, the success and positive image of Korean popular culture in Taiwan involved it in the political domain when a hit song by a Korean group, Clone, was used as a campaign song for Chen, the incumbent prime minister, during his election campaign in 2000. It is said that the Korean group's popularity among young Taiwanese and its powerful and energetic image fit well with Chen's intention to reach out to the young constituencies. At the same time, Korea's successful political transition from an authoritarian to a democratic regime in the late 1980s was used as a reference for Chen's campaign, which emphasized the change of regime.[39]

Korean popular culture's success is also often explained in terms of cultural proximities among Asian countries. In particular, the focus of Korean TV dramas on family lives and their depiction of social relationships based largely on Confucian ideology supposedly contribute to their popularity overseas because family themes cater to a wider array of audiences including both old and young people, and because Asians supposedly share the Confucian cultural tradition. In fact, my informants in China and Taiwan attested that the family theme and perceived cultural proximity are the reasons Korean TV dramas have a wider range of viewers compared to Japanese dramas, which are consumed mostly by teenagers and people in their early twenties. While this kind of explanation makes sense to some extent, the actual degree of cultural proximity based on shared cultural tradition can be questionable. First of all, the three-generation families that are somehow frequently portrayed in TV dramas exported overseas are rarities in contemporary South Korea.

Hence, the premise of Korean familial relationships that other Asian audiences imagine is a fallacy. Moreover, in contemporary China and Taiwan, such extended family life is largely in memory, not in reality. If Korean dramas appeal to the old population in those countries, it is probably because they can fantasize about their secret longing to be treated with respect and care in a traditional Confucian manner through the dramas whose stories are a construction rather than a reality in Korea.

The similarities in social relations and issues that connect other East/Southeast Asians with Koreans through TV dramas are perhaps closely related to the rapid socioeconomic and political transformations that those countries have undergone in their modern history. Issues such as generational and gender conflicts, social inequality, dissolution of family relationships, Westernization, and identity questions are common in many Asian countries. Thus, the ways that Korean dramas deal with such issues may generate a feeling of cultural proximity based on shared modernization experiences rather than common cultural traditions. This does not mean, however, that there are no shared cultural commonalities. Despite the loss of old cultural traditions, East/Southeast Asia, especially the greater Chinese region, still seems to share certain social values and customs, at least ideally. This becomes obvious when individuals express their familiarity with Korean dramas in contrast to Western dramas.[40]

Cultural proximity is also discussed in conjunction with cultural translation. Some Chinese scholars argue that the success of *hanryu* is related to the Korean media's ability to translate Western culture to suit the Chinese taste.[41] They insist that Western culture is too different from Chinese culture; thus, its direct importation is not successful because of the nonnegotiable cultural distance. The Koreanized version of Western popular culture, however, reinterprets and mediates the Western culture in an "Asian" way, which Chinese consumers can readily accept and relate to. Thus, the cultural proximity between Korea and China effectively builds bridges between the West and China as well. This argument is interesting in the sense that Japan has long claimed this role of "cultural interpreter" between Asia and the West.[42] Yet, according to my Chinese informants, Japanese popular culture and its interpretation of Western pop culture have alienating elements to them, which generates a feeling of distance. They are too postindustrial, too Westernized, and too individualistic to the extent that they seem incomprehensible and weird. On the contrary, Korea still seems to retain cultural similarities with China while it is Westernized enough to transmit and mediate information from the West to China. As I mentioned, Korea's "in-between" stance, in terms of the development of cultural industry and economy, eases its connection with some Asian neighbors such as China.

Implications of the Korean Wave

The "Korean wave" is an indication of new global- and regional-level transformations in the cultural landscape. At the global level, it signifies multidirectional transnational cultural flows in which the previous cultural "peripheries" began to have a presence and a voice in the cultural "centers." The fact that the transnational influx of Korean popular culture to the United States has been facilitated not only by Korean Americans but also by other Asian-American groups whose countries of origin have experienced *hanryu* exemplifies this point.[43] What *hanryu* also symbolizes is a regionalization of transnational cultural flows as it entails Asian countries' increasing acceptance of cultural information from neighboring countries that share similar economic and cultural backgrounds rather than from economically and politically powerful (Western) others. Overall, new cultural formation is in the making, and the Korean wave is a first sign of how a country "in-between" can find a niche and reposition itself as an influential cultural mediator and creator in the midst of global cultural transformation.

Hanryu also has many practical ramifications. For example, it brings about changes in the images of Korea. Before the Korean wave, many neighboring Asians either did not know much about Korea or knew only a few simple, often stereotypical things about Korea, for example, about the Korean War and political instability. But after having seen contemporary Korean lives through dramas and movies, the images of Korea have changed a great deal. My Taiwanese and Chinese informants told me they learned that Korea is an economically developed modern nation with unique lifestyles and moral and behavioral codes. This better understanding of Korea sometimes leads to a more systematic study of Korea and Korean culture. Some of my Chinese and Japanese informants actually learned Korean in order to understand Korea better and become friends with Koreans. Therefore, intercultural understanding and sometimes personal-level friendship are formed through the consumption of popular culture. In conjunction, Korean waves help businesses related to Korea as well as Korean industries. For example, the travel industry benefits from the increasing travel to Korea. In many cases, the trip is tied to meeting one's favorite star idols (fan-club meetings or observing their favorite stars making dramas or films) or visiting the famous places where certain dramas and movies were shot. This is usually combined with shopping and further sightseeing. In addition, the sales of Korean products, especially the ones that famous Korean stars advertise, increase a great deal. For instance, with the success of Korean dramas, movies, and music in the greater Chinese region, Samsung cell phones, LG electronic goods, and De Bon cosmetics have considerably expanded their market shares. Therefore, the popularity of pop cultural products has significant repercussions in other industries and intangible arenas.

While Korean waves have generally induced positive outcomes, they have also had negative impacts such as misunderstandings and stereotypes. For example, most of my Taiwanese and Chinese informants think that most Koreans live with extended family members as the three-generation household is frequently portrayed in Korean dramas, while the reality in Korea is far from it. They also think that Korean men are wife-beaters (again, certain dramas depict such scenes) and Korean women's social status is very low to the extent that they expressed pity for them. There is always a danger of seeing and understanding others through the looking glass of pop culture; thus, unless the media images are supplemented by personal-level contacts and communication, the risk of cultural misunderstanding lurks.

The media industry's awareness of these complex issues as well as its pursuit of economic profit has resulted in an increasing number of co-productions in recent years, especially among the Korean, Japanese, Taiwanese, and Chinese industries. Featuring of Asian stars with various national backgrounds in domestic productions as well as co-financing and co-production of films and TV dramas have become common practices. These are expected to secure and expand markets in Asia for the involved parties, which is another indication of regionalization of intra-Asian cultural production and dissemination.

Conclusion

I have examined the complex reasons for the emergence of the Korean wave and its ramifications. Then, what is the future of Korean waves? Are they going to fade away, as some of my informants predicted? Or, are they going to continue? It is difficult to predict because the future of Korean waves is contingent upon many variables. For example, factors such as changes in local cultural needs, the ability of Koreans and others to produce high-quality popular cultural products, and the intricacies of political and economic situations in the region will affect the future of Korean waves. If the local Chinese/Taiwanese cultural industry can produce good dramas, films, and music, it will not only dominate the Chinese market but also will penetrate the Korean and/or Japanese markets, which might become another interesting example of multidirectional cultural flows. If the Korean cultural industry maintains its energy, vision, and capital, it may continue to exert an influence in the region and beyond. Moreover, the political fusion and fission as well as economic cooperation and rivalry among Asian countries could reformulate the cultural landscape. While the future is an open book, many of my informants predicted that the Korean waves as a distinctive phenomenon would eventually disappear, but, just like the Japan fever, it will be integrated into everyday life (in the case of Hong Kong and Taiwan, at least). Yet, the history and context of Korean waves and Japan fever are different, so their paths might be different. No matter what happens in the future, one of the critical significances of the Korean wave is that it challenged the existing binary division between dominant and dominated cultures, center and periphery, and unidirectional flows of cultural influence. Korean waves cross many boundaries (territorial, political, cultural, theoretical) and have constructed new kinds of relations across borders including multidirectional cultural regionalization. Although it is premature to discuss their legacies, as their beginning was unique, perhaps their legacies will be unique as well, intersecting national, regional, and global cultures in a new way.

Epilogue

Korea, Northeast Asia, and the Long Twentieth Century

Charles K. Armstrong

In 1930—what in hindsight turned out to be the halfway point of Japanese colonial rule in Korea—a British writer named H.B. Drake published a travelogue, *Korea of the Japanese*. "England," he wrote of the world's then greatest power, "knows nothing of Korea. Yet Korea is worth knowing. It focuses so many problems, focuses them so clearly."[1] And so it has been. From the late nineteenth century, the Korean peninsula has almost continuously been the focus of regional and global geopolitical problems, including three major wars by the mid-twentieth century and an ongoing low-level conflict—threatening at times to erupt again into all-out war. While the Anglophone world may know a bit more about Korea than did Drake's contemporaries seventy years ago, our knowledge still does not match Korea's regional and global significance.

Northeast Asia is a peculiar place in the contemporary world. Viewed with Korea at its center, Northeast Asia's paradoxical features appear all the more prominently. The end of the cold war in Europe, exemplified by German unification, provides a striking contrast to the continued confrontation over a divided Korean peninsula. Geopolitics—in the old-fashioned, nineteenth-century sense of conflict over territory demarcated by clear boundaries—lives on in Northeast Asia, despite the era of globalization and its diminishing of territoriality. This is above all because of the Democratic People's Republic of Korea (DPRK)—a barrier reef of unreformed, Marxist-Leninism in a sea of market economies. And yet, some of the region's constituent parts are at the leading edge of global trends. China has become one the most important global centers of manufacturing and has sustained the highest consistent levels of economic growth in the world. Japan rebounded from more than a decade of economic stagnation in the early 2000s, and it is still the world's second largest economy. South Korea, now a manufacturing and high-tech powerhouse in its own right, has the world's highest per capita rates of broadband Internet usage.

Although historical animosities and distrust among China, South Korea, and Japan, not to mention Russia, persist, in recent years, the conversations among the respective governments have tended to focus more on free trade areas and increasing cooperation at all levels. At the same time, transnational flows of goods, capital, culture, and people in the region flourish. Mongolia is building infrastructure and attracting foreign investors in a shift toward becoming the Canada of China—Mongolia's various provinces, like Canada's, already trade more with the country's giant southern neighbor than with each other. Having wallowed in Yellow Peril, the depressed Russian Far East may finally be busier with learning how to overcome its disadvantages by taking advantage of nearby Chinese labor and markets. Even North Korea, despite its longstanding isolationism, appears to be fitfully emerging from its shell. Obviously, Northeast Asia lacks the institutionally based open regionalism we see in Europe or Southeast Asia, but that, too, may be changing, as this volume has shown.

It also needs to be kept in mind that Korea has been more than a source of conflict and discord among the major countries surrounding the peninsula. Throughout this volume, we have seen that Korea has also been a force for bringing the region together. This has not always been at the initiative of Koreans, nor in their interests. But any vision of regional unity has inevitably put Korea at the center. From the 1870s onward, control over Korea was critical to Japanese plans for expansion into the continent, and after 1910 Korea was the most important part of the Japanese colonial empire. For the Russian empire as well, Korea (along with Manchuria) was a valued strategic prize in Asia. With the collapse of Japanese imperial power at the end of World War II, the Korean peninsula became one of the first objects of Soviet-American strategic rivalry in Asia, and the site of the first hot war of the cold-war era. A divided nation in a divided region, the two Koreas in the cold war period succeeded, for a time, in being at the center of regional cooperation in their respective blocs. North Korea in the 1950s was the focus of the highest level of Sino-Soviet cooperation in any third country. South Korea in the 1970s and 1980s—assisted greatly by the United States and Japan—appeared to vindicate American-led containment and capitalist development in the region. Indeed, a major difference between Northeast Asian regionalism in the early twenty-first century and various attempts at regional integration in the past hundred years is that now (South) Korea can pursue regional cooperation in its own interest and is not merely the object of the regional ambitions and rivalries of its more powerful neighbors.

To be sure, the relative strength of South Korea (much less North Korea), whether measured by economic power, military might, or political clout, is far below that of China and Japan—to say nothing of the United States, which is still an enormous presence in the region. Russia, while its GDP is now less than South Korea's, has recently begun to reclaim its regional influence as well, and at some point Russia's military power, natural resources, and population could make it once again a significant regional presence. As the American influence in Northeast Asia ineluctably declines relative to China, a recovering Japan, a reemerging Russia, and a more assertive South Korea, a strictly "realist" or power-political view of Northeast Asia might suggest that the region will once again become an arena of great power rivalry; that local conflicts are likely to increase; and that Korea will again be caught in the middle.[2] In other words, the twenty-first century might begin to look much like the nineteenth. But the dynamics of the region and the world have changed considerably since Korea first became the object of geopolitical rivalries in the late nineteenth century. Perhaps most important, Korea is different.

Late Choson Korea was a largely self-contained, deeply conservative, agrarian monarchy with a weak sense of national identity among its general population and a fractious elite.[3] Choson's people and its leaders knew little about the outside world, and the monarchy's attempts to adjust to the rapid changes around the peninsula at the very end of the nineteenth century were too little, too late to retain Korean autonomy, and, ultimately, to avoid the country's loss of sovereignty. A half-century of Japanese domination was followed by an even longer period of national division, which has not yet ended. In the meantime, however, both Koreas have cultivated a powerful sense of national identity, and South Korea at least has become a sophisticated, economically advanced society determined to assert its place in the world. Neither North nor South Korea can easily be manipulated by foreign powers as Choson was, and a unified Korea would be a major regional player in its own right.[4]

Predictions about the future of this dangerous region are themselves dangerous, but a few trends seem to stand out. First, barring a devastating event on the peninsula such as war (a grim prospect, but not outside the realm of possibility), Korea—whether the South alone or a unified peninsula—will continue to be an important and increasingly independent actor in the region and will not lapse into its old role of "a shrimp crushed between whales," as the Korean proverb puts it. Second, the relative balance of power in the region appears likely to shift away from the United States and toward China. Nowhere is this trend more evident than on the Korean peninsula itself, where China has replaced the United States as South Korea's largest trading partner, and where U.S. plans to reduce and redeploy its military forces, perhaps ultimately to remove them from the peninsula altogether, are rapidly moving forward. Japan, too, imports more from China than from the United States, and even if China surpasses Japan as the world's second largest economy (as some predict), Sino-Japanese economic cooperation will remain a critical engine for regional prosperity.[5] Nor is Russia's presence to be discounted. After a decade of paying little attention to the region following the Soviet collapse, Russia started to reestablish its presence in Northeast Asia, first by establishing diplomatic relations with South Korea, and subsequently in forums such as the six-party talks on North Korea's nuclear program, which began in 2003. In any event, Russia will play a critical role locally as a source of energy, including oil and natural gas, especially for Korea and Japan, which lack such resources of their own, but above all for a resource-devouring China. Overall, then, the countries and areas within Northeast Asia may well draw closer together, while the U.S. presence could decline to a position more indicative of its geographical distance.

Finally, the flow of goods, information, cultural products, and people in all directions appears unstoppable, and likely to increase. Again, Korea offers a telling example: by 2003, more South Korean students were studying in China than in the United States, and this trend shows little sign of abating.[6]

Amid this broadening regionalism, Korea has been and will remain at the center. But unlike in the past, Korea now has the opportunity to function as a facilitator of regional cooperation. Certainly, playing such a role has been the expressed interest of recent South Korean governments, especially the government of Roh Moo Hyun, with its dreams of Korea becoming the "hub" of a dynamic regional economy. Whether reality will match Korean ambitions remains to be seen. A more pessimistic scenario would see Korea squeezed between the complementary economies of Japan and China.

Many uncertainties remain. Historical animosities and rivalries among China and Japan, Korea and Japan, China and Russia have hardly disappeared. No effective institutional mechanism for resolving critical security issues yet exists. China's economic power creates competition as well as opportunities for Korea and Japan, as well as tremendous ecological pressures. Korea's political and economic presence in the region is unlikely to rival or surpass that of China or Japan in the foreseeable future; its most important role would be that of facilitator or catalyst (a promoter of free trade areas, an organizer of security dialogue) rather than of regional leader. The remarkable export success of South Korea's popular culture may have a long-term regional impact, or it may be a passing fad. And it is not clear what role, if any, the "overseas Koreans"—who number some two million in China, 700,000 in Japan, and 500,000 in the former Soviet Union—will play in the process of regional integration, despite longstanding attempts on the part of both Korean governments to mobilize the support of ethnic compatriots abroad.[7]

The biggest question of all is the future of Korean division, which is to say, the future of North Korea. To paraphrase Mark Twain, rumors of the DPRK's imminent demise have so far been exaggerated. Notwithstanding "collapsist" scenarios favored by many Western scholars and experts, fifteen years after the fall of the Berlin Wall North Korea was still with us. Futurology on North Korea has become a cottage industry, but basically forecasts come down to three possibilities: sudden implosion, gradual reform, or war. The latter scenario would mean devastation for the peninsula and much of the surrounding region, and none of the governments in the region, including the United States, favors a military solution to the Korean problem (although the United States officially has not ruled it out). "Regime change" triggered by popular protests and removal of the current government by internal political forces, akin to those that swept communist Eurasia from Berlin to Ulan Bator between 1989 and 1991, could still sweep North Korea. But who can pinpoint clear signs of mobilizable internal dissent in the DPRK?

Gradual reform is the scenario for North Korea favored by the governments of China and South Korea, which have the most to lose if North Korea implodes or war breaks out. These two have contributed the greatest resources (economic and political) to try to keep North Korea from disintegrating. By the early 2000s, North Korea showed some signs of pursuing limited reform in the economic realm. Whether these measures will continue, and whether they give the DPRK a new lease on life, leading to a "soft landing" for the regime and eventually peaceful unification with the South, are open questions. But regardless of what happens in North Korea, a new infrastructure of broad regionalism is being built in Northeast Asia among South Korea, China, Japan, Russia, and Mongolia. North Korea can voluntarily join in this growing regionalism or not. At some point, it may find that it has no choice.

The twentieth century—a century of war, colonization, and superpower antagonism—was not kind to Korea. For Korea and Northeast Asia, the violence and turmoil commenced as early as the Sino-Japanese War of 1895 (or even the Sino-Japanese and Korean-Japanese diplomacy of the 1870s, or perhaps even the Russian expansion to the Pacific and the Meiji Restoration of the 1860s). The conflicts and divisions set into motion have yet to be entirely resolved in the early twenty-first century. Whether or not, for a Western-centered world, the twentieth century appeared to be a "short" century, lasting roughly from 1914 to 1991,[8] for Northeast Asia it has been a long one.[9] Nevertheless, a growing regionalism has gone some way toward overcoming the divisive legacies of imperial conflict, colonization, and the cold war. Even the most intractable conflict at the core of the region—the divided Korean peninsula—has been moving toward some measure of alleviation, if not resolution. If that zigzagging trend persists, Northeast Asia's long twentieth century may finally come to an end.

Notes

Notes to Chapter 1

1. Carter J. Eckert, Ki-baik Lee, Young Ick Lew, Michael Robinson, and Edward W. Wagner, *Korea Old and New: A History* (Seoul: Ichokak, 1990), p. 42.

2. For Japan, see Shiraishi Taichiro, ed., *Wakoku no tanjō* (Tokyo: Yoshikawa kobunkan, 2002); Suzuki Yasutani, ed., *Wakoku to Higashi Ajia* (Tokyo: Yoshikawa kobunkan, 2002); Mori Kimiaki, ed., *Wakoku kara Nihon e* (Tokyo: Yoshikawa kobunkan, 2002); Ishikawa Akiyasu, *Nihon shi no kangaekata* (Tokyo: Kodansha, 2003). For England, see *Cambridge History of England* (Cambridge: Cambridge University Press, 1966); Michael Mann, *Social Power*, 2 vols. (Cambridge: Cambridge University Press, 1986); S.E. Finer, *The History of Government*, 2 vols. (Oxford: Oxford University Press, 1996).

3. See the contrasting conceptions of the Chinese world order by John King Fairbank, ed., *The Chinese World Order: Traditional China's Foreign Relations* (Cambridge: Harvard University Press, 1968); and Morris Rossabi, *China Among Equals* (Berkeley: University of California Press, 1983).

4. Samuel Huntington, *The Clash of Civilizations and Remaking of World Order* (New York: Simon and Schuster, 1997).

5. It is interesting to see that some Japanese writings published on the 150th anniversary of the Perry visit and the Treaty of Amity reevaluate this event more in terms of the beginning of friendship and cooperation rather than naval coercion, which had been the common perception in the past. See, for example, Kato Yuzo, *Bakumatsu to kaikoku* (Tokyo: Iwanami shoten, 2004), and Takashi Inoguchi, "Awed, Inspired and Disillusioned: Japanese Scholarship on American Politics," in *The Political Culture of Foreign Area and International Studies*, ed. Richard Samuels and Myron Weiner (Washington, DC: Brassey's, 1992), pp. 57–74.

6. For the Western notion of sovereignty, see Stephen Krasner, *Organized Hypocrisy* (Princeton: Princeton University Press, 1999); Takashi Inoguchi, "Peering into the Future by Looking Back: The Westphalian, Philadelphian and Anti-Utopian Paradigms," *International Studies Review* 2, no. 2 (1997), pp. 173–91.

7. Kawamura Hirotada, *Kinsei Nihon no Sekaizo* [World Maps of Early Modern Japan] (Tokyo: Pelican sha, 2003).

8. Kamiya Atsuyuki, *Bakuhansei kokka no Ryūkyū shihai* (Tokyo: Azekura shobo, 1990); Robert Sakai, "The Ryukyu (Liyuch'iu) Islands as a Fief of Satsuma," in Fairbank, *Chinese World Order*, pp. 112–34.

9. Tashiro Kazui, *Kinsei Nitchō tsūkō bōeki shi no kenkyū* (Tokyo: Sobunsha, 1981); Chun Haejong, "Sino-Korean Tributary Relations: The Ch'ing Period," in Fairbank, *Chinese World Order*, pp. 90–111.

10. For the Korean world order, see Hahm Chaibong, chapter 3 in this volume; and Kim Key-Hiuk, *The Last Phase of the East Asian World Order: Korea, Japan and the Chinese*

Empire, 1860–1882 (Berkeley: University of California Press, 1980); Kimura Kan, *Chosen/Kankoku Nationalism to "shōkoku" ishiki* (Kyoto: Minerva shōbo, 2002).

11. For the Vietnamese world order, see Alexander Woodside, *Vietnam and the Chinese Model* (Cambridge: Harvard University Press, 1988).

12. For the Japanese world order, see Arano Yoshinori, ed., *Kinsei Nihon to Higashi Ajia* (Tokyo: University of Tokyo Press, 2003); Marius B. Jansen, *Japan and Its World* (Princeton: Princeton University Press, 1980); Ronald P. Toby, *State and Diplomacy in Early Modern Japan* (Princeton: Princeton University Press, 1984). For early Meiji politics, see Banno Junji, *Kindai Nihon no kokka kōsō* (Tokyo: Iwanami shōten, 1996).

13. Akira Iriye, "Japan's Drive to Great-Power Status," in *The Cambridge History of Japan*, vol. 5: *The Nineteenth Century*, ed. Marius B. Jansen (Cambridge: Cambridge University Press, 1989), p. 743.

14. Richard Samuels, *Rich Nation, Strong Army* (Ithaca: Cornell University Press, 1994).

15. Quoted in Marlene Mayo, "The Korean Crisis of 1873 and Early Meiji Foreign Policy," *Journal of Asian Studies* 31, no. 4, pp. 793–820.

16. Quoted in Nakatsuka Akira, *Nisshin sensō no kenkyū* (Tokyo: Iwanami shōten, 1968), p. 28.

17. Quoted in Carmen Blacker, *The Japanese Enlightenment: A Study of the Writings of Fukuzawa Yukichi* (Cambridge: Cambridge University Press, 1964), p. 136.

18. Quoted in Shumpei Okamoto, *The Japanese Oligarchy and the Russo-Japanese War* (New York: Columbia University Press, 1970), p. 48.

19. *Mainichi shimbun,* February 10, 2004, p. 5.

20. *Sankei shimbun,* February 10, 2004, p. 3; *Sankei shimbun,* February 11, 2004, p. 3.

21. Iriye, "Japan's Drive to Great-Power Status," p. 750.

Notes to Chapter 2

1. G.A. Tkacheva, "Immigranty na Dal′nem Vostoke Rossii v 20–30-e godi XX veka" [Immigrants in the Russian Far East in the 1920s and 1930s], *Vestnik DVO RAN*, no. 5 (1997), p. 22.

2. Ibid., p. 99.

3. A.G. Larin, *Kitaitsy v Rossii* [The Chinese in Russia] (Moscow: Institut Dal′nego Vostoka RAN, 2000), p. 15.

4. A.N. Heyfets, *Sovetskaia Rossiia i sopredel′ nye strany Vostoka (1918–1920)* [Soviet Russia and the Neighboring Countries of the East (1918–1920)] (Moscow: Nauka, 1964), p. 356.

5. A. Buiakov, "Kazhdyi kitaets mechtal stat′ politseiskim" [Every Chinese Dreamed of Becoming a Policeman], *Vladivostok,* April 19, 1996, p. 9.

6. Larin, *Kitaitsy v Rossii*, pp. 22–36.

7. *Pis′ma i bumagi Imperatora Petra Velikogo* [Letters and Papers of Emperor Peter the Great] (St. Petersburg and Moscow, 1887–1910), vol. 1, pp. 253–54.

8. S.C.M. Paine, *Imperial Rivals: China, Russia, and Their Disputed Frontier* (Armonk, NY: M.E. Sharpe, 1996), p. 32.

9. Quoted in ibid., p. 63.

10. Li Hung Chang [Li Hongzhang], *Memoirs of the Viceroy* (London, 1913), p. 134.

11. "Pervye shagi Russkogo imperializma na Dal′nem Vostoke" [The First Steps of Russian Imperialism in the Far East], *Krasnyi arkhiv* 52, no. 3 (1932), pp. 43, 78–83.

12. Ibid., p. 119.

13. "Vsepoddaniishii doklad Voennogo Ministra v 1900 godu" [Most Humble Report by the Minister of War in 1900], March 14, 1990; quoted in Paine, *Imperial Rivals*, p. 96.

14. Quoted in B.D. Pak, *Rossiia i Koreia* [Russia and Korea] (Moscow: GRVL, 1979), pp. 33–34.

15. I.A. Goncharov, *Fregat "Pallada." Ocherki puteshestviia* [Frigate *Pallada:* Notes of a Journey] (Moscow, 1951), p. 587.

16. See Pak Chon Khe, *Rossiia i Koreia. 1895–1898* [Russia and Korea. 1895–1898] (Moscow: Moskovskii Gosudarstvennyi Universitet, 1993), p. 35.

17. Ibid., p. 44.

18. Ibid., p. 49.

19. "Instruktsiia poslanniku v Pekine S. Popovu ot 1 iiulia 1883 g." [Instruction to the Envoy in Beijing S. Popov of July 1, 1883]; quoted in A.L. Narochnitskii, *Kolonial'naia politika kapitalisticheskikh derzhav na Dal'nem Vostoke 1860–1895* [Colonial Policy of Capitalist Powers in the Far East 1860–1895] (Moscow: AN SSSR, 1956), p. 289.

20. Pak, *Rossiia i Koreia,* p. 83.

21. Ibid., p. 83.

22. Ibid., p. 85.

23. B.D. Pak, *Rossiiskaia diplomatiia i Koreia (1860–1888)* [Russian Diplomacy and Korea (1860–1888)] (Irkutsk: Irkutskii pedagogicheskii institut, 1998), p. 176.

24. Ibid., p. 177.

25. Special conferences were convened to discuss the most import policy issues. They were usually presided over by the tsar or a grand duke, and ministers and other high-ranking officials were invited. The conferences' decisions signed by the tsar were subject to immediate implementation by all government agencies.

26. Pak, *Rossiia i Koreia,* p. 113.

27. Ibid., pp. 13–15.

28. Ibid., p. 115.

29. A.C. Nahm, *Korea: Tradition and Transformation* (Elizabeth, NJ: Hollym, 1988), pp. 188–89.

30. Seung-Kwon Synn, *The Russo-Japanese Rivalry Over Korea, 1876–1904* (Seoul: Yuk phub sa, 1981), pp. 20–21.

31. Ibid., p. 22.

32. Pak Chon Khe, *Russko-iaponskaia voina 1904–1905 i Koreia* [The Russo-Japanese War 1904–1905 and Korea] (Moscow: Vostochnaia literatura, 1997), pp. 50–51.

33. Ibid., p. 52.

34. Ibid., pp. 90–91.

35. Kuropatkin, while disagreeing on methods of securing Russian interests in Manchuria, saw it as the center of Russian efforts in the Far East.

36. Pak, *Russko-iaponskaia voina,* pp. 90–91.

37. Ibid, p. 83.

38. Ibid., p. 113.

39. S.O. Kurbanov, *Rossiia i Koreia. Kliuchevye momenty v istorii rossiisko-koreiskikh otnoshenii, seredina XIX–nachala XX stoletii* [Russia and Korea. Key Aspects of the History of Russian-Korean Relations, Middle of the Nineteenth to the Beginning of the Twentieth Centuries) (Orient, 2000), available at http://asiapacific.narod.ru/countries/koreas/russia_korea.htm (accessed February 20, 2005).

40. P. Rossov, *Koreia v kontse 1905 g. i nachale 1906 g.* [Korea at the End of 1905 and the Beginning of 1906] (Harbin, 1906); P. Rossov, *Natsional'noe samosoznanie koreitsev* [The National Self-Consciousness of Koreans] (St. Petersburg, 1906); P. Vaskevich, *K voprosu o sovremennom sostoianii Koreii* [On the Current Situation in Korea] (Vladivostok, 1906); V.D. Pesotskii, *Koreia nakanune anneksii* [Korea on the Eve of Annexation] [N.p., 1910]; N.V. Kiuner, *Statisiko-geograficheskii i ekonomicheskii ocherk Korei, nyne iaponskogo*

general-gubernatorstva Chiosen [Statistical, Geographical, and Economic Outline of Korea, Currently a Japanese General Governorship Choson], parts 1–2 (Vladivostok, 1912).

41. Quoted in Pak, *Rossiia i Korea*, p. 39.

42. B.D. Pak, *Koreitsy v Rossiiskoi imperii* [Koreans in the Russian Empire] (Moscow: Mezhdunarodnyi tsentr koreevedeniyia Moskovskii Gosudarstvennyi Universitet, 1993), p. 106.

43. Pak, *Rossiia i Korea*, p. 68.

44. Pak, *Koreitsy v Rossiiskoi imperii*, p. 102.

45. Ibid., p. 103.

46. Ibid., p. 106.

47. Quoted in ibid., p. 109.

48. V.V. Grave, *Kitaitsy, koreitsy i iapontsi v Priamur´e* [Chinese, Koreans, and Japanese in the Amur Region] (St. Petersburg, 1912), p. 137.

49. Quoted in Pak, *Koreitsy v Rossiiskoi imperii*, p. 113.

50. Ibid., pp. 115–16.

Notes to Chapter 3

1. *Yun Ch'iho ilgi* [Yun Ch'iho's Diary], November 1, 1893 (Seoul: Kuksa p'yonch'an wiwonhoe, 1973).

2. See, for example, Kenneth M. Wells, *New God, New Nation: Protestants and Self-Reconstruction Nationalism in Korea, 1896–1937* (Honolulu: University of Hawaii Press, 1990); and Chong-sik Lee, *The Korean Workers' Party: A Short History* (Stanford: Hoover Institution Press, 1978).

3. James Palais, *Politics and Policy in Traditional Korea* (Cambridge: Harvard University Press, 1975).

4. In 1801, Hwang Sa-yong, a Roman Catholic, wrote a letter to the French bishop in Beijing asking for French military intervention on behalf of those being persecuted by the Choson government. The letter was discovered before it could be delivered and Hwang was caught, tried, and executed for treason.

5. Quoted in Hilary Conroy, *The Japanese Seizure of Korea: 1868–1910* (Philadelphia: University of Pennsylvania Press, 1960), pp. 23–24.

6. Kim Yong-jak, *Hanmal nashonolism yongu: sasang kwa hyonshil* [A Study of Late Choson Nationalism: Theory and Reality] (Seoul: Chonggye, 1989), p. 34.

7. The Choson courts' intransigence in the face of the Meiji government's repeated attempts to establish "friendly" relations led to the rise of a movement calling for the invasion of Korea, or "Seikan Ron" in Japan with far-reaching consequences for Japanese domestic politics as well as Korean-Japanese relations (Conroy, *Japanese Seizure of Korea*).

8. Palais, *Politics and Policy*, p. 181.

9. Quoted in Lew Young Ick, "The Conservative Character of the 1894 Tonghak Peasant Uprising: A Reappraisal with Emphasis on Chon Bongjun's Background and Motivation," *Journal of Korean Studies*, no. 7 (1990), p. 168.

10. Lew Young Ick, "Yuan Shi-kai's Residency and the Korean Enlightenment Movement, 1885–1894," *Journal of Korean Studies* 5 (1984), pp. 77–78.

11. *Yun Ch'iho ilgi*, February 2, 1884.

12. Li Hongzhang brokered the first treaty between Choson and the United States in 1882, as well as the treaty between Choson and France in 1886.

13. *Sungjonwon ilgi* [Records of the Royal Secretariat], Kojong 13 nyon 2 wol 5 il jo [Entry for the 5th day of the 2nd month of the 13th year of Kojong's reign]), quoted in Kim, *Late Choson Nationalism*, p. 70.

14. Palais, *Politics and Policy*, p. 259.

15. Kim, *Late Choson Nationalism*, p. 102.

16. Ibid., p. 103.

17. Kim Yun-sik, who was in China at the time as the head of the learning mission, and quickly contacted Li Hongzhang on Queen Min's behalf.

18. *Yun Ch'iho ilgi*, September 28, 1894.

19. *Yun Ch'iho ilgi*, September 27, 1894.

20. Kim, *Late Choson Nationalism*, p. 336.

21. *Kojong shillok, gwon 35, gonyang yi nyon samwol cho* [Records of the Reign of Kojong, Book 35, 2nd year of Gonyang, 3rd Month Entry] (Seoul: T'amgudang, 1970).

22. *Yun Ch'iho ilgi*, December 28, 1889. See also *Yun Ch'iho ilgi*, November 18, 1905, (October 16, 1905), against Uibyong (June 16, 1906), against protest against protectorate, November 27, 1905.

23. The Chinese Exclusion Act was in force until 1924, when a new immigration law passed by the U.S. Congress banned the immigration of all Asians. This act was repealed only in 1943 and Chinese immigration was permitted again, albeit with a quota of 105 per year. The banning of immigration from Asia took place simultaneously with the opening of immigration from eastern and southern Europe, hitherto excluded.

24. *Yun Ch'iho ilgi*, February 14, 1890.

25. *Yun Ch'iho ilgi*, May 7, 1902.

26. Andre Schmid, *Korea Between Empires: 1895–1919* (New York: Columbia University Press, 2002), p. 88.

27. Cited in ibid.

28. Chung Yonghwa, "Munmyonkaehwaron ui dot: Yun Ch'iho ilgirul chungsimuro" [The Trap of the Theory of Civilization and Enlightenment: With an Emphasis on Yun Ch'iho's Diary], *Kukchechongchi nonchong* 41, no. 4 (2001), p. 309.

29. *Yun Ch'iho ilgi*, June 2, 1905, September 7, 1905.

30. Schmid, *Korea Between Empires*, p. 88.

31. Sin Ch'ae-ho, *Yoksanonsoljip: Toksa sillon oe 35 p'yon* [Collected Works of History: 35 Volumes of the Toksa sillon] (Seoul: Hyondai silhaksa, 1995), p. 12.

32. Ibid., p. 13.

33. Ibid.

34. Clark Sorensen, "National Identity and the Creation of the Category 'Peasant' in Colonial Korea," in *Colonial Modernity in Korea*, ed. Gi-Wook Shin and Michael Robinson (Cambridge: Harvard University Press, 1999), pp. 288–310.

35. See, for example, Kenneth Wells, ed., *South Korea's Minjung Movement: The Culture and Politics of Dissidence* (Honolulu: University of Hawaii Press, 1995).

36. See Hahm Chaibong, "Anti-Americanism in South Korea: Historical Roots and Future Prospects," in *Korean Attitudes Toward the United States: Changing Dynamics*, ed. David I. Steinberg (Armonk, NY: M.E. Sharpe, 2005).

37. See, for example, Carter J. Eckert, *Offspring of Empire: The Koch'ang Kims and the Colonial Origins of Korean Capitalism, 1876–1945* (Seattle: University of Washington Press, 1991).

Notes to Chapter 4

Versions of this chapter were presented as papers at the annual meeting of the Association for Asian Studies in April 2002, and at the workshop on Northeast Asia between Regionalism and Globalization: Korea at the Center (1890–present), held at Princeton University in May 2003. The author greatly appreciates the comments and suggestions that were offered at both forums.

1. The Korean *silhak* (practical learning) scholar and tributary envoy Pak Chi-won

estimated the amount of silver brought by annual tribute missions to be 100,000 ounces of silver. See Gari Ledyard, "Hong Taeyong and His 'Peking Memoir,'" *Korean Studies* 6 (1982), p. 88. For a description of Sino-Korean tribute trade during the Qing period, see Zhang Cunwu, *Qing-Han zongfan maoyi* [Qing-Korean Tribute Trade] (Taipei: Institute of Modern History, 1978). See also Hae-jong Chun, "Sino-Korean Tributary Relations in the Ch'ing Period," in *The Chinese World Order: Traditional China's Foreign Relations*, ed. John K. Fairbank (Cambridge: Harvard University Press, 1968), pp. 91–112.

2. Before the Hideyoshi invasions (1592–98), Japanese merchants were allowed to call at three Korean ports—Tongnae (near Pusan), Ungchon, and Ulsan. Trade was restricted to Pusan (Tongnae) after the invasions. See James Palais, *Confucian Statecraft and Korean Institutions: Yu Hyongwon and the Late Choson Dynasty* (Seattle: University of Washington Press, 1996), p. 32.

3. For a thorough discussion of trade between Choson Korea and Tokugawa Japan, see Chong Song-il, *Choson hugi tae-Il muyok* [Late Choson Trade with Japan] (Seoul: Sinsowon, 2000). See also Palais, *Confucian Statecraft*, pp. 31–32.

4. Chun, "Sino-Korean Tributary Relations," p. 108. See also Key-hiuk Kim, *The Last Phase of the East Asian World Order* (Berkeley: University of California Press, 1980), pp. 10–11.

5. Yu Wentai was "a Chinese pilot who had been engaged with Koreans for a long period of time." Yu left the *General Sherman* at the mouth of the Taedong River and returned to China. See Yongkoo Kim, *The Five Years' Crisis, 1866–1871: Korea in the Maelstrom of Western Imperialism* (Inchon: Circle, 2001), pp. 61, 62. For a British account of coastal smuggling, see Sir Edward Hertslet, "Korea," in "Korea, the Ryukyu Islands, and North-East Asia, 1875–1888," *British Documents on Foreign Affairs: Reports and Papers from the Foreign Office Confidential Print*, Part I, Series E, vol. 2, ed. Ian Nish (Frederick, MD: University Publications of America, 1989–1994), p. 3 [hereafter *British Docs*].

6. For example, see the 1881 memorial of King Kojong (r. 1864–1907) to the Qing Board of Rites:

> Our people are poor. Our resources are meager. We do not produce gold or silver, pearls or jade. Nor have we an abundant supply of rice, grain, cloth, and silk. The products of our country hardly meet our own needs. If they are allowed to be exported overseas, it would lead to the eventual depletion of our domain and make the preservation of our feeble country even more difficult. (*Chouban yiwu* [A Complete Account of the Management of Barbarian Affairs] 81:11a–b, in T.C. Lin, "Li Hung-Chang: His Korea Policies, 1870–1885," *Chinese Social and Political Science Review* 29, no. 2 [July 1935], p. 204)

Lin concludes, "in the opinion of the Korean Government, there was no economic basis for a Korean-foreign trade" (ibid., pp. 204–5).

7. Hall to Parkes, February 28, 1883, *British Docs.*, p. 118.

8. Cho Ki-jun, "The Impact of the Opening of Korea on Its Commerce and Industry," *Korea Journal* 16, no. 2 (1976), p. 29.

9. For a comparison of the changes in the amounts of trade carried out in various treaty ports, see *Inchonshisa* [History of Inchon City] (Inchon: Inchon chikhalshi, 1993), p. 1241.

10. In the early part of the Open Port period, one *koku* (*sok*), or 4.96 bushels, of rice cost less than half a yen in Korea, but could be sold for ¥6–8 in Japan. Peter Duus, *The Abacus and the Sword: The Japanese Penetration of Korea, 1895–1910* (Berkeley: University of California Press, 1995), p. 254. See also Han U-gun, *Han'guk kaehanggi ui sangop yon'gu* [Commerce in Open Port Period Korea] (Seoul: Ilchogak, 1970), pp. 262–80, and Yoshino Makoto, "Chōsen kaikokugo no kokumotsu yūshutsu ni tsuite" [Korean Grain Exports During the Open Port Period], *Chōsenshi Kenkyūkai ronbunshū*, no. 12 (December 1975), pp. 33–60.

11. Unless otherwise indicated, all trade figures are taken from a combination of the following sources: China, Imperial Maritime Customs, *Returns of Trade and Trade Reports*

(Shanghai: Inspector General of Customs, 1885–1894); British Foreign Office, *Diplomatic and Consular Reports on Trade and Finance* (later *Diplomatic and Consular Reports*) 1884–1910; Kim Kyong-t'ae, ed., *Tongsang hwich'an: Han'gukp'yon* [Consular Reports: Korea], 10 vols. (Seoul: Yogang ch'ulp'ansa, 1987); *Kankoku kakukō bōeki gaikyō* [The General Condition of Korea's Trade] (Seoul: Japanese Colonial Bureau, 1906) (Royal Library (Kyujanggak) at Seoul National University No. 20265); *Kankoku shutchō chōsa hōkokusho* [Investigative Report of Reconnaissance of Korea] (Osaka: Osaka Tax Bureau, 1909), at Kyujanggak No. 20740; Korean Customs Service, *Yunghui wonnyon Han'guk oeguk muyok yolam* [Survey of Korea's Foreign Trade, 1907] (1908?)—Korean Customs Service Museum. For a thorough discussion of these sources and how they were used to arrive at figures for Choson Korea's foreign trade, see Kirk Larsen, "From Suzerainty to Commerce: Sino-Korean Economic and Business Relations During the Open Port Period (1876–1910)," Ph.D. dissertation, Harvard University, 2000.

12. For example, in 1889, Korean rice exports were valued at around ¥78,000 while its imports of rice topped ¥200,000. The source of this rice was originally Japan, but Korea also obtained rice from China and even Indochina.

13. For a brief examination of the qualities of beans that made them amenable for export, see British Foreign Office, *Corea: Report for the Year 1896 on the Trade and Commerce of Corea*, Diplomatic and Consular Reports on Trade and Finance, 1897 [hereafter *British Consular Reports*; the year listed is the year in the title of the report, not the year the report was published], pp. 3–4.

14. Yi Yang-ja, "Ch'ong ui tae Choson kyongje chongch'i wa Won segi" [Yuan Shikai and Qing Economic Policies Toward Korea], *Pusan sahak*, no. 8 (1984), p. 150; British Foreign Office, *Report on the Commercial Condition of the Ports of Fusan and Wonsan*, Miscellaneous Series, no. 318 (1894), p. 4.

15. *British Consular Reports*, 1894, p. 4.

16. A British report in 1890 pointed out that Korean rice, cleaned and polished by Japanese mills in Korean treaty ports, was often mixed with Japanese rice in Japan where it "finds its way eventually to Europe in increasing quantities" (*British Consular Reports*, 1890, p. 3).

17. Sakurai Gunnosuke, "Chosen jiji" [Current Affairs in Korea], in *Soul e namgyodun kkum* [Dreams of Seoul Left Behind], ed. and trans. Han Sang-il (Seoul: Kon'guk taehakkyo, 1993), p. 269.

18. Duus, *Abacus and the Sword,* pp. 328–29. For other descriptions of the port, see Isabella Bird Bishop, *Korea and Her Neighbors* (Seoul: Yonsei University Press, 1970 [1898]), pp. 23–30; Sakurai Gunnosuke, "Chosen jiji," pp. 263–75.

19. For a brief summary of the incident, see Kirk Larsen, "The Law of Nations: Tool of Qing Imperialism in Choson Korea (and Beyond)" (paper presented at the workshop on China's Interactions with the World Internationalization, Internalization, Externalization, Berlin, 2001), pp. 22–26; see also Qin Yuguang, "Hwagyo" [Overseas Chinese], *Chungang ilbo*, September 24, 1979, p. 5; Sun Chong-mok, *Han'guk kaehanggi toshi pyonhwa kwajong yon'gu* [Urban Change and Development in Open Port Period Korea] (Seoul: Iljisa, 1982), p. 108; Academia Sinica, Institute of Modern History, ed. *Qingji Zhong-Ri-Han guanxi shiliao* [Historical Materials on Chinese-Japanese-Korean Relations During the Qing Period], 11 vols. (Taipei: Zhong yang yan jiu yuan jin dai shi yan jiu suo, 1972), pp. 1258–60 [hereafter *ZRHGX*].

20. See Pusan chikhalshisa p'yonch'an wiwonhoe, *Pusanshisa* [History of Pusan City] (Pusan: Pusan chikhalshisa p'yonch'an wiwonhoe, 1989), p. 836. According to the best available figures, the Japanese share of Korea's exports from Pusan never fell below 87 percent. In the case of imports into Korea, Chinese merchants mounted a short-lived challenge to Japanese supremacy in the port around the turn of the century, but their share of the imports into Pusan never rose above 20 percent. By the end of the Open Port period, mer-

chants from Western countries had established a presence in Pusan as part of the larger pattern of increasing direct involvement in Korea. However, their share of Pusan's imports never amounted to more than one-quarter of all imports into the port.

21. For an introduction to the opening and development of Wonsan, see Sun, *Toshi pyonhwa kwajong yon'gu*, pp. 117–21; Martina Deuchler, *Confucian Gentlemen and Barbarian Envoys: The Opening of Korea, 1875–1885* (Seattle: University of Washington Press, 1977), pp. 54–64; Duus, *Abacus and the Sword*, pp. 330–31.

22. China, Imperial Maritime Customs, *Returns of Trade and Trade Reports* (Shanghai: Inspector General of Customs, 1885–1894), "Report for the Year 1893," p. 672 [hereafter *CSR*].

23. For example, around the turn of the century, the Japanese population of Wonsan numbered around 1,600 while only 70 Chinese resided in the port. See "Wun-san," *Korea Review* (1901), p. 61. The number of Japanese in Wonsan had increased to 3,257 by 1906; see *Korea Review* (1906), p. 196.

24. British Foreign Office, *Report on the Commercial Condition of the Ports of Fusan and Wonsan*, 1894, p. 7.

25. There is some evidence pointing to regional differences in "brand" loyalty, but more research on Korean consumption patterns needs to be conducted before this conclusion can be anything more than speculative. British observers noted that the "mark" on piece goods was an important determination of their popularity. Piece goods marked with "FFF" were favored in Wonsan while the "KK" mark prevailed in Pusan. See British Foreign Office. *Report on the Commercial Condition of the Ports of Fusan and Wonsan*, p. 7.

26. *CSR*, 1893, p. 637; *British Consular Reports*, 1886, p. 2; *British Consular Reports*, 1897, p. 1.

27. For a discussion of currency during the Choson period, see James Palais, *Politics and Policy in Traditional Korea* (Cambridge: Harvard University Press, 1975), pp. 160–67. In 1875, the Korean government treasury held 144 yang of gold, 126,848 yang of silver, and 108,424 yang of copper (Palais, *Politics and Policy*, p. 206).

28. A British report noted in 1888 that "amongst the Chinese and Japanese passengers outwards by every steamer there are always some who take gold, in greater or lesser quantities, on their persons which is never reported to the customs" (*British Consular Reports*, 1888, p. 4); see also *British Consular Reports*, 1892, p. 5.

29. *British Consular Reports*, 1891, p. 7; see also *British Consular Reports* for 1885, 1888, 1896, 1898, passim; see also *CSR*, 1884–1893, passim.

30. *CSR*, 1893, pp. 620–21.

31. *CSR*, 1891, p. 633.

32. Larisa V. Zabrovskaia, "1899 Treaty and Its Impact on the Development of the Chinese-Korean Trade (1895–1905)," *Korea Journal* 31, no. 4 (1991), pp. 33–34.

33. Duus, *Abacus and the Sword*, p. 250.

34. See *British Consular Reports*, 1893, p. 7.

35. *CSR*, 1888, p. 544; *CSR*, 1890, p. 348.

36. *CSR*, 1886, p. 463.

37. *British Consular Reports*, 1888, p. 3; British Foreign Office, *Report of a Visit to Fusan and Yuensan*, p. 8.

38. George Alexander Lensen, *Balance of Intrigue: International Rivalry in Korea and Manchuria, 1884–1899*, vol. 1 (Tallahassee: University Presses of Florida, 1982), p. 72. See also British Foreign Office, *Report of a Visit to Fusan and Yuensan*, p. 1; *British Consular Reports*, 1892, p. 2.

39. *British Consular Reports*, 1888, p. 6; British Foreign Office, *Report on the Commercial Condition of the Ports of Fusan and Wonsan*, pp. 7–8.

40. Angus Hamilton, *Korea* (London: William Heinemann, 1904), p. 173; *British Consular Reports*, 1901, p. 6.

41. *Korea Review* (1906), p. 118.

42. The actual port that was opened was located near the tiny fishing village of Chemulpo. Inchon is the name of a nearby town. Both names are used interchangeably in the literature.

43. For descriptions of the difficult approach to Inchon, see J.C. Hall, "A Visit to West Coast and Capital of Korea," *Transactions of the Asiatic Society of Japan* 11 (1883), p. 148. It took, on average, more than an hour (and cost at least $1) for a small boat to reach the shore from where steamships and other large vessels had to drop anchor. See G. James Morrison, "Some Notes of a Trip to Corea, in July and August 1883," *Journal of the North-China Branch of the Royal Asiatic Society* n.s., 18 (1883), p. 141.

44. H.A.C. Bonar, "Notes on the Capital of Korea," *Transactions of the Asiatic Society of Japan* 11 (1883), p. 243. See also William Franklin Sands, *Undiplomatic Memories: The Far East, 1896–1904* (London: John Hamilton, 1904), p. 29.

45. *Inchonshisa*, p. 1241. See also Sun, *Toshi pyonhwa*, p. 141; and Jinsenfu, *Jinsenfushi* [History of Jinsen (Inchon)] (Jinsen [Inchon]: Jinsenfucho, 1933), pp. 921–23.

46. Duus, *Abacus and the Sword*, p. 276. As early as 1884, Korea's first newspaper, *Hansong sunbo*, noted that Inchon was filled with the signboards of Chinese merchants and piles of their goods were everywhere. However, since the Chinese found nothing of value to trade for their goods, payment had to be made in specie, a fact that dismayed many customers (*Hansong sunbo*, January 30, 1884, p. 163).

47. *Inchonshisa*, pp. 1239–40.

48. See Larsen, "The Law of Nations," pp. 26–34.

49. Zabrovskaia, "1899 Treaty," p. 32. The lack of competition in the banking sector and the Japanese practice of openly discriminating against Chinese merchants in their banks was a perennial subject of complaint by the Chinese commercial community. See Ma Tingliang, "Hancheng dengchu shanggongye qingxing" [Conditions of Industry and Commerce in Seoul], *Shangwu guangbao*, no. 27 (1906), pp. 16–18.

50. Ma Tingliang, "Chaoxian Renchuan shangwu qingxing" [Commercial Conditions in Inchon, Korea], *Shangwu guangbao* (1907), pp. 13, 15–17.

51. For a history of Choson government attempts to control and profit from ginseng, see Yang Sang-hyon, "Tae-Han chaegukji naejangwon chaejong kawlli yon'gu" [Financial Administration of the Royal Court in the Great Han Empire], Ph.D. dissertation, Seoul National University, 1997, pp. 15–86. Exports of Korean ginseng to China was a practice that dated back centuries, but it was only in the eighteenth century that ginseng was cultivated (as opposed to gathered from the wild) on any significant scale. For a detailed examination of the various types of ginseng and the process of ginseng cultivation, see C.T. Collyer, "The Culture and Preparation of Ginseng in Korea," *Transactions of the Korea Branch of the Royal Asiatic Society* 1, no. 3 (1903), pp. 18–30.

52. Ginseng exports accounted for an average 6 percent of the value of all of Korea's exports during the period 1896–1910. For examples of ginseng smuggling, see Merrill to Detring, February 5, 1886, *Merrill's Letterbooks*, Book 1, pp. 267–69; *Korea Review* (1903), pp. 503, 507; *Korea Review* (1906), p. 354.

53. *British Consular Reports*, 1894, p. 9; 1895, p. 5.

54. *British Consular Reports*, 1897, p. 11.

55. Kim Kyong-t'ae, ed., *Tongsang hwich'an: Han'gukp'yon* [Consular Reports: Korea], vol. 10, pp. 366–74.

56. Bishop, *Korea and Her Neighbours*, p. 31; *Korea Review* (1901), p. 13. See also Ch'oe Song-yon, *Kaehang kwa yanggwan yôkjông* [Western-style Buildings in Open Port Period Korea] (Inchon: Kyonggi munhwasa, 1958), 105–7; William Richard Carles, *Life in Corea* (London and New York: Macmillan, 1888), p. 20; Tan Que, "Tongshuntai yu jiu Han jiehuan" [Tongshuntai's Loans to Korea], *Hanhua chunqiu* 4 (1964), p. 27.

57. *British Consular Reports*, 1897, p. 8; for another statement attesting to the signifi-

cance attached to these three import items, see *Korea Review* (1901), p. 4.

58. Sugiyama Shinya, "Textile Marketing in East Asia, 1860–1914," *Textile History* 19, no. 2 (Autumn 1988), p. 282.

59. Furuta Kazuko, "Shanghai: The East Asian Emporium for Lancashire Goods: A Statistical Analysis" (paper presented at the Conference on Commercial Networks in Asia, 1850–1930, Atami, Japan, 1994), pp. 3, 11.

60. Chinese merchants based in Japan repeatedly called for official representation in Korea as a precondition for their setting up shop there. See *ZRHGX*, p. 1349.

61. Kazuko, "Shanghai," p. 15.

62. One reason for the popularity of Japanese yarn, as one contemporary observer noted, was "due to the manner in which it is twisted—from left to right, which is alleged to suit the manipulation of the Corean spindle. English yarn, being twisted in the opposite direction, is said to get loosened and tangled in the process" (*British Consular Reports*, 1897, p. 10).

63. An 1889 source notes: "This Japanese yarn is sold all over the country by Japanese peddlers thoroughly conversant with the language, in packets of 26 lbs., any Corean commodity being taken in exchange, and this system suits both parties" (*British Consular Reports*, 1899, p. 11). Imports of yarn, relative to other cotton imports, would peak around the turn of the century (averaging nearly 30 percent of all cotton imports in 1899 and 1900) but still averaged nearly one-fifth of all cotton goods imports for the period 1895–1910.

64. The term "piece goods" is often used rather loosely in the literature. Sometimes it refers to a particular (but often unspecified) type of cotton cloth that is either woven by hand (in the case of Chinese Nankeens, for example) or that resembles hand-woven cloth. At other times, "piece goods" appears to refer to a wider variety of cotton textiles, sometimes the entire class of cotton textiles as a whole.

65. See, for example, *British Consular Reports*, 1895, p. 5.

66. *British Consular Reports*, 1897, p. 9.

67. For an assessment of the British "entrepreneurial failure" approach and the "comparative advantage" approach to explaining British decline in Asian textile markets, see Bruce L. Reynolds, "The East Asian 'Textile Cluster' Trade, 1868–1973: A Comparative Advantage Interpretation," in *America's Trade in Historical Perspective*, ed. Ernest R. May and John K. Fairbank (Cambridge: Harvard University Press, 1986), pp. 129–50. For another long-term explication of the "comparative advantage" approach, see Young-il Park, and Kym Anderson, "The Experience of Japan in Historical and International Perspective," in *New Silk Roads: East Asian and World Textile Markets*, ed. Kym Anderson (Cambridge: Cambridge University Press, 1992), pp. 15–29. A more general consideration of how the British middle class adopted upper-class values of rural leisure and abandoned the values and practices responsible for their dramatic worldwide success can be found in Martin Wiener, *English Culture and the Decline of the Industrial Spirit* (Oxford: Oxford University Press, 1981).

68. The 100,000 pounds sterling (approximately ¥990,000) worth of Japanese yarn imported into Korea in 1898 reduced the demand, according to one estimate, for foreign-made shirtings by 150,000 pounds (approximately ¥1,485,000) (*British Consular Reports*, 1898, p. 9).

69. Sugiyama Shinya, "Textile Marketing in East Asia, 1860–1914," *Textile History* 19, no. 2 (1988): 282, 294. In addition to cotton cloth, Korean grasscloth, along with large quantities of grasscloth imported from China, gradually replaced British lawns and muslins in the Korean market. See *British Consular Reports*, 1907, p. 4; 1908, p. 5.

70. Tang Entong, "Hanguo Renchuan shangwu qingxing" [Commercial Conditions in Inchon], *Shangwu guangbao*, 1908, no. 2, p. 13.

71. See Furuta Kazuko, "Inchon Trade: Japanese and Chinese Merchants and the Shanghai

Network" in *Commercial Networks in Modern Asia*, ed. Shinya Sugiyama and Linda Grove (Richmond: Curzon, 2001), pp. 71–95.

72. Seoul was also officially designated as an Open Port in 1907. However, given the already substantial foreign commercial presence in the city and its environs, the impact of its official opening (aside from streamlining the collection of customs revenues) was minimal.

73. See, for example, *CSR*, 1888, p. 514.

74. *British Consular Reports*, 1899, p. 15.

75. Duus, *Abacus and the Sword,* p. 318.

76. Yi Hon-chang, "Kaehanggi shijang kujo wa ku pyonhwa e kwanhan yon'gu" [Market Structure and Transformation in the Enlightenment Period], Ph.D. dissertation, Seoul National University, 1990, p. 374.

77. For an examination of Myer and Company and its activities in Korea, see Kim Chong-gi, "Choson chongbu-ui tokil ch'agwan toip (1883–1894)" [Choson Korea's Solicitation of Loans from Germany (1883–1894)], *Han'guksa Yongu* 39 (December 1982), pp. 83–120. For more on Tongshuntai's transportation and shipping ventures, see Keijofu, *Keijofushi* [History of Keijo (Seoul)] (Tokyo: Shonando shoten, 1934, 1936, 1941), p. 617; *Yongsanguji* [History of Yongsan] (Seoul: Yongsangu, 1992), pp. 462–63.

78. The following account of the construction and operation of telegraph lines in Korea is drawn from Lin Mingde, *Yuan Shikai yu Chaoxian* [Yuan Shikai and Korea] (Taipei: Institute of Modern History, Academia Sinica, 1984), pp. 227–34; Kim Chong-gi, "1876–1894 nyon Ch'ong ui Choson chongch'aek yon'gu" [Qing Policies Toward Choson Korea, 1876–1894], Ph.D. dissertation, Seoul National University, 1994, pp. 137–39; Yi, "Chong ui tae Choson kyongje chongch'i wa Won segi," pp. 133–144.

79. *Korea Review* (1902), pp. 30, 77, 126.

80. "News Calendar," *Korea Review* (1901), p. 312.

81. For example, some rumors pointed to the belief that "smoke from the railway engines dries up the heavens." See "News Calendar," *Korea Review* (1902), p. 267.

82. For example, see Korea, Chief Commissioner of Korean Customs, *Report on the Trade of Korea and Abstract of Statistics for the Year 1905* (Seoul, 1906), p. 4, and Diplomatic and Consular Reports, *Report for the Year 1899*, p. 17.

83. *British Consular Reports*, 1908, p. 10; see also *British Consular Reports*, 1909, p. 10. Merchants in Inchon also complained that much-needed harbor improvements in the port were deliberately stalled so as to facilitate trade in Japan-dominated Pusan.

84. Hamilton, *Korea*, pp. 18–19.

85. Japanese imports of railroad material, for example, constituted the third largest import into Korea for most of the Protectorate period.

86. For an example of Chinese complaints about the disadvantages caused by the Japanese banking monopoly, see Ma, "Hancheng dengchu shanggongye qingxing," pp. 16–18.

87. Duus, *Abacus and the Sword*, 270.

Notes to Chapter 5

1. L.L. Wade and B.S. Kim, *Economic Development of South Korea: The Political Economy of Success* (New York: Praeger, 1978), p. vi.

2. See, for example, Edward S. Mason et al., *The Economic and Social Modernization of the Republic of Korea* (Cambridge: Harvard University Press, 1980), chap. 2.

3. Guenther Stein, *Made in Japan* (London: Methuen, 1935), pp. 181, 191.

4. Simon Kuznets in *Economic Growth and Structural Change in Taiwan: The Postwar Experience of the Republic of China*, ed. Walter Galenson (Ithaca: Cornell University Press, 1979), p. 49.

5. Ibid., p. 53.

6. Walter LaFeber places the United States as the hidden third partner in the Anglo-Japanese Alliance in *The Clash: U.S.-Japanese Relations Throughout History* (New York: Norton, 1998).

7. The "grand area" was a concept used in Council on Foreign Relations planning in the early 1940s for the postwar period. See Laurence H. Shoup and William Minter, *Imperial Brain Trust: The Council on Foreign Relations and U.S. Foreign Policy* (New York: Monthly Review Press, 1977), pp. 135–40.

8. Although I have been writing about hegemony for two decades, I found in Robert Latham's *The Liberal Moment: Modernity, Security, and the Making of Postwar International Order* (New York: Columbia University Press, 1997) a particularly cogent analysis of postwar American hegemony. In particular, Latham emphasizes the simultaneous embrace of segregation at home (until the civil rights movement), various authoritarian allies abroad, and an "external state" of American military bases, within a general conception of the "free world" and liberal hegemony.

9. Burke, as quoted in Albert O. Hirschman, *National Power and the Structure of Foreign Trade* (Berkeley: University of California Press, 1980 [1945]), pp. ix–x.

10. Especially in *Across the Pacific: An Inner History of American-East Asian Relations* (New York: Harcourt, Brace & World, 1967), his most brilliant and original book; but see also *Pacific Estrangement: Japanese and American Expansion, 1897–1911* (Cambridge: Harvard University Press, 1972), *After Imperialism* (Cambridge: Harvard University Press, 1965), and the deeply revisionist *Power and Culture: The Japanese-American War, 1941–45* (Cambridge: Harvard University Press, 1981). All these books operate on the terrain of intercultural imagery and conflict.

11. Iriye, *Pacific Estrangement,* pp. viii, 18–19, 26–27, 35–36. In fact, the United States was for the Japanese both "a model and an object of their expansion." Iriye has a remarkably benign view of both American and Japanese expansion, terming the former "peaceful" and "liberal" because it sought only commercial advantage—that is, what I call hegemony (ibid., pp. 12–13, 36).

12. *Power and Culture*, pp. 1–2; he writes that from the Meiji Restoration to 1941 Japan wanted to integrate itself with the regime of the great powers, which he connotes as a policy of "international cooperation" or "interdependence."

13. Ibid., pp. 3–4, 15, 20, 25–27. Iriye dates Japanese plans for an exclusive Northeast Asian regional hegemony from 1936, but according to him it still did not have a blueprint in 1939, and was still dependent on the core powers in the system until the middle of 1941.

14. Ibid., p. 15.

15. LaFeber, *The Clash*.

16. Iriye, *Power and Culture*, pp. 148–50. What I would call hegemony Iriye calls "Wilsonian internationalism."

17. At the time, the leader of the small "Japan Lobby," Harry Kern, said of the U.S.-Japan relationship, "'remote control' is best" (Harry Kern, "American Policy Toward Japan," 1948, a privately circulated paper, in Pratt Papers, box 2, Yale University, Beinecke Rare Book and Manuscript Library). Kern's quotation marks on "remote control" refer to George Sansom's use of the term.

18. The exception would be industrial reparations policy, which was a key element in the early development of the cold war in Europe, but which was rejected outright in East Asia by late 1946 because it would benefit Japan's communist or communizing neighbors at the expense of democratizing Japan.

19. William S. Borden, *The Pacific Alliance: United States Foreign Economic Policy and Japanese Trade Recovery, 1947–1955* (Madison: University of Wisconsin Press, 1984). Borden and Michael Schaller did original work on the "great crescent" program (Acheson and the State Department used the term several times in 1949–50). See Michael Schaller,

The American Occupation of Japan: The Origins of the Cold War in Asia (New York: Oxford University Press, 1985). I have set out my ideas here at greater length in *The Origins of the Korean War*, vol. 2: *The Roaring of the Cataract, 1947–1950* (Princeton: Princeton University Press, 1980), chaps. 2 and 5.

20. Peter Booth Wiley, *Yankees in the Land of the Gods: Commodore Perry and the Opening of Japan* (New York: Viking, 1990), pp. 60, 492. The 1876 reference is to Japan's unequal treaty with Korea, enforced by gunboats anchored off Inchon harbor. Others, of course, have made the same point about the late 1940s as Japan's "second opening."

21. Chonsa p'yonch'an wiwonhoe, *Han'guk chonjaeng-sa* [History of the Korean War], vol. 1, *Haebang kwa kon'gun* [Liberation and the Establishment of the Army] (Seoul: Kukpang-bu, 1967), pp. 247–303.

22. Bruce Cumings, *The Origins of the Korean War*, vol. 1: *Liberation and the Emergence of Separate Regimes, 1945–1947* (Princeton: Princeton University Press, 1981), chap. 5.

23. National Archives, 740.0019 Control (Korea) file, box 3827, Marshall's note to Acheson of January 29, 1947, attached to Vincent to Acheson, January 27, 1947.

24. John W. Dower, *Empire and Aftermath: Yoshida Shigeru and the Japanese Experience, 1878–1954* (Cambridge: Council on East Asian Studies, Harvard University, 1979), p. 316. Japan lost about 2 million people during the entire Pacific War.

25. At the 139th meeting of the National Security Council, April 8, 1953, "The President expressed the belief that there was no future for Japan unless access were provided for it to the markets and raw materials of Manchuria and North China." Secretary of Treasury Humphrey wanted the United States to be "aggressive" in providing Japan and West Germany with a secure position where they could "thrive, and have scope for their virile populations." In some respects, it seemed to him, "we had licked the two wrong nations in the last war." Whereupon, "Mr. Cutler [special assistant to the president] inquired whether the Council wished to go further than this and adopt a policy which would look to the restoration of Japan's lost colonial empire." Ike said no, probably not (Eisenhower Presidential Library, Eisenhower Papers [Whitman file], National Security Council Series, box 4).

26. John G. Roberts, "The 'Japan Crowd' and the Zaibatsu Restoration," *Japan Interpreter*, no. 12 (Summer 1979), pp. 384–415.

27. Charles S. Maier, "The Politics of Productivity: Foundations of American International Economic Policy after World War II," in *Between Power and Plenty: Foreign Economic Policies of Advanced Industrial States*, ed. Peter J. Katzenstein (Madison: University of Wisconsin Press, 1978), p. 45.

28. See Kennan's remarks in "Transcript of Roundtable Discussion," U.S. Department of State, October, 6, 7, and 8, 1949, pp. 25, 47, in Carrollton Press, *Declassified Documents Series*, 1977, 316B.

29. U.S. Central Intelligence Agency, ORE 43–48, May 24, 1948, in HST/PSF file, Memos 1945–49, box 255, Harry S. Truman Library, Independence, Missouri.

30. Economic Cooperation Administration, unsigned memorandum of November 3, 1948, in Dean Acheson Papers, box 27, Harry S. Truman Library.

31. Central Intelligence Agency, ORE 69–49, "Relative U.S. Security Interest in the European-Mediterranean Area and the Far East," July 14, 1949, in HST/PSF file, Memos 1945–49, box 249, Harry S. Truman Library.

32. David P. Calleo and Benjamin M. Rowland, *America and the World Political Economy: Atlantic Dreams and National Realities* (Bloomington: Indiana University Press, 1973), pp. 198–202.

33. Draft paper, NSC 48, October 26, 1949, in NSC materials, box 207, Harry S. Truman Library.

34. *Oriental Economist* (Tokyo), June 24, 1950.

35. Truman Library, Acheson Papers, box 65, memoranda, Kennan to Acheson, August 21, 1950 (emphasis added).

36. Donald S. Macdonald, *U.S.-Korean Relations from Liberation to Self-reliance: The Twenty-year Record: An Interpretative Summary of the Archives of the U.S. Department of State for the Period 1945 to 1965* (Boulder, CO: Westview Press, 1992), pp. 26, 28–31.

37. James W. Morley, *Japan and Korea: America's Allies in the Pacific* (New York: Walker, 1965), pp. 40, 48–49, 52.

38. Jung-en Woo, *Race to the Swift: State and Finance in Korean Industrialization* (New York: Columbia University Press, 1991), pp. 76–77. Komer was with the CIA Office of National Estimates in the 1950s, but moved to the NSC in 1960.

39. Macdonald, *U.S.-Korean Relations from Liberation to Self-reliance*, pp. 31–32.

40. Gustav Ranis, "Industrial Sector Labor Absorption," *Economic Development and Cultural Change* 21, no. 3 (April 1973), pp. 402–3.

41. Chalmers Johnson rightly called attention to this Manchukuo group in his seminal work *MITI and the Japanese Miracle* (Berkeley: University of California Press, 1982).

42. Quoted in Woo, *Race to the Swift*, p. 99.

43. Carter Eckert, *Offspring of Empire: The Koch'ang Kims and the Colonial Origins of Korean Capitalism, 1876–1945* (Seattle: University of Washington Press, 1991), p. 254.

44. Woo, *Race to the Swift*, p. 134.

45. Ibid., pp. 138–39.

46. See David Noble, *Forces of Production: A Social History of Industrial Automation* (New York: Knopf, 1984).

Notes to Chapter 6

1. *Hankook Ilbo* (August 20, 2002) (English edition available at http://times.hankooki.com/times.htm); "Kim to Ask ASEM Leaders for Cooperation in 'Iron Silkroad' Plan" Yonhap in English (September 19, 2002); and "Reconnection of Inter-Korean Railroads Spur Economic Exchange," Yonhap (August 30, 2002), translated in Foreign Broadcasting Information Service.

2. The World Bank defines infrastructure "to include the sectors of transport, water and sanitation, power, telecommunication, and irrigation." See Christine Kessides, *The Contributions of Infrastructure to Economic Development: A Review of Experience and Policy Implications* (Washington, DC: World Bank, 1993), p. ix.

3. For a comprehensive survey of Japan's postwar legacy, see Kobayashi Hideo, "The Postwar Economic Legacy of Japan's Wartime Empire," in *The Japanese Wartime Empire, 1931–1945*, ed. Peter Duus et al. (Princeton: Princeton University Press, 1996), pp. 314–34. See also Bruce Cumings, "The Legacy of Japanese Colonialism in Korea," in *The Japanese Colonial Empire, 1895–1945*, ed. Ramon H. Myers and Mark R. Peattie (Princeton: Princeton University Press, 1984), pp. 479–96. Carter Eckert's work remains the best example in English. See Eckert, *Offspring of Empire: The Koch'ang Kims and the Colonial Origins of Korean Capitalism, 1876–1945* (Seattle: University of Washington Press, 1991). In Japanese, many essays in the eight-volume Iwanami series *Kindai Nihon to Shokuminchi* [Modern Japan and Its Colonies], ed. Kobayashi Hideo et al. (Tokyo: Iwanami shoten, 1992–93) touch on the issue. See also Yamamoto Yuzo, *Nihon shokuminchi keizaishi kenkyū* [Economic History of Japan's Colonies] (Nagoya: Nagoya Daigaku shuppankai, 1992).

4. See, for example, Christopher Howe, "Japan's Economic Experience in China Before the Establishment of the People's Republic of China: A Retrospective Balance Sheet," in *Japan and World Depression*, ed. Ronald Dore and Radha Sinha (London: Macmillan, 1987), pp. 155–77.

5. Ramon Myers, "Creating a Modern Enclave Economy: The Economic Integration of Japan, Manchuria, and North China, 1932–1945," and Nakamura Takafusa, "The Yen Bloc, 1931–1941," both in Duus et al., *The Japanese Wartime Empire, 1931–1945*, pp. 136–170,

171–187. In a series of stimulating essays, Bruce Cumings pioneered the study of colonial origins of the Northeast Asian economy. See Cumings, "The Origins and Development of the Northeast Asian Political Economy: Industrial Sectors, Product Cycles and Political Consequences," *International Organization* 38, no. 1 (Winter 1984), pp. 1–40.

6. The term *infura* used today in Japan is a postwar creation, as is the term *shakai kiban* (societal basics).

7. Matsuura Shigeki, *Meiji no kokudo kaihatsu shi* [History of Land Development During Meiji] (Tokyo: Kajima shuppankai, 1992).

8. Clarence B. Davis and Kenneth E. Wilburn, Jr., with Ronald E. Robinson, ed., *Railway Imperialism* (New York: Greenwood Press, 1991); Daniel R. Headrick, *The Tools of Empire: Technology and European Imperialism in the Nineteenth Century* (New York: Oxford University Press, 1981).

9. On the South Manchuria Railway Company we now have Y. Tak Matsusaka's excellent study, *The Making of Japanese Manchuria, 1904–1932* (Cambridge: Harvard University Press, 2001). There are too many works in Japanese to list them all.

10. For a lucid account in English on railway development in colonial Korea, see Shinohara Hatsue, "Highway versus Development: Railroads in Korea under Japanese Colonial Rule," in *Chicago Occasional Papers on Korea*, ed. Bruce Cumings (Chicago: University of Chicago Center for East Asian Studies, 1990), pp. 33–57.

11. Takahashi Yasuyaka, "Shokuminchi no tetsudo to kaiun" [Colonial Railways and Marine Transport], in Kobayashi, *Kindai Nihon to Shokuminchi*. Takahashi examines this subject in a longer book, *Nihon shokuminchi tetsudo shiron* [History of Japanese Colonial Railways] (Tokyo: Nihon keizai hyōronsha, 1990), p. 12.

12. Bruce Cumings, *The Origins of the Korean War* (Princeton: Princeton University Press, 1981), vol. 1, pp. 13–14.

13. Quoted in Takahashi, *Nihon shokuminchi tetsudo shiron*, pp. 348–49.

14. Michael Barnhart, *Japan Prepares for Total War* (Ithaca: Cornell University Press, 1987).

15. *Nihon doboku kensetsu ko shi* [A Draft History of Civil Engineering in Japan], quoted in Hirose Teizō, "Gunju keiki to denryoku kensetsu kōji" [War Profits and Electric Power Constructions], in *Doboku: Sangyō no sakaishi 12* [Civil Engineering: The Social History of an Industry], ed. Tamaki Motoi (Tokyo: Nihon keizai hyōronsha, 1993). Interestingly, in the period 1936–45, the resource devoted to military facilities took a close second.

16. Barbara Molony, *Technology and Investment: The Prewar Japanese Chemical Industry* (Cambridge, MA: Council on East Asian Studies, Harvard University, 1990).

17. Hirose, "Gunju keiki to denryoku kensetsu kōji," p. 155. Large numbers of Korean laborers were required for these projects, leading to the migration of hundreds of thousands from the southern part of Korea. The Suiho Dam project alone forced 70,000 people to move, and inundated an area of 198 square kilometers. On Noguchi and his activities in Korea, see Molony, *Technology and Investment*.

18. As many as one thousand laborers were estimated to have died during the construction.

19. By the end of the war some thirteen years later, however, only half of the targets were met. See *Nihonjin no kaigai katsudo ni kansuru rekishiteki chōsa: Chōsen 8* [A Historical Survey of Japanese Activities Overseas: Korea 8] (Tokyo: Ōkurashō Kanrikyoku, 1950), pp. 137–39.

20. Quoted in Takahashi, *Nihon shokuminchi tetsudō shiron*, p. 107.

21. "Ton-Zu sen no kaitsu to Kita-Chōsen" [Opening of the Tonghua-Tumen Line and North Korea], *Chugai shō gyō shimpō* (September 4, 1933).

22. On the early history of Pusan and Inchon, see Hashiya Hiroshi, "Pusan, Inchon no keisei [Development of Pusan and Inchon]," in Kobayashi Hideo et al., *Kindai Nihon to Shokuminchi*, vol. 6.

23. *Shimonoseki shi shi* [History of Shimonoseki City], quoted in "Kan-Mo, Kita Kyūshū Fieldwork Shiryō" [Shimonoseki, Moji, Northern Kyushu: Fieldwork Materials] (available at www1.ocn.ne.jp/~apuro21/fw07.htm, accessed February 20, 2005).

24. "Hokushi kōwan chōsa no ken" [Survey of Harbors in North China] (June 18, 1936), Riku Man mitsu dai-nikki, available on the Japan Center for Asian Historical Records (JACAR) database (www.jacar.go.jp).

25. See Tamaki, *Doboku*; Wang Kuang, *Zhongguo de haiyun* [Marine Transport in China].

26. Horiuchi Daihachi, "Tōa kōtsū ittaika" [Integration of Transportation in East Asia], *Kōtsū bunka* 12 (October 1940), pp. 101–2.

27. Horiuchi, "Tōa kōtsū ittaika," pp. 101–4.

28. For a list of these participants, see Nichi-Man-Shi Kōtsu Kondankai Dai-ichi Chōsakai Jimukyoku, comp., *Tōa kyōeiken nai kōtsuryō tōkei (1936–1940)* [Statistics of Transport Traffic in the East Asian Co-prosperity Sphere] (Tokyo: Nihon Sōeki Shinko Kyōkai, 1942).

29. Nagasaki Sōnosuke, "Nichi-Man-Shi renraku unyu kaigi no gaikyō" [A Brief on the Japan-Manchukuo-Korea Transportation Conference], *Tōa denkitsūshin zasshi* 1, no. 2 (1940), pp. 25–26.

30. Horiuchi, "Tōa kōtsū ittaika," pp. 105–7.

31. Andre Sorensen, *The Making of Urban Japan: Cities and Planning from Edo to the Twenty-First Century* (London: Routledge, 2002).

32. Examples include Ichii Osamu, *Tōa kokudo keikaku* [Land Planning in East Asia] (Tokyo: Dobunkan shuppanbu, 1941); Kōseikai, *Daitōa kokudo keikaku no kenkyū* [Land Planning in Greater East Asia] (Tokyo: Heibonsha, 1943).

33. The best introduction on this subject is Hatano Sumio, "Tōa shinjitsujo to chiseigaku" [New Order in East Asia and Geopolitics], in *Nihon no 1930 nendai* [Japan in the 1930s], ed. Miwa Kimitada (Tokyo: Sairyūsha, 1980), pp. 13–47.

34. Manshūkoku Sōmuchō Keikausho, "Sōgō ritchi keikaku sakutei yōkō" [Outlines of Comprehensive Land Planning] (June 1940); "Sōgō ritchi keikaku ni tsuite" [On Comprehensive Land Planning] (March 7, 1940), in *Shiryō Kokudo keikaku* [Historical Documents on Land Planning], comp. Sugai Shirō (Tokyo: Taimeidō, 1975), pp. 1–18.

35. See Chalmers Johnson, *MITI and the Japanese Miracle* (Stanford: Stanford University Press, 1982).

36. "Nichi-Man-Shi keizai kensetsu yōkō" (Cabinet Resolution on October 3, 1940), in Ishikawa Junkichi, ed. *Kokka sōdoin shi shiryō* [Documents on National General Mobilization], vol. 4, pp. 1083–85.

37. Sugai Shirō, ed., *Kokudo keikaku no keika to kadai* [Process and Issues of Land Planning] (Tokyo: Taimeidō, 1975). For a brief discussion in English, see Kent Calder, *Crisis and Compensation: Public Policy and Political Stability in Japan, 1949–1986* (Princeton: Princeton University Press, 1988), pp. 386–90.

38. Kikakuin, "Kokudo keikaku settei yōkō" (Cabinet approval on September 24, 1940) Kikakuin Kenkyūkai, comp., *Kokubō kokka no kōryō* (Tokyo: Shin Kigensha, 1941), pp. 150–51; also, Sugai, *Shiryō Kokudo keikaku*.

39. Kikakuin, "Chūō keikaku soan" [The Central Plan: A Draft] (October 1943), in Sugai, *Shiryō Kokudo keikaku*, p. 105. Although no specific reason was provided in the plan, it did stipulate the criteria for selecting sites of future capital: it had to be away from major industrial zones.

40. Kikakuin, "Kōkai-Bōkai chiiki kokudo keikaku yōkōan" [Draft Outline of Land Planning in the Yellow Sea-Bohai Region] (October 10, 1942), in Sugai, *Shiryō Kokudo keikaku*, pp. 74–85.

41. "Jūyō butshitsu yido mikomi ryō," appended to Kikakuin, "Chūō keikaku soan" (October 10, 1943), in Sugai, *Shiryō Kokudo keikaku*, pp. 191–93.

42. Su Zongzhou, "Dongbei tianluwang zhi yanju" [A Study of Railway Networks in Northeastern China] *Dongbei jingji* 1, no. 3 (June 1947).

43. See Harada Katsumasa, "Kaisetsu," in *Dai Tōa jūkan tetsudō kankei shorui* [Documents Concerning A Trans-Greater East Asian Railway], comp. Harada (Tokyo: Fuji shuppan, 1988), pp. 7–8; it also contains sketches of the plan. On the Greater East Asian Reconstruction Exposition, see Ōya Giichi, "Dai-Tōa Kensetsu Hakurankai tokoro tokoro" [On the Greater East Asian Reconstruction Exposition], *Chōsen*, no. 328 (September 1942), p. 56.

44. Satō Ojirō, "Daitōa kōtsū taisaku ikensho" [Recommendations for Transportation in Greater East Asia], in *Daitōa Kensetsu Shingikai Kankei Shiryō* [Documents Concerning the Greater East Asian Reconstruction Forum] (Tokyo: Ryukei shosha, 1995), vol. 2, pp. 122–23.

45. Papers presented at a recent conference on the Eurasian Railway network in Helsinki are available at www.geocities.com/kaky_ry/symposium/ (accessed February 20, 2005). See also Harada Katsumasa, *Tetsudo* [Railway] (Tokyo: Nihon keizai hyōronsha, 1988), pp. 202–9.

46. Yumoto Noboru, "Daitōa jūkan tetsudo kensetsu ron" [On Building a Trans-Greater East Asian Railway], *Kagakushugi kōgyō* 6, no. 3 (March 1942), pp. 36–43.

47. Koshizawa Akira, *Zhongguo Dongbei dushi jihua shi* [History of Urban Planning in Northeastern China] trans. Huang Shimeng (Taipei: Dajia chubanshe, 1986).

48. Chang Kai-ngau, *Last Chance in Manchuria* (Stanford: Hoover Institution Press, 1989).

49. Ōkurasho Kanrikyoku, *Nihonjin no kaigai katsudo ni kansuru rekishiteki chōsa*. On the overall background and content, see Kobayashi Hideo "Nihonjin no kaigai katsudo ni kansuru rekishiteki chōsa," in *1940-nendai no Tō-Ajia: Bunken kaidai* [East Asia in the 1940s: Introduction to Sources], ed. Imura Tetsurō (Tokyo: Ajia kenzai kenkyūjo, 1997). On the background of the volumes on Korea, see Namiki Masato's pieces in the same volume. This series became the subject of a legal dispute in the 1970s. Despite calls from historians, the Japanese Ministry of Finance sought a court injunction that effectively stopped a publisher from reprinting the whole series on the grounds of government copyright protection. In 1986 a Korean publisher in Seoul published a complete set of reprints, effectively breaking the Japanese government ban.

50. Ōkurasho Kanrikyoku, *Nihonjin no kaigai katsudo ni kansuru rekishiteki chōsa*, vol. 11.

51. Cumings, "Northeast Asian Political Economy"; Eckert, *Offspring of Empire*.

52. One outstanding exception is Matsumoto Toshirō, *"Manshūkoku" kara shin-Chūgoku e: Ansan tekkōgyō kara mita Chūgoku tōhoku no sanhen katei, 1940–1954* [From "Manchukuo" to New China: Reorganization of Northeastern China as Seen From the Anshan Steel Works, 1940–1954] (Nagoya: Nagoya daigaku shuppankai, 2000). It is based on extensive Japanese and Chinese primary sources.

53. In 1945 the Soviet and Nationalist governments signed an agreement that put the trunk railway network in Manchuria under the Sino-Soviet joint venture Chinese Changchun Railway (CCR) Company for thirty years. Over one thousand Soviet managers and technicians worked in the company, and established a management system on the Soviet model but suited to Chinese needs. This cooperation improved efficiency and reduced cost. Moreover, the company became a model for railway managers in China, as the government dispatched over 10,000 managers and workers to learn from the experience. Mao himself likened the CCR to "a training school for the preparation of Chinese cadres in railroad and industry." Mao's comment was made in a conversation with Stalin in late 1949. See Odd Arne Westad, ed., *Brothers in Arms: The Rise and Fall of the Sino-Soviet Alliance, 1945–1963* (Stanford: Stanford University Press, 1998), p. 315. See also *Dangdai Zhongguo de tiedao shiye* [Railway Enterprise in Contemporary China] (Beijing: Zhongguo shehui kexue chubanshe, 1988), pp. 22–27. The question remains, of course, how much earlier Japanese management techniques were retained.

54. Alfred Perlman, an American railway manager who investigated the South Ko-

rean railways under contract with the UN Korean Reconstruction Agency shortly after the conclusion of World War II, spoke highly of the Japanese railway hardware. But he suggested Korean railway managers should be sent to the United States because the Japanese railway management was "extremely inefficient" compared to the American system. See Day & Zimmermann Co., *Report no. 5002 to His Excellency, Syngman Rhee, President, on the Condition, Rehabilitation, and Further Development of Certain Elements in the Industry of the Republic of Korea* (Philadelphia: Day & Zimmermann, 1949), p. 426.

55. Edwin W. Pauley, *Report on Japanese Assets in Soviet-Occupied Korea to the President of the United States, June 1946* (Washington, DC: U.S. Government Printing Office, 1946), p. 15.

56. Roy E. Appleman, *South to the Naktong, North to the Yalu* (Washington, DC: Office of the Chief of Military History, 1960), p. 261.

57. On economic cooperation and assistance from the Soviet union to China, see Deborah A. Kaple, "Soviet Advisors in China in the 1950s," and Shu Guang Zhang, "Sino-Soviet Economic Cooperation," in Westad, ed., *Brothers in Arms*, pp. 117–40, 189–226; for North Korea, see Karoly Fendler, "Economic Assistance from Socialist Countries to North Korea in the Postwar Years: 1953–1963," in *North Korea: Ideology, Politics, Economy*, ed. Han S. Park (Englewood Cliffs, NJ: Prentice Hall, 1996), pp. 161–74. Fendler gives a list of mostly industrial projects in North Korea partially funded by "fraternal" socialist countries. These projects include railway repair work by China in 1954 and the Tumen River bridge, as well as the railway between Shinchon and Kangwon, both built in 1959 by the Soviet Union.

58. *Dangdai Zhongguo de shuiyun shiye* [Water Transportation in Contemporary China] (Beijing: Zhongguo shehui kexue chubanshe, 1988).

59. Hisashi Sato, "Japan's Interest in Developing Eurasian Railway Connections" (paper presented at the Eurasian Railways Symposium, Helsinki, April 3–4, 2002, available at www.geocities.com/kaky_ry/symposium/sato.html, accessed February 20, 2005).

60. Some of the most infamous incidents associated with Japan's infrastructure building were in Southeast Asia—especially the Thai-Burmese Railway, popularized by the film *The Bridge over the River Kwai*. Casualties among local workers also ran high in Japanese-occupied East Asia. See Tamaki, *Doboku*, pp. 147–48, 150, 154–55, 157, 169, 189–98.

61. *Dangdai Zhongguo de shuiyun shiye*, p. 270. Data on the Japanese embassy in China are available at www.mofa.go.jp/mofaj/gaiko/oda/kunibetu/gai/h06gai/h06gai023.html1993/.

62. The current competition over proposed routes of future oil pipelines to Northeast Asia is reminiscent of the railway geopolitics of an earlier period. See James Brooke, "The Asian Battle for Russia's Oil and Gas," *New York Times*, January 3, 2004, p. C1.

63. See, for instance, "DPRK Said 'Actively Publicizing' Sinuiju, Rail Link as Routes to 'Life of Abundance,'" *Chosŏn Ilbo,* translated in FBIS-EAS-2002-1010.

64. For instance, Furui Tadao, ed., *Tōhoku Ajiashi no saihakken: rekishizō no kyōyū o motome* [Rediscovering Northeast Asian History: Search for a Common Historical Vision] (Tokyo: Yūshindō, 1994).

65. For an example of early advocacy of the Japan Sea Economic Zone, see Matsuo Shōsaburō, *Nihonkai chūshin ron* [The Japan Sea as the Center] (Tokyo, 1942 [1921]).

Notes to Chapter 7

1. Among the plethora of works on the subject, the place to start is David Dallin, *The Rise of Russia in Asia* (New Haven: Yale University Press, 1949).

2. Mark Mancall, *Russia and China: Their Diplomatic Relations to 1728* (Cambridge: Harvard University Press, 1971); S.C.M. Paine, *Imperial Rivals: China, Russia, and Their Disputed Frontier* (Armonk, NY: M.E. Sharpe, 1996); Alexander Lukin, *The Bear Watches*

the Dragon: Russia's Perceptions of China and the Evolution of Russian-Chinese Relations Since the Eighteenth Century (Armonk, NY: M.E. Sharpe, 2003).

3. George Lensen, *The Russian Push Toward Japan: Russo-Japanese Relations, 1697–1875* (Princeton: Princeton University Press, 1959); idem, "Japan and Tsarist Russia—the Changing Relationships, 1875–1917," *Jahrbücher für Geschichte Osteuropas* 10 (1962), pp. 337–48.

4. George Lensen, *Balance of Intrigue: International Rivalry in Korea and Manchuria, 1884–1899* (Tallahassee: University Press of Florida, 1982).

5. Boris Slavinskii, *Sovetskaia okkupatsiia kuril' skikh ostrovov (avgust'–sentiabr' 1945 goda): documental' noe issledovanie* [The Soviet Occupation of the Kuril Islands (August–September 1945)] (Moscow: Lotos, 1993), pp. 59–66, citing various military archives (for example: Moskovskoe otdelenie Tsentral'nogo voenno-morskogo arkhiva, *fond* (f) 129, *delo* (d) 17777, *list* (l). 2, for the documents on the abrupt cancellation of the Hokkaido operation). See also Tsuyoshi Hasegawa, *The Northern Territories Dispute and Russo-Japanese Relations*, 2 vols. (Berkeley: University of California International and Area Studies, 1998).

6. Shen Zhihua, "Sino-Korea Conflict and Its Resolution During the Korean War," *Cold War International History Project Bulletin* 14/15 (Winter 2003–Spring 2004), pp. 9–24. See also Odd Arne Westad, ed., *Brothers in Arms: The Rise and Fall of the Sino-Soviet Alliance 1945–1963* (Stanford: Stanford University Press, 1998).

7. Why the United States in East Asia did not seek to form a multilateral NATO-like alliance but to rely on bilateral arrangements is beyond the scope of this essay. See C. Hemmer and P.J. Katzenstein, "Why Is There No NATO in Asia? Collective Identity, Regionalism, and the Origins of Multilateralism," *International Organization* 56, no. 3 (2002), p. 575.

8. Steven Levine, *Anvil of Victory: The Communist Revolution in Manchuria* (New York: Columbia University Press, 1987), p. 68. See also Odd Arne Westad, *Decisive Encounters: The Chinese Civil War, 1946–1950* (Stanford: Stanford University Press, 2003), p. 166; and Norman M. Naimark, *The Russians in Germany: A History of the Soviet Zone of Occupation* (Cambridge: Harvard University Press, 1995).

9. Kathryn Weathersby, interviewed by Chong-Sik Lee, "What Stalin Wanted in Korea at the End of World War II," *Korea Focus* (1993), p. 41.

10. United States Department of State, *North Korea: A Case Study in the Techniques of Takeover* (Washington, DC: U.S. Government Printing Office, 1961 [1951]), p. 2; Dae-Sook Suh, "A Preconceived Formula for Sovietization: North Korea," in *The Anatomy of Communist Takeovers*, ed. John Hammond (New Haven: Yale University Press, 1975).

11. *Intelligence Summary North Korea* (ISNK), no. 1 (December 1, 1945), p. 6, in National Archives and Records Administration (NARA), Record Group 319. See also Levine, *Anvil of Victory*.

12. Erik van Ree, *Socialism in One Zone: Stalin's Policy in Korea, 1945–1947* (Oxford: Berg, 1989), which makes excellent use of Soviet memoirs; Charles K. Armstrong, *The North Korea Revolution, 1945–1950* (Ithaca: Cornell University Press, 2003), which uses captured North Korean documents and stresses Korean agency. See also Michael Sandusky, *America's Parallel* (Alexandria, VA: Old Dominion, 1983); Wada Haruki, *Kin Nichisei to Manshū kōnichi sensō* [Kim Il Sung and the Anti-Japanese War in Manchuria] (Tokyo: Heibonsha, 1992).

13. Gavril Korotkov (Institute of Military History, Moscow) claimed to have found classified materials in the Russian Defense Ministry archives indicating that Stalin discussed invasion plans with Kim during the latter's visit to Moscow in March 1949. See Kathryn Weathersby, "Soviet Aims in Korea and the Origins of the Korean War, 1945–50: New Evidence from the Russian Archives," Cold War International History Project

(CWIHP), working paper no. 8 (November 1993), citing *Yonhap,* translated in FBIS-SOV-93-119 (June 23, 1993), p. 14. (Korotkov has still not published this material, according to a personal communication from Kathryn Weathersby.) Someday, we may learn of discussions to "unify" the peninsula in 1945. See also Bruce Cumings, *The Origins of the Korean War,* 2 vols. (Princeton: Princeton University Press, 1981, 1990); Weathersby, "New Russian Documents on the Korean War," *Cold War International History Project Bulletin,* nos. 6–7 (1995–96), including Cumings and Weathersby, "An Exchange on Korean War Origins," pp. 120–22. Park Myongnim, *Hanguk chonjaengui palpal kwa kiwon* [The Outbreak and Origins of the Korean War] (Seoul: Nanam, 1997); Wada Haruki, *Chōsen sensō zenshi* [Complete History of the Korean War] (Tokyo: Iwanami, 2002); Chen Jian, "The Sino-Soviet Alliance and China's Entry into the Korean War," CWIHP, working paper no. 1 (1991); Hao Yufan and Zhai Zhihai, "China's Decision to Enter the Korean War: History Revisited," *China Quarterly,* no. 121 (March 1990), pp. 94–115; Alexandre Y. Mansourov, "Communist War Coalition Formation and the Origins of the Korean War" (Ph.D. dissertation, Columbia University, 1997); and D.C. Kim, "Beneath the Tip of the Iceberg: Problems in Historical Clarification of the Korean War," *Korea Journal* 42, no. 3 (2002), pp. 60–86.

14. *"Industries in North Korea,"* p. 29, in NARA, Record Group 497, box 462.

15. Van Ree, *Socialism in One Zone.*

16. Cf. Armstrong, *North Korea Revolution,* and Andrei Lankov, *From Stalin to Kim Il Sung: The Formation of North Korea 1945–1960* (London: Hurst, 2002).

17. Mitsuhiko Kimura, "From Fascism to Communism: Continuity and Development of Collectivist Economic Policy in North Korea," *Economic History Review* 42, no. 2 (1999), pp. 69–86.

18. Lankov, *From Stalin,* pp. 39–40, citing Center for the Study and Preservation of Documents of Contemporary History [RTsKhIDNI], f. 17, op. 128, d. 1148, ll. 20–45.

19. John J. Stephan, *The Russian Far East: A History* (Stanford: Stanford University Press, 1994).

20. Lankov, *From Stalin,* pp. 111–35.

21. United States Department of State, *North Korea,* p. 62.

22. Van Ree, *Socialism in One Zone,* p. 164.

23. One estimate of Soviet aid to North Korea was 567 million rubles by 1972. N.E. Bazhanova, *Vneshekonomicheskie sviazi KNDR: v poiskakh vykhoda iz tupika* [Foreign Economic Ties of the Korean Democratic People's Republic: In Search of a Way Out of the Dead End] (Moscow: Nauka, 1993), p. 16. South Korean estimates of Soviet aid to North Korea for the period 1945–70, including credits and grants, are $1 billion, with an additional $500 million said to have been received from China (Lankov, *From Stalin,* p. 63). See also Armstrong, *North Korean Revolution,* pp. 153–54.

24. When Hamhung, an East German–reconstructed city (1955–62), threatened to become more attractive than Pyongyang, the DPRK leadership diverted substantial German-donated materials to the capital. "New Evidence on North Korea," *Cold War International History Project Bulletin* 14/15 (Winter 2003–Spring 2004), p. 26.

25. George M. McCune, *Korea Today* (Cambridge: Harvard University Press, 1950), p. 214.

26. Edwin W. Pauley, *Report on Japanese Assets in Soviet-Occupied Korea to the President of the United States, June 1946* (Washington, DC: U.S. Government Printing Office, 1948), p. 17.

27. McCune, *Korea Today,* p. 216.

28. George G.S. Murphy, *Soviet Mongolia: A Study of the Oldest Political Satellite* (Berkeley: University of California, 1966). Murphy details Soviet atrocities in Mongolia, yet he also notes that "the Soviet government has shown continuing concern to keep its

advisors and workers in the background and to train as rapidly as possible a Mongol work force to run Outer Mongolia's industry" (p. 152). See also S.G. Luzianin, *Rossiia-Mongoliia-Kitai v pervoi polovine XX v.: Politicheskie vzaimootnosheniia v 1911–1946 gg.* [Russia-Mongolia-China in the First Half of the Twentieth Century: Political Interrelations 1911–1946] (Moscow: IDV RAN, 2000).

29. Robert A. Rupen, *Mongols of the Twentieth Century* (Bloomington: Indiana University Press, 1964), pp. 261–62.

30. Shu Guangzhang, "Sino-Soviet Economic Cooperation," in Westad, *Brothers in Arms*, pp. 197–98.

31. Ibid., pp. 202, 211.

32. Ken Coates, ed., *China and the Bomb* (Atlantic Highlands, NJ: Spokesman, 1986); John Wilson Lewis and Xue Litai, *China Builds the Bomb* (Stanford: Stanford University Press, 1988).

33. RTsKhSDNI, f. 2, op. 1, d. 720, l. 44, cited in Tatiana G. Zazerskaia, *Sovetskie spetsialisty i formirovanie voenno-promyshlennogo kompleksa Kitaia (1949–1960 gody)* [Soviet Specialists and the Formation of the Military Industrial Complex in China [1949–1960]) (St. Petersburg: Peterburgskii gos. universitet, 2000), pp. 120–21.

34. "China's Nuclear Ambition Grows," *Risk Report* 1, no. 9 (November 1995).

35. N.T. Fedorenko, "Stalin i Mao Zedun" [Stalin and Mao Zedong], *Novaia i noveishaia istoriia*, no. 5 (1992), p. 101.

36. Goncharenko adds that during the enmity of the 1960s, when both sides exposed dirty secrets about the other, Moscow and Beijing avoided revealing details of their military cooperation. Even during the documents gold rush of the 1990s, he writes, "the military aspect of the alliance has remained terra incognita." Nonetheless, he concludes that "the transfer of military technology from the Soviet Union to China was more extensive than was earlier thought" (Goncharenko, "Sino-Soviet Military Cooperation," in Westad, *Brothers in Arms*, pp. 141–64).

37. Constantine Pleshakov, "Nikita Khrushchev and Sino-Soviet Relations," in Westad, *Brothers in Arms*, p. 236.

38. David Wolff, "'One Finger's Worth of Historical Events': New Russian and Chinese Evidence on the Sino-Soviet Alliance and Split, 1948–1959," Cold War International History Project (CWIHP), working paper no. 30 (2000), p. 23.

39. *Foreign Relations of the United States*, 1961–63, vol. 7, p. 801. On U.S. government reactions to China's pending acquisition of the bomb, including arguments in favor of a preemptive strike, see the remarkable declassified documents at www.gwu.edu/~nsarchiv/NSAEBB/NSAEBB38/.

40. Goncharenko, "Sino-Soviet Military Cooperation," pp. 141–64.

41. Zazerskaia, *Sovetskie spetsialisty*, esp. pp. 109–23.

42. Vladislav Zubok and Constantine Pleshakov, *Inside the Kremlin's Cold War* (Cambridge: Harvard University Press, 1996), p. 227, citing RTsKhSDNI, f. 5, op. 49, d. 134, l. 92.

43. See www.china-defense.com. See also Deborah A. Kaple, *Dream of a Red Factory: The Legacy of High Stalinism in China* (New York: Oxford University Press, 1994). In October 1966, China tested its first nuclear missile.

44. As Zazerskaia notes, however, Lewis and Xue claim the decision not to provide a prototype bomb was made in early 1958 (Lewis and Xue, *China Builds the Bomb*, p. 61).

45. David Holloway, personal communication, April 2003. See also Holloway, *Stalin and the Bomb: The Soviet Union and Atomic Energy, 1939–1956* (New Haven: Yale University Press, 1994). In the 1960s and 1970s, tensions with the Soviet Union appear to have spurred Chinese efforts to develop *tactical* nuclear weapons. *Bulletin of the Atomic Scientists* 56, no. 6 (2000), pp. 78–79.

46. Bhabhani Sen Gupta, *Nuclear Weapons? Policy Options for India* (New Delhi: Sage, 1983); George Perkovich, *India's Nuclear Bomb: The Impact on Global Proliferation* (Berkeley: University of California Press, 1999); Raj Chengappa, *Weapons of Peace* (HarperCollins Publishers India, 2000).

47. "The Soviet Union has the bomb," stated Deng Xiaoping in 1957. "Where does the significance lie? It lies in the fact that imperialists are afraid of it. Are the imperialists afraid of us? I don't think so. . . . The United States stations its troops on Taiwan because we have no atom bombs or guided missiles" (as quoted in Dingli Shen, "The Current Status of Chinese Nuclear Forces and Nuclear Policy," Princeton University Center for Energy and Environmental Studies, report no. 247 [February 1990]). See also Roger Digman, "Atomic Diplomacy During the Korean War," *International Security* 13, no. 3 (1988–89), pp. 50–91.

48. David E. Sanger and William J. Broad, "Evidence Is Cited Linking Koreans to Libya Uranium," *New York Times*, May 23, 2004, p. A1.

49. For comprehensive accounts of the 1994 crisis from American perspectives, see Leon V. Sigal, *Disarming Strangers: Nuclear Diplomacy with North Korea* (Princeton: Princeton University Press, 1998), and Joel S. Wit, Daniel B. Poneman, and Robert L. Gallucci, *Going Critical: The First North Korean Nuclear Crisis* (Washington, DC: Brookings Institution Press, 2004).

50. Georgii Kaurov, "A Technical History of Soviet-North Korean Nuclear Relations," in *The North Korean Nuclear Program: Security Strategy and New Perspectives from Russia*, ed. James Clay Moltz and Alexandre Y. Mansourov (London: Routledge, 2000), 15.

51. Valery I. Denisov, "Nuclear Institutions and Organizations in North Korea," in ibid., p. 21.

52. The consensus among Russian experts was that the North Koreans did not have the technology to build nuclear weapons, even if they possessed sufficient weapons-grade plutonium (ibid., p. 25).

53. Natalia Bazhanova, *Kiroe son Puk Han kyongje* [North Korean Economy at the Crossroads], trans. Yang Chuyong (Seoul: Hanguk kyongje sinmunsa, 1992), p. 22, based on statistics from the Soviet Trade Ministry archives.

54. Ibid., p. 24.

55. John Yoon Tai Kuark, "A Comparative Study of Economic Development in North and South Korea During the Post-Korean War Period" (Ph.D. dissertation, University of Minnesota, 1966), p. 55.

56. Chen Jian and Yang Kuisong, "Chinese Politics and the Collapse of the Sino-Soviet Alliance," in Westad, *Brothers in Arms*, p. 264.

57. Annette Baker Fox, *The Power of Small States: Diplomacy in World War II* (Chicago: University of Chicago Press, 1959).

58. Yoon T. Kuark, "North Korea's Industrial Development During the Post-War Period," in *North Korea Today*, ed. Robert A. Scalapino (New York, Praeger, 1963), p. 62.

59. Chin O. Chung, *P'yongyang Between Peking and Moscow: North Korea's Involvement in the Sino-Soviet Dispute, 1958–1975* (University: University of Alabama, 1978), p. 29.

60. Qiang Zhai, *China and the Vietnam Wars, 1950–1975* (Chapel Hill: University of North Carolina Press, 2000), pp. 71–73.

61. Pleshakov, "Nikita Khrushchev and Sino-Soviet Relations," in Westad, *Brothers in Arms*, p. 234.

62. Balázs Szalontai, "'You Have No Political Line of Your Own': Kim Il Sung and the Soviets, 1953–1964," *Cold War International History Project Bulletin* 14/15 (Winter 2003–Spring 2004), pp. 87–137.

63. Ibid., p. 87.

64. Chung, *P'yongyang Between Peking and Moscow*, pp. 68–80.

65. Chae-Jin Lee, *China's Korean Minority: The Politics of Ethnic Education* (Boulder, CO: Westview, 1986), p. 87.

66. Soviet embassy in DPRK, Report, August 1962, in Arkhiv Vneshnei Politiki Rossiiskoi Federatsii (AVPRF), f. 0102, op. 16, pap. 87, d. 29.

67. Chung, *P'yongyang Between Peking and Moscow*, p. 56.

68. Ibid., pp. 56–57.

69. Ibid., p. 65.

70. Soviet embassy in DPRK, Report, February 5, 1962, in AVPRF, f. 0102, op. 16, pap. 87, d. 29.

71. Soviet embassy in DPRK, Report, April 5, 1962, in AVPRF, f. 0102, op. 16, pap. 87, d. 29.

72. Chung, *P'yongyang Between Peking and Moscow*, pp. 70–77.

73. Soviet embassy to the DPRK, Report, February 5, 1962, in AVPRF, f. 0102, op. 16, pap. 87, d. 29.

74. Hungarian embassy to the DPRK, Report, January 19, 1962, in KTS, 5 doboz, 5/bc, 002255/1962, trans. Balázs Solantai for Cold War International History Project, www.wilsoncenter.org. Party officials in the East European satellites also were troubled by what they saw as the undue influence of China over the DPRK. See, for example, the GDR Foreign Ministry, Extra-European Department, Korea Section, "The Position of Leadership of the KWP on the Fundamental Issues of Our Epoch," December 2, 1963, in MfAA A 7174, German Foreign Ministry archives.

75. At the level of economic interaction, there was no significant falling out between the Soviet Union and North Korea at this time. Soviet trade with the DPRK remained steadily high between 1961 and 1964, whereas Sino-Soviet trade dropped sharply. See Chung, *P'yongyang Between Peking and Moscow*, p. 93.

76. Soviet embassy in DPRK, Report, October 18, 1964, in AVPRF, f. 0102, op. 16, pap. 87, d. 230.

77. German Federal archives, GDR embassy Annual Report, 1963, SAPMO-BA, DY 30, IV A2/20/251.

78. GDR embassy in DPRK, December 19, 1963, in MfAA A 7126.

79. Mitchell Lerner, "Failure of Perception: Lyndon Johnson, North Korean Ideology, and the Pueblo Incident," *Diplomatic History* 25, no 4 (fall 2001): 664–65.

80. "North Korea Holds Up Highway," *Far Eastern Economic Review*, May 27, 2004, pp. 8–9.

Notes to Chapter 8

1. Robert Scalapino, *The Foreign Policy of Modern Japan* (Berkeley: University of California Press, 1977).

2. Takashi Shiraishi, *Umi no teikoku* [The Marine Empire] (Tokyo: Chuko Shinsho, 2000); Masaru Tamamoto, "Ambiguous Japan: Japanese National Identity at Century's End," in *International Relations Theory and the Asia-Pacific*, ed. John Ikenberry and Michael Masutandino (New York: Columbia University Press, 2002), pp. 191–212.

3. Junosuke Yasukawa, *Fukuzawa Yukichi no Ajia ninshik* [Fukuzawa Yukichi's Perception of Asia] (Tokyo: Kobunken, 2000).

4. Ibid., pp. 119–33.

5. Junji Banno, *Nihon no rekishi 13: Kindai Nihon no shuppatsu* [History of Japan 13: Departure of Modern Japan] (Tokyo: Shogakukan, 1993), pp. 238–311.

6. Taichiro Mitani, "Higashi Ajia chikishugi no rekishiteki kosatsu to sono shoraieno tenbo" [A Historical Study of East Asian Regionalism and Its Outlook], working paper, Center for Contemporary Korean Studies, Wasada University, Tokyo, 2002.

7. Kenichi Goto, "Kindai Niho-Tonan Ajia kankei shiron josetsu" [On the History of Japan-Southeast Asian Relations], in *Nashonarizumu to kokumin kokka* [Nationalism and Nation-State], ed. Tsuchiya, Kenji (Tokyo: Tokyo University Press, 1994), pp. 38–40;

Victor Koschmann, "Asianism's Ambivalent Legacy," in *Network Power: Japan and* Asia, ed. Peter J. Katzenstein, and Takashi Shirashi (Ithaca: Cornell University Press, 1997), pp. 83–110.

8. Keiichi Eguchi, *Nihon no rekishi 14: Futatus no taisen* [History of Japan 14: Two World Wars] (Tokyo: Shogakukan, 1993), pp. 351–52.

9. Bruce Cumings, "Japan and Northeast Asia into the Twenty-First Century," in Katzenstein and Shirashi, *Network Power*, pp. 136–68.

10. Japanese MOFA (Ministry of Foreign Affairs), *Ohira sori no Chugoku homon* [Prime Minister Ohira's Visit to China: Responses of Foreign Press] (Tokyo: Department of Intelligence and Culture, Ministry of Foreign Affairs, December 19, 1979), pp. 11–36.

11. Masayoshi Ohira, *Ohira Masayoshi kisoroku: Denkihen* [Memoir of Ohira Masayoshi: Biography] (Tokyo: Ohira Kisoroku Kankokai, 1982), pp. 85–86.

12. Makoto Iokibe, "Fukuda Takeo: Seisaku no shosha, seiso no hasha" [Takeo Fukuda: Winner in Policy, Loser in Political Strife], in *Sengo Nihon no saisho tachi* [Premiers in the Postwar Era], ed. Akio Watanabe (Tokyo: Chuokoronsha, 1995), pp. 291–93.

13. Victor Cha, *Alignment Despite Antagonism* (Stanford: Stanford University Press, 1999).

14. Chong-sik Lee, *Japan and Korea: The Political Dimension* (Stanford, CA: Hoover Institution Press, 1985), pp. 69–73.

15. Ibid., p. 71.

16. Chae-jin Lee and Hideo Sato, *U.S. Policy Toward Japan and Korea* (New York: Praeger, 1982), pp. 40–41.

17. Lee, *Japan and Korea*, pp. 80–82.

18. Ibid., pp. 100–101.

19. Kenneth B. Pyle, *The Japanese Question: Power and Purpose in a New Era* (Washington, DC: AEI Press, 1996), pp. 88–89.

20. Yasuhiro Nakasone, "Sengo no sokessan kara 21 seiki sekai no Nihon e" [From Total Evaluation of the Postwar Period to Twenty-first Century Japan], *Jiyu minshu* (March 1984), p. 30.

21. Hakuki Inoki, "Saikin no Chogoku josei" [Current Trends in China], *Kokumin gaiko* (June 1984), pp. 25–26.

22. Yasuhiro Nakasone, *Tenchi yujo: Gojunen no sengo seiji wo karata* [Talking About Fifty Years of Postwar Politics] (Tokyo: Bungei Shunju, 1995), p. 449.

23. Lee, *Japan and Korea*, pp. 129–35.

24. Masao Okonogi, "Shin Naengjonhaui Hanmiil chaeje [Korea–United States–Japan System in the New Cold War]," in *Sijang, kukka, kukjecheje* [Market, the State, and International System], ed. Chung-in Moon and Masao Okonogi (Seoul: Asiatic Research Center, 2002), pp. 191–216.

25. Mike M. Mochizuki, "American and Japanese Strategic Debates: The Need for a New Synthesis," in *Toward a True Alliance*, ed. Mochizuki (Washington, DC: Brookings Institution, 1997), pp. 56–64.

26. Ichiro Ozawa, *Nihon kaizo keikaku* [A Plan for Reforming Japan] (Tokyo: Kodansha, 1993).

27. Mochizuki, "American and Japanese Strategic Debates," pp. 60–62.

28. Shintaro Ishihara and Mahathir Mohamad, "'No' to ieru Ajia" [Asia That Can Say "No"] (Tokyo: Kobunsha, 1994), pp. 36–40; Shoichi Watanabe, "Ajia kyoenken no michi" [Way to the Asian Common Prosperity Sphere], in *Ajia kyoenken no jidai* [The Age of Asian Common Prosperity Sphere], ed. Kyu Eikan and Shoichi Watanabe (Tokyo: PHP kenkyusjo, 1994), pp. 169–86.

29. Chung-seok Yun, "Choson minzoku ni totte no kaso tekikoku Nihon" [Japan, the Imaginary Enemy for Koreans], *Sapio* (June 1991), pp. 7–9; Katsuhiro Kuroda, "Kankoku, 'Nihon shutekiron' no Shini: Han nichi nashorarizumu ni tayoru nanboku wakai mudo no

ayausa" [The Real Meaning of Koreans' 'Japan as a Main Enemy': The Weakness of the South-North Reconciliation Mood Relying on Anti-Japan Nationalism], *Voice* (April 1992), pp. 116–25.

30. Jung-Hoon Lee and Chung-in Moon, "Responding to Japan's Asian Policy: The Korean Calculus," in *Japan's Asian Policy*, ed. Takashi Inoguchi (New York: Palgrave, 2002), p. 151.

31. Japanese Ministry of Foreign Affairs, *1998 Diplomatic Bluebook: Japanese Diplomacy with Leadership Toward the New Century, an English version* (Tokyo: Urban Connections, 1999).

32. Katzenstein and Shirashi, *Network Power*.

33. JETRO (Japan External Trade Organization), www.jetro.go.jp/ec/j/invest,/ accessed March 25, 2004.

34. Tetsushu Kosiba, "Ajia taiheyo keizaiken ni okeru Nihon kigyo no jigyo nettowakuka" [Emerging Business Networks of Japanese Firms in the Asia-Pacific Zone], *Sekai keizai hyoron* (August 1996), pp. 40–57.

35. Japanese Ministry of Foreign Affairs, *Wagakuni no seifu kaihatsu enjo* [Japan's Official Development Assistance] (Tokyo, 2000).

36. Chung-in Moon, "Conclusion: A Dissenting View on the Pacific Future," in *Pacific Dynamics: The International Politics of Industrial Change*, ed. Stephan Haggard and Chung-in Moon (Boulder, CO: Westview Press, 1989), pp. 359–74; Mitchell Bernard and John Ravenhill, "Beyond Product Cycles and Flying Geese: Regionalization, Hierarchy, and the Industrialization of East Asia," *World Politics* 47, no. 2 (1995), pp. 171–209.

37. ROK Ministry of Foreign Affairs and Trade, *Oikyo* baekseo [White Paper on Diplomacy] (each year from 1997 to 2002) (Seoul).

38. Jae-hyun Baek, "Yolsimhi polowa ilbonae bachinun 155 ok dallo" [Hard-earned 15.5 Billion Dollars Is Being Taken Away by Japan], *Monthly Choson* (October 1996), pp. 309–10.

39. Yukiko Fukagawa, *Kankoku: Senshinkoku keizairon* [Korea: A Developed Economy] (Tokyo: Nihon keizai shimbunsha, 1997).

40. Jeong-yeon Shim, "FDI in Korea Continues to Increase in the First Half of 2002," *Korea Insight* 4, no. 8 (2002), pp. 1–4.

41. Saburo Okita, *Kan taiheyo koso no genjo* [The Current Status of the Pan-Pacific Design] (Tokyo: Kodansha, 1982), p. 28.

42. Keizai Kikakucho, ed., *Chiiki shugi taito ka deno Nihon no sentaku* [Japan's Choice Under the Resurgence of Regionalism] (Tokyo: Okurasho insatsukyoku, 1989), pp. 191–93.

43. Yong Deng, "Japan in APEC," *Asian Survey* 37, no. 4 (April 1997), pp. 353–67.

44. Koschmann, "Asianism's Ambivalent Legacy," p. 83.

45. Tatsumi Okabe, Sakutaro Tanino and Kazuki Kasuya, "Zadankai: Posto reisen to Ajia-Taiheiyo no shinchoryu" [Round-Table Talk: Post-Cold War and the New Asia-Pacific Trend," *Gaiko Forum* (February 1991), pp. 12–25.

46. Yotaro Kobayashi, "'Sai Ajiaka' no susume" [Japan's Need for "Re-Asianization"], *Foresight* (April 1991), pp. 44–46.

47. Shintaro Ishihara and Akio Morita, *The Japan That Can Say No* (New York: Simon and Schuster, 1991).

48. Japanese Ministry of Foreign Affairs, *1998 Diplomatic Bluebook*.

49. Ibid.

50. Young-hee Kim, "AMF oe korina?" [Why Do We Fear the AMF?], *Joongang Daily*, December 2, 1998, p. 5.

51. Lee and Moon, "Responding to Japan's Asian Policy," p. 157.

52. Ministry of International Trade and Industry, *White Paper on International Trade* (Tokyo, 2001 [in Japanese]); JETRO, *AFTA-Progress of ASEAN Economic Integration and Prospects* (Tokyo, 2001).

53. Masahiro Kondo, "Nikkan FTA ni taisuru kankokugawa kara mita eikyo, Kitai to kadai" [The Influences, Expectations, and Challenges of Japan–Korea FTA: A South Korean Perspective], *Nagasaki keizai* (January 2003), pp. 24–31; Ippei Yamazawa, "Japan–Korea FTA," *Focus Japan* (January–February 2001); T. Nakajima and O.K. Kwon, "An Analysis of the Economic Effects of Japan–Korea FTA," ERINA Discussion Paper no. 0101e, Economic Research Institute for Northeast Asia, Niigata, 2001; In-kyo Cheong, *Han Il FTA ui Kyungjaejeok Hyokwawa jeongchaek shisajom* [Economic Effects and Policy Implications of Korea–Japan FTA] (Seoul: KIEP, 2001).

54. Nao Ishizaki, "Nikkan jiyu boeki kyotei no teiketsu wa jitsugen suruka?" [Can Japan and Korea Make a Free Trade Agreement?], *Chiiki Kasseika Journal* (July 2000), pp. 52–55.

55. Kondo, "Nikkan FTA ni taisuru kankokugawa kara mita eikyo, Kitai to kadai."

Notes to Chapter 9

1. Chung Jae Ho, "Chungguk oe pusang, Miguk oe kyonje, Hanguk oe tillema" [China's Emergence, America's Restraint, Korea's Dilemma], *Shin donga* (October 2000), p. 260.

2. Gilbert Rozman, "Japan and South Korea: Should the U.S. Be Worried About Their New Spat in 2001?" *Pacific Review* 15, no. 1 (2002), pp. 1–28.

3. Yoshida Kenichi, "Tairitsu zofukushita 'amachua seiji'" ["Amateur Politics" Which Have Increased Confrontation], *Sekai shuho*, March 2, 2004, pp. 10–13.

4. Chae-jin Lee, *China and Korea: Dynamic Relations* (Stanford, CA: Hoover Institution Press, 1996), pp. 112, 145.

5. Joon Yong Park, "Soviet Russia's Policies Toward the Korean Peninsula," in *The Soviet Union and East Asia in the 1980s*, ed. Jae Kyu Park and Joseph H. Ma (Seoul: Kyungnam University Press, 1983), p. 81.

6. Charles E. Ziegler, *Foreign Policy and East Asia: Learning and Adaptation in the Gorbachev Era* (Cambridge: Cambridge University Press, 1993), p. 116.

7. Victor D. Cha, *Alignment Despite Antagonism: The U.S.-Korea-Japan Security Triangle* (Stanford: Stanford University Press, 1999), pp. 188–90.

8. Ibid., p. 195.

9. Gilbert Rozman, "Japan's Quest for Great Power Identity," *Orbis* 46, no. 1 (Winter 2002), pp. 73–91.

10. Il Yung Chung, ed., *Korea and Russia: Toward the Twenty-first Century* (Seoul: Sejong Institute, 1992).

11. Byung Chul Koh, "Northeast Asia in the Post-Cold War Era: Minimum Order and Optimum Order," *Korean Journal of Defense Analysis* 3, no. 2 (Winter 1991), pp. 105–22.

12. Gilbert Rozman, "Decentralization in East Asia: A Reassessment of Its Background and Potential," *Development and Society* 31, no. 1 (June 2002), pp. 1–22; idem, "Troubled Choices for the Russian Far East: Decentralization, Open Regionalism, and Internationalism," *Journal of East Asian Affairs* 11, no. 2 (Summer/Fall 1997), pp. 537–69; idem, "Northeast China: Waiting for Regionalism," *Problems of Post-Communism* 45, no. 4 (July–August 1998), pp. 3–13; idem, "Backdoor Japan: The Search for a Way Out via Regionalism and Decentralization," *Journal of Japanese Studies* 25, no. 1 (Winter 1999), pp. 3–31.

13. *ERINA Report* 1–49 (1994–2002).

14. *Ilbon pogoso* [Japan Report] (Seoul: Shinhan chonghap yonguso, 1998).

15. *Zolotoi rog*, October 15, 2002, p. 15.

16. Sang-Chuel Choe, "The Evolving Urban System in Northeast Asia," in *Emerging*

World Cities in Pacific Asia, ed. Fu-chen Lo and Yue-man Yeung (New York: United Nations University Press, 1996), pp. 498–519.

17. Alice H. Amsden, *Asia's New Giant: South Korea and Late Industrialization* (Oxford: Oxford University Press, 1989); Meredith Woo-Cumings, *The Developmental State* (Ithaca: Cornell University Press, 1999).

18. Gilbert Rozman, "China's Quest for Great Power Identity," *Orbis* 43, no. 3 (Summer 1999), pp. 383–402.

19. In the wake of conferences on a shared culture based on use of Chinese characters (*kanji bunka ken*), despite the rarity of their use in Korea today, Funabashi Yoichi of *Asahi shimbun* was among the most enthusiastic in predicting regional fusion in his book *Ajia taiheiyo fyujon* [Asia-Pacific Fusion] (Tokyo: Chuokoronsha, 1995).

20. Bae Ho Hahn and Chae-Jin Lee, "Japan and Korea," in *The Korean Peninsula and the Major Powers*, ed. Bae Ho Hahn and Chae-Jin Lee (Seoul: Sejong Institute, 1998), pp. 33–68.

21. Qi Mei, "Jianxi dangqian daguo guanxi zhong zengzhi he anquan insu" [Analysis of the Political and Security Factors in Current Great Power Relations], *Shijie jingji yu zhengzhi*, no. 2 (1998), pp. 21–24.

22. Vl. F. Li, *Rossiia i Koreia v geopolitike evraziiskogo Vostoka* [Russia and Korea in the Geopolitics of the Eurasian East] (Moscow: Nauchnaia kniga, 2000).

23. Michael J. Green, *Japan's Reluctant Realism: Foreign Policy Challenges in an Era of Uncertain Power* (New York: Palgrave, 2001), pp. 122–24.

24. Samuel S. Kim, ed., *East Asia and Globalization* (Lanham, MD: Rowman & Littlefield, 2000).

25. Keun-Sik Kim, "Inter-Korean Relations and the Future of the Sunshine Policy," *Journal of East Asian Affairs* 16, no. 1 (Spring/Summer 2002), pp. 98–119.

26. Lee Jong Won, "The Possibility of Regional Security Framework on the Korean Peninsula," *Rikkyo hogaku*, no. 61 (2002), pp. 150–86.

27. Christopher W. Hughes, "Japan and North Korea Relations from the North-South Summit to the Koizumi-Kim Summits," *Asia-Pacific Review* 9, no. 2 (November 2002), pp. 61–78; Gilbert Rozman, "Japan's North Korea Initiative and U.S.-Japanese Relations," *Orbis* 47, no. 3 (Summer 2003), pp. 527–39.

28. Ogane Shin, "Kim Dai Jung seiken wa do hyoka sareruka?" [How Should the Kim Dae Jung Regime be Evaluated?], *Sekai shuho*, April 1, 2003, p. 47.

29. *Asahi shimbun*, March 6, 2003, p. 15.

30. Ibid., p. 14.

31. Ibid., March 5, 2003, p. 15.

32. Shigemura Toshimitsu, "Hokai ni mukau Beikan domei kankei" [U.S.-South Korean Alliance Relations Heading for a Breakup], *Sekai shuho*, March 2, 2004, pp. 14–17.

33. *Nihon keizai shimbun*, March 2, 2003, p. 18.

34. *Sankei shimbun*, January 27, 2003, p. 3.

35. *Mainichi shimbun*, June 5, 2003, p. 2.

36. "Ratchi kaiketsu wa Katei Gaimusho de wa dekinai" [The Abductions Cannot be Resolved by the Presumed Foreign Ministry], *THEMIS*, no. 6 (2003), pp. 84–85; Okonogi Masao, "Kitachosen mondai no shindankai to Nihon gaiko" [The New Stage of the North Korean Question and Japan's Diplomacy], *Kokusai mondai*, no. 5 (2003), pp. 2–13.

37. "Beichu ga nerau 'Kim Jung Il seiken hokai' no shinario" [The United States and China Cannot Aim at the Scenario of "Breaking Up the Kim Jong Il Regime"], *THEMIS*, no. 6 (2003), pp. 16–17.

Notes to Chapter 10

1. See Nicholas Eberstadt and Richard J. Ellings, eds., *Korea's Future and the Great Powers* (Seattle: University of Washington Press, 2001).

2. Thucydides, *History of the Peloponnesian War*, trans. Rex Warner (New York: Penguin Books, 1982), p. 402.

3. Samuel S. Kim, "North Korea in 1994: Brinkmanship, Breakdown and Breakthrough," *Asian Survey* 35, no. 1 (January 1995), pp. 13–27.

4. On power transitions, see Robert Gilpin, *War and Change in World Politics* (Cambridge: Cambridge University Press, 1981); A.F.K. Organski, *World Politics* (New York: Knopf, 1968), ch. 14; Joshua Goldstein, *Long Cycles: Prosperity and War in the Modern Age* (New Haven: Yale University Press, 1988); George Modelski, "The Long Cycle of Global Politics and the Nation-State," *Comparative Studies in Society and History* 20 (April 1978), pp. 214–35; William Thompson, *On Global War: Historical–Structural Approaches to World Politics* (Columbia: University of South Carolina, 1988); Paul Kennedy, *The Rise and Fall of the Great Powers: Economic Change and Military Conflict from 1500 to 2000* (New York: Random House, 1987); and Charles Kupchan, *The Vulnerability of Empire* (Ithaca: Cornell University Press, 1994).

5. For realist analyses along this line with some variations, see Richard K. Betts, "Wealth, Power, and Instability: East Asia and the United States after the Cold War," *International Security* 18, no. 3 (Winter 1993/94), pp. 34–77; Aaron L. Friedberg, "Ripe for Rivalry: Prospects for Peace in a Multipolar Asia," *International Security* 18, no. 3 (Winter 1993/94), pp. 5–33; idem, "Will Europe's Past Be Asia's Future?" *Survival* 42, no. 3 (Autumn 2000), pp. 147–59; and Barry Buzan and Gerald Segal, "Rethinking East Asian Security," *Survival* 36, no. 2 (Summer 1994), pp. 3–21.

6. According to Gen. Gary Luck, former Commander of U.S. Forces Korea, another Korean war would cost $1 trillion in economic damage and a million human casualties, including 52,000 U.S. military casualties; cited in Victor D. Cha and David C. Kang, "The Korea Crisis," *Foreign Policy* (May/June 2003), p. 24.

7. See Samuel S. Kim, "China's Path to Great Power Status in the Globalization Era," *Asian Perspective* 27, no. 1 (March 2003), pp. 35–75.

8. For further discussion in the context of South Korea and East Asia, see Samuel S. Kim, ed., *Korea's Globalization* (New York: Cambridge University Press, 2000) and *East Asia and Globalization* (Lanham, MD: Rowman & Littlefield, 2000).

9. For a full English text, see Yonhap News Agency, March 9, 2000.

10. To call this return visit a "promise" is a stretch. The Joint Declaration merely states that Chairman Kim Jong Il would visit Seoul "at an appropriate time." In other words, Kim Jong Il will decide what constitutes "an appropriate time" without violating the letter, if not the spirit, of the Joint Declaration.

11. For a full elaboration of such a synthetic theory of national identity, see Lowell Dittmer and Samuel S. Kim, "In Search of a Theory of National Identity," in *China's Quest for National Identity*, ed. Dittmer and Kim (Ithaca: Cornell University Press, 1993), pp. 1–31.

12. William Bloom, *Personal Identity, National Identity and International Relations* (New York: Cambridge University Press, 1990); Dittmer and Kim, *China's Quest for National Identity*; Peter Katzenstein, ed., *The Culture of National Security: Norms and Identity in World Politics* (New York: Columbia University Press, 1996); Jill Krause and Neil Renwick, eds., *Identities in International Relations* (New York: St. Martin's Press, 1996); Yosef Lapid and Friedrich Kratochwil, eds., *The Return of Culture and Identity in IR Theory* (Boulder, CO: Rienner, 1996); Ilya Prizel, *National Identity and Foreign Policy: Nationalism and Leadership in Poland, Russia and Ukraine* (New York: Cambridge University Press,

1998); Rodney Bruce Hall, *National Collective Identity: Social Constructs and International Systems* (New York: Columbia University Press, 1999); Alexander Wendt, *Social Theory of International Politics* (New York: Cambridge University Press, 1999); and Samuel Huntington, *The Clash of Civilizations and the Remaking of World Order* (New York: Simon and Schuster, 1996).

13. See Katzenstein, *The Culture of National Security*; Ted Hopf, "The Promise of Constructivism in International Relations Theory," *International Security* 23 (1998), pp. 171–200; Paul Kowert, "National Identity: Inside and Out," *Security Studies* 8 (1999), pp. 1–34; and Michael C. Desch, "Culture Clash: Assessing the Importance of Ideas in Security Studies," *International Security* 23 (1998), pp. 141–70.

14. For a detailed discussion, see Samuel S. Kim, "The Making of China's Korea Policy in the Era of Reform," in *The Making of Chinese Foreign and Security Policy in the Era of Reform, 1978–2000*, ed. David M. Lampton (Stanford: Stanford University Press, 2001), pp. 371–408.

15. Samuel S. Kim, "China as a Regional Power," *Current History* 91, no. 566 (September 1992), pp. 247–52.

16. You Ji, "China and North Korea: A Fragile Relationship of Strategic Convenience," *Journal of Contemporary China* 10, no. 28 (August 2001), p. 391.

17. Cai Jianwei, ed., *Zhongguo da zhanlue: lingdao shijie da lantu* [China's Grand Strategy: A Blueprint for World Leadership] (Haikou: Hainan chubanshe, 1996), p. 200.

18. See Zong Hairen (pseudonym), "Hu Jintao Writes to Kim Jong-il to Open Door to Six-Party Talks," *Hong Kong Hsin Pao*, August 28, 2003, translated in Foreign Broadcast Information Service, CHI-2003-0828, August 29, 2003.

19. Ronald Grigor, "Provisional Stabilities: The Politics of Identities in Post-Soviet Eurasia," *International Security* 24, no. 3 (Winter 1999–2000), p. 149.

20. Elizabeth Wishnick, "Russian–North Korean Relations: A New Era?" in *North Korea and Northeast Asia*, ed. Samuel S. Kim and Tai Hwan Lee (Lanham, MD: Rowman & Littlefield, 2002), pp. 139–62.

21. For an English text of the Moscow Declaration, see Korean Central News Agency, August 4, 2001 (available at www.kcna.co.jp/contents/archives).

22. See Masaru Tamamoto, "Japan's Uncertain Role," *World Policy Journal* 8 (Fall 1991), pp. 584–85.

23. See Michael H. Armacost and Kenneth B. Pyle, "Japan and the Unification of Korea: Challenges for U.S. Policy Coordination," in *Korea's Future and the Great Powers*, ed. Nicholas Eberstadt and Richard J. Ellings (Seattle: University of Washington Press, 2001), p. 128.

24. Joseph S. Nye Jr., "East Asian Security: The Case for Deep Engagement," *Foreign Affairs* 74, no. 4 (July/August 1995), p. 98. The conceptual foundation of the report may be found in the antidecline thesis expounded in idem, *Bound to Lead: The Changing Nature of American Power* (New York: Basic Books, 1990).

25. See "Review of United States Policy Toward North Korea: Findings and Recommendations," unclassified report by Dr. William J. Perry, U.S. North Korea policy coordinator and special adviser to the president and the secretary of state, Washington, DC, October 12, 1999 (available at www.state.gov/www/regions/eap/991012_northkorea_rpt.html, accessed February 21, 2005).

26. North Korea Advisory Group (Representative Benjamin A Gilman, chair), "Report to the Speaker of the House of Representatives," November 1999 (available at www.fas.org/nuke/guide/dprk/nkag-report.htm, accessed February 21, 2005).

27. Robert Manning, "United States–North Korean Relations: From Welfare to Workfare?" in Kim and Lee, *North Korea and Northeast Asia*, pp. 61–88.

28. Ashton B. Carter and William J. Perry, *Preventive Defense: A New Security Strategy*

for America (Washington, DC: Brookings Institution Press, 1999), pp. 123–24. A footnote for this statement explains that Ashton Carter was not present for the meeting referred to here, so Perry "tells this story himself" (p. 123).

29. U.S. Department of Defense, *Quadrennial Defense Review Report*, September 30, 2001 (available at www.defenselink.mil/pubs/qdr2001.pdf, accessed February 21, 2005).

30. Selig Harrison, *Korean Endgame: A Strategy for Reunification and U.S. Disengagement* (Princeton: Princeton University Press, 2002), p. 102.

31. See Lee Young-sun, "Is Korean Reunification Possible?" *Korea Focus* 3, no. 3 (May–June 1995), p. 13; and Park Young-ho, "International Perceptions of Korean Unification Issues," *Korea Focus* 6, no. 1 (January–February 1998), pp. 72–80.

32. The classical exposition of such a functional approach to a working peace system is David Mitrany, *A Working Peace System* (Chicago: Quadrangle 1966 [1943]).

Notes to Chapter 11

1. Tsuneo Akaha, "Japan's Policy Toward North Korea: Interests and Options," in *The Future of North Korea*, ed. Akaha (London: Routledge, 2002), pp. 77–94.

2. Tsuneo Akaha, "Beyond Self-Defense: Japan's Elusive Security Role under the New Guidelines for US-Japan Defense Cooperation," *Pacific Review* 11, no. 4 (Fall 1998), pp. 461–83.

3. Tsuneo Akaha, "Japan's Policy Toward North Korea."

4. Gilbert Rozman, "Japan's North Korea Initiative and U.S.-Japanese Relations," *Orbis* (Summer 2003), p. 538.

5. Murayama Tomiichi, "Beyond My Visit to Pyongyang," *Japan Quarterly* 47 (April–June 2000), pp. 3–10.

6. "N. Korea Says It Refused Japan Normalization Plan," Reuters, Tokyo, December 1, 2000; cited in *Nautilus Daily Report*, December 2, 2000.

7. A provisional English translation of the joint declaration is available from the Japanese Foreign Ministry's at www.mofa.go.jp/region/asia-paci/n_korea/pmv0209/pyongyang.html (accessed February 21, 2005).

8. Japanese Foreign Ministry, www.mofa.go.jp/mofaj/kaidan/s_koi/n_ korea_02/sengen.html (accessed September 18, 2002).

9. Takesada Hideji, "Kitachosen no senryaku kara mita Nitcho shunokaidan no igi" [The Significance of the Japan–North Korea Summit from the Perspective of North Korean Strategy], in *Kitachosen o meguru hokutoajia no kokusai kankei to Nihon* [International Relations in Northeast Asia Regarding North Korea, and Japan], ed. Hirama Yoichi and Sugita Yoneyuki (Tokyo: Akashi shoten, 2003), p. 35.

10. Junko Takahashi, "Tokyo Hopes for Another Meeting," *Japan Times*, August 30, 2003 (available at www.JapanTimes.com/cgi-bin/getarticle.pl5?nn20030830a7.htm, accessed February 21, 2005).

11. Masao Okonogi, "Nitcho Shunokaidan no Seika to Tenbo" [The Results of the Japan–North Korea Summit and Prospects], in *Tohokuajia Jidai eno Teigen: Senso no Kiki kara Heiwa Kochiku e* [Proposal for the Era of Northeast Asia: From Crisis of War to Construction of Peace], ed. Kinhide Mushakoji, Suh Sung, Shuji Matsuno, and Xia Gang (Tokyo: Heibonsha, 2003), pp. 47–48.

12. Wada Haruki, *Hokutoajia kyodo no ie* [A Northeast Asian Common House] (Tokyo: Heibonsha, 2003), p. 166.

13. Kan Sang-jung, *Nitcho-kankei no kokufuku: naze kokko seijoka kosho ga hitsuyo nanoka* [Overcoming Japan-North Korea Relations: Why Are Diplomatic Normalization Talks Necessary?] (Tokyo: Shueisha, 2003), pp. 176–181.

14. Takesada, "Kitachosen no senryaku kara mita Nitcho shunokaidan no igi," p. 35.

15. *Yomiuri shimbun*, August 25, 2003 (available at www.yomiuri.co.jp/politics/news/20030825ia23.htm, accessed August 25, 2003).

16. During his European tour in mid-August, Prime Minister Koizumi obtained the endorsement of German, Polish, and Czech leaders for Japan's call for a package resolution of the nuclear and abduction issues. Japan attached particular importance to these three countries because they all had diplomatic ties with North Korea (*Yomiuri shimbun*, August 22, 2003 [available at www.yomiuri.co.jp/politics/news/20030821ia21.htm, accessed August 23, 2003]).

17. James Brooke and David E. Sanger, "Japan Urges North Korea to Rejoin Disarmament Talks," *New York Times,* February 12, 2005 (available at www.nytimes.com/2005/02/12/international/asia/12korea.htm, accessed February 12, 2005).

18. *Yomiuri shimbun,* February 17, 2005 (available at www.yomiuri.co.jp/politics/news/20050217it13.htm, accessed February 17, 2005).

19. Brooke and Sanger, "Japan Urges North Korea to Rejoin Disarmament Talks."

20. On August 27, 2003, Foreign Minister Junko Kawaguchi stated that Japan should participate in a multilateral agreement on nonaggression, noting that the United States was opposed to a bilateral nonaggression treaty with North Korea (*Sankei shimbun*, August 28, 2003 [available at www.sankei.co.jp/news/030828/morning/28pol002.htm, accessed August 28, 2003]).

21. Author conversation with William Perry, San Francisco, August 18, 2003.

22. Hisahiko Okazaki, "Japan-South Korea Security Cooperation: A View Toward the Future," in *Korea-Japan Security Relations: Prescriptive Studies*, ed. Sang-woo Rhee and Tae-hyo Kim (Seoul: New Asia Research Institute, 2002), pp. 89–97; Victor Cha, "The Positive and Preventive Rationales for Korea-Japan Security Cooperation: The American Perspective," in Rhee and Kim, *Korea-Japan Security Relations*, pp. 99–122. These observers also discuss constraints on Japanese–South Korean defense ties.

23. Cha, "Positive and Preventive Rationales," p. 103.

24. Quoted in Hideshi Takesada, "Korea-Japan Defense Cooperation: Prospects and Issues," in Rhee and Kim, *Korea-Japan Security Relations*, p. 126.

25. Ralph Cossa, ed., *U.S.-Korea-Japan Relations: Building toward a Virtual Alliance* (Washington, DC: Center for Strategic and International Studies, 1999).

26. See, for example, Okazaki, "Japan-South Korea Security Cooperation," p. 93; Cha, "Positive and Preventive Rationales," p. 103.

27. See Jason U. Manosevitz, "Japan and South Korea: Security Relations Reach Adolescence," *Asian Survey* 18, no. 5 (September 2003), pp. 801–25.

28. Another twentieth-century legacy of Japan yet to be brought to a peaceful conclusion is the dispute with Russia over the Northern Territories (southern Kuriles).

Notes to Chapter 12

The author thanks the four editors for useful comments and Sheena Chestnut for research assistance.

1. The inclusion of North Korea in President George W. Bush's "axis of evil" in January 2002, though portrayed extremely negatively, has nevertheless elevated the status of North Korea in world affairs.

2. The official designation of Sino–South Korean relations was upgraded from a "cooperative partnership" forged in 1998 to a *"comprehensive* cooperative partnership" (*quanmian hezuoxing huoban guanxi*) during Premier Zhu Rongji's visit to Seoul in 2000. The new designation was officially ratified during President Roh Moo Hyun's state visit to China in July 2003. According to Chinese sources, *"comprehensive* cooperative partner-

ship" is considered the second best designation—only after the "traditionally amicable ties" (*chuantong youhao guanxi*)—accorded by Beijing. See Zhang Jianhua, ed., *Jiejue zhongguo zaidu mianlin de jinyao wenti* [On the Resolution of the Urgent Problems China Has Faced Again] (Beijing: Jingji ribao chubanshe, 2000), pp. 523–25.

3. For Seoul's hedging, see Jae Ho Chung, "The Korean-American Alliance and the "Rise of China": A Preliminary Assessment of Perceptual Changes and Strategic Choices," Occasional Papers, Asia/Pacific Research Center, Stanford University, February 1999 (available at http://aparc.stanford.edu/publications, accessed February 21, 2005); and Jae Ho Chung, "South Korea Between Eagle and Dragon: Perceptual Ambivalence and Strategic Dilemma," *Asian Survey* 41, no. 5 (September–October 2001), pp. 778–79. On the other hand, Alastair I. Johnston, and Robert S. Ross have characterized Seoul as shying away from hedging between Washington and China. For their point, see "Conclusion," in *Engaging China: The Management of an Emerging Power*, ed. Johnston and Ross (London: Routledge, 1999), p. 288.

4. See Kurt M. Campbell and Mitchell B. Reiss, "Korean Changes, Asian Challenges and the U.S. Role," *Survival* 43, no. 1 (Spring 2001), pp. 59–60, 63.

5. Zbigniew Brzezinski, Lee Hamilton, and Richard Lugar, *Foreign Policy into the 21st Century: The United States Leadership Challenge* (Washington, DC: Center for Strategic and International Studies, 1996), p. 49. See also Eric A. McVadon, "China's Goals and Strategies for the Korean Peninsula," in *Planning for a Peaceful Korea*, ed. Henry D. Sokolski (Carlisle, PA: Strategic Studies Institute, February 2001), pp. 149, 169.

6. While China denies any aspiration to become a hegemon, it is nevertheless willing to assign itself a "great-power" (*daguo*) status. See Ye Zicheng, "Zhongguo shixing daguo waijiao zhanlue shi zai bixing" [It Is Inevitable That China Perform Great-Power Diplomacy], *Shijie jingji yu zhengzhi*, no. 1 (2000), pp. 10–11; and Yongjin Zhang and Greg Austin, *Power and Responsibility in Chinese Foreign Policy* (Canberra: Asia Pacific Press, 2001).

7. See Huang Zunxian, *Chaoxian celue* [The Strategy for Korea] (Seoul: Kunkook University Press, 1977), p. 47.

8. China's bombardments of Quemoy and Matsu in 1954–55 and 1958, as well as sporadic crossfire along the demilitarized zone on the Korean peninsula, are examples of such conflictual atmosphere.

9. See David A. Baldwin, "Neoliberalism, Neorealism, and World Politics," in *Neorealism and Neoliberalism: The Contemporary Debate*, ed. Baldwin (New York: Columbia University Press, 1993), pp. 3–25.

10. Debates continue unabated as to whether such perceptions are real or mere myths. The bottom line, however, is that Chinese policy makers seem to have acted on what is called "siege mentality." See Fei-Ling Wang, "Self-Image and Strategic Intentions: National Confidence and Political Insecurity," in *In the Eyes of the Dragon: China Views the World*, ed. Yong Deng and Fei-Ling Wang (Lanham, MD: Rowman and Littlefield, 1999), pp. 21–46.

11. China's failed effort to maintain quasi-neutrality between the Soviet Union and the United States during 1946–47 is a good illustration of the powerful systemic constraints.

12. See Chae-Jin Lee, *China and Korea: Dynamic Relations* (Stanford, CA: Hoover Institution Press, 1996), pp. 10–21; Zhihua Shen, "China Sends Troops to Korea: Beijing's Policy-Making Process," in *China and the United States: A New Cold War History*, ed. Xiaobing Li and Hongshan Li (Lanham, MD: University Press of America, 1998), pp. 13–47; and Xiaobing Li, Allan R. Millet, and Bin Yu, eds., *Mao's Generals Remember Korea* (Lawrence: University Press of Kansas, 2001).

13. The same can be said of the Seoul-Taipei-Pyongyang triangle although there is no evidence that the relationship as such was viewed at the time as a triangle. For the concept of "strategic triangle," see Lowell Dittmer, "The Strategic Triangle: An Elementary Game-Theoretical Analysis," *World Politics* 33, no. 4 (July 1981), p. 489.

14. The Chinese term for its foreign policy stance during this period was "leaning to one side" (*yibiandao*), referring to aligning unconditionally with the Soviet Union for its socialist leadership. The South Korean catchphrase at the time was "anti-Communist reunification" (*ban'gong tong'il*).

15. Joseph Camilleri, *Chinese Foreign Policy: The Maoist Era and Its Aftermath* (Oxford: Martin Robertson, 1980), ch. 5.

16. See Shi Yuanhua, "Lun xinzhongguo zhoubian waijiao zhengce de lishi yanbian" [The Evolution of China's Foreign Policy Toward Its Periphery], *Dangdai zhongguoshi yanjiu*, no. 5 (2000), pp. 38–50.

17. Except for 1967–69, when the radicalization of ideology reached its zenith, North Korea generally maintained a more amicable relationship with China than with the Soviet Union. See Liu Jinzhi, Zhang Minqiu, and Zhang Xiaoming, *Dangdai zhonghan guanxi* [Contemporary Sino-Korean Relations] (Beijing: Zhongguo shehuikexue chubanshe, 1998), pp. 41–44.

18. For North Korea's ideological emulation, see Glenn D. Paige, "North Korea and the Emulation of Russian and Chinese Behavior," in *Communist Strategies in Asia*, ed. A. Doak Barnett (New York: Praeger, 1963), pp. 228–62; and Yang Ho-min, "Mao Zedong's Ideological Influence on Pyongyang and Hanoi: Some Historical Roots Reconsidered," in *Asian Communism: Continuity and Transition*, ed. Robert A. Scalapino and Dalchoong Kim (Berkeley: Institute of East Asian Studies, University of California, 1988), pp. 37–66.

19. See Chin O. Chung, *Pyongyang Between Peking and Moscow: North Korea's Involvement in the Sino-Soviet Dispute, 1958–1975* (Birmingham: University of Alabama Press, 1978).

20. See Lee Sang-Ok, *Jonhwan'gi eui hangook woegyo* [Korea's Diplomacy in an Era of Transition] (Seoul: Life and Dream, 2003), p. 184.

21. Jae Ho Chung, "South Korea–China Economic Cooperation: The Current Situation and Its Implications," *Asian Survey* 28, no. 10 (October 1988), p. 1036.

22. See Nancy Bernkopf Tucker, *Taiwan, Hong Kong, and the United States, 1945–1992* (New York: Twayne, 1994), ch. 7; and James Mann, *About Face: A History of America's Curious Relationship with China, from Nixon to Clinton* (New York: Knopf, 1999), ch. 2.

23. Parris H. Chang, "Beijing's Policy Toward Korea and PRC-ROK Normalization of Relations," in *The Changing Order in Northeast Asia and the Korean Peninsula* (Seoul: Institute for Far Eastern Studies, 1993), p. 163, cited in Lee, *China and Korea*, p. 68.

24. See Robert S. Ross, *Negotiating Cooperation: The United States and China 1969–1989* (Stanford: Stanford University Press, 1995), ch. 3.

25. See Tai Sung An, *North Korea: A Political Handbook* (Wilmington, DE: Scholarly Resources, 1983), pp. 79, 85–87.

26. National Unification Board, ed., *Bukhan pyonlam* [Survey of North Korea] (Seoul, 1984), pp. 129–31.

27. See Lee, *China and Korea*, p. 105.

28. See Lee Beom-chan, "Hanso kyoryu hyonhwanggwa hwakdae bang-an" [The Current Situation of South Korean-Soviet Bilateralism and the Measures for Expansion], *Kongsangwon yongu* (May 1987), p. 15.

29. See Chi-jeong Park, "Han-junggong min'gan gyoryu hwakdae bang'an" [Measures to Expand Nongovernmental Exchanges Between South Korea and China], *Jungguk yongu* 5 (1986), p. 44; and Ilpyong J. Kim, "Policies Toward China and the Soviet Union," in *The Foreign Policy of the Republic of Korea*, ed. Youngnok Koo and Sung-joo Han (New York: Columbia University Press, 1985), pp. 202–3, 209–10.

30. See Lee, "Hanso kyoryu hyonhwanggwa hwakdae bang'an," p. 15; and Kim Young-moon, "Choegun jungso-ui daehan jongchaek" [Recent Policies of China and the Soviet Union Toward Korea], *Tongil munje yongu* 11 (April 1984), p. 36 (originally quoted in *Nepszabadsag*, December 29, 1978).

31. As one analyst points out, "[T]he economic success of East Asia derived from its open economic policy has influenced many nations to rethink how they ought to go about achieving economic development. . . . Nowhere is the resulting change in thinking more apparent than in China." See Dwight H. Perkins, *China: Asia's Next Economic Giant?* (Seattle and London: University of Washington Press, 1986), pp. 5–6.

32. Author's interview with a scholar from the CASS. A Korean source suggests that Liu Guoguang, an influential economist with political clout, paid a visit to Seoul in 1980, but this could not be independently substantiated. See Lee Ho, *Han jung so gan eui bukbang woegyo silche* [The Real Story of Korea's Diplomacy with China and the Soviet Union] (Seoul: Cheil Media, 1997), pp. 193–94.

33. See Chung, "Junggong eui daehan insik," p. 79; and Shin Myung-soon, "Hangukgwa junggong eui gwangye gaeson e gwanhan yongu" [Study on How to Improve Korea's Relations with Communist China], *Hanguk gwa gukje jongchi* 1, no. 1 (January 1985), p. 59.

34. For the "trading world" as an alternative to the "military world," see Richard Rosecrance, *The Rise of the Trading State: Commerce and Conquest in the Modern World* (New York: Basic Books, 1986).

35. For China's hypersensitivity to sovereignty, see Peter Van Ness, "China and the Third World," in *China and the World: Chinese Foreign Policy Faces the New Millennium*, ed. Samuel S. Kim (Boulder, CO: Westview, 1998), pp. 158–59; and Hongying Wang, "Multilateralism in Chinese Foreign Policy: The Limits of Socialization," *Asian Survey* 40, no. 3 (May/June 2000), p. 486.

36. The quote is from Carol Lee Hamrin, "China Reassesses the Superpowers," *Pacific Affairs* 56, no. 2 (Summer 1983), pp. 210, 212. For the centrality of the 1982 turnaround, see Tucker, *Taiwan, Hong Kong and the United States,* ch. 7–8, and Jia Qingguo and Tang Wei, *Lashou de hezuo—zhongmei guanxi de xianzhuang yu qianjing* [Intricate Cooperation: The Current Situation of Chinese-U.S. Relations and Prospects] (Beijing: Wenhua yishu chubanshe, 1998), pp. 22–23.

37. See Wang Xuhe and Ren Xiangqun, *Guo zhi zun—xin zhongguo waijiao jishi* [The Prestige of China: Chronicles of New China's Diplomacy] (Hangzhou: Zhejiang renmin chubanshe, 1999), ch. 5; and Wang Taiping, *Xinzhongguo waijiao wushinian* [Fifty Years of New China's Foreign Relations] (Beijing: Beijing renmin chubanshe, 1999), vol. 1, pp. 33–37.

38. On this line of argument, see Samuel S. Kim, "China and the Third World: In Search of a Neorealist World Policy," in Kim, *China and the World*, pp. 189–205; and Zhu Hongqian, "China and the Triangular Relationship," in *The Chinese View of the World*, ed. Hao Yufan and Huan Guocang (New York: Pantheon Books, 1989), pp. 42–43.

39. See, for instance, Jonathan Goldstein, ed., *China and Israel 1948–1998: A Fifty-Year Perspective* (Westport, CT: Praeger, 1999); and Rizal Sukma, *Indonesia and China: The Politics of a Troubled Relationship* (London: Routledge, 1999).

40. According to this author's counting of the articles in *Shijie zhishi* published by China's Ministry of Foreign Affairs between 1979 and 1991, among the thirty-seven articles concerning the Korean peninsula, nine were on reunification and twenty (seven for 1979–85 and thirteen for 1986–91) were on South Korea, while only eight (seven in 1979–85 and one in 1986–91) were devoted to China's long-time ally, North Korea.

41. See Wu Linggeng, "Yazhou sixiaolong jingji qiji puoxi" [Analyzing the Economic Miracle by Asia's Four "Little Dragons"], *Hongqi* (April 1987), pp. 29–32; and Pu Zhengluo, Wang Rui, and Cong Ronglian, *Yazhou sixiaolong yu waixiangxing jingji* [Asia's Four Little Dragons and Their Outward-Oriented Economies] (Beijing: Zhongguo duiwai jingji maoyi chubanshe, 1990).

42. See Bruce Cummings, "The Political Economy of China's Turn Outward," in Kim, *China and the World*, pp. 246–47.

43. Hwang Byung-Tae, "Hanjung gyungje sum'eun juyok eun deungsopyong adeul"

[Deng Xiaoping's Son Is the Hidden Hand Behind South Korea-China Economic Cooperation], *Shindong-a* (March 1996), p. 471.

44. Charles Lipson, "International Cooperation in Economic and Security Affairs," *World Politics* 37, no. 1 (October 1984), pp. 1–23.

45. See Robert Kleinberg, *China's "Opening" to the Outside World: The Experiment with Foreign Capitalism* (Boulder, CO: Westview, 1990); and Yang Jisheng, *Deng Xiaoping shidai—zhongguo gaige kaifang ershinian jishe* [The Era of Deng Xiaoping: Chronicles of Twenty Years of Reform and Opening] (Beijing: Zhongyang bianyi chubanshe, 1998), vol. 1, ch. 3.

46. See Eul Yong Park, "Foreign Economic Policies and Economic Development," in Koo and Han, eds., *The Foreign Policy of the Republic of Korea,* pp. 125–27.

47. See Chung, "South Korea-China Economic Cooperation," p. 1047.

48. See Hao Yufan, "China and the Korean Peninsula," in Hao and Huan, eds., *The Chinese View of the World,* p. 198.

49. During 1979–91, China scored a total trade surplus of US$3.265 billion with South Korea, while that of South Korea was only US$711 million.

50. For China's occasional act of giving North Korea some face, see Qi Xin, "Cong jieji shijian kan zhonghan guanxi" [Chinese–South Korean Relations Seen in Light of the Hijacking Incident], *Qishi niandai* (June 1983), p. 55.

51. See Jae Ho Chung, "Sino–South Korean Economic Cooperation: An Analysis of Domestic and Foreign Entanglements," *Journal of Northeast Asian Studies* 9, no. 2 (1990), pp. 73–74.

52. See *Joong-ang Ilbo*, May 26, 1987, and *New York Times*, November 22, 1987.

53. This was suggested in Chae-jin Lee, "China's Policy Toward North Korea: Changing Relations in the 1980s," in *North Korea in a Regional and Global Context*, ed. Robert A. Scalapino and Hongkoo Lee (Berkeley: University of California Press, 1986), pp. 180–225, esp. p. 205.

54. Gu Weiqun, "Security in the Asian-Pacific Region," in Hao and Huan, *Chinese View of the World*, pp. 25–26. See also Jianwei Wang and Xinbo Wu, "Against Us or With Us: The Chinese Perspective of America's Alliances with Japan and Korea," Discussion Papers, Asia/Pacific Research Center (May 1998), pp. 34–35.

55. A "romantic triangle" refers to a relationship of amity between one pivotal player (China) and two "wing" players and enmity between the latter. See Hong Yung Lee, "The Emerging Triangle among China and Two Koreas," in *Korea and the World: Beyond the Cold War*, ed. Young Whan Kihl (Boulder, CO: Westview, 1994), pp. 97–110.

56. For a Chinese account that defines China-North Korean relations as "special," see Liu, Zhang, and Zhang, *Dangdai zhonghan guanxi*, p. 103.

57. For details of the politics of normalization, see Jae Ho Chung, *Between Ally and Partner: South Korea-China Relations and the United States* (forthcoming), ch. 6.

58. In 2004, South Korea's total cumulative investment in the United States of US$17.1 billion was overtaken by that in China, with US$17.9 billion. China is the largest recipient of South Korea's overseas investment while South Korea is the seventh-largest destination for China's outbound investment.

59. See *Hankyoreh sinmun*, June 8, 2000; *Munwha ilbo*, September 3, 2001; and *Zhongguo jingji shibao*, June 14, 2000. On the "garlic war," see Jae Ho Chung, "How China Responds to Trade Sanctions: Decoding the Sino–South Korean 'Garlic War,'" in *China and Globalization: An IPE Approach*, ed. David Zweig and Chen Zhimin (London: RoutledgeCurzon, 2006), ch. 8.

60. On such concerns, see Nan Liming, "Hanguo dui zhongguo de wenhua kangyi" [South Korea's Cultural Objection to China], *Yazhou zhoukan* (Asia Weekly), July 25, 2004, pp. 16–17; *Dong-a Ilbo*, December 3, 2003, August 25 and December 25, 2004; *Joong-ang Ilbo*, December 4, 2003; and *Washington Post*, September 23, 2004. On the goals of the

Northeast Project, see Ma Dazheng, ed., *Zhongguo dongbei bianjiang yanjiu* [Study of China's Northeastern Border Areas] (Beijing: Zhongguo shehuikexue chubanshe, 2003).

61. A Chinese official's comment is interesting in this regard: "[E]ven a thin lip (North Korea) could still be better than nothing in protecting one's teeth (China)." For a Western analysis that characterizes North Korea as China's "lipstick," see Andrew Scobell, "China and North Korea: The Limits of Influence," *Current History* (September 2003), p. 278.

62. See, for instance, Chae-Jin Lee and Stephanie Hsieh, "China's Two-Korea Policy at Trial: The Hwang Chang Yop Crisis," *Pacific Affairs* 74, no. 3 (Fall 2001), pp. 321–41.

63. The ideal situation—better than ménage à trois—would be one where the levels of cooperation and cultural internalization are to be maximized among all three states, although the latter would be much more difficult to attain. See Alexander Wendt, *Social Theory of International Politics* (Cambridge: Cambridge University Press, 1999), pp. 254–55.

64. See Gerald Segal, "Northeast Asia: Common Security or à la Carte?" *International Affairs* 67, no. 4 (1991), pp. 756, 763; Patrick M. Cronin, "Pacific Rim Security: Beyond Bilateralism?" *Pacific Review* 5, no. 3 (1992), p. 211; and Gilbert Rozman, *Northeast Asia's Stunted Regionalism* (Cambridge: Cambridge University Press, 2004).

65. For a chart on country membership in Northeast Asian multilateral forums, see Samuel S. Kim, "North Korea and Northeast Asia in World Politics," in *North Korea and Northeast Asia*, ed. Kim and Tai Hwan Lee (Lanham, MD: Rowman and Littlefield, 2002), p. 14.

66. Edward A. Olsen, "Korean Security: Is Japan's Comprehensive Security Model a Viable Alternative?" in *The U.S.-Korean Alliance: Time for A Change*, ed. Doug Bandow and Ted Galen Carpenter (New Brunswick, NJ: Transaction, 1992), pp. 146, 148. One key goal of South Korea's *nordpolitik* was to "expand the horizons of South Korea's foreign policy, which were hitherto limited to the countries like the United States and Japan." See the Ministry of Information, "Great Strides Made during the First Five Years of the Roh Tae Woo Presidency," *Backgrounder*, no. 94 (February 8, 1992), p. 10.

67. See Jae Ho Chung, "China's Ascendancy and the Korean Peninsula: From Re-evaluation to Re-alignment?" in *Power Shift: China and Asia's New Dynamics*, ed. David Shambaugh (Berkeley: University of California Press, 2005).

68. See Li Qiang, "Chaoxian bandao wenti sifang huitan de xianzhuang yu qianjing" [The Current Situation of and Prospects for the Four-Party Talks over the Korean Problem], *Dangdai yatai*, no. 3 (1999), pp. 33–37; and Chen Fengjun and Wang Chuanzhao, *Yatai daguo yu chaoxian bandao* [Great Powers of the Asia-Pacific and the Korean Peninsula] (Beijing: Beijing daxue chubanshe, 2002), pp. 340–47.

69. See *International Herald Tribune*, January 10, 2003; and *New York Times*, February 13, 2003.

70. *The Defense White Paper*, published annually by South Korea's Ministry of National Defense, generally devotes four to five pages to briefly outlining China's military modernization and intermilitary exchanges. No trace of security concern is evident.

71. *Choson Ilbo*, January 5, 2003.

72. See Chung, "South Korea Between Eagle and Dragon," pp. 783–85.

73. While South Koreans have demonstrated realist mind-sets, relative-gains diplomacy, and reactive nationalism toward the United States, this has been much less true of their dealings with China. This crucial disparity remains to be explained. For the above three characteristics, see Victor Cha, "The Security Domain of South Korea's Globalization," in *Korea's Globalization*, ed. Samuel S. Kim (Cambridge: Cambridge University Press, 2000), pp. 236–40.

74. See *1995 Sejong Survey* (Seoul: Sejong Institute, 1995), p. 78; *1997 Sejong Survey* (Seoul: Sejong Institute, 1997), p. 11.

75. *Hanguk, Jungguk, Ilbon gungmin uisik josa baekso* [White Paper on the National Consciousness Survey in Korea, China and Japan] (Seoul: Korea Broadcasting System and Yonsei University, December 1996), pp. 431, 436.

76. See, for instance, Seymour Martin Lipset, *American Exceptionalism: A Double-Edged Sword* (New York: Norton, 1996), ch, 7.

77. See William Watts, *Americans Look at Asia* (Washington, DC: Asia Society Washington Center, 1999), p. 42.

78. See *1997 Sejong Survey*, p. 12; and *Dong-a Ilbo*, December 5, 2000.

79. See Jae Ho Chung, "How America Views South Korea–China Bilateralism" (available atwww.brookings.edu/fp/cnaps/papers/chung2003.htm). The list of fifth-six interviewees has also been appended.

80. America's unilateral dominance in the postcollapse crisis management, however, may seed some great-power rivalry, thus reducing the prospect of genuine reunification. The most popular (38%) choice of the American elite interviewed by the author during 2002–3 was to send in UN forces for crisis management.

81. Jonathan D. Pollack and Young Koo Cha, *A New Alliance for the Next Century: The Future of U.S.-Korean Security Cooperation* (Santa Monica: RAND, 1995); and *Alliance Diversification and the Future of the U.S.-Korean Security Relationship*, ed. Charles Perry, Jacquelyn K. Davies, James L. Schoff, and Toshi Yoshihara (Dulles, VA: Brassey's, 2004).

82. The regional manifestation of "China's rise," however, may come much earlier than its global impact.

83. Not making choices prematurely refers to enhancing the transparency on the knowns and maintaining strategic ambiguity on the unknowns. This posits future South Korean–Chinese relations as an evolutionary learning process. See Samuel S. Kim, "The Making of China's Korea Policy in the Era of Reform," in *The Making of Chinese Foreign and Security Policy*, ed. David M. Lampton (Berkeley: University of California Press, 2001), pp. 373–404.

84. Russia's reaction is also a variable, but it seems unlikely for Moscow to side with Pyongyang unconditionally. It will certainly be much less willing than China.

85. Unlike during 1993–94, China has not so much stressed the "limited" nature of its influence over North Korea this time around. In fact, a *Renmin ribao* article boasted that a quarter of North Korea's trade was conducted with China, and that Beijing was well equipped with the potential power to resolve the Korean problem. At the IAEA's Board of Governors meeting, China voted in favor of putting the North Korean issue on the discussion agenda for the UN Security Council (January 20 and 21, 2003, available at, www.peopledaily.com.cn/other/archjive.html).

86. Despite China's more forthcoming position on the North Korean problem—including the three-day suspension of oil supply to North Korea—how far Beijing will go to jeopardize its relationship with Pyongyang is difficult to foresee.

87. Since the sixteenth congress of the Chinese Communist Party in late 2002, China appears to have been making sincere efforts to put relations with the United States on the top of its agenda, even concerning the North Korean conundrum.

88. If we subscribe to a realist forecast, the persistence of anarchy in Northeast Asia would lead to a dangerous possibility. See John J. Mearsheimer, *The Tragedy of Great Power Politics* (New York: Norton, 2001), pp. 396–402.

89. Nicholas Eberstadt and Richard J. Ellings, "Assessing Interests and Objectives," in *Korea's Future and Great Powers*, ed. Eberstadt and Ellings (Seattle and London: University of Washington Press, 2001), pp. 320–40.

Notes to Chapter 13

1. Natalia Bazhanova, *Vneshneekonomicheskie sviazi KNDR* [The Foreign Economic Relations of North Korea] (Moscow: Vostochnaia literatura, 1992).

2. Nikita Khrushchev, *Memuary* [Memoirs] (Moscow: Mezhdunarodnye otnosheniia, 1991), pp. 342–45.

3. *The USSR in Struggle for Peace, International Security, and Disarmament (1946–1977)* (Moscow: Znanie, 1978), pp. 226, 309, 352–53, 374.

4. Georgi Kim, ed., *Situatsiia na Koreiskom poluostrove* [The Situation on the Korean Peninsula] (Moscow: Institut Vostokovedeniia, 1981), pp. 16, 24, 31, 38.

5. Russian State Archive for Contemporary History (RGANI), File 8, List 6, units of storage (u. of s.) 262, pp. 32–33.

6. RGANI, File 8, List 6, u. of s. 119, p. 40.

7. E. Bazhanov, *Kitai i vneshnii mir* [China and the Foreign World] (Moscow: Mezhdunarodnye otnosheniia, 1990), pp. 301–5.

8. *Koreiskaia problema* [The Korean Problem] (Moscow: CC CPSU, August 14–15, 1984).

9. *Materialy 27 siezda KPCC* [Materials of the Twenty-seventh Communist Party Congress] (Moscow: Politizdat´, 1986), pp. 9–11, 19–20.

10. Mikhail Gorbachev, *O glavnykh napravleniiakh vnutrennei i vneshnei politiki* [On the Principal Directions of Domestic and Foreign Policy] (Moscow: Politizdat´, 1989), pp. 4–8.

11. E. Bazhanov, "Light in the Tunnel," *Vestnik,* no. 9 (1991), pp. 12–13.

12. *Pravda,* October 25, 1986.

13. RGANI, File 8, List 9, u. of s. 253, pp. 18–19.

14. RGANI, File 8, List 9, u. of s. 253, pp. 20–22.

15. RGANI, File 8, List 9, u. of s. 309, p. 215.

16. *Pravda,* September 18, 1988, p. 1.

17. *Materialy po seminara mezhdunarodnym problemam* [Materials for a Seminar on International Problems] (Moscow: Mezhdunarodnye otnosheniia, 1988), pp. 302–3.

18. V. Andreev and V. Osipov, "Druzhba i sotrudnichestvo mezhdu narodami SSSR i KNDR" [Friendship and Cooperation between the Nations of the USSR and the DPRK], *Problemy dal'nego vostoka,* no. 4, 1986, pp. 26–27.

19. O. Davidov and V. Mikheev, "Nekotorye aspekty Severokoreiskoi vneshnei politiki v svete mezhdunarodnykh otnoshenii na Dal'nem Vostoke" [Certain Aspects fo North Korean Foreign Policy in Light of International Relations in the Far East], *Problemy dal'nego vostoka,* no. 7, 1987, pp. 18–19.

20. *Za rubezhom,* June 20, 1988, p. 9.

21. RGANI, File 8, List 6, u. of s. 153, p. 80.

22. Bazhanova, *Vneshneekonomicheskie sviazi KNDR,* pp. 10–88.

23. *Pravda,* August 6, 1990, p. 6.

24. RGANI, File 8, List 6, u. of s. 205, p. 162.

25. V. Lobov, "Kto dobivaetsia prevoskhodstva?" [Who Will Prevail?], *Krasnaia zvezda,* July 14, 1988, p. 4.

26. *Pravda,* May 4, 1989, p. 5.

27. RGANI, File 8, List 6, u. of s. 109, pp. 17–18.

28. *Pravda,* December 16, 1990, p. 1.

29. *Komsomol'skaia pravda,* April 28, 1991, p. 3.

30. *Trud,* April 20, 1991, p. 1.

31. Evgeny P. Bazhanov, *Aktual'nye problemy mezhdunarodnykh otnoshenii* [Current Problems of International Relations] (Moscow: Nauchnaia kniga, 2001), vol. 1, p. 207.

32. *Moscow News,* January 2, 1992, p. 4.

33. Evgeny Bazhanov, *Evoliutsiia Rossiiskoi vneshnei politiki v 1990e* [The Evolution of Russian Foreign Policy in the 1990s] (Moscow: Nauchnaia kniga, 1999), pp. 4–6.

34. Evgeny Bazhanov and Natalia Bazhanova, "Russia and Asia in 1992," *Asia Survey* 33, no. 1 (January 1993), pp. 91–109.

35. Anatoly Shutov, ed., *Diplomaticheskii ezhegodnik—1996* [Diplomatic Yearbook: 1996] (Moscow: Nauchnaia kniga, 1996), pp. 12–14.

36. Bazhanov, *Evoliutsiia Rossiiskoi vneshnei politiki,* pp. 8–9.

37. Evgeny Bazhanov and Natasha Bazhanov, "The Evolution of Russian-Korean Relations," *Asia Survey* 34, no. 9 (September 1993), pp. 789–90.

38. Anatoly Torkunov, ed., *Istoriia Korei* [The History of Korea] (Moscow: ROSSPEN, 2003), pp. 390–401.

39. Evgeny Bazhanov, *Prospects of the General Situation in Northeast Asia and the Korean Peninsula* (Moscow, 1997), pp. 11–14.

40. Alexandr Zadokhin, ed., *Uchenye zapiski* [Scholarly Notes] (Moscow: Nauchnaia kniga, 2001), pp. 120–30.

41. Bazhanov and Bazhanov, "Evolution of Russian-Korean Relations," p. 792.

42. Evgeny Bazhanov, "Russia and North Korea," in *KPF on Record* (Seoul: KPF, 1996), pp. 34–41.

43. Ibid., p. 40.

44. Bazhanov, *Aktual′nye problemy mezhdunarodnykh otnoshenii,* vol. 1, pp. 216–19.

45. Ibid., pp. 219–25.

46. *Segodnia,* November 4, 1994, p. 6.

47. Anatoly Torkunov, *Problemy bezopasnosti na Koreiskom poluostrove* [Problems of Security on the Korean Peninsula] (Moscow: ROSSPEN, 1995), pp. 20–21.

48. Evgeny Bazhanov, ed., *Rossiisko-koreiskii otnosheniia* [Russian-Korean Relations] (Moscow: Nauchnaia kniga, 1997), p. 28.

49. *Pravda,* September 6, 1996, p. 6.

50. Vladimir Putin, *Kontseptsiia vneshnei politiki Rossiiskoi Federatsii* [The Concept of Foreign Policy in the Russian Federation] (Moscow: Diplomaticheskii Vestnik, July 2000), pp. 4–16.

51. Ibid., pp. 9–10.

52. Evgeny Bazhanov, *Prioriteti Rossii v meniaiushemsia mire* [Russia's Priorities in the Changing World] (Moscow: Nauchnaia kniga, 2000), pp. 16–18.

53. Igor Ivanov, *Novaia Rossiiskaia diplomatiia* [New Russian Diplomacy] (Moscow: OLMA-PRESS, 2002), pp. 158–59.

54. *Rossiia i mezhkoreiskii otnosheniia* [Russia and Inter-Korean Relations] (Moscow: Fond Gorbacheva, 2003), p. 41.

55. See the views of influential Russian experts on the issue in James Clay Moltz and Alexander Y. Mansurov, eds., *The North Korean Nuclear Program* (New York: Routledge, 2000).

56. Vladimir F. Lee, "Russia's Far East in Contemporary Russia-Korean Relations," in *Politics and Economies in the Russia Far East,* ed. Tsuneo Akaha (New York: Routledge, 1997), pp. 198–207.

57. Yury Fokine and Evgeny Bazhanov, ed., *4ii Rossisko-koreiskie forum* [The Fourth Russian-Korean Forum) (Moscow: Nauchnya Kniga, 2002), pp. 15–19, 23–25.

58. Anatoly Shutov, ed., *Nauchnie zapiski* [Scientific Notes] (Moscow: Nauchnaia kniga, 2003), pp. 20–23.

59. Ibid., p. 24.

60. Ibid., p. 26.

61. Ibid., p. 27.

62. *Diplomaticheskii Vestnik,* July 2000, pp. 62–63.

63. Ibid., pp. 65–66.

64. Evgeny Bazhanov, ed., *Koreiskii faktor* [The Korean Factor] (Moscow: Nauchnaia kniga, 2003), pp. 23–24.

65. *Itogi,* August 2001, pp. 18–19.

66. *Diplomaticheskii Vestnik,* August 2001, pp. 58–59.

67. Ibid., p. 59.

68. *Rossiiskaia gazeta,* May 20, 1999, p. 3.

69. ITAR-TASS, March 1, 2001.

70. Valery Denisov, "Rossiiskaia Federatsiia–Respublika Koreia: partnerstvo prodvigaetsia" [The Russian Federation–Republic of Korea: The Partnership Moves Forward], in *Diplomaticheskii ezhegodnik 2001* [Diplomatic Yearbook 2001], ed. Iurii Fokin (Moscow: Nauchnaia kniga, 2001), pp. 280–85.

71. Bazhanov, *Koreiskii faktor,* pp. 30–31.

72. Ibid., p. 32.

73. Kang Won Sik, *Rossiia i Koreia* [Russia and Korea] (Moscow: Koros, 2002), pp. 205–8.

74. Vladimir Lee, ed., *Povorotnii moment v Koree* [The Turning Point in Korea] (Moscow: Nauchnaia kniga, 2001), pp. 12–14.

75. Foreign Broadcast Information Service, DR/EAS (2000–0918).

76. Lee, *Povorotnii moment v Koree*, pp. 17–18.

77. Ibid., pp. 20–21.

78. Vladimir Miasnikov, *Dogovornymi statiami podtverdili* [The Contractual Articles Are Confirmed] (Moscow: IDV, 1996), pp. 412–13, 418–19.

79. Ludmila Zabrovskaia, *Proekt Tumangan* [Tumen River Project] (Moscow: IDV, 1993), pp. 100–110.

80. Evgeny Bazhanov, *Aktual'nye problemy mezhdunarodnykh otnoshenii* (Moscow: Nauchnaia kniga, 2002), vol. 3, pp. 242–43.

81. *Nezavisimaia gazeta*, July 22, 2003, p. 1.

82. *Kommersant-Daily*, August 29, 2003, p. 1.

83. *Izvestia*, July 24, 2003, p. 3; *Rossiiskaia gazeta*, July 24, 2003, p. 4.

84. Svetlana Dolgopolova, "Kim Chen Ir razigrivaet iadernuiu kartu" [Kim Jong Il Plays the Nuclear Card], *Smysl'*, no. 13 (September 1–15, 2003), p. 8.

85. See the interview with Russia's ambassador to South Korea, *Joonggang Daily,* August 7, 2003, p. 3.

Notes to Chapter 14

1. Joseph Ferguson, "The Diaoyutai-Senkaku Islands Dispute Reawakened," *Asia Media*, February 4, 2004.

2. Gilbert Rozman, "The Northeast Asian Regional Context for Environmentalism: Assessing Environmental Goals against Other Priorities in the 1990s," *Journal of East Asian Studies* 1, no. 2 (August 2001), pp. 13–30.

3. Ken Conca, "Environmental Confidence Building and Regional Security in Northeast Asia," in *Ecological Security in Northeast Asia*, ed. Miranda A. Schreurs and Dennis Pirages (Seoul: Yonsei University Press, 1988), pp. 41–66.

4. Shin-wha Lee, "Environmental Regime-building in Northeast Asia: A Catalyst for Sustainable Regional Cooperation," *Journal of East Asian Studies* 1, no. 2 (August 2001), pp. 31–61.

5. Samuel S. Kim, "Regionalization and Regionalism in East Asia," *Journal of East Asian Studies* 4, no. 2 (August 2004), p. 40.

6. Portions of this section are drawn from Shin-wha Lee, "A New Diplomacy? Environmental Regime-Building in Northeast Asia," in *International Environmental Cooperation Politics and Diplomacy in Pacific Asia*, ed. Paul Harris (Boulder: University of Colorado Press, 2002), pp. 203–20; and Lee, "Environmental Regime-Building in Northeast Asia."

7. Lyuba Zarsky, "The Domain of Environmental Cooperation in Northeast Asia," Nautilus Institute, May 1995 (available at www.nautilus.org/archives/papers/enviro/zarsky_domain.html, accessed March 21, 2004).

8. Garrett Harding, "The Tragedy of the Commons," *Science* 162, no. 3859 (December 1968), pp. 1243–48.

9. Peter Hayes and Lyuba Zarsky, "Regional Cooperation and Environmental Issues in Northeast Asia," Institute on Global Conflict and Cooperation, IGCC Policy Papers, Working Paper PP05, October 1993 (available at http://repositories.cdlib.org/igcc/PP/PP05/, accessed February 21, 2005).

10. www.me.go.kr, accessed February 21, 2005.

11. "Sandstorms Blanket Northern China, Korea," Big News Network.com, March 21, 2004 (available at http://feeds.bignewsnetwork.com/?sid=047967127955057e/, accessed February 21, 2005).

12. "Yellow Dust Issue and International Cooperation," *Korea Times*, March 13, 2001, p. 1.

13. Esook Yoon and Hong Pyo Lee, "Environmental Cooperation in Northeast Asia: Issues and Prospects," in Schreurs and Pirages, *Ecological Security in Northeast Asia*, pp. 67–88; GESAMP (IMO.FAO, UNESCO-IOC/WMO/WHO/IAEA/UN/UNEP Joint Group of Experts on the Scientific Aspects of Marine Environmental Protection), "A Sea of Troubles," January 2001 (available at http://gesamp.imo.org/no70/report.pdf, accessed February 21, 2005).

14. Mark J. Valencia, "Ocean Management Regimes in the Sea of Japan: Present and Future," July 1998 (available at www.nautilus.org/archives/papers/energy/ValenciaESENAY2.html, accessed March 25, 2004).

15. Tak-Whan Han, "Assessment of Environmental Cooperation in North-East Asia," in *Proceedings of Kyobo International Symposium of Review Environmental Cooperation in Northeast Asia and Prospects for the New Millennium* (Seoul: Kyobo Foundation for Education and Culture, 2000).

16. Hyon-Jin Kim, "Marine Environmental Cooperation in Northeast Asia" (paper presented at the ESENA Workshop: Energy-Related Marine Issues in the Sea of Japan, Tokyo, July 1998) (available at www.nautilus.org/archives/papers/energy/KimESENAY2.html, accessed May 30, 2005).

17. World Resource Institute (WRI), *World Resources, 1989–1999* (Oxford: Oxford University Press, 1999).

18. In addition to the region's energy vulnerability, cross-border environmental problems arising from the burning of fossil fuel are the main causes behind the region's wide attraction to nuclear energy in that the nuclear power plants do not emit sulfur dioxide or greenhouse gases (Lee, "Environmental Regime-Building in Northeast Asia").

19. The ESCAP is an intergovernmental forum in the Asia Pacific region, which aims to promote economic and technological development in the region.

20. TumenNet, RAS/98/G31—Tumen River Strategic Action Program (available at www.tumennet.org/project/proj_index.htm, accessed February 21, 2005).

21. China's "Agenda 21—White Paper on China's Population, Environment, and Development in the 21st Century" was adopted at the Executive Meeting of the State Council of the People's Republic of China on March 25, 1994.

22. Peter M. Haas, "Prospects for Effective Marine Governance in the Northwest Pacific Region" (paper presented at ESENA Workshop Energy-Related Marine Issues in the Sea of Japan, Tokyo, July 1998) (www.nautilus.org/archives/papers/energy/HaasESENA2/html).

23. The following paragraphs concerning the prospects for regional cooperation are elaborated from Lee, "Environmental Regime-building in Northeast Asia."

24. Tae-Yeon Hwang, "International Environmental Organizations," in *International Organizations and Korean Diplomacy*, ed. Young Kwan Yoon and Byung Moo Hwang [in Korean] (Seoul: Mineum Sa, 1996), pp. 529–54.

25. A significant example has been the major role that South Korea has played during 1987–89 and 1993–97 as a member state of the Governing Council of the UNEP.

26. Korean Ministry of Foreign Affairs and Trade, *Global Environmental Information* [in Korean], no. 30, 1999.

27. The Northeast Asian Conference of Environmental Cooperation (NEACEC), an annual meeting between working-level officials from the environmental ministries of NEA countries (except North Korea), has pursued intergovernmental exchanges of information and policy on national and regional environmental affairs. It was established in 1992 as a result of annual seminars on environmental science held from 1988 to 1991 by the Korean government in cooperation with the Japanese government. See Sangmin Nam, "Ecological Interdependence and Environmental Governance in Northeast Asia: Politics vs. Cooperation," in Harris, *International Environmental Cooperation Politics*, pp. 167–202.

28. Gilbert Rozman maintains that "[w]e must avoid naïve environmentalism, assuming that progress on this issue [environmentalism] is independent of other cooperation or can disregard the power of nationalism in pursuit of still weakly-embedded forces of localism and globalization" ("Northeast Asian Regional Context," p. 27).

29. See Samuel S. Kim's chapter in this volume.

30. Rozman, "Northeast Asian Regional Context."

31. Lee, "Environmental Regime-building in Northeast Asia."

Notes to Chapter 15

This research was funded by research and travel grants from the Korea Foundation (Advanced Research Grant), California State University at Dominguez Hills (RSCAAP Summer Research Grant), and Stanford University's Korean Studies Center. I am grateful for their support. I am also deeply indebted to my friends and informants, whose kindness, generosity, and openness made my fieldwork pleasant and memorable.

1. For a summary and analysis of the *hanryu* discourses in South Korea, see Cho-Han Haejoang, "Modernity, Popular Culture and East-West Identity Formation: A Discourse Analysis of Korean Wave in Asia," *Korean Cultural Anthropology* 35, no. 1 (2002), pp. 3–38.

2. Ulf Hannerz, *Cultural Complexity: Studies in the Social Organization of Meaning* (New York: Columbia University Press, 1992); David Morley and Kevin Robins, *Spaces of Identity: Global Media, Electronic Landscapes and Cultural Boundaries* (New York: Routledge, 1997).

3. Korean waves refer to the popularity of South Korean popular culture both in East and Southeast Asia. But, due to limitations of time and resources, this time, I could not conduct fieldwork in the Southeast Asian region including Vietnam, Thailand, Singapore, Indonesia, and Malaysia, where *hanryu* is reported to be visible. Thus, my analysis of *hanryu* in this chapter focuses on the phenomenon observed in East Asia.

4. See Arjun Appadurai, *Modernity at Large: Cultural Dimensions of Globalization* (Minneapolis: University of Minnesota Press, 1996); Fredric Jameson, *Postmodernism, or the Cultural Logic of Late Capitalism* (Durham: Duke University Press, 1997).

5. See John Tomlinson, *Cultural Imperialism: A Critical Introduction* (Baltimore: Johns Hopkins University Press, 1991).

6. Paul Gilroy, *The Black Atlantic: Modernity and Double Consciousness* (Cambridge: Harvard University Press, 1993).

7. Orientalism is perhaps one of the critical roots of the West's lack of interest in Asian popular culture. Asia has long been associated with either the exotic past or the faceless, monotonous machines, represented by Japanese advanced technology; see Koichi Iwabuchi, *Recentering Globalization: Popular Culture and Japanese Transnationalism* (Durham: Duke University Press, 2002).

8. Dorinne Kondo, "The Aesthetics and Politics of Japanese Identity in the Fashion Industry," in *Re-Made in Japan*, ed. Joseph Tobin (New Haven: Yale University Press, 1992),

pp. 176–203; Sunaina Maira, "Hanna and Hip Hop: The Politics of Cultural Production and the Work of Cultural Studies," *Journal of Asian American Studies* 3, no. 3 (November 2000), pp. 329–69; Pak Tae-gyon, *Japanimation i segyerul chibaehanun iyu: atom eso slam dunk kkaji* [The Reason Japanimation Rules the World: From Atom to Slam Dunk] (Seoul: Kilbok, 1998); David Desser, "Consuming Asia: Chinese and Japanese Popular Culture and the American Imaginary," in *Multiple Modernities: Cinemas and Popular Media in Transcultural East Asia*, ed. Jenny Kwok Wah Lau (Philadelphia: Temple University Press, 2003), pp. 179–99.

9. Jung-Sun Park, "Korean American Youths' Consumption of Korean and Japanese TV Dramas and Its Implications," in *Feeling "Asian" Modernities: Transnational Consumption of Japanese TV Dramas*, ed. Koichi Iwabuchi (Hong Kong: Hong Kong University Press, 2004), pp. 275–300.

10. David Harvey, *The Condition of Postmodernity* (Oxford: Basil Blackwell, 1989).

11. David Morley and Kevin Robins, *Spaces of Identity: Global Media, Electronic Landscapes and Cultural Boundaries* (New York: Routledge, 1997).

12. Ibid.; Iwabuchi, *Recentering Globalization.*

13. Hong Kong films' popularity in East/Southeast Asia continued throughout the early 1990s. See Esther Yau, ed., *At Full Speed: Hong Kong Cinema in a Borderless World* (Minneapolis: University of Minnesota Press, 2001); Iwabuchi, *Recentering Globalization.*

14. Japanese contemporary pop culture is largely based on Western, especially American, pop culture. Thus, in terms of cultural form, and, to some extent, content, Japanese pop culture has many resemblances to Western pop culture. Yet, as scholars have argued, some Japanese think that their way of appropriating and modifying Western culture to suit the taste of Asian as well as Japanese audiences is uniquely "Japanese" and perhaps that ("domestication" of borrowed cultural forms and contents) is what characterizes Japanese pop culture (see Iwabuchi, *Recentering Globalization*; Tobin, *Re-Made in Japan*). In this sense, Japanese cultural dominance in Asia may not be necessarily an outright challenge to the Western cultural hegemony. Indeed, in a way, it contributes to the continuation of Western influence in the region. Yet, Japanese pop culture also has elements that are distinguishable from those in Western pop culture, and, perhaps due to the common Asian background, Japanese cultural influence is accepted and appropriated differently than that of the West in Asia. Moreover, Japanese pop culture competes against Western pop culture for market share in Asia. In this sense, Japanese pop culture undermines Western hegemony.

15. For example, "Star, a Hong Kong-based company which began broadcasting in August 1991, has effectively constructed the Asia region; stretching from Turkey to Japan, from Mongolia to Indonesia, it encompasses thirty-eight countries" (Morley and Robins, *Spaces of Identity*, p. 16).

16. Iwabuchi, *Recentering Globalization*, p. 4.

17. Japan's music and television markets are the second largest in the world, if European countries are not considered one unit.

18. Some argue that in some parts of Asia, such as Taiwan and Hong Kong, Japanese pop cultural influence is stronger than that of the West. See Iwabuchi, *Recentering Globalization.*

19. George Li, "Korean TV Dramas in Taiwan" (paper presented at the seminar on the Digital Era: Suggestions for the Korean Broadcasting Industry, Naksan, Korea, June 2001).

20. According to my Japanese informant, who works at a network TV station, his company had sold few TV dramas before 1996. But when the demand grew in Taiwan, things changed drastically. An employee of another Japanese network TV station also told me that nowadays her company has almost run out of stock of old dramas as most of their dramas were already sold to Taiwan.

21. The popularity of Korean music in Taiwan preceded the success of Korean dramas by a couple of years. For the young Taiwanese audience, at least, their familiarity with

Korean music may have affected their consumption of Korean dramas. Yet it is the synergistic effect of different genres of Korean popular culture that resulted in *hanryu*.

22. A Korean drama, *Sarangi mwogillae* [What Is Love?], was already a big hit in China in 1997. But the term *hanryu* was coined a couple of years later, as it took time for the combined effects of Korean pop cultural genres, such as music, TV dramas, and movies, to be felt as a social phenomenon.

23. Most countries have regulations for the importation of foreign media products, but the degree of the Chinese government's regulations for and censorship of foreign programs is higher and more intense than those of many other countries.

24. See Wang Xuanjing, "'Hanliu' yu 'Huafeng'" [Korean Waves" and "Chinese Wind], *Dangdai Hanguo* (Winter 2002), pp. 72–73; Yao Ying, "Hanliu: bei wenhua baozhuang de shangye" [Korean Waves: Commercialism in the Form of Culture], *Shanghai jingji yanjiu*, no. 7 (2002), p. 69, pp. 75–79; Yi Mei, "Cong 'Hanliu' re tan qi" [A Discussion of 'Korean Waves'], *Shi shi*, pp. 27–30.

25. The consumption of foreign movies, dramas, and songs by pirate copies in China is very extensive. Information of and knowledge about foreign popular culture spreads fast despite the government banning and low "official" sales figures of those cultural products.

26. Most Chinese informants mentioned these points when they explained why Korean pop culture has become so popular.

27. Some Korean informants told me that the Chinese government began to implicitly sanction the importation of Korean popular culture in recent years as its popularity noticeably increased.

28. Cho-Han Haejong, "Modernity, Popular Culture and East-West Identity Formation: A Discourse Analysis of Korean Wave in Asia," *Korean Cultural Anthropology* 35, no. 1 (2002), pp. 3–38.

29. See Jung-Sun Park, "Change in South Korean Citizenship and Its Implications" (paper presented at the annual meeting of the Association for Asian Studies, San Diego, March 2000).

30. Interviews with individuals who work in the media industry in Korea and Taiwan.

31. See Chae-bok Pak, "A Study on the Competitiveness of Korean Television Programs: The MBC Case," M.A. thesis, Graduate School of Mass Communications, Yonsei University, Seoul, Korea, 2001. Nowadays, Korean dramas are distributed to many countries beyond the Asian region, including Europe, the United States, South America, Uzbekistan, Kazakhstan, Turkey, Jordan, Lebanon, and Egypt. In the Asian region, Indonesia and Malaysia are becoming burgeoning markets besides the old greater Chinese region and Vietnam, Thailand, Myanmar, and Cambodia. While most overseas audiences watch Korean dramas because of their favorite stars and/or story lines, certain directors have become "brands" of their own. So overseas buyers would buy anything that they make.

32. My Taiwanese informant told me that they edit Japanese dramas anyway despite the Japanese companies' guidelines.

33. Urban Asian youth, in particular, share similar consumer tastes and their increasing buying power places them at the center of the consumption of transnational popular cultures.

34. Indeed, Korean TV drama producers take pride in their ability to create "good and beautiful" scenes.

35. Despite some Hong Kong informants' prediction of the fast waning of the Korean wave during my fieldwork in 2003, it still seems to be going strong as of 2005. A recently aired Korean period drama, *Daejanggeum* (Jewel in the Palace), was such a big hit that its last episode "opened a new chapter in Hong Kong television history" by marking the highest TV drama ratings ever (47%). Vivien Chow, "Finale Puts Biggest Jewel in Broadcast Crown," *South China Morning Post*, May 4, 2005. The success of the drama consequently triggered a craze for Korean court food, which is a main theme of the drama, and Korea in general. See Vivien Chow, "TV Series Fuels Exodus to South Korea," *South China Morn-*

ing Post, April 11, 2005; idem, "Businesses Discover Jewel in the Crown of Obsession with Korea," *South China Morning Post,* April 11, 2005.

36. Some Japanese media people acknowledge that the "melodramatic" elements in Korean dramas, which supposedly awaken Japanese "nostalgia," are what have made Korean TV dramas successful in Asia and, simultaneously, why Japanese dramas have lost popularity there. In fact, I was told that the majority of Asian audiences still prefer love stories more than anything else, and recent Japanese TV dramas, which focus more on the individual psyche and psychological issues, have lost their appeal.

37. So Hyon-ch'ol, Interview documents for his special TV program on Korean waves aired on KBS, 2001, p. 16.

38. Interview with a Korean informant in Taiwan. My informant said that during the 2002 World Cup, Taiwanese people overtly expressed negative feelings toward the success of the Korean soccer team, and, to some extent, toward Korea. He thinks that it was a manifestation of Taiwanese jealousy of Korea's economic and cultural power, which is rooted in Taiwanese economic competition with Korea for the same economic niche.

39. So Hyon-chol, author interview.

40. While cultural proximity has some relevance in the East/Southeast Asian region, we should not assume an unquestionable cultural proximity that automatically connects people in the region because the presumably shared cultural traditions of the region have undergone rapid and extensive changes, generating multiple local variations.

41. Yao, "Discussion"; Yi, "Korean Waves."

42. Iwabuchi, *Recentering Globalization.*

43. Jung-Sun Park, "Korean American Youth and Transnational Flows of Popular Culture Across the Pacific," *Amerasia Journal* 30, no. 1 (2004), pp. 147–69.

Notes to Epilogue

1. H.B. Drake, *Korea of the Japanese* (London: John Lane, 1930), p. 8.

2. Suisheng Zhao, *Power Competition in East Asia: From the Old Chinese World Order to Post-Cold War Regional Multipolarity* (New York: St. Martin's Press, 1998), p. 231.

3. James B. Palais, *Politics and Policy in Traditional Korea* (Cambridge: Harvard University Press, 1975).

4. Selig Harrison, *Korean Endgame: A Strategy for Reunification and U.S. Disengagement* (Princeton: Princeton University Press, 2002), p. 347.

5. Jason T. Shaplan and James Laney, "China Trades Its Way to Power," *New York Times,* July 12, 2004, p. A 19.

6. Author's communication with ROK Foreign Minister Ki-Moon Ban, April 8, 2004.

7. For a recent example of this, see the section on "Bolstering Cultural Diplomacy and Assisting Ethnic Communities Abroad," in the ROK National Security Council report *Peace, Prosperity and National Security: National Security Strategy of the Republic of Korea* (May 2004), p. 70.

8. Eric J. Hosbawm, *The Age of Extremes: A History of the World, 1914–1991* (New York: Pantheon Books, 1994).

9. Giovanni Arrighi uses this term in a different sense, referring to cycles of global economic hegemony, in *The Long Twentieth Century: Money, Power, and the Origins of Our Times* (London: Verso, 1994).

About the Editors and Contributors

Tsuneo Akaha is professor of international policy studies and director of the Center for East Asian Studies at the Monterey Institute of International Studies, California. He is the author and editor of numerous books and articles dealing with the international relations of Northeast Asia, Japanese foreign and security policies, Russo-Japanese relations, and the Korean peninsula. He is currently spearheading an international research project on "Cross-border Human Flows in Northeast Asia: A Human Security Perspective."

Charles K. Armstrong is associate professor of history at Columbia University, where he specializes in modern Korean, East Asian, and international history. His recent books include *Korean Society: Civil Society, Democracy and the State* (ed., 2002) and *The North Korean Revolution, 1945–1950* (2003). He is currently completing a book on the history of North Korean foreign relations.

Evgeny P. Bazhanov is vice president of the Diplomatic Academy and director of the Research Institute of Contemporary International Studies, Foreign Ministry of Russia. From 1970 to 1985 he served as a diplomat in Singapore, the United States, and China, and from 1985 to 1991 he was an adviser on foreign policy for Mikhail Gorbachev. He is the author of 83 books and over 100 articles on politics and international relations.

Hahm Chaibong is professor of political science at Yonsei University in Seoul, Korea, currently on leave as the director of the Division of Social Sciences Research and Policy at UNESCO, Paris, France. He is the author of *Confucianism, Capitalism and Democracy* (2000, in Korean) and co-editor of *Confucianism for the Modern World* (2003).

Jae Ho Chung is professor of international relations and director of the Center for International Studies at Seoul National University, Korea. He is the author of *Central Control and Local Discretion in China* (2000) and is currently working on a book entitled *Between Dragon and Eagle: South Korea-China Bilateralism and the United States.*

Bruce Cumings is the Norman and Edna Freehling Professor of History at the University of Chicago. He is the author of *The Origins of the Korean War* (1981, 1990), *War and Television* (1992), *Korea's Place in the Sun: A Modern History* (1997), *Parallax Visions: Making Sense of American-East Asian Relations* (1999), and *North Korea: Another Country* (2003), and is the editor of the modern volume of the *Cambridge History of Korea* (forthcoming).

Takashi Inoguchi is professor of political science at the Institute of Oriental Culture, University of Tokyo. He has published many books, including *Reinventing the Alliance* (co-edited with G.J. Ikenberry, 2003) and *American Democracy Promotion* (co-edited with Michael Cox and G.J. Ikenberry, 2000). He is also the editor of two journals, *Japanese Journal of Political Science* and *International Relations of the Asia-Pacific*.

Samuel S. Kim teaches in the Department of Political Science at Columbia University, where he is also senior research scholar in the Weatherhead East Asian Institute. His recent publications include *Korea's Democratization* (ed., 2003), *The International Relations of Northeast Asia* (ed., 2004), and *Inter-Korean Relations: Problems and Prospects* (ed., 2004).

Stephen Kotkin teaches European and Asian history at Princeton University, where he also directs the Russian and Eurasian Studies Program. He initiated the present volume, and has co-edited two other works in this series: *Mongolia in the Twentieth Century: Landlocked Cosmopolitan* (1999) and *Rediscovering Russia in Asia: Siberia and the Russian Far East* (1995).

Kirk W. Larsen is Korea Foundation Assistant Professor of History and International Affairs at the George Washington University. He received his Ph.D. in history from Harvard University. His monograph *Tradition, Trade and Empire: The Qing Empire and Choson Korea* is forthcoming.

Shin-wha Lee is associate professor in the Department of Political Science and International Relations, Korea University. She has served as a special adviser to the Rwandan Independent Inquiry appointed by UN Secretary-General Kofi Annan and a consultant to the ASEAN+3 East Asian Vision Group. Her most recent publication is *Human Security Matters: The Ethical, Normative and Educational Frameworks for the Promotion of Human Security in East Asia* (2004).

Alexander Lukin is associate professor in the Department of Comparative Political Science and director of the Center for East Asian Studies of Moscow State Institute of International Relations. His most recent book is *The Bear Watches the Dragon: Russia's Perceptions of China and the Evolution of Russian-Chinese Relations Since the Eighteenth Century* (2003).

Chung-in Moon is professor of political science and director of the Institute of Modern Korean Studies, Yonsei University. He has published 20 books and over 190 articles in edited volumes and such scholarly journals as *World Politics*, *International Studies Quarterly*, and *Journal of Asian Studies*. His publications include *State, Market and Just Growth* (2003) and *Understanding Korean Politics* (2001).

Jung-Sun Park is associate professor of Asian Pacific Studies at California State University at Dominguez Hills. Her research interests include transnationalism, (im)migration, popular culture, identity, and citizenship. She is author of *Chicago Korean Americans: Identity and Politics in a Transnational Community* (2005). She has also published articles on transnational flows of Korean/Asian popular culture, Korean/Asian American identity politics, and Japanese animation in *Amerasia Journal*, *Yoksa bipyong* (Critical Review of History), and *Yuriika* (Eureka: Poetry and Criticism).

Gilbert Rozman is Musgrave Professor of Sociology at Princeton University, where he has taught since 1970. His writings center on comparisons and bilateral relations and perceptions in Northeast Asia. His most recent book is *Northeast Asia's Stunted Regionalism: Bilateral Distrust in the Shadow of Globalization* (2004).

Seung-won Suh is associate professor of political science at Kanto Gakuin University in Japan. His publications include *Japanese Economic Statecraft toward China* (forthcoming), *Chinese Politics and East Asia* (co-authored in Japanese, 2004), *Economic Reform of North Korea* (co-authored in Korean, 2002), and "Economic Statecraft, Domestic Politics and Japan's China Policy Since the late 1970s" (in English, *Kanto Gakuin Law Review*, October 2002).

Daqing Yang is associate professor of history and international affairs at the George Washington University. He teaches modern Japanese history and is author of *Technology of Empire: Telecommunications Networks and Japanese Expansion* (forthcoming).

Index